THE EICHMANN TRIAL RECONSIDERED

The Eichmann Trial Reconsidered

EDITED BY REBECCA WITTMANN

UNIVERSITY OF TORONTO PRESS
Toronto Buffalo London

ISBN 978-1-4875-0849-4 (cloth)   ISBN 978-1-4875-3837-8 (EPUB)
                                 ISBN 978-1-4875-3836-1 (PDF)

Library and Archives Canada Cataloguing in Publication

Title: The Eichmann trial reconsidered / edited by Rebecca Wittmann.
Names: Wittmann, Rebecca, 1970– editor.
Series: German and European studies.
Description: Series statement: German and European studies | Includes
   bibliographical references.
Identifiers: Canadiana (print) 20210226528 | Canadiana (ebook)
   20210226722 | ISBN 9781487508494 (cloth) | ISBN 9781487538378
   (EPUB) | ISBN 9781487538361 (PDF)
Subjects: LCSH: Eichmann, Adolf, 1906–1962 – Trials, litigation, etc. |
   LCSH: Trials (Genocide) – Jerusalem. | LCSH: Holocaust, Jewish
   (1939–1945)
Classification: LCC KMK44.E33 E33 2021 | DDC 364.15/1092 – dc23

The German and European Studies series is funded by the DAAD with
funds from the German Federal Foreign Office

Deutscher Akademischer Austauschdienst
German Academic Exchange Service

University of Toronto Press acknowledges the financial assistance to its
publishing program of the Canada Council for the Arts and the Ontario
Arts Council, an agency of the Government of Ontario.

For John, Charlie, and Nora

Contents

Acknowledgments   ix

Introduction   3
REBECCA WITTMANN

Part I: Eichmann on Trial

1 Coming to Terms with the "Banality of Evil": Implications
   of the Eichmann Trial for Social Scientific Research on
   Perpetrator Behaviour   19
   JAMES E. WALLER

2 From History to Story: When the "Architect" of the Holocaust
   Became His Own "Witness"   32
   FABIEN THÉOFILAKIS

3 Revisiting Eichmann and Zionism: Contexts, Strange
   Encounters, and Their Afterlives   50
   MICHAEL BERKOWITZ

Part II: Eichmann and Jurisprudence

4 Prosecuting "Crimes against the Jewish People": The Eichmann
   Trial and the History of a Legal Concept   75
   LAURA JOCKUSCH

5 The Eichmann Trial: Towards a Jurisprudence of Victims as
   Eyewitnesses to Genocide   104
   LEORA BILSKY

6 What Makes a Prosecution an International Landmark Trial?
Reflections on the Tensions between Legal Proceedings,
Politics, and Historical Facts   122
RUTH BETTINA BIRN

Part III: Eichmann and Geopolitics

7 The Eichmann Trial's Impact Reconsidered   153
BOAZ COHEN

8 The Eichmann Trial and the Relations between the Federal
Republic of Germany and Israel: A Positive or Negative
Influence?   169
DOMINIQUE TRIMBUR

9 The Impact of the Eichmann Trial on Relations between
Israel and the Federal Republic of Germany   190
RONI STAUBER

10 The Impact of the Eichmann Affair on Arab
Holocaust Discourse   207
ESTHER WEBMAN

Part IV: Representing Eichmann

11 Remaking Eichmann: Memories of Mass Murder and the
Transatlantic Student Movements of the 1960s   231
THOMAS PEGELOW KAPLAN

12 From 2-Inch to YouTube: The Audiovisual Documentation
and Broadcast of the Eichmann Trial   253
LIAT BENHABIB

Contributors   267

Acknowledgments

This volume would not have been possible without the extraordinarily diligent and careful work of both Stephanie Corazza and Ramneek Sodhi, and I am deeply indebted to them both. I would also like to thank the Department of History, the Jackman Humanities Institute, the Centre for Jewish Studies, and the Munk School of Global Affairs at the University of Toronto, and the German Historical Institute in Washington, DC.

THE EICHMANN TRIAL RECONSIDERED

Introduction

REBECCA WITTMANN

In his essay entitled "From History to Story: When the 'Architect' of the Holocaust Became His Own "Witness," Fabien Théofilakis quotes from a chilling excerpt of Adolf Eichmann's trial notes: Eichmann writes, "Historians of all confessions ... will study the trial down to the last detail still for fifty years and more. And you will see, it will be interpreted according to the Zeitgeist in one way or another."

Despite all his ridiculous assertions and lies, Eichmann was certainly right about that. But it is not only the trial that consumes us. The fascination with Adolf Eichmann – the man, the Nazi, the bureaucrat, the facilitator, the murderer – seems to exceed that of almost any other major Holocaust perpetrator. Why is that, exactly? Is the Eichmann trial solely responsible? Or is Hannah Arendt's interest in Eichmann the main reason why countless biographies continue to appear on the subject of this enigma, why we feel compelled to understand what motivated him?

The Eichmann Trial Reconsidered examines the origins, course, and implications of the trial of Adolf Eichmann: captured by the Israelis in Argentina in May 1960, Eichmann was brought before the Jerusalem District Court in April 1961, sentenced, and finally hanged in May 1962. Bringing together leading international authorities, this volume assesses the very considerable scholarship conducted on the subject of the trial over the years. It examines not only the legal significance of the trial (the doctrine of universal jurisdiction is one of its main contributions to the evolution of international law) but the man himself, our fascination with him, and the legacy of the trial in Israel and beyond. This volume is singular in its examination of the topic of Eichmann because it is the first and only interdisciplinary and multidisciplinary examination of the question of motivation by scholars across the fields of history, film studies, political science, sociology, psychology, and law. But rather than asking what "really" drove Eichmann – and countless other

Holocaust perpetrators – to participate in the organization of mass murder, we ask how that question has shaped perceptions of Eichmann, the trial, and international law. Ultimately, then, the volume turns the question of Eichmann's motivation inside out. While perpetrator motivation studies abound, we seek a new and richer understanding of why and how our fascination, incomprehension, and subsequent (often futile) need to understand motivation has shifted, distorted, or clarified public and scholarly perceptions of Eichmann and his sensational trial. We do indeed examine motivation, but not just that of Eichmann; while part I takes up the question of what drove Eichmann, parts II–IV explore the motivation of prosecutors, lawyers, diplomats, students, and neighbouring countries before, during, and long after the trial had ended.

Because both Eichmann and the trial are known to us mainly through the eyes of Hannah Arendt in her controversial *Eichmann in Jerusalem*, her inescapable notion of the "banality of evil" and its lingering, ever-present impact on theories of perpetrator motivation and legal confrontations with Nazi defendants are also examined in this volume. However, the scholars here do not attempt yet another analysis of whether or not this theory holds water; instead, they seek to go beyond understanding Eichmann through the Arendtian lens, and adopt a different perspective in order to better understand who Eichmann was, how we have come to perceive him, and how our understanding of "Eichmann the man" has influenced recent historical events. Eichmann becomes at once, in this volume, an intersection and starting point for studying, for example, diplomatic relations between Israel and West Germany, the media, and the cause of growing tensions between the Israelis and the Arabs.

Brought together here are the musings and assertions of scholars – beyond just historians, thankfully – at the forefront of research on perpetrator motivation, Nazi trials, the possibility of justice, the philosophy of evil, and our lingering and persistent need to understand not only the how but the why. What we do not see a lot of in the existing literature is a contextualizing of Eichmann temporally and geopolitically: this volume attempts to rectify that lack. This book is about how Eichmann forged and fostered Israeli identity, and puts Eichmann at the centre of an exploration of German versus Israeli jurisprudence; it puts Eichmann at the centre of the exploration of national Israeli (and Arab!) identities and politics; it puts him at the centre of the struggle and conflict between states – German, Israeli, and Arab. This is at once a transnational, international and supranational study of Eichmann.

Extending over two years, the Eichmann trial was an electrifying event in Israeli society and a significant contributor globally both to understanding the Holocaust and the development of international law. The trial also occasioned considerable debate globally and generated new prominence to what was only just becoming known as "the Holocaust." In this regard, the trial became a focal point for what was subsequently denoted as a "coming to terms with the Holocaust." This book examines just how effectively – and with what lasting results – this "coming to terms" transpired. It looks at the trial itself and its historical context, but also considers the legal, historical, and cultural perspectives on topics such as the evolution of war crimes proceedings, the impact of broadcast media, the depiction of Eichmann in Arendt's famous account of the trial, and the transformation of historical consciousness about the Holocaust.

Obviously, the questions "why" and "how" remain at the heart of virtually all scholarly inquiry into the genesis and execution of the Holocaust, and in some ways, there will always remain a rupture between what we know to have happened and our ability to comprehend how it was that so many were not only willing but wanting to envision, plan, and create hell on earth in the form of an Auschwitz – or a Treblinka or a Belzec. This is not to say that we cannot comprehend: Claude Lanzmann's insistence that it is obscene to even ask why is a deeply limiting and ultimately empty dictum, since scholars will of course always be consumed with the why. Even Lanzmann is not immune to pondering it, precisely because of his refusal to engage the question. But let us turn our attention to this very difficult dilemma, especially in relation to Adolf Eichmann: does it, in fact, matter what motivated him? What kind of a person was he? A banal thoughtless clown, as Arendt would have us believe, or a calculating, sly, ambitious, and ideologically driven antisemite, as recent biographies by David Cesarani or Bettina Stangneth have argued?[1] Does the dissection of Eichmann's personality and motives bring us closer to an understanding of how and why? Our preoccupation with Eichmann and his motives (or lack thereof) is the product of two distinct problems, one tangible and the other much less so. First, trials of those accused of mass atrocities have the impossible requirement of quantifying and assessing individual guilt in the face of large-scale, collective perpetration, and invariably do not create a nuanced and realistic picture of the defendant on the stand. Second, we remain deeply uncomfortable with the upsetting arguments of a motiveless perpetrator, especially when made by Hannah Arendt in her blunt, insensitive, and often unmeasured style. These two factors together have created a perpetrator in Adolf Eichmann who is so much larger than life (ironically, considering Arendt's thesis) that his role as symbol for the Holocaust endures. He is the personification of our incomprehension, our confusion, our debates about the how and the why; yet he is also the efficient, successful, bureaucratic head of deportations, whose ability to coordinate and execute mass murder fulfils our stereotypes of German transportation efficiency and of the inevitability of death for the victims of the Holocaust, as inevitable as the phrase, " the trains have left the station" – trains he coordinated – in which both no one and everyone is responsible.

Nazi trials are in large part responsible for creating comforting but often distorted representations of Holocaust perpetrators. Simply put, desk murderers are incredibly difficult to prosecute, and even harder to convict. German Nazi trials (my area of research) have shown this again and again: those who did not show individual initiative, who did not in some way commit excessive crimes of sadism or brutality, would not be convicted as perpetrators and would either get a slap on the wrist as accomplices, or be acquitted. This is evident at the Auschwitz trial in 1963, where the adjutant to the camp commander – the biggest fish on the stand, Robert Mulka – is convicted as an accomplice and receives time served, whereas sadists, defendants like Oswald Kaduk and Josef Klehr, much smaller fish in comparison, are sentenced to life in prison as perpetrators. Their crimes were much easier to identify, quantify, and cringe at – real murderers in our midst – than those of the camp bureaucracy.[2] The Majdanek trial in 1975 had a similar outcome, lasting six long years, resulting in numerous acquittals and only one life sentence for a sadistic female guard. By the time the Demjanjuk case began in 2009, German courts had enacted some major amendments, making it possible to try him as an accomplice; but this case is riddled with problems. Those who have done research on other kinds of Nazi trials will concur that bureaucratic killers make for terrible defendants, at least for prosecutors: if their motives cannot be concretely proven as sadists, or antisemites, or ideologues – and bureaucrats can always deny these motives – then they are invariably subject to much lesser convictions. What is astounding is that Eichmann was convicted and sentenced to death at all, based on his profile, his representation of himself, and the evidence against him regarding his motives. Eichmann simply took the mundane route that virtually every Nazi defendant did, also in the German trials, which was to portray himself as an order-follower. The great victory of the Eichmann trial is, in fact, that a desk killer was convicted. But the need to define him as an ideologue, an anti-Semite, and even a bloodthirsty killer was still very much evident at the trial, and represents not only one of the confines of the law but one of the deep impulses of humanity: find the tangible evil.

As this volume demonstrates, there is no contemplating Adolf Eichmann without first thinking of Hannah Arendt's theory of the "banality of evil." Arendt met with enormous resistance not only from those who were victims of the Holocaust, and could not accept that their fate had not been in the hands of a monster, but from scholars who had struggled to forefront what antisemitism had wrought upon civilization, in a world where people were much more consumed with Stalin's Cold War than with Hitler's Holocaust. Others (most famously, Zygmunt Bauman in *Modernity and the Holocaust*) then expanded upon and refined Arendt's theory, explaining the Holocaust to be a result of modern society – bureaucracy, technocracy, banality – rather than an aberration of it. During the escalating Cold War, historians and philosophers all had eureka moments in which they recognized the paralysing and blinding effects of totalitarianism, with its millions of silently complicit, passive minions who allowed themselves to be swept into collective indifference toward or, worse, collaboration with and participation in acts of mass atrocity.

Much has changed since then. Without exception, recent literature examining Eichmann's life, career, behaviour, and motivations has sought to show that Arendt was utterly wrong about Eichmann's banality. He was, according to Hans Safrian (*Eichmann's Men*, 1993), Irmtrud Wojak (*Eichmann's Memoiren*, 2001), and David Cesarani (*Becoming Eichmann*, 2006), a calculating, merciless (if weak-stomached) anti-Semite, firmly convinced by Hitler's vision of a Judenrein Reich. More recently, Deborah Lipstadt's *The Eichmann Trial* and Bettina Stangbeth's *Eichmann vor Jerusalem*, in different ways and to varying degrees, uphold this trend. Through the examination of new evidence such as Eichmann's testimony, his personnel files, and the Sassen interviews, recent scholarship presents a very different Eichmann from the one Arendt presented. It would follow that Arendt's theory of banality is thoroughly discredited, dead, and finally long gone. But this is not so. Her infuriating and appalling observations of a man somewhat befuddled by the charges against him, only partially responsible for his actions – responsibility shared, in her view, by the victims and their leaders themselves – cannot be completely shaken. How and why can this be?

Much scholarship on the Holocaust in general is shaped by this tug of war between those historians, social scientists, and philosophers who wish to pull the rope toward ideological arguments (see, for example, Michael Thad Allen's *The Business of Genocide*, Edward Westermann's important article "'Ordinary Men' or 'Ideological Soldiers?,'" and, most spuriously, Goldhagen's *Hitler's Willing Executioners*) and those who, on the other side, pull the rope back to discuss utterly different and varying types of perpetrator motivation: careerism, opportunism, peer pressure, obedience to authority, fear of a violent state, and professional and economic greed (Christopher Browning's *Ordinary Men*, James Waller's *Becoming Evil*, Götz Aly's *Hitler's Beneficiaries*). Psychologist James Waller's essay in this volume is one example: he argues that we should not dismiss Hannah Arendt so easily, for she has much to teach social scientists about evil. The more recent books on Eichmann and the Eichmann trial also follow this pattern, some arguing their cases more successfully than others. But is this question – was antisemitism at the core of people's active participation, collaboration, and passive complicity in the Holocaust, or were other factors more central? – still relevant, useful, or answerable? Perhaps our goalposts should be shifted from finding the correct answer to complicating the picture and recognizing that the only way to understand the Holocaust – and at least attempt to understand we must – is to refuse a simple explanation that satisfies and comforts us. No group of perpetrators as enormous, multinational, and diverse as the one that implemented the Final Solution can easily be categorized as possessing one overarching motivation.

Sergio Minerbi's *The Eichmann Trial Diary* is a relatively recent publication which sheds light on both problems mentioned earlier: the need for prosecutors to portray an individual on trial for mass crime as a monster, and the reality of Eichmann's personality. What makes this diary fascinating is the immediacy of the events being described; unlike any other account of the trial, with the exception perhaps of the film *The Specialist*, this book takes the reader directly back into the courtroom. Minerbi, an Italian journalist, was clearly sceptical and disgusted by the man, but, unlike Arendt, he lets the trial's events speak for themselves. He leaves the reader with this chilling anecdote, one of many: when asked by Judge Halevy if he was an antisemite, Eichmann answered, "No, certainly not. But to be uncompromising was a virtue ... I chose the path dictated by the circumstances. Any other position would have appeared to be insubordination ... Today I wonder why such large segments of the population lack civic courage, and why the authorities were able to act so brutally."[3]

Although it is certainly possible to interpret Eichmann's statement as an outright lie, it is still impossible to ignore the cold, distanced tone of a consummate bureaucrat. This distancing is what Arendt tried to clarify in a radio discussion conducted by Joachim Fest on 9 November 1964 (on the anniversary of Kristallnacht). Fest wanted her to address her critics, which she was loath to do, but she insisted on saying this much: "He wanted to participate. He wanted to be able to say 'we,' and this participation, this wanting to say we was enough to commit the greatest of crimes … This feeling of power, that comes in acting together, is not absolute evil, it is completely human. But it is also not good. There is definite desire in this kind of acting together … And so I would say, that the real perversion in this participation is the act of functioning. And the desire to be a functionary, this desire was most evident in Eichmann."[4]

Bettina Stangneth probes the question at the heart of all books about Eichmann and his trial, books attempting to comprehend the kind of person it takes to perpetrate crimes on such a mass scale. Using the now famous Sassen papers, Stangneth shows a man who was unrepentant, deeply committed to the extermination of the Jews, and still thoroughly entrenched in a community of old Nazis who firmly believed that Hitler had been on the right track.[5] At one point Eichmann tells Sassen that if he had been able to oversee and order the murder of all 10.3 million Jews in Europe, then he would have been happy – a statement which Stangneth interprets as a sign of his ideological motivation, but which Arendt would no doubt have seen as more proof of Eichmann's desire to participate, please, and succeed at all costs. Interestingly, Minerbi's *Diary* also makes mention of the Sassen interview, as it was used by prosecutor Gideon Hausner to make Eichmann confess to his rabid antisemitism; Eichmann simply denies ever having said that he was motivated by anti-Jewish fanaticism, an approach which appears to exhaust Hausner (and possibly convince Arendt).

Historians, philosophers, psychologists – scholars invested in examining the notion of evil – struggle with Eichmann. Eichmann has become the perfect symbol of the desk killer, representing in one man the debate that scholars of the Holocaust have engaged in since the magnitude of the crime was realized: how was this possible, and why did so many participate?

This volume attempts to answer some of these questions. With the question of motivation at its core – in particular, why and how Eichmann's motivations have so captured the media, the public, and scholarly fascination – this book examines the man himself, Arendt's analysis of the trial and the enduring power of her interpretation of events (if only to be refuted), and the trial's effects and aftermath in Israel and beyond, and in the realm of national and international law.

Part I, "Eichmann on Trial," leads off discussion of these debates. The three scholars represented here – James Waller, Fabien Théofilakis and Michael Berkowitz – are not unanimous in their opinions of Hannah Arendt and Adolf Eichmann. Rather, their competing arguments reflect the scholarly community's divided responses to Arendt. On the one hand, James Waller, a psychologist who writes extensively on the theory of evil, is unwilling to dismiss Arendt, arguing that "Arendt's work influenced a generation of social scientists to believe that the sources of evil are not mysterious or profound but fully within our grasp." We are forced to ask, What does Arendt mean by the "banality of evil?" This has to be read in context of her description of "radical evil" in *Origins of Totalitarianism* – as being the kind of evil which dreams up and then creates places like Auschwitz. Someone like Eichmann does not fall into the category of the mastermind, according to Arendt. Although scholars continually acknowledge that ordinary men and women can be horribly evil, it seems that we are still deeply reluctant to accept Arendt's version of Eichmann's evil. Despite the many flaws in her understanding of Eichmann, largely due to the lack of information available to her at the time about Eichmann's statements to Sassen in South America, Waller cautions that we should not entirely discard Arendt's thesis.

Fabien Théofilakis and Michael Berkowitz, on the other hand, both argue against Waller's position. Théofilakis takes aim at Arendt's portrayal of Eichmann as a motiveless man, or at her face-value acceptance of his representation of himself. As Théofilakis argues, the thousands of pages of notes that Eichmann made throughout the trial do not provide us with a clear picture of an antisemitic ideologue, but they do show a man determined to present an image of himself as a "cog in the wheel." In sum, "these notes constitute the missing link between the Eichmann in Argentina who regretted in 1957 not having killed all the 10.3 million Jews of Europe, and the one who played the 'cautious bureaucrat' before the entire world." How so? Because Eichmann used his considerable historical knowledge and became the leading provider of evidence and information about his role in the Final Solution. In this way he could also forcefully shape his own defence and the representation of his character at the trial. And so, what we see here is a man determined, through his keen sense of self-preservation, to take himself out of the ranks of big fish like Hitler and Himmler and into the ranks of the small men. Clearly, he was successful in this self-portrayal if not in the verdict against him, whose outcome we all know, but in the court of public opinion, which in some ways has had a more lasting effect than his death sentence. Eichmann as "ordinary," a "disappointment," a balding old man, and, finally, as immortalized by Arendt, a man who was not an antisemite. Perhaps this is the real root of our fascination with Eichmann: that he misrepresented himself so successfully, and that such a keen and insightful observer as the philosopher Hannah Arendt could have been fooled by him and in turn led us all astray.

Michael Berkowitz takes exception to the "theory" that Eichmann was a Zionist. The essay reserves particular disdain for Slavoj Žižek and, of course, the one everyone loves to hate (even more than Žižek!),

Hannah Arendt. Berkowitz' piece provokes some important questions: Does labelling Eichmann a real Zionist mean that he was not an anti-semite, had no real ideological motivation, or was even sympathetic toward the Jews? Does anyone really believe that the main perpetrators of the Holocaust were ever anything but opportunistic and shrewd, especially in their early relations with Jews? We of course know that there was some indecision about what to do with the Jews until the Final Solution was decided upon and implemented, but this does not mean that Eichmann initially hoped to spare all of the Jews. So does the problem lie in the notion that Eichmann was a real Zionist, who understood exactly what that meant, or in the possibility that he thought he was one? Why is it crucial that we prove Arendt wrong about Eichmann's lack of antisemitism? Is this only to set the historical record straight, or is it also to insist that he had to embody a different, radical kind of evil in order to do what he did?

I am reminded of Zygmunt Baumann's controversial and often inflammatory 2001 epilogue to *Modernity and the Holocaust*, entitled "The Duty to Remember: But What?" In it, Baumann contends that the Israeli nationhood depends too heavily, and perilously, on victimhood for its self-identity.[6] Does the contention that Eichmann was a Zionist in some way make the Zionist vision less innocent, and put it into cahoots with Nazism? Is this why Rudolf Kastner (discussed in this volume by both Boaz Cohen and Michael Berkowitz) was so vilified, because he was a dangerous symbol of a version of the state of Israel that was not entirely a victim? In some ways, the notion of Eichmann as a Zionist brings us back to Arendt's other contention, the flipside of this portrayal of Eichmann, that the Jewish Council leaders were as bad as Nazis, reflected in her description (quoted by Berkowitz) of Leo Baeck as the "Führer of the Jews." We are all deeply uncomfortable with these conflations, and Arendt made them both. The grey zone, the blurring of lines between perpetrators and victims in any real way, is deeply troubling, especially when it comes from an outsider like Arendt or Žižek rather than an insider like Primo Levi. How do we move forward here?

Part II, "Eichmann and Jurisprudence," contemplates the legal legacy of the trial and its enormous resonance and shattering impact on Israel, on West Germany, and on the law itself. Laura Jockusch examines the notion of the Eichmann trial as the "Jewish Nuremberg." She places the Eichmann trial in a wider historical perspective by discussing the prehistory of the category "crimes against the Jewish people," which stood at the centre of the trial and distinguished the Israeli proceedings from the Allied war crimes trials that had taken place a decade and a half earlier. Leora Bilsky addresses the role of witnesses in light of the framework of "jurisprudence of atrocity." In contrast to previous scholarship, which has sharply distinguished the legal from the historical or didactic role of testimony given by victims during the Eichmann trial, her work adopts a framework based on collective crimes, and investigates the changing role of the victim as witness. She thus illuminates these distinctive crimes, which are characterized by mass murder and the separation – both physical and psychological – of the victimizer from his victims. The District Court of Jerusalem in the Eichmann case granted witnesses this new role by juxtaposing the dry Nazi documents discussing effective methods and numbers with horrifying stories conveyed by victims and survivors. In this manner, the encounter that could not have taken place during actual events was recreated in the courtroom.

Ruth Bettina Birn takes a sharp turn away from most scholarly literature, including the articles in this volume; rather than criticizing Arendt's portrayal of Eichmann, she argues that the prosecution got it largely wrong on all fronts because it was influenced by political considerations that led them to exaggerate Eichmann's role in the Holocaust. She documents the crimes of which Eichmann was wrongfully accused and for which he was wrongfully convicted, and argues that the defence did not enjoy equality of arms. For Birn, the prosecution's haphazard selection of historical documents led to distorted views on the chain of command within the SS and Police, and on Eichmann's position in this apparatus, a distortion that could easily have been avoided had the prosecution simply used the documentation available to them rather than been motivated by political interests.

Part III, "Eichmann and Geopolitics," examines the trial's influence on postwar national identity politics in Israel, the surrounding Arab world, and Germany. In his essay, Boaz Cohen challenges the enduring perception of the Eichmann trial as effecting profound change on Israel, a kind of cultural trauma and awakening to the Holocaust. Cohen argues the Holocaust was already a major feature in the private life of many Israelis, and was present on a communal level and in the public sphere. Survivors, as a major segment of Israeli society, had a distinct presence that was apparent in Israel's public sphere. This essay demonstrates that an active body of survivors dedicated itself to ensuring Holocaust commemoration and awareness in Israeli society, and that their voice was heard.

Dominique Trimbur's piece considers the state of affairs between West Germany and Israel in relation to the trial, in the form of a diplomatic history; he argues that while the trial did indeed influence Germany in terms of financial and military support, it had little further effect on diplomatic ties between the countries. While it did serve to formalize relations, he sees the responses of both countries as examples of Realpolitik at work. Roni Stauber, on the other hand, examines the shift in relations between Germany and Israel because of the trial. It was in fact Fritz Bauer, attorney general of the State of Hesse and staunch advocate of Nazi trials, who insisted to the German government that Eichmann had gone into hiding and should be tried in West Germany. But according to Irmtrud Wojak, Bauer's biographer, German chancellor Konrad Adenauer refused to look into this further and was determined not to have Eichmann tried in Germany. Wojak argues that Adenauer, though a victim of Nazi persecution himself, felt it better to act defensively than aggressively in relation to such a high-ranking Nazi, largely because the mood in Germany in the 1950s was all about a *Schlußstrich* – putting an end – to Nazi trials. And indeed, according to Stauber, the more defensive strategy worked in relation to Israel as well. Ben-Gurion was determined to use the trial to get more support for Israel, and knew he had to be strategic; once Eichmann's location was known and the Mossad snatched him, the Israeli prime minister and Foreign Ministry went to work examining how best to improve Israel's political interests, particularly in regard to relations with West Germany. They were well aware of the anxiety of West German leaders that the trial might awaken hatred of Germany, so Ben-Gurion took a very warm and positive approach to the Federal Republic, repeatedly acknowledging the moral distinction between Nazi Germany and the new democratic Germany. Stauber argues that this had tremendous impact on Adenauer's decision to expand support for Israel, and especially to supply the Jewish state with sophisticated new weapons.

Esther Webman turns her gaze eastward, to the Arab discourse surrounding the trial and the Holocaust. Webman examines what she considers to be the curious fascination of the Arab press with the Holocaust She contends that the Arab debate on the Holocaust had a significant impact on the subsequent development of Holocaust discourse in the Arab world, reinforcing particularly the alleged Zionist-Nazi collaboration theme, the equation of Zionism with Nazism, the comparison between the Holocaust and the *Nakba*, and the accusation that Israel and Zionists were exploiting the Holocaust while fostering feelings of guilt among the Germans for material and political gains. Moreover, it proves that the Holocaust discourse in the Arab world was subordinated to the political struggle against Israel and Zionism and was linked to increasing antisemitic attitudes.

Part IV, "Representing Eichmann," assesses the aftermath of the Eichmann trial and particularly its lasting legacy on the world stage.

In his piece on the student movements of the 1960s, Thomas Pegelow Kaplan re-examines two strains of scholarly inquiry: first, the common conclusion that the Eichmann trial represented a fundamental shift in the ways in which German and American societies confronted the Hitler regime's genocidal crimes; second, the portrayal of the 1960s student revolts as an additional factor in the transformation of collective memories of German mass crimes. Pegelow Kaplan examines the transnational elements to this political activism, and traces how American and West German student organizers transferred images of Eichmann in their interactions. He demonstrates how the activists' remaking of Eichmann influenced the movements' ongoing radicalization and was, in turn, impacted by it. He argues that the naming of mass crimes and the portrayals of Eichmann had a profound impact on evolving societal Holocaust memories, perpetrator imagery, and processes of "coming to terms" with this genocide.

Finally, Liat Benhabib examines the extraordinarily important video documentation of the trial, which, after all, was the means by which most people – including Israelis themselves – witnessed it. She argues that crucial errors were made from beginning to end, errors which resulted in large parts of the trial being omitted from the documentation. This means that many iconic moments of the trial, as documented by Arendt, have disappeared from the visual record forever. Yad Vashem digitized and made available the 241 hours of tape on YouTube; but how will our understanding of the trial be shaped in decades to come if the visual record is incomplete?

This brings us back to Eichmann the man, and to the question of motivation and why it consumes us. Perhaps James Waller – who has immersed himself in the study of perpetrator motivation and what makes ordinary men commit extraordinary evil, perhaps get to the root of why Arendt, warts and all – cannot be dismissed as easily as we would like. After all, according to Waller, "Arendt's work influenced a generation of social scientists to believe that the sources of evil are not mysterious or profound but fully within our grasp." We are forced to contemplate, What does Arendt mean by the "banality of evil?" Waller is engaged in a difficult and commendable task: to actually come to some kind of understanding of what evil is, how it functions, and how it can be banal; in a way, an attempt to answer the question that Claude Lanzmann would have us not ask: why? Although Eichmann was convicted, sentenced to death, and executed, scholars – and the general public – remain profoundly uneasy about the notion of banality as motivation. In fact, in many ways, as countless undergraduate students often observe when they see a form of banal evil surfacing in Chris

Browning's *Ordinary Men*, it is much more terrifying and immoral than a radical evil that declares itself openly.[7] A conscience that is fully functioning, but is simply "the other way around" as Waller explains, is so alienating and we are so estranged from it that we wish to deny it. We now have ample evidence that Arendt should not have accepted Eichmann's representation of himself as a follower; but, as Waller states, "The fact that Eichmann was not the 'banal bureaucrat' that he pretended to be does not automatically, as some would argue, discredit Arendt's concept of the banality of evil." Why are we so eager to do so?

Despite the fact that this book seeks to go far beyond simply the motivation question, in many ways it remains at the heart of all of the articles in this book; our lack of clarity on Eichmann's motivations radiates inward as we examine human evil and complicity, and outward as we look at the cultural, historical, and geopolitical influence of the trial of this man. We cannot escape it.

We know that scholars and the public alike are fascinated with Eichmann the "man" and also Arendt as philosopher of evil. What we don't see a lot is a contextualizing of Eichmann, temporally and geopolitically. Boaz Cohen's article is not really about Eichmann or the trial itself, but rather about the young Israeli state and how it was not silent about the Holocaust. Cohen's goal in his essay is to disprove the myth of silence (in Israel), and throughout it contextualizes Eichmann's trial as a result of what Israeli society was like before the trial itself. Although this may seem ironic, the lack of discussion of the Eichmann trial itself highlights its very questionable importance. Perhaps the Eichmann trial was not so novel, ground-breaking, and silence-breaking as we thought. In fact, Cohen's extensive discussion of the Kastner trial in 1950s Israel and his overall challenge to myths about silence in Israel about the Holocaust serve to further contextualize and help us better understand what the Eichmann trial meant in Israel. Laura Jockusch examines how the decision to put Eichmann on trial in Israel caused discordance within the international Jewish diaspora. With the exception of Arendt, most Jews were in agreement that they were not singled out as victims at Nuremberg, but at the Eichmann trial they were, and this was what caused disputes about Jewish identity and law. Esther Webman examines the national discourses and national tensions that arose from the Eichmann trial in Israel; she demonstrates that the trial was not just about notions of evil, trying Nazi war criminals, or the persona of a criminal either: it actually had wide-reaching, tangible repercussions that we may not immediately think of. She suggests that the trial played a role in Arab-Jewish affairs and that the trial reinforced Arab hatred of the Jews and of the state of Israel. As such, Webman, like all the contributors here, pushes past the boundaries of Western discourses on Eichmann, the trial, and the Holocaust. While the "why" remains central to our grappling with the Holocaust, engaging in a more far-reaching examination of the motivation question's after-effects on the world stage is long overdue. This is the contribution of *The Eichmann Trial Reconsidered*.

NOTES

1 David Cesarani, *Becoming Eichmann: Rethinking the Life, Crimes, and Trial of a "Desk Murderer"* (Cambridge, MA, 2007), and Bettina Stangneth, *Eichmann vor Jerusalem: Das unbehelligte Leben eines Massenmörders* (Hamburg, 2011).
2 For more on the Auschwitz trial, see Devin O. Pendas, *The Frankfurt Auschwitz Trial, 1963–65: Genocide, History, and the Limits of Law* (Cambridge, MA), and Rebecca Wittmann, *Beyond Justice: The Auschwitz Trial* (Cambridge, MA, 2005).
3 Sergio Minerbi, *The Eichmann Trial Diary: An Eyewitness Account of the Trial that Revealed the Holocaust* (New York, 2011), 153.
4 Ursula Ludz and Thomas Wild, eds., *Hannah Arendt und Joachim Fest: Eichmann war von empörender Dummheit: Gespräche und Briefe* (Munich, 2010), 38–9.
5 Stangneth, 16.
6 Zygmunt Bauman, *Modernity and the Holocaust* (Ithaca, NY, 2001).
7 Christopher Browning, *Ordinary Men: Police Battalion 101 and the Final Solution in Poland* (New York, 1998).

PART I

Eichmann on Trial

1 Coming to Terms with the "Banality of Evil": Implications of the Eichmann Trial for Social Scientific Research on Perpetrator Behaviour

JAMES E. WALLER

Introduction

Social scientific research on perpetrator behaviour has consistently affirmed that the origins of extraordinary evil cannot be isolated in the extraordinary nature of the collective, the influence of an extraordinary ideology, psychopathology, or a common, homogeneous, extraordinary personality.[1] We are then left with the most discomforting of all realities – ordinary, "normal" people committing acts of extraordinary evil. The notion of the "ordinariness" of those who commit extraordinary evil was first given life in the early 1960s when a noted political philosopher posited an obedient, indifferent, and mundane personality to explain the atrocities of the Holocaust. The philosopher's name is Hannah Arendt (1906–1975) and her conception of the "banality of evil" would fundamentally challenge our understanding of who commits extraordinary human evil.

Hannah Arendt was one of about 37,000 German Jews who emigrated from Germany in 1933. She first went to France, where, with Youth Aliyah, she worked for the immigration of Jewish refugee children to Palestine. Interned during the war at Gurs, in Vichy France, she escaped, made her way to the United States in 1941, and secured US citizenship in 1951. Arendt's field of study was philosophy and she counted among her mentors Rudolf Bultmann, Martin Heidegger, and Karl Jaspers. Over time, she emerged as a prominent political philosopher and theoretician who focused much of her very productive academic life on the question of behaviour in totalitarian regimes.[2]

In 1961, Arendt – then numbered among the most important intellectuals in the United States – was commissioned by *The New Yorker* magazine to cover the sensational trial of Adolf Eichmann in Jerusalem. Eichmann was a major bureaucrat charged with implementing the

Final Solution. After receiving paramilitary training near the Dachau concentration camp, he found a more glamorous position in the powerful SS security service. While there, Eichmann gradually became the acknowledged "Jewish specialist" of the Third Reich. With the takeover of Austria in 1938, he was sent to Vienna to promote Jewish emigration. Eichmann developed a method of "forced emigration" that was financed by confiscation of Jewish property – simultaneously putting fear into the Jewish population *and* destroying their economic well-being. He was later named head of the Department for Jewish Affairs in the Gestapo (Department IV B4), a position he would hold from 1941 to 1945. In that role, Eichmann was responsible for the implementation of Nazi policy toward the Jews in Germany and all occupied territories – including the deportation of millions of Jews to concentration and extermination camps.

Following the defeat of Nazi Germany, Eichmann was arrested and confined to an American internment camp. Because his name and role were not yet well known, however, Eichmann managed to escape and flee to Argentina. Eventually abducted by Israeli Mossad secret service agents in Argentina in May 1960, he was brought to Israel to stand trial. He faced fifteen charges, for crimes against the Jewish people, for crimes against humanity, and for war crimes. Eichmann's trial opened on 11 April 1961 and ended on 14 August of that same year. He was found guilty and sentenced to death (Israel allows the death penalty only for crimes of genocide). An appeal of his death sentence was rejected in May 1962. Eichmann was hanged in the Ramla prison at midnight on 13 May–1 June 1962. His body was cremated and his ashes spread over the sea, outside the territorial waters of Israel.

While covering the legal and technical aspects of the Eichmann trial, Arendt also explored the wider themes inherent in the trial – the nature of justice, the behaviour of Jewish leadership during the Nazi regime, and the nature of evil itself. In 1963, the five articles serialized in *The New Yorker* were published, in revised and expanded form, as a book, *Eichmann in Jerusalem: A Report on the Banality of Evil*. The next year, the book was published in a follow-up version that carried a postscript and reply to the heated controversy that followed Arendt's original work.

What were the critics so exercised about? Much of the furore stemmed from Arendt's critique of Jewish leadership during the Holocaust. She claimed that far fewer than 6 million Jews would have died if Jewish leaders had not cooperated to various degrees with Nazis like Eichmann. The subsequent visceral reactions of those who took her comments as accusations that the Jews had gone passively to their deaths or murdered themselves made sensational headlines – "Self-Hating Jewess

Writes Pro-Eichmann Series for New Yorker Magazine" proclaimed one Jewish newspaper.[3] Her passing characterization of Jewish resistance during the Holocaust as inconsequential inflamed a controversy all out of proportion in relation to the self-described "sadly limited subject" of her book – the trial of Adolf Eichmann.[4]

Hidden by the sensationalism of the debate over Jewish passivity during the Holocaust ran a deeper issue of contention that *was* directly related to the subject of her work. Specifically, a substantial number of critics questioned her explanation of the *why* of the Holocaust. Arendt located the *why* in the nature of the bureaucratic mind – a world of operations without consequences, information without knowledge. In other words, mindless perpetrators doing what they are ordered and expected to do without being personally involved, committed, or aware of the terrifying destruction they are executing.

Arendt argued that what was frightening about Eichmann was not how unusual or how monstrous he was but, rather, how extremely *ordinary* he was. In his personal manner, he had little in common with the dramatic antisemitism or florid lust for killing of some other Nazi leaders. He was not evil personified. Neither was he a deranged Jew-killer. Half a dozen psychiatrists had certified him as "normal" – "More normal, at any rate, than I am after having examined him," one of them was reported to have said.[5] Eichmann was, in Arendt's view, a drab drone committed to industriousness and efficiency, a featureless functionary particularly steadfast in obeying and carrying out assigned duties and orders. "Except for an extraordinary diligence in looking out for his personal advancement," Arendt wrote," he had no motives at all."[6] It was the discovery that there was nothing to discover that turned the Eichmann trial into such a shocking experience.

Unpacking the "Banality of Evil"

Exactly what did Arendt mean by the "banality of evil"? The phrase did not appear in *The New Yorker* articles. Notwithstanding its prominence in the subtitle, and hints of the concept from the first chapter on, the phrase itself appeared only once in the book, at the very end: "It was as though in those last minutes he was summing up the lesson that this long course in human wickedness had taught us – the lesson of the fearsome, word-and-thought-defying *banality of evil*" (emphasis in original).[7] Arendt must have thought that the meaning of her phrase was obvious, since she did not define or explain it. Most readers, however, were – and still are – puzzled by the exact meaning of the "banality of evil."

We can begin to unpack Arendt's conception of the banality of evil by saying that it seems clear she did *not* mean several things. She did not mean that Eichmann's evil was trite, hackneyed, or stale. She did not mean that his evil was not immoral or grossly wrong. Nor did she use the word, as some critics charged, as a form of clever apologetics to make Eichmann into an everyday functionary – interchangeable with other unimportant people and their passive followers. Nor did she use it to mean that evil itself was banal or to make the Holocaust just one more example of everyday evil in human history. Finally, she obviously did not use it to hide or reveal any particular thesis or doctrine or as a precise theoretical explanation.

So what did Arendt mean by the "banality of evil?" By "banal," she meant a strictly factual contrast with "diabolical," "demonic," or "instinctively evil." As Susan Neiman has suggested, "banal" is less a definition of evil and more a theodicy that suggests "that the sources of evil are not mysterious or profound but fully within our grasp."[8] In other words, Arendt meant to counter the prevailing tradition of thought – literary, theological, and philosophical – about the phenomenon of evil and place it more squarely in "the ordinary." Psychoanalyst Elisabeth Young-Bruehl affirms that, for Arendt, the term "banal" did not mean "commonly occurring," but rather meant "commonplace" or "ordinary."[9] Peter Novick wove together Arendt's remarks from other publications and lectures to argue that by "the banality of evil" Arendt meant

> the phenomenon of evil deeds, committed on a gigantic scale, which could not be traced to any particularity of wickedness, pathology, or ideological conviction in the doer, whose only personal distinction was a perhaps extraordinary shallowness … However monstrous the deeds were, the doer was neither monstrous nor demonic … [Evil] can spread over the whole world like a fungus and lay waste precisely because it is not rooted anywhere … It was the most banal motives, not especially wicked ones (like sadism or the wish to humiliate or the will to power), which made Eichmann such a frightful evil-doer.[10]

Perhaps the greatest clarification, however, comes from the recognition that Arendt's conception of "banality" was less a description of the nature of evil and more a description of the nature of the man who committed the evil. In other words, she did not apply the term "banal" to the crimes themselves but, rather, to the origins – the causes and motivations – behind the man who perpetrated them. For Arendt, the "ordinary" banality of Eichmann's evil was twofold. First, Eichmann's evil was normal, prosaic, or matter-of-fact within the disfigured reality of the Nazi worldview. Second, Eichmann's evil was rationalized as good because it was obedient or because it served a larger purpose. Rather than a sadistic monster, Eichmann was a person strongly committed to personal fulfilment through a bureaucratic career. Not a raving ideologue animated by demonic antisemitism or a deranged madman, but simply an ambitious bureaucrat who did his duty and followed orders.

Contrary to expectations, Eichmann also was *not* a man without a conscience. As a matter of fact, it was his "good" conscience (though certainly not one that valued of all human life) that compelled him to follow what he felt to be his "duty" toward his superiors. In other words, his conscience worked "the other way around." He had not organized the killing because he particularly hated Jews or because he had somehow been forced to do so. Rather he did his job simply, and thoughtlessly, because he was a person "dutybound" to a social hierarchy committed to such extraordinary evil. The banality of his personality kept him from having compunction or even second thoughts about his "job." As Arendt wrote, "He would have had a bad conscience only if he had not done what he had been ordered to do – to ship millions of men, women and children to their death with great zeal and meticulous care."[11] This is why Eichmann continually made it clear that he felt he did no wrong. He would not have felt the slightest remorse had the Nazis won and had he been able to carry out the Final Solution.

Arendt reasoned that anyone could have filled Eichmann's role and that his evil was "banal" precisely because insertion into a social hierarchy committed to such evil made it normal and legitimate. This is why, in her view, Eichmann was not a madman. His deeds were monstrous, but Eichmann himself was thoroughly ordinary. In Arendt's words: "The trouble with Eichmann was precisely that so many were like him, and that the many were neither perverted nor sadistic, that they were, and still are, terribly and terrifyingly normal."[12]

The Banality of Eichmann's Evil

How applicable is Arendt's concept of the "banality of evil" to Eichmann specifically? The eminent Holocaust historian Raul Hilberg, for one, believes that Arendt did not recognize the magnitude of what Eichmann had done in the Final Solution in organizing the mass deportations of Jews from all corners of occupied Europe to the Polish extermination camps. "She did not," Hilberg wrote, "discern the pathways that Eichmann had found in the thicket of the German administrative machine for his unprecedented actions. She did not grasp the dimensions of his deed. There was no 'banality' in this 'evil.'"[13]

Similarly, Norman Podhoretz wrote that "no person of conscience could have participated knowingly in mass murder: to believe otherwise is to learn nothing about the nature of conscience ... no banality of a man could have done so hugely evil a job so well; to believe otherwise is to learn nothing about the nature of evil."[14] Echoing many who expressed concern about Arendt's criticism of Israel (criticism understood as bordering on antisemitic and racist) as well as her ahistorical comments, Yaacov Lozowick argued that her "position was the result of ideological considerations, not careful scholarship."[15] Most recently, Deborah Lipstadt, while holding that Arendt's "evaluation of the trail is actually more complex than those who have vilified her would acknowledge," has agreed that Eichmann was no mere passive actor, but an intentional agent, motivated not just by ordinary desires for professional advancement, but by deep-seated antisemitism.[16]

Clearly, Arendt had uncritically accepted Eichmann's representation of himself. Attending only the start of the trial, she neglected to understand that Eichmann did not simply follow orders but initiated creative new policies; that he was well-aware of what he was doing and, to a point, even proud of his accomplishments. By all accounts, he carried out his assigned duties with unyielding persistence, considerable ingenuity, and undying loyalty to the vision of the Final Solution. As Lipstadt concludes, "In Eichmann's case her [Arendt's] analysis seems strangely out of touch with the reality of his historical record."[17]

The Banality of Evil beyond Eichmann

If Arendt's conclusions about Eichmann were wrong, does that necessarily mean that her conception of the banality of evil was wrong as well? Certainly, her conception of evil was almost entirely new. As Stephen Miller has pointed out, before the Enlightenment, most theological and philosophical thinking about the nature of evil rested on the assumption that evildoing is the product of strong passions – pride, ambition, envy, or hatred.[18] During the Enlightenment and well into the nineteenth century, Western thinkers began to suggest that evil grew less out of our dark passions and more from unjust social conditions. This belief sounded a more hopeful note as it held out the possibility of eradicating evil through social and political transformations. The events of the Holocaust, though, shattered this more hopeful conception and cried for a new conception of evil – whether it be secular, religious, philosophical, or experiential. For many, it appeared that Arendt had found one.

The fact that Eichmann was not the "banal bureaucrat" that he pretended to be does not automatically, as some would argue, discredit Arendt's concept of the banality of evil. Even if she misunderstood her star example of the banality of evil, the conception itself may still serve as a powerful insight about how ordinary people come to commit extraordinary evil. As Christopher Browning has argued, "the 'banality of evil' is a concept that survives her [Arendt's] historical shortcomings."[19]

It should be remembered that Arendt's hypothesis of the obedient, indifferent, and mundane banal Nazi certainly does not apply to all Nazis, and certainly not any more than it applied to Eichmann. Such a sweeping judgment can lose the important distinctions, exceptions, qualifications, and nuances that are inherent in the complexity of understanding perpetrators of extraordinary evil. As it turns out, however, the awkward truth of the banality of evil is much more accurate and broadly applicable than we would hope. It had been apparent in the courtrooms at Nuremberg and it had surfaced again and again in the subsequent German postwar trials against other perpetrators of Nazi genocidal policies.

Recent research by historian Dick de Mildt, for example, meticulously reviewed the cases of 129 German citizens put on trial in the late 1940s and early 1950s before West German courts on suspicion of involvement in the mass murder policies of Nazi Germany. De Mildt concluded that, by and large, the background profiles of the men and women who were involved in either one – or both – of these mass murder campaigns evidenced the same banality of evil that Arendt used to (mis)characterize Eichmann. They were not idealists or killers of conviction. Rather, they were killers by circumstance and opportunity. "Instead of matching the image of the paranoiac ideological warriors so often invoked when describing the fieldworkers of Nazi genocide," de Mildt writes, "their background profile far more closely matches that of rather ordinary citizens with a well-developed calculating instinct for their private interests ... The key word which springs to mind when reviewing the criminal biographies of the 'Euthanasia' and *Aktion Reinhard* hangmen is not 'idealism' but 'opportunism.'"[20]

In addition to the significant amount of comparative archival work I have done in perpetrator behaviour over the years, I have now interviewed face-to-face over 225 alleged or convicted perpetrators of genocide and mass atrocity from a wide range of countries in Latin America and the Great Lakes Region of Africa, the former Yugoslavia, and Northern Ireland. That work has affirmed that the banality of evil thesis is not unique to Nazi Germany. Rather, it transcends culture, place, time, people, and history. Killers of circumstance and opportunity are the norm rather than the exception. When it appears, idealism and conviction most often emerge as justifications for committing atrocities; consequence rather than cause.

In summary, perhaps Arendt's coinage of the phrase "banality of evil" was unfortunate. Its lack of clarity leaves it open to many interpretations. For all of her critics, though, her *conception* of the banality and ordinariness of perpetrators of extraordinary evil has withstood the test of time. She suggests that the commission of extraordinary evil has a universalism that transcends groups, culture, psychopathology, and personality. Arendt leaves us with the crucially insightful recognition that ordinary people in extraordinary circumstances can perform extraordinarily evil deeds. Its durability is most telling in that it runs counter to our unwillingness, even our inability, to believe in the "ordinariness" of people who perpetrate such extraordinary evil. We would rather maintain that extraordinary individuals, very much *unlike* you and me, commit extraordinary evil. We can then distance *us* from *them* and rest in the reassurance that extraordinary evil cannot be duplicated in "ordinary" groups or cultures or in individuals with seemingly "normal" human capacities. As the novelist Leslie Epstein wrote in 1987, "the outrage ... that greeted Arendt's thesis when applied to Adolf Eichmann indicates the depth of our need to think of that bureaucrat as different from ourselves, to respond to him, indeed, as a typical character in Holocaust fiction – a beast, a pervert, a monster."[21]

The Structure of a Social Scientific Revolution

Peter Baehr has argued that Arendt "loathed the social sciences," particularly sociology, finding them pretentious and obfuscating.[22] Arendt took issue with what she saw as social scientific explanations built on deterministic theories of causality that denied the existence of human freedom. In *The Human Condition*, Arendt wrote that the social sciences "[aimed] to reduce man as a whole, in all his activity, to the level of a conditioned and behaving animal."[23]

Regardless of her feelings regarding the social sciences, qualified in large part by her conflation of a variety of disciplinary object domains and perspectives, it is clear that her conception of the banality of evil was influenced greatly by the notion of the bureaucratic "machinery of destruction," a notion developed by a political scientist often credited with founding the field of Holocaust studies – Raul Hilberg. Moreover, Arendt's conception of the banality of evil was resonant with emerging social scientific trends emphasizing the power of the situation in understanding human behaviour. While the Eichmann trial recentred Holocaust narratives about victims' experiences rather than perpetrators' acts, her conception of the banality of evil would ally well with the social sciences' most salient demonstrations of situationism – a core tenet that emphasizes the power of the situational forces over human behaviour.

The emphasis that Hilberg and Arendt placed on the power of social structures received "experimental" validation in Stanley Milgram's three-year study, begun while the Eichmann trial was in process, on obedience to authority. Milgram (1933–1984), then a young social psychologist at Yale University, posed a simple, but intriguing, research question: How far would ordinary Americans go in inflicting harm on a perfectly innocent stranger if an authority figure told them to do so?

To probe this question empirically, Milgram devised a "learning" experiment in which unwitting subjects were led to believe that they were administering increasingly severe, but "corrective" electrical shocks to another "volunteer" subject (in reality, an accomplice of the experimenter). The experimenter/"authority figure" explained that the shocks were intended to test the effects of punishment on learning. In the initial experiment, twenty-six out of forty participants (65 per cent) obeyed the experimenter's orders that they shock the "learner," in steadily increasing magnitude, to the point of maximum, perhaps even life-threatening, punishment. In a series of more than twenty studies, Milgram could not devise a variation in which no subjects would obey the experimenter fully. Testing more than a thousand individuals in a variety of obedience conditions, Milgram found that obedience to authority is deep-seated and often insidious in human behaviour without regard to age, gender, or level of education.[24] While recent critiques of the validity of his studies have become popular (though poorly argued), Milgram's main findings have been replicated at least forty times in subsequent research studies around the world.[25]

Milgram's findings joined those of Hilberg and Arendt to show how social structures produce immensely destructive behaviour. In Milgram's words: "After witnessing hundreds of ordinary people submit to the authority in our experiments, I must conclude that Arendt's conception of the banality of evil comes closer to the truth than one might dare imagine ... That is, perhaps, the most fundamental lesson of our study: ordinary people, simply doing their jobs, and without any particular hostility on their part, can become agents in a terrible destructive process."[26] He concludes, "while there are enormous differences of circumstance and scope, a common psychological process is centrally involved in both [his laboratory experiments and Nazi Germany] events."[27] It is important to note that the implications of Milgram's work were not about understanding Eichmann per se but were about understanding Arendt's general conception of the banality of evil.

Several years later, the social psychologist Philip Zimbardo explored similar issues related to the power of the situation in his 1971 Stanford Prison Experiment (SPE), a simulation in which he investigated how the immediate social context of prison life – its roles, rules, and norms – might transform the people within it.[28] Under realistic circumstances, twenty-one male undergraduates were randomly assigned to play the role of a prisoner or guard during the study. Although neither group received instructions about how to behave, some "prisoners" and "guards" soon acted like their real-world counterparts. Many of the prisoners became increasingly resigned, ineffectual, apathetic, submissive, and depressed. Despite their knowledge that they might just as easily have been randomly assigned as prisoners, about a third of the eleven guards took on cruel, callous, sadistic, dominating, authoritarian, tyrannical, coercive, and aggressive roles. This moral drift and brutality escalated daily, demoralizing the mock prisoners to such an extent that Zimbardo aborted the study – planned to last two weeks – after only six days.

The SPE demonstrated the evil that ordinary people can be readily induced into doing to other ordinary people within the context of socially approved roles, rules, and norms, a legitimizing ideology, and institutional support that transcends individual agency. It also demonstrated that the egregious brutality of some perpetrators does not automatically indicate an *inherent*, pre-existing brutality; not everyone playing a brutal role has to have sadistic traits of character. Rather, brutality can be a consequence, not only a cause, of being in a duly certified and legitimized social hierarchy committed to extraordinary evil. In other words, the nature of the tasks of extraordinary evil may have been sufficient to produce that brutality even if the perpetrators were not initially sadists. It was a vicious social arrangement, and not the pre-existing viciousness of the participants, that led to the cruel behaviours exhibited by the guards.

Zimbardo's debt to Arendt's conception of the banality of evil is clear in his 2007 book-length treatment of the SPE. He writes:

Arendt's phrase "the banality of evil" continues to resonate because genocide has been unleashed around the world and torture and terrorism continue to be common features of our global landscape. We prefer to distance ourselves from such a fundamental truth, seeing the madness of evildoers and senseless violence of tyrants as dispositional characters within their personal makeup. Arendt's analysis was the first to deny this orientation by observing the fluidity with which social forces can prompt normal people to perform horrific acts.[29]

Clearly, Arendt's work influenced a generation of social scientists to believe, in Neiman's words, that the sources of evil are not mysterious or profound but fully within our grasp.[30] David Cesarani argues that Arendt's "notion of the 'banality of evil,' combined with Milgram's theses on the predilection for obedience to authority, *straitjacketed* [italics mine] research into Nazi Germany and the persecution of the Jews for two decades."[31] On the contrary, I maintain that, where Cesarani sees a straitjacket, there was really the shaping of a paradigm in the social sciences under Arendt's influence; the structure of a social scientific revolution that would move us from exceptionalism to universalism in our attempt to understand the origins of perpetrator behaviour.

For the generations of social scientists beyond Milgram and Zimbardo, Arendt's conception of the banality of evil had a transformative disciplinary influence that still impacts their work, both conceptually and methodologically. Couched in the vocabulary of Thomas Kuhn's landmark *The Structure of Scientific Revolutions*, Arendt bequeathed to social science a paradigm that shaped the fundamental assumptions, as well as the shared exemplars (or models of good research), of how we approach and understand perpetrator behaviour.[32] That is, she gave us the language, conceptual framework, theories, methods, and limits of how we understand the perpetration of extraordinary evil. In so doing, she shaped, and continues to shape, the very fields of disciplinary knowledge that she so often excoriated.

Conclusion

As Lindsay Macumber has argued, "Arendt has been nothing short of demonized by scholars."[33] In this essay I have argued that such demonization, where it exists, stems from indictments of Arendt's personal biases as well as her misunderstanding of the subject of her work, Adolf Eichmann. I have also argued, however, that neither of these planks for demonization justifies the jettisoning of Arendt's conception of the banality of evil. That conception, quite apart from its origin in Arendt's personal views or her characterization of Eichmann, has stood the test of time. As Lipstadt asserts, "Her [Arendt's] contention that many of the perpetrators were not innately monsters or diabolical creates but 'ordinary' people who did monstrous things not only seems accurate but is the accepted understanding among most scholars of the perpetrators."[34]

NOTES

1 For a review, see James E. Waller, *Becoming Evil: How Ordinary People Commit Genocide and Mass Killing*, 2nd ed. (New York, 2007).

2 For additional background on the life of Hannah Arendt, see Elisabeth Young-Bruehl's *Hannah Arendt: For Love of the World*, 2nd ed. (New Haven, CT, 2004).

3 Peter Novick, *The Holocaust in American Life* (New York, 1999), 134.

4 Hannah Arendt, *Eichmann in Jerusalem: A Report on the Banality of Evil* (New York, 1963). See her postscript, especially p. 283 and following, in the 1964 revised and enlarged edition published by Penguin Books. All subsequent quotes and page numbers in this essay refer to the Penguin edition.

5 Arendt, *Eichmann in Jerusalem*, 25.

6 Ibid., 287.

7 Ibid., 252.

8 Susan Neiman, *Evil in Modern Thought: An Alternative History of Philosophy* (Princeton, 2002), 303.

9 Elisabeth Young-Bruehl, "From the Pariah's Point of View: Reflections on Hannah Arendt's Life and Work," in *Hannah Arendt: The Recovery of the Public World*, ed. Melvyn Hill (New York, 1979), 17.

10 Novick, *The Holocaust in American Life*, 135.

11 Arendt, *Eichmann in Jerusalem*, 25.

12 Ibid., 276.

13 Raul Hilberg, *The Politics of Memory: The Journey of a Holocaust Historian* (Chicago, 1996), 150.

14 Norman Podhoretz, "Hannah Arendt on Eichmann: A Study in the Perversity of Brilliance," *Commentary* (1963): 206.

15 Yaacov Lozowick, "Malicious Clerks: The Nazi Security Police and the Banality of Evil," in *Hannah Arendt in Jerusalem*, ed. Steven E. Aschheim (Berkeley, 2001), 216.

16 Deborah Lipstadt, *The Eichmann Trial* (New York, 2011), 164.

17 Ibid., 169.

18 Stephen Miller, "A Note on the Banality of Evil," *WQ: The Wilson Quarterly* 12 (Autumn 1998): 54–9.

19 Christopher R. Browning, "Introduction," in Leonard S. Newman and Ralph Erber's *Understanding Genocide: The Social Psychology of the Holocaust* (New York, 2002), 4.

20 Dirk Welmoed de Mildt, *In the Name of the People: Perpetrators of Genocide in the Reflection of Their Post-War Prosecution in West Germany* (London, 1996), 311.
21 Quoted in Miller, "A Note on the Banality of Evil," 55.
22 Peter Baehr, *Hannah Arendt, Totalitarianism, and the Social Sciences* (Stanford, 2010), 3.
23 Hannah Arendt, *The Human Condition* (Chicago, 1958), 45.
24 Milgram's experiments on obedience to authority were originally published with the innocuous title "Behavioral Study of Obedience" (*Journal of Abnormal and Social Psychology* 67 [1963]: 371–8). The complete and most authoritative account of Milgram's series of studies on obedience to authority can be found in his book *Obedience to Authority: An Experimental View* (New York, 1974).
25 See, for instance, Gina Perry's highly speculative *Behind the Shock Machine: The Untold Story of the Notorious Milgram Psychology Experiments* (New York, 2013).
26 Milgram, *Obedience to Authority*, 6.
27 Ibid., 175.
28 Philip Zimbardo, "Pathology of Imprisonment," *Society* 6 (1972): 4, 6, 8.
29 Philip Zimbardo, *The Lucifer Effect: Understanding How Good People Turn Evil* (New York, 2007), 288–9.
30 Neiman, *Evil in Modern Thought*, 303.
31 David Cesarani, *Becoming Eichmann* (Cambridge, MA, 2004), 15.
32 Thomas S. Kuhn, *The Structure of Scientific Revolutions* (Chicago, 1962).
33 Lindsay Macumber, "Banality Reconsidered: The Process from Ambivalence to Compliance, or 'It is Pointless to Swim against the Stream'" (paper presented at the Centre for Jewish Studies Graduate Conference at the University of Toronto, 18 April 2012.
34 Lipstadt, *The Eichmann Trial*, 169.

2 From History to Story: When the "Architect" of the Holocaust Became His Own "Witness"[1]

FABIEN THÉOFILAKIS

Introduction: Adolf Eichmann, No Ordinary Defendant

When the trial of Adolf Eichmann began in Beit Ha'am on the morning of 11 April 1961, everyone looked expectantly at the glass booth. However the spectators were quickly disappointed by the defendant, whose image seemed far removed from that of the intimidating SS (Schutzstaffel) officer they were expecting. Many journalists and Israeli citizens felt the same disillusion that police officer Avner Less had noticed when he first saw Eichmann during the preliminary investigation:

> I considered and studied Eichmann thoroughly. Actually this man is a deception. I imagined him as something completely else. Bigger in stature, more imposing in terms of appearance and presence, yes, perhaps arrogant in his behaviour. I expected to face a devil, and I now have to state that Eichmann had neither horn nor clubfoot. If I had met him on the street, I would not have not even paid him attention – he would have melted into the masses. But perhaps it is this anonymity, that made him so dangerous, this inner impulse to become somebody.[2]

To be sure, the formerly young officer in his smart black SS uniform, whom Prime Minister David Ben-Gurion introduced as "the architect of the Final Solution," was now a decrepit man in his fifties. With his thick glasses and dark suit and tie, he looked quite ordinary, resembling a civil servant in a public administration.

Few people, however, noticed the notepad that awaited the defendant in the booth. This notebook was a subtle indication of the unusually large volume of writing that Eichmann would produce during his trial. Throughout the 121 sessions of his trial, Eichmann handled pens of different calibres, bombarded his lawyer with notes, and entrenched himself behind thick stacks of files. Even fewer people knew that the defendant was also a graphomaniac: between his arrival in Israel on 22 May 1960 and his execution on 31 May 1962, he wrote more than 8,000 pages. This writing, together with his *Argentinien Papiere*,[3] constituted his corpus. During his questioning, Eichmann wrote "Meine Memoiren" (128 pages), which he later completed with a testimony about his escape. He also read the 3,564-page preliminary investigation to his trial and signed his initials to page after page. Between the end of the trial and the judgment on 15 December, Eichmann wrote a second version of his memoirs, titled "Idols," which was 1,206 pages in length. Even his death sentence did not put a stop to this intense autobiographic activity: before his hanging, he wrote several more manuscripts.

None of the twenty-four Nazi defendants at the Nuremberg trial were such prolific writers, even those who had occupied much higher positions of responsibility within the regime. At the request of the Allied legal authorities in 1946, Hans Frank (former governor-general of the General Government territory in occupied Poland) wrote a twenty-five-page memo recalling his experiences and activities in Nazi Germany. Also at Nuremberg, Ernst Kaltenbrunner produced a twenty-seven-page overview of his life and career during the Third Reich. Rudolf Höss, commander of the Auschwitz complex, provides an example that contrasts with Eichmann's obsessive writing: while in jail, Höss wrote only a short autobiography for the Polish court.[4] But neither at the Nuremberg trial nor in the following trials of Nazi perpetrators did any of the accused take advantage of the opportunity to explain his or her past actions to the same extent as Eichmann.

The former SS officer's writing frenzy was not limited to *pro domo* pleadings. Eichmann's prolific inclinations spread, first and foremost, in relation to the legal proceedings of his trial, and he wrote in order to aid his defence. Eichmann dedicated the same amount of energy to writing memoranda and critically analysing the documents produced by the prosecution after the hearings and on the weekends as he did to taking notes for his defence counsel during the sessions. In his glass booth, in his cell at Beit Ha'am, and also behind bars in the prison in Ramla, Eichmann sharpened his weapons of pen and paper and prepared for his final battle. This written confrontation with his judges, prosecutors, and victims thus provides a unique archive for anyone wishing to understand how the trial was viewed from inside the glass booth. To date, these thousands of pages have been overlooked and unused by historians. Aside from historiographical and practical reasons, the fact that Eichmann's notes have been underutilized can be explained by considering two questions: what kind of history do the notes allow us to write and how can they be used?

Eichmann's notes do not allow us to solve the mystery he posed to the "world of the sufferers."[5] They do not lay bare the ideological justification of antisemitism; they do not contain a confession of guilt; and they do not reveal the ways in which an ordinary man was transformed into one who perpetrated genocide. However, they do reveal something else entirely: they allow us to understand to what extent Eichmann was playing a role in Jerusalem, and, specifically, what role that was. In other words, they allow us to see how he *worked*, in order to comprehend how Eichmann presented himself in court and the way that he experienced his trial and sought to manipulate his image. Finally, these notes allow us to consider the reasons why the accused chose his defence strategy, a strategy which reveals a far from "banal" figure.

Hannah Arendt's analysis, which has caused rivers of ink to flow about Eichmann and the nature of perpetrators in Nazi Germany, brought about an interpretation of the trial that shielded the defendant. It presented him as a paradigmatic character – a new kind of persecutor, the "desk perpetrator" – who performed his job without any ideological motive or exterminating will. Because of the way the totalitarian system functioned, by bureaucratizing its massive crime apparatus, the regime made its "civil servants" unaccountable. Despite several highly relevant remarks and a careful reading of the trial documents, Hannah Arendt moved from her theory of a totalitarian system to examining the defendant, instead of taking account of what Eichmann really said. However, she appears to have attended only a quarter of the sessions, mostly at the beginning of the trial,[6] so her conclusions about Eichmann were based on limited observation on the spot and on the transcript of the sessions. For instance, she wrote, "Despite all the efforts of the prosecution, everybody could see that this man was not a 'monster,' but it was difficult indeed not to suspect that he was a clown."[7] The neglected corpus of Eichmann's notes allows us to step beyond Arendt's perspective and take a deeper look at the man in the glass booth. A much different Eichmann emerges from these pages. He was no ordinary defendant. In contrast to those tried at Nuremberg, he took part in the legal proceedings and wielded influence beyond that of a typical defendant. Eichmann sought to be involved in every step of the judicial procedure. In doing so, he used all the legal tools he had to defend himself and, in the end, produced an unprecedented corpus of notes, memorandums, and charts commenting on his time in jail as well as in the defendant's box. Through his notes we learn not about the facts of the case but about his assessment of the protagonists, his existential position, and the meaning he imparted on the trial.

This essay, based on the notes that Eichmann took between March 1961 and March 1962, reads these writings as wartime writings, arguing that during this time Eichmann was engaging in his last battle against the *Reichsfeinde* (enemies of the Reich). The weapons that he used were not military but rather discursive tools; to Eichmann, finality was not merely the extermination of his enemies, but also the fight and struggle for its interpretation. This essay presupposes that these notes constitute the missing link between the Eichmann in Argentina, who regretted in 1957 not having killed all the 10.3 million Jews of Europe, and the one who played the role of "cautious bureaucrat" in front of the entire world. Although Eichmann had had an opportunity in Argentina to develop a version of his actions in Europe between 1932 and 1945, the fact that he was confronted with "the Jew" for a second time – and this time in a completely reversed balance of power – obliged him to adapt his discourse. His notes now give us the possibility to analyse how he was *thinking* during the trial. To what extent do the notes express a tension between the strategic constraints of the legal arena and the underlying will of the defendant to claim an inheritance?

Archive of a Trial: When the Defendant Assisted His Counsel for the Defence

Placed in the context of their production, the notes reveal an unfolding defence strategy. Even if the answers and reactions of Robert Servatius (Eichmann's defence counsel) are missing, the notes reveal a process characterized by a shortage of time and a lack of manpower, which transformed the defendant into an expert on his own case. The prosecution team, which included Gideon Hausner and three other prosecutors, could rely on the work conducted by the police (the Office 06); in contrast Servatius was the only counsel for the defence. Servatius was, however, experienced in trials of Nazi war criminals; at the International Military Tribunal in Nuremberg he defended Fritz Sauckel as well as the Nazi Party as a criminal organization, Professor Karl Brandt for charges of participating in the euthanasia program, and Paul Pleider, the Reichsbeauftragter für Kohle. A young lawyer named Dieter Wechtenbruch assisted Servatius. However, after the first few weeks, the latter went to Europe to take part in the questioning of the sixteen German witnesses for the defence; he did not return until the last sessions at the end of July.

Eichmann's counsel had a considerable workload: Servatius had seven months to learn the file, work with the approximately 1,600 documents chosen by the public prosecutor, and gather his own evidence and witnesses. One week after the trial had begun, Eichmann complained to his counsel about the conditions in which they had to work:

> The prosecution against me is so *massive*, as to be far-fetched. As if [erasure] I were Himmler or even Hitler!
>
> But I *have to* defend myself against this madness. I have no means for that. The defence should have more assistants, *who must be paid by the Israel State, which let me be kidnapped*.[8]

This configuration between "us" and "them" had the effect of building team spirit between Eichmann and his defence counsel. They joined together to fight what Eichmann saw as an "unequal struggle."

The defendant put his clerical obsession to use by handling the bulk of the documentation, and thus participated, to an unprecedented degree, in the work of his own defence. Away from the cameras, Eichmann examined sources, which he sorted and divided into groups. He listed documents, indicated their deficiencies, and questioned their authenticity. Eichmann's work as the document specialist determined the pace of Servatius' work. Regretting that the prosecution had not communicated the number of documents in advance, Eichmann did not hesitate to push his lawyers in order to keep up with the timetable:

> I am very late in the processing of files. I have seen, from more than 1,500 documents, only 400 until now.
>
> Please urgently request documents so that I can work at least on Saturday and Sunday on what will be due at the beginning of the next week. In the absence of documents I can consequently object to nothing.[9]

As well, the former SS officer developed his own system to handle the volume of documents, using his experience as *Referent* (department head) at the Reich Security Main Office (RSHA) to do so. Out of the public prosecutor's classification system, he established another logic of utilization, that is, of interpretation. In preparation for the sessions, which Hausner organized by country, Eichmann worked on the selected documents, which he called the *Länderakten*. He informed his defence that he "could gather together these documents into files" and had "classified also all the *Länderdokumente*."[10] He even proposed a holistic system of organization that could classify the entire defence, as he thought, into seven thematic groups, including personnel data, career, and role in antisemitic policies. This system seems to correspond to the order of the files in Servatius' archives.

Eichmann paid much attention to detail. While planning for his questioning by Servatius at the end of June, he suggested a didactic "distribution of the projects," which combined themes with documents. For instance, Project "Zur Person" would be included with document no. 22; Project "Deutschland II" with document no. 874 (the affidavit of Huppenkothen, a witness for the defence); Project "Deutschland V" with documents about Austria, unless Servatius wanted to "introduce all of them one after another."[11] This capacity to rethink the documentation has to do with Eichmann's mindset – the idea that he was still mobilizing for war. In the late 1950s in Argentina, Eichmann had considered returning to Germany to go to trial, and then to start a new political career for the Fourth Reich. He prepared for this future by keeping up with the National Socialist historiography.

The reversed function of counsel between lawyer and client stimulated the document production. In late May 1961, Eichmann wrote memos and drew detailed organization charts which encapsulated three advantages he saw to his involvement: his expertise in the subject matter, his time-saving method of organizing evidence, and his control over his line of defence. Indeed, Eichmann's knowledge became a considerable asset to the defence team: he chose the exculpatory evidence and defined the battle order, and the defence counsel aligned itself to his plans. Thus, Eichmann held the balance of power in his relationship with his defence team.

Eichmann also maintained his role as auxiliary in court, where he acted as the devoted, emotionless stenographer of his own case. In the notes passed by the policeman sitting on his left, Eichmann asked Servatius to show him pictures to identify, expressed his interpretation of various documents, and referred his counsel to notes about the evidence to be summoned. In this quite uncommon and interactive way, the defendant reacted to the narrative that was taking shape in court. Scrawled on random sheets of paper, the notes are characterized by the use of colours, capital letters, and expressive handwriting, reflecting Eichmann's emotional involvement in the process. These are not the notes of a "cautious bureaucrat" or a "common criminal."

Eichmann made the most of his key role. Out of all the players in the courtroom (prosecution, defence, judges), only Eichmann had been an actor in the antisemitic policies that began in 1933, meaning that he was personally familiar with the events of the Holocaust. This strategic advantage allowed him to use his command of historiography – the main source of knowledge for judges, the defence, and the prosecution – in an indirect way. Because he knew what his opponents and adversaries knew, he was always ahead of the curve, which gave him a certain amount of flexibility to adapt his narrative and find the best balance between credibility and deceit. In particular her relied on two reference works for the preliminary investigation: *The Final Solution: The Attempt to Exterminate the Jews of Europe, 1939–45,* by Gerald Reitlinger, and *Das Dritte Reich und seine Diener,* edited by Léon Poliakov and Joseph Wulf.[12] Eichmann had read these books in Argentina in preparation for the Sassen discussions.[13] In Jerusalem he continued his extraordinary "dialogue" with these historians. He used their works to analyse the prosecution's documentation, to counter its interpretation of his actions, and to determine other lines of interrogation and response.

During his "struggle" – which is how he viewed his trial – Eichmann repeated a tactic he had used at the Referat IVB4 and he used it well: bluffing. If trial was Eichmann's ultimate struggle to push forward a narrative of the National Socialist years, the documents he produced became "this dreadful ammunition"[14] to reduce the adversary to silence, and afterward to lead the offensive. Between the ruses of war and legal rules, Eichmann did not only try to furnish evidence in Israel, he also opposed another *régime de vérité.*

When Eichmann Told His "Story"

In the prolific, often redundant, notes produced by the defendant are a number of autobiographical details that allow us to trace his life's path. For the purpose of the trial, Eichmann, then fifty-five years old, reconstructed a narrative of his life. He presumed, of course, a teleological continuity (I became what I am, because I could not become somebody else) and he integrated the legal constraints under which he operated by proposing a discourse acceptable for his lawyer and the court. This shifts the issue from the truth of the discourse to its credibility.

Eichmann's notes reach back to the origins of his political engagement in the 1920s, at other times to his birth date in 1906, and even as far back as his ancestors. By mid-1960 he had written for Servatius two successive notes with the evocative titles: "My position toward the facts until 1945 and the start of my intellectual development"[15] and "My present position to the facts taking into account my experience."[16] In his completed project the accused presented three key points to rehabilitate his image. First he listed reasons for his support of Nazism, which he presented as a necessity; next he stressed his positive development since the end of the war (I am no longer who I was); finally he introduced the idea of "destiny" (*Schicksal*). For Eichmann, destiny referred to the human struggle with forces that exceed it and thus, in some ways, remove individual responsibility. Introducing the concept of "destiny" made Eichmann merely "a plaything of destiny, in the eternal interplay between cause and consequence."[17] This mirrors, on a larger scale, his other line of defence: that of the small *Befehlsempfänger* (one who received commands), who had no control in the decision-making process but was simply the underling of Nazi dignitaries. These three points served to depoliticize and denazify Eichmann's commitment during the Third Reich and to explain – that is, to rehabilitate – his actions between 1932 and 1945.

Eichmann attempted to present Nazism in a way that de-emphasized racial politics, viewed in 1961 as the most destructive part of Nazi ideology and practices and of his own responsibility. In doing so, he offered his vision of Nazism in opposition to the one developed by the prosecution, which situated the destruction of European Jews as a fundamental objective of the regime.

In order to explain "how it could happen,"[18] Eichmann considered – in a classic way – the Treaty of Versailles as the source of all evil, and in particular as the cause of the rise of nationalism in Germany. He pointed out the inability of the Weimar Republic to move past the German defeat and cited the economic crisis that (with seven million unemployed) had brought about the "mass pauperization of the German people."[19] In this depressed economic environment, Eichmann argued, integration of the masses into politics became a necessity, a situation reflected in the fight between two political parties – the NSDAP (National Socialist German Workers' Party, or Nazi Party) and the Communist Party – for hegemony in Germany. Through mass mobilization, the former SS officer assigned to antisemitism the function of "catalyst," a secondary motive until the Nazi takeover of power. However, he acknowledged that the fact that "the Jew carried no more and no less guilt … as others, was not to be said."[20] By separating the fight against communism and Jews, Eichmann eliminated entirely the antisemitic ideology that formed a significant component of Nazism as well as the dynamic of annihilation that began in 1941. (In 1961, many historians, influenced by the intentionalist school of thought, argued that the Nazi extermination project began in 1939.) Therefore, Eichmann could introduce himself in the following way: "In this context I have to say that such an idea as the physical destruction of Jews was so completely alien to me that it didn't even come to my mind. When I heard the 'Führerbefehl' for the first time, the words and ideas were frightening for me."[21]

In this context, the link between German history and Eichmann's individual path was presented as normal. Like many others, Eichmann had let himself be taken over by the "nationalist channels" and had joined the NSDAP in 1932 in Austria only because of the negative fallout of the Treaty of Versailles. He was then, little by little, overtaken by National Socialist ideology until he could no longer – and no longer wanted to – think differently. He became a "good and reliable SS-man," then "a good and reliable SS-officer."[22] This trajectory was marked by obedience to his superiors in the SS, then to the regime through the RSHA. As Eichmann explained, "My initial voluntary involvement then became a legal obligation and at the start of the war ... a coercion, which I couldn't escape."[23] Wrapped up in the integrative logic of the totalitarian system, defending his country, bound by his duty, the SS *Obersturmbahnführer* was not responsible for his actions because he was acting for the regime: absolute obedience had become "second nature."[24] It is the line of defence Eichmann would summarize with the *Befehlsempfänger* argument – that he was a small cog in the extermination machine. This is why the man who was initially responsible for a "political solution"[25] to the "Jewish Question" became the man involved in the Final Solution.

Eichmann Posing for Posterity: Why Did Eichmann Fight? Whom Did He Fight?

Eichmann's writings reveal how he viewed his trial in Jerusalem and the stakes he placed on it. His notes show that he perceived a dramatic struggle between him and the court – in other words, between Nazism and the "Jewish people." Immersed in an a priori hostile environment, Eichmann paid attention to any individual with power or in a position of public authority. Early in June 1961 he gave his counsel an amazing gallery of written portraits of the main protagonists: he was drawn to Hausner's "sad, nice and deep" eyes, and he described "the old expert on international law" as "solidity itself." Among the judges, he preferred Yitzhak Raveh, whose eyes often met his; he noted the "clever appearance of his head" and his "friendly voice." In fact, all of the Jewish actors involved in the proceedings, from the police officers to his guards, impressed Eichmann due to their absence of spite and brutality, which stood in contrast to the customs and manners of the "German police." "I have to say, God damn!, astonishing people,"[26] he remarked in a note.

This collective attitude of Jews was incomprehensible to Eichmann and he asked his counsel to explain it to him. But this perception also shows Eichmann's realization of the fact that the time for justice had come. In the face-to-face interactions he had during the trial, Eichmann assumed that he understood which role the prosecution wanted him to play to further their narrative of the Holocaust and fulfil the political finality of his trial. On the fifth day of the sessions, he announced to his counsel:

The *prosecution argues thus*:

1) The RSHA was responsible for *all* Jewish matters
2) The *Referent* for Jewish issues at the RSHA was Eichmann (I was in the Amt IV of the RSHA)
3) Ergo he is responsible for *each* Jewish issue.[27]

He refused to lend himself to this "game" that transformed him into a cog in a world that was not his. He was concerned only with three of the fifteen charges, hence the verbal confrontation levelled at Hausner during his cross-examination.

The Court of the Jewish State, however, was not the only adversary Eichmann faced. He intended to set himself apart from those Nazis who rejected Nazism during their trials and thus broke their oath of loyalty. Facing his judges, Eichmann was also confronted with Nazism, but he wished to be the one who did not surrender or lie. Not rejecting Nazism in its entirety would be, Eichmann believed, a way to carry on the legacy of National Socialism. Well aware of the major trials at the end of the war, he attached particular importance to Nuremberg because, in his mind, that trial resulted in the treason of his comrades. They sacrificed the Nazi ideal and brought evidence against absentees in order to save their "organic life." During the preparation for his own trial, Eichmann examined the number of victims suggested in Nuremberg and wrote to Servatius, "The more the defendants lied about their former superiors and also comrades of pretty much the same official position, the bigger the trust that these cowards expected to win for themselves from the occupying forces."[28]

Yet, Eichmann argued that he was on trial in Jerusalem fifteen years later because of his absence at Nuremberg. He explained that, at Nuremberg, his comrades shamelessly passed off their responsibilities to him. Without knowing it, they played into the hands of the Israeli "enemy" by making Eichmann the "scapegoat."[29] Eichmann did not put himself in the same category as the "lying Wisliceny," "The Becker, Veesermayer, and Winkelmann, and their inferior cowardice," and Globke.[30] Servatius endeavoured to confuse the issue of responsibility but Eichmann did not lay the blame on the other members of his office; he stood up for what he had done. During his trial, he intended to denounce, but not "betray." He would not provide any new names or tell any secrets. In some ways, the attitude of his superiors toward justice allowed Eichmann to play the last of Hitler's soldiers – a role he assumed with confidence – and led him to conceive of Jerusalem as the anti-Nuremberg.

Eichmann never ceased defending himself because he believed he was fighting for his honour and his family, but above all for truth and posterity. In that sense, the defendant and his prosecutors were in agreement on one point: the case number 40/61 would be a trial for the history books. The corpus contains notes that reflect the defendant's state of mind and the way in which he included his *Weltanschauung* (worldview) in his trial, which makes the finality of his struggle explicit. By early June, halfway through the trial, his counsel told Eichmann that he was fighting for his life. Eichmann responded:

> Whether I struggle or not, I am not stupid enough to not know that my current life is already lost, in *any case*. Nothing matters: if I sleep, watch out, or look in the air during the flood of lies in my glass booth, so-called dock. The result is in any case the same …
>
> *No, to fight for my life* is for me out of the question in Israel, because the decision has already been made a long time ago …
>
> A library of books will write legends about me for the time being. Until the nets become friable, the web-spinning spiders dry out due to the absence of new food. But life is eternal; a new spider will start with the net of the truth. *That is important to me.*[31]

By presenting himself as a soldier of the truth, Eichmann continued the National Socialist struggle by rehabilitating the work of his department and denouncing the proceedings in Israel as victor's justice. In this way, he used the glass booth as a stage. Several clues suggest that he wanted his name to go down in history – and not only as a "cautious bureaucrat."

Nazism after the Holocaust and the Defeat of the Third Reich: The Contradictions of Eichmann's Autobiographical Illusion in Court

Three arenas for confrontation seemed to guide Eichmann's strategy: the utilization of documents to draw up short-term plans, clashes with witnesses in court, and his own questioning as a witness at the end of the trial. That Eichmann continued to be a Nazi long after the end of the National Socialist regime demonstrates the importance of his notes and impacts how they can be interpreted. If one considers that Eichmann was still operating with a Nazi mentality, then a critical analysis of his notes should refer to the relationship between what he said and what he wrote, and should attend to the discrepancy between what he stated publicly and how he viewed himself according to the Nazi value system.

One of the arguments Eichmann put forward to prove he was not legally responsible for what he was accused of dealt with his position in the Nazi apparatus and the functioning of the administration. According to the *Führerprinzip*, every member of the Nazi organization had to unquestioningly obey his superiors, and at the top, the *Führer* – a principle that provided the hierarchical organization with its strong structure.[32] As one of the most famous specialists of constitutional law in the Third Reich, Theodor Maunz, declared in 1943, "The command of the Führer … is the absolute center of the present legal order."[33] In fact, Eichmann referred to this concept to defend himself by distinguishing between what he did as a civil servant and what he thought as a person. In a note to Servatius he tried to explain what was meant by the expression *im Auftrag* (on behalf of), concluding, "All of them have been commissioned and have orders, to write *i. A.* of the leader."[34] Eichmann compared the values of the Nazi regime to the administration in any other political regime.

According to the *Führerprinzip*, obedience was a positive virtue. To Eichmann, obedience determined the nature of his work and reflected his attachment to the regime's ideology. If Eichmann was such an essential specialist and became such a well-known symbol of the deportation of the Jews – if he were such a good Nazi civil servant, in other words – it is precisely because he was "working towards the Führer."[35] But Eichmann was not just a zealous bureaucrat; he also initiated policies to meet the wishes of Hitler (and other leaders including Himmler, Heydrich, and Kaltenbrunner) as he perceived them. Or, he attempted to turn loosely and indistinctly phrased wishes into RSHA policy. This helped him explain why he still tried to deport the Hungarian Jews at the end of the war against Himmler's order that deportations be stopped. (Himmler hoped this act would make negotiations with the Allies easier.) But in the democratic framework of the rule of law, this justification could not be considered as an extenuating circumstance.

When Eichmann portrayed the Third Reich administration as a machine in which every servant was a "robot," he glossed over a fundamental dimension of the bureaucratic apparatus – the "sub-bureaucracy." According to French sociologist Pierre Bourdieu, this "sub-bureaucracy" seems to have a priori a position of inferiority toward its central superiors, as local knowledge and networks "allowed [it] to stop orders from above and information from below."[36] So Eichmann was not only desk-bound, but also a field man, who wished to know everything through the reports he liked to read. He used the knowledge he obtained as a political tool to make his name (the "Eichmann Kommando") synonymous with the deportation of Jewish populations. According to Bourdieu, this "kind of gatekeeper position ... allows [him] to intercept what suits [him], to let go through what suits [him]," and gives him the possibility to divert power to his benefit, that is, to create for him room between the lines and the levels.[37] In Jerusalem, Eichmann only reflected the dimension of the civil servant, who holds a permanently ambiguous position. He could speak in his name and on behalf of the institution to which he belongs. By evoking only the delegate function of administrative power, he hid the fact that he could "steal a legitimate personality in order to accomplish the interests of a physical personality." The notes allow us to understand that Nazi bureaucracy could be considered not only rational and clear, as Eichmann would have us believe, but also "spoiled" and corrupted. When the delegation of authority multiplied, it also multiplied the diversions and abuses of power. In this respect, the delegate task of signing that was so often highlighted by Eichmann's defence could appear as a "guarantee chain," which would protect him as well as allow him a margin of autonomy.

Eichmann's posturing and defence strategies betray a Nazified way of thinking if we consider them not for what they literally say but for what they mean (showing the opposition between the signified and the signifier) and if we analyse the position of the defendant in terms of bureaucratic apparatus and operation. Pierre Bourdieu's work demonstrates that "the bureaucratic play ... involves a degree of disinclination or of uncertainty."[38] Every bureaucrat, in applying the rule, always has a choice between two extreme (theoretical) limits: the full application of a regulation, without regard for the special circumstances of the case, or the formal or informal exemption. Even in the most regulated and hierarchical administrations, rule cannot support all of the cases, and therefore "can only be applied through the action of the agents responsible for implementing them."[39] Even the "cautious bureaucrat" is never only a mere functionary but someone with "freedom to play." On which principle was this civil servant's authority based? Did he fall into the camp that simply identified with the rules, or did he enjoy a degree of freedom? According to the principle set out by Max Weber, "one obeys the rule when the interest to obey it outweighs the interest to disobey it." Thus, if Eichmann always obeyed, as he said he had done (that is, he was subjected as much as possible to the rules of his institution and reduced as far as possible in his freedom), it was not because of any bureaucratic lack of interest, but because he benefited from this obedience. Namely, he was bringing to life an ideology in which he believed and for which he was ready to kill or sacrifice himself, if asked. Eichmann was far from a puppet or servant; he understood quite well how to use the bureaucratic particularities under Nazism to achieve his aims as well as to shrug off his responsibilities twenty-four years later.

As we have seen, Eichmann's utilization of documents provides us with a way to see how he made good use of his knowledge of the "Final Solution of the Jewish Question" and of the strategy from which his line of defence was drawn, the "small cog" argument. However, Eichmann not only rejected charges of genocidal responsibility, he also applied himself to defusing another of the prosecution's charges: his direct participation in the Final Solution. He opposed this charge despite the fact that he ordered massive deportations of Jews to the Eastern Front while knowing their fate. The tactic he used, based on his knowledge of the *Lingua Tertii Imperii* as analysed by Victor Klemperer, is similar to the approach of the exegete. For example, he employed the expression *Sonderbehandlung* (special treatment), which could mean physical extermination in Nazi jargon. In a note, he detailed six different meanings of this term, of which "Auschwitz" signified the last one.[40] Eichmann used these lexical variants to create intellectual distance and to finesse his commitment to the killing of European Jews. Thus, he subsequently became a "technician" of the Final Solution, one who neither killed nor gave the order to kill.

As Haïm Gouri points out, "Eichmann was facing a threefold enemy: the wartime documents, the Sassen document, and the record of his interrogation by Section 06."[41] Indeed, the Sassen discussions could appear as death blows to his defence, because they came from the defendant himself. Between April and November 1957, in Buenos Aires, Eichmann openly discussed his role in the Holocaust, for which he took full responsibility; these discussions could have easily destroyed his line of defence. But in Jerusalem he refuted the authenticity of the Sassen document and took advantage of the prosecutor's mistake – which was to introduce the whole discussion as the defendant's comments. With his counsel, Eichmann endeavoured to enter into evidence only what he himself had said. Servatius successfully ensured that the court would only uphold pages proofread or written by Eichmann (meaning 196 pages out of the 796 introduced by Hausner). Eichmann was far from a person "who did not think." On the contrary, he revealed that he was able to reflect on what he took part in from a first-person perspective. He opportunistically assumed the role of the bureaucrat in his line of defence, that is, he was simply, dispassionately, following orders and his actions were indistinguishable from those of other agents, thus removing personal responsibility in his participation in the genocidal process.

Apparently, Eichmann took an unusual approach toward the trial's many witnesses: he ostentatiously refused to address them face to face, which shocked the observers. He did not look at the witnesses, and his counsel avoided submitting them to cross-examination. Perhaps Eichmann felt that he had everything to lose if he appeared as the "immoral witness" in contrast to these "moral witnesses"? His written notes allow us to better understand his strategic choice because they confirm that, in fact, Eichmann paid very close attention to some witnesses. Toward his "enemy" he took on the characteristics of a chameleon: he showed nothing, but listened to everything. He planned to let the enemy play its trump cards in order to note any flaws and refine his "counter-attack." The witness statements from sessions 51 to 62, in conjunction with the case of Hungary, provide the most significant examples.

Eichmann's reactions in the heat of the moment show the contempt that he had for these survivors and the reasons why he displayed chameleon-like qualities. He did not acknowledge the witnesses because in his perception of the trial as a battle he wished to avoid hand-to-hand combat. His manifest insensitivity corresponds then to a triple refusal: refusal to accept the witness as an equal, which would force the Nazi to defend himself to a Jew; refusal of the discursive register, which amounts to excluding any pathos or empathy toward the victim and to confine oneself to the realm of facts; and the refusal of contradictory interpretations, which could lead one to lose control over the legal arena. Asserting the veracity of the documents against the statements of survivors was another means for Eichmann to stay true to his Nazi roots and to affirm his historical otherness.

Toward witnesses who questioned his line of defence, Eichmann opposed a quasi-systematic parry: he denounced the distorted connection of the witness statements to historical truth to call into question the position of the witness himself. Three elements can be distinguished in this denunciation. The first one consisted of pointing out the propensity of the witness to provide an unreliable reconstruction of the past, which transformed his or her statement into a "fairy tale" in which Eichmann was the would-be attacker. To fend off a witness summoned in the case pertaining to atrocities in Slovakia, he discredited the witness' interpretation in the following way:

The witness is fantasizing:

1) He babbles on about the Red Cross commission
2) Of course Eichmann stood in the middle
3) He is playing the dolt, who doesn't know exactly anything.[42]

The defendant very often levelled a charge of perjury against witnesses, both individually and collectively. This led Eichmann to challenge the judges, claiming the prosecution simply resorted to fabrication to suit its purposes.[43]

In the end, Eichmann's notes show how his system of defence and his interpretation of the witnesses' statements were based on his own conceptions of the events, which allowed him to detect the prosecution's "fabrications." These notes underline the extent to which Eichmann had developed a de-realizing link with the truth, historical as well as legal. In so doing, the notes reveal the process that led to Eichmann's silence and to his position of seeming exteriority: the more the enemy tried to introduce the defendant as "the architect of the Final Solution," the more it reinforced Eichmann's decision not to be led through what was, from his perspective, a minefield. Eichmann wrote that these witness statements were intended to "fry" him, but he affirmed that he had the "skin of an elephant."[44] Eichmann's denunciation of these "lies" constituted a system of defence based on the denial of what others had to say and of the judicial process., Eichmann believed that the trial was his last battle and that the only solution was frontal assault, that is, to take the floor again. Thus, he focused his whole attention on the examination by his counsel and the cross-examination by the public prosecutor.

Conclusion

The study of Eichmann's defence through an analysis of his notes does not entirely dispel the mystery of the man in the glass booth, but it does reveal how the defendant was subjected to strong internal tensions: Eichmann sought to appear as a cog in the Nazi machine, but at the same time an important and necessary one. His explanations of documents, the memos for his counsel, and the reactions he wrote down on the spot tell us that Eichmann had only been obeying orders, but also remind us that the "extermination machine" could not have worked so well without his participation.

Eichmann used the glass booth as a stage. He inquired about media coverage of his trial and contemplated what he should state in order to garner newspaper coverage. Several clues suggest that Eichmann's prolixity was designed to ensure that his name would go down in history. As Eichmann wrote to Servatius on 7 June 1961, "Historians of all confessions and many other people will study the trial down to the last detail for fifty years or more. And as you will see, it will be interpreted according to the *Zeitgeist* in one way or another."[45] This essay is an attempt to consider the trial in a new perspective, not in the way that the defendant would have expected, but by critically applying these writings to Eichmann himself.

NOTES

1 Started in 2011, this research project on the Eichmann trial has been carried out with a fellowship at the International Institute for Holocaust Research in Yad Vashem (March–April 2013) and a fellowship from the Fritz Thyssen Stiftung in Berlin (2013–14). I warmly thank Deborah Barton for her thorough rereading of this new version in English. This text had been written in 2011.

2 Avner Werner Less, *Lüge! Alles Lüge! Aufzeichnungen des Eichmann-Verhörers: Rekonstruiert von Bettina Stangneth* (Zurich-Hamburg, 2012), 114. Unless otherwise indicated, all translations are my own.

3 The "Argentinien Papiere" is the corpus constituted of writings and testimonies produced by Adolf Eichmann during his stay in Argentina (1950–60). See Bettina Stangneth, *Eichmann vor Jerusalem: Das unbehelligte Leben eines Massenmörders* (Zurich-Hamburg: 2011); Christian Gerlach, "The Eichmann Interrogations in Holocaust Historiography," *Holocaust and Genocide Studies* 15 (2001–3): 428–53.

4 Rudolf Höss, *Kommandant in Auschwitz* (Munich, 1958).

5 Haïm Gouri, *Facing the Glass Booth: The Jerusalem Trial of Adolf Eichmann* (Detroit, 2004), 145. The first edition of this book was published in 1964.

6 She arrived in Israel on 8 April and left it on 6 May. She returned for the period 17–24 June, but attended only three sessions because the trial was interrupted for a few days. See Claude Klein, *Le cas Eichmann: Vu de Jérusalem* (Paris, 2012), 204.

7 Hannah Arendt, *Eichmann in Jerusalem: A Report on the Banality of Evil* (New York, 1965), 54.

8 Bundesarchiv Koblenz (BArch), All Proz 6/165, 4/19/61, 340.

9 BArch, All Proz 6/165, 4/25/61, 316, 319.

10 BArch, All Proz 6/169, 132.

11 BArch, All Protz 6/165, 6/14/61, 108.

12 Eichmann also used Léon Poliakov and Joseph Wulf, *Das Dritte Reich und die Juden: Dokumente und Aufsätze* (Berlin, 1955).

13 Between April and November 1957 Eichmann was in Buenos Aires,
   invited by Willem Sassen (a former Waffen-SS member who had escaped
   to Argentina, where he worked as journalist), to attend meetings with
   another Nazis. The aim of these weekly discussions was to rehabilitate
   National Socialism by denouncing the "six million lie."
14 Gouri, *Facing the Glass Booth*, 52.
15 BArch K, All Proz. 6/164, 143–50.
16 BArch K, All Proz. 6/164, 151–64.
17 BArch K, All Proz. 6/164, 146.
18 BArch K, All Proz. 6/164, 6/15/61, 5.
19 Ibid.
20 Ibid, 13.
21 BArch K, All Proz. 6/164, 143–50.
22 Ibid, 144.
23 Ibid, 146.
24 BArch K, All Proz. 6/164, 151.
25 Ibid, 157.
26 BARch, All Proz 6/254, 6/5/61, 2–3.
27 BARch, All Proz 6/165, 4/17/61, 333.
28 BARch, All Proz 6/166, 3/22/61, 13.
29 BARch, All Proz 6/165, 5/25/61, 166.
30 BARch, All Proz 6/165, 6/7/61, 252.
31 BArch K, All Proz 6/254, 6/7/61, 4–5.
32 See Adolf Hitler, *Mein Kampf* (Munich, 1926), vol. 2, chap. 4.
33 Arendt, *Eichmann in Jerusalem*, 24.
34 BArch K, All Proz. 6/165, 332–3.
35 On this notion, see Ian Kershaw, "'Working towards the Führer':
   Reflections on the Nature of the Hitler Dictatorship," *Contemporary
   European History* 2, no. 2 (1993): 103–18.
36 Pierre Bourdieu, "Cours du 7 novembre 1991," in *Sur l'Etat: Cours au
   Collège de France, 1989 – 1992* (Paris: 2012), 446.
37 Ibid.
38 Pierre Bourdieu, "Droit et passe-droit," *Actes de la recherche en sciences
   sociales* 88 (1990): 86–96.
39 Ibid.
40 BARch, All Proz 6/165, 251.
41 Gouri, *Facing the Glass Booth*, 207.
42 BARch, All Proz 6/165, 140.
43 BARch, All Proz 6/165, 5/28/61, 234.
44 BARch, All Proz 6/163, 4/26/61, 128.
45 BARch, All Proz 6/254, 6/7/61, 4–5.

3 Revisiting Eichmann and Zionism: Contexts, Strange Encounters, and Their Afterlives

MICHAEL BERKOWITZ

Contrary to a point of view in current intellectual discourse, particularly among those concerned with what can broadly be called "theory," Adolf Eichmann did not believe in the benefit or rectitude of a Jewish state in Palestine. When it was expedient he could support requests of Zionists or help facilitate the emigration of the Jews out of Central Europe to Palestine – but this was mainly to lessen his own load, and to be seen as leading a kind of work that boosted his stock in the SS (Schutzstaffel). In this regard, his administration of the Holocaust in Vienna is crucial. For those vested with the fate of fellow Jews, however, dealing with Eichmann ultimately meant either emigration from the Nazi orbit or transport to ghettos, concentration camps, and facilities that existed for no purpose other than murder. Historian Doron Rabonovici has tackled head-on the question of whether or not, or to what extent, European Jewry's Nazi-appointed representatives "cooperated in their own destruction" in their extensive and complex interactions with Eichmann – in which they possessed little leverage to influence such arrangements. "Eichmann's Jews," he concludes, "when confronted with what seemed to be a choice between certain death or cooperation, usually chose to deal with Nazi authorities in the hope that their actions would turn out to be the lesser evil."[1] What is unfathomable, though, is the often-repeated contention that Eichmann was a staunch advocate of Zionism, bolstering the organized efforts of Jews to settle in Palestine on a Jewish/national basis – as Eichmann and his legal defence team propounded, and as famously echoed by Hannah Arendt.[2]

To be sure, the fiftieth anniversary of the Eichmann trial in Jerusalem is an opportune moment to reflect on the complex relationships between the history of the Jews and the history of the Holocaust,[3] and the real and imagined connections between the attempted annihilation of European Jewry, the Zionist movement, and the young state of Israel's struggle to deal with its immediate past. One of Eichmann's calling cards was his claim that he knew more about the Jews than the average German, or even SS-man.[4] It is true that he came to learn, or at least absorb, a fair amount. We are well aware that Eichmann professed to be a "Jewish expert," that he fancied himself as having unusual insight into Jewish history, the current state of Jewish affairs in the 1930s and 1940s, and where they were headed. Much of the rationale for this mix of belief, bluster, and, frankly, nonsense – which Eichmann succeeded in mobilizing to his advantage, up to a point – was that he knew a thing or two about Zionism in particular. Hannah Arendt noted, in one of her cryptic, ironic statements, that among the few books Eichmann claimed to have read in their entirety were Theodor Herzl's polemic that launched the Zionist movement, *Der Judenstaat*, written in 1896, and Adolf Boehm's *Die zionistische Bewegung*, a sympathetic account of the movement's development by one of its stalwarts. She was bemused that Eichmann had read just a couple of books, and that he did not even possess a clear recollection of them, often confusing Boehm's quasi-historical work with Herzl's pamphlet.[5] Arendt, though, was not simply being ironic – she ventured into grotesque terrain by alleging that Herzl's *Judenstaat* had "converted" Eichmann "promptly and forever to Zionism."[6] My concern here is mainly with the reception and afterlife of this comment. Throwing light on juxtapositions of "Eichmann and Zionism" provides not only a chance to correct Arendt and later distortions, but also an opportunity to knit together the history of the Jews, the development and repercussions of Nazi policy, the history of the Holocaust, and postwar attempts by Jews to confront their recent past. Zionism was, in fact, highly significant in both the making and undoing of Adolf Eichmann.

In earlier work I argued that the Nazis, including Hitler, were more interested in Zionism than many scholars assume. This interest persisted through the Second World War and even influenced a concerted attempt to explain away the Holocaust.[7] The Nazis made a deliberate effort in June 1944 to portray Zionism as the world's most venal conspiracy, and as distinctly threatening to Germany, thereby causing them to take what they described as lethal but appropriate action.[8] Eichmann may have contributed in some small way to this with the report he filed with Herbert Hagen upon his trip to Cairo in 1937. Richard Evans, some years ago, began wrestling with the problem of Nazism's imagination of Zionism when he explored the charges regarding Chaim Weizmann's "declaration of war" against the Nazis that surfaced in the context of the *Historikerstreit*.[9] More importantly, the scholarship of Klaus-Michael

Mallmann and Martin Cüppers has shown conclusively that if the Nazis had had the means, they would have slaughtered all the Jews of Palestine.[10] The point here is that the work of several scholars should have put to rest the charges of a long-term, meaningful Zionist "collusion" with Nazism,[11] even when acknowledging exceptions such as the "Transfer Agreement" and the temporary stay given to the youth *aliyah* program in Germany, as discussed by Brian Amkraut.[12] Although it is possible to speculate on the reasons behind the recurrent charge of "collusion," there is little doubt that part of the reason why this phantom of "Zionism and Nazism" continues to reappear stems from the legacy of Eichmann and Arendt's canonical treatment of the trial.

An ironic and bizarre aspect of Eichmann's defence while in the dock in Jerusalem was his claim that he had been a Zionist. One of the formulations of this insipid argument was that if he had been ordered to carry out the evacuation of Jews to Palestine, he happily would have done so. In effect, Eichmann crudely conflated his keyhole knowledge of the Zionist movement and the fact that he had dealt with a number of Zionists – in some cases facilitating emigration to Palestine – with the claim that he adhered to Zionism as a legitimate cause. This was an absurd, even offensive tack. But there was a germ of substance to this notion, at least in Eichmann's own mind and in the trajectory of his career, in seeing a distinctive confluence with Zionism.

I believe that greater emphasis should be placed on the fact that Eichmann's assumption of responsibility for expediting Jewish emigration, which included an option for Palestine, was complemented by a number of factors beyond his control. The sense that he spearheaded the entire phenomenon has accumulated over time. At the very moment when he came onto the scene in Vienna there were fervent efforts by Viennese Jews to prepare the ground for emigration.[13] Perhaps even more important was intense British and American pressure, as well as Zionist organizational efforts[14] to alleviate the deepening crisis, which Hitler could not simply ignore.[15] The appalling decimation of the Austrian Jewish community in the immediate wake of the Anschluss was strongly registered in the west, as evinced by full-page ads in London's *Jewish Chronicle* and elsewhere (see figures 3.1–3.3).[16] Eichmann's superiors in Berlin were inclined to grease the gears of his bureaucratic assembly line in part because specific funds raised for the purpose immediately went into Nazi hands.[17] (See figure 3.4.)[18] As of 29 April 1938, £115,071 had been raised by British Jewry alone.[19] I would go so far as to say that the pressure to extricate Jews from Vienna was ferocious, as the once stolid community became homeless and impoverished,[20] even "starved," with lightning

3.1. Source: Appeal for Austrian Jewry, N.M. Rothschild & Sons, New Court, London, E.C.4.

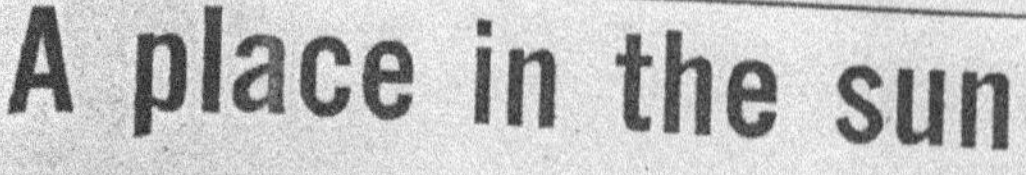

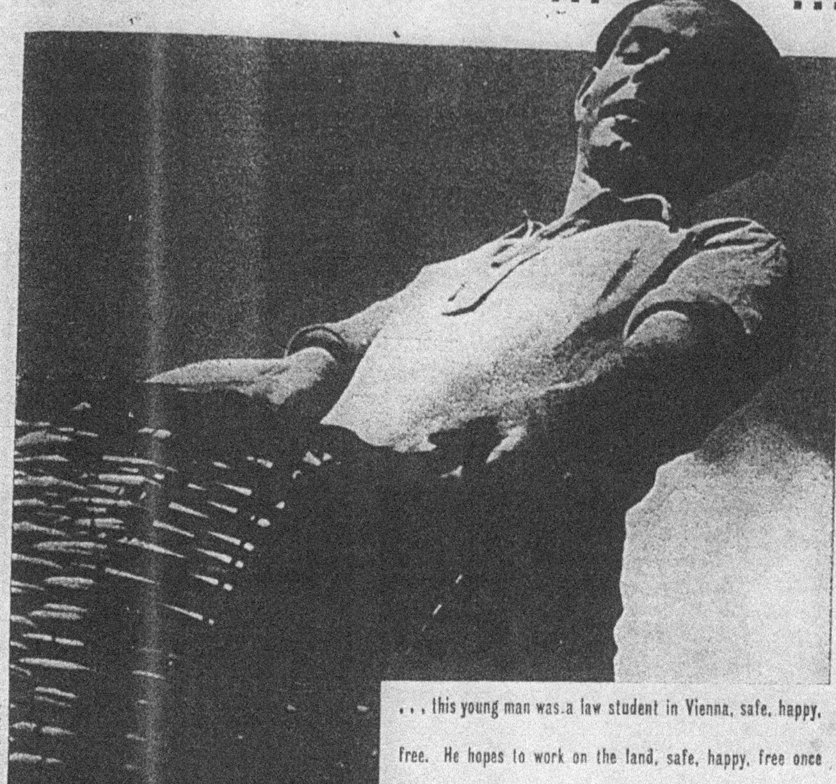

3.2. Source: Appeal for Austrian Jewry, N.M. Rothschild & Sons, New Court, London, E.C.4.

The end is not yet...

TO-DAY in Austria persecution is raging. A persecution of 200,000 of our fellow Jews: a persecution more ruthless, because more perfectly organised, than any before. A whole community—children and old alike, women and girls as well as men—is facing the threat of extirpation. Is facing almost certain destitution, or at best a life made intolerable by discrimination and insult.

With your help we can deliver them out of the hand of the oppressor. We can bring them forth to a kinder land. To a future. But only with your help. We must have money... quickly. Their plight grows daily more desperate. Please give to the utmost of your capacity.

CONTRIBUTIONS TO THE APPEAL FOR

AUSTRIAN JEWRY

should be sent to N. M. ROTHSCHILD & SONS, *New Court, London, E.C.4*

3.3. Source: Appeal for Austrian Jewry, N.M. Rothschild & Sons, New Court, London, E.C.4.

3.4. Source: Appeal for Austrian Jewry, N.M. Rothschild & Sons, New Court, London, E.C.4.

speed.[21] Moreover, it was apparent to numerous observers that Nazi leaders disagreed about how to handle the Jews,[22] causing heightened "tension"[23] and "confusion" between officials.[24] To no small extent, Eichmann's work also complemented efforts of the Nazi Gauleiter of Vienna, Josef Bürckel,[25] and others to mollify the perception of "the hell which is Austria" for Jews.[26] In sum, my point is that an even stronger case may be made that the circumstances in which Eichmann found himself were critical to the perception of his supposed enthusiasm for Zionism.

But however inconsistent or marginal, Eichmann's encounters with Zionists and Zionism contributed to his being eagerly sought by the State of Israel. His brushes and engagements with German-speaking Zionists also helped to assure that he would be subject not only to vengeance, but to a public, judicial procedure.[27] One of the points I wish to underscore is that although it was important that Eichmann had become known to a number of Jews and those in positions of authority, in diverse settings, it was especially important that he was familiar to a small but influential segment of German and Austrian Zionists who later became establishment figures in Israel. He was known to the cohort that was likely to be influential in the security and judicial apparatus of the young state.

His dealings with Zionism contributed to the limited proof that Eichmann would have been able to muster for his self-definition as a "Jewish expert." Allow me to be very clear: he was no Jewish expert, and he was no Zionist, or Zionist sympathizer by any conventional standard. Zionism was to Eichmann a means of emigration, and his claim to being sympathetic to concerns of Zionists was a short-term means of placating tensions. He was never, as has been expressed or insinuated by some who have written on the relations between the Nazis and the Zionists, in some type of collusion with those in the movement. There is no reason to take seriously, say, Leni Brenner's accusation that David Cesarani whitewashed the reputed collusion between Eichmann and Zionism.[28] There are scores, if not hundreds, of comments on the internet that likewise do not merit our serious attention. In several of these comments, Tom Segev's book *The Seventh Million*, which tells the story of Eichmann's mission to Palestine, has been wrenched out of context.[29] But perhaps we would be wise to dwell for a moment on Slavoj Žižek's thoughts on Eichmann and Zionism, as Žižek is one of the notable cultural critics of our day, published by reputable presses. While he styles himself as a gadfly, Žižek nevertheless carries weight as a public intellectual, one seen as bridging the worlds of scholarship and popular culture.

Žižek and others are confident, even proud, of remarks identifying Eichmann with Zionism, remarks presented as being consistent with Hannah Arendt's *Eichmann in Jerusalem,* and, some believe, Tom Segev's much-lauded *The Seventh Million.* In *The Parallax View,* Žižek avers that the "stain of injustice" which forever marks Israel as outcast from the comity of nations is encapsulated in Eichmann's attempted mission to Palestine, which had been thoughtfully analysed by several scholars. Žižek boldly contends that the date 26 September 1937 should be inscribed as particularly important to anyone concerned with antisemitism. He explains why:

On that day Adolf Eichmann and his assistant boarded a train in Berlin in order to visit Palestine. Heydrich himself gave Eichmann permission to accept an invitation from Feivel Polkes, a senior member of the Hagana (the Zionist secret organization), to visit Tel Aviv and discuss the coordination of German and Jewish organizations to facilitate the Jews' emigration to Palestine. Both the Germans and the Zionists wanted as many Jews as possible to move to Palestine. The Germans wanted them out of Western Europe, and the Zionists themselves wanted the Jews in Palestine to outnumber the Arabs as quickly as possible. (The mission failed because due to some violent unrest the British blocked access to Palestine. But Eichmann and Polkes did meet days later in Cairo, and discussed coordination of German and Zionist activities.) Is not this weird incident the supreme case of how Nazis and radical Zionists shared a common interest – in both cases, the purpose was a kind of "ethnic cleansing," that is, to change fundamentally the ratio of ethnic groups of the population?[30]

No, this is not "the supreme case of how Nazis and radical Zionist shared a common interest." Žižek is wrong, or at least misleading, on several counts. On the most basic level, Eichmann was dedicated to "relentlessly" removing Jews from German-held territory, no matter what their destination. This point is seconded not only by scholars who have focused primarily on Eichmann but also by historians concerned with specific contexts of his activity, such as Jonathan Steinberg, writing on Italy, and Mark Mazower, on the Balkans.[31] In addition, we know that the policy of allowing Jews to emigrate to Palestine was superseded by the directive for their mass murder. The Jews of Palestine, too, were slated for execution by the Nazis in the expected aftermath of the Nazi conquest of the Middle East. Žižek's claim is misleading, as well, because he takes no notice of a cardinal belief among many Zionists, and even many observers of the movement, that "Palestine was the land without a people for a people without a land." In fact, there was an item with precisely this vacuous slogan in the *Zionistische Rund-schau*, the short-lived newspaper "sponsored" by Eichmann himself,[32] to which I refer below. I myself have interrogated this myth.[33] Still, it was widely and sincerely held.

For those who were more sophisticated or had had actual experience with Palestine, other competing strategies, even among Zionists, were common. Many assumed that Zionism could be accommodated within the Arab population of Palestine. Even more popular, however, was the notion that the Zionists would actually be welcomed by the indigenous population as bearers of modern progress, especially with respect to the benefits of technology, education, public health, and medicine. Those familiar with the history of Zionism know that the form of the move-ment originally favoured by Ahad Ha-Am was the fostering of a small, distinctly non-conventional "national" cultural centre in Palestine. But the discourse of Zionism since the so-called Uganda proposal or scheme of 1903 was that Zion and Zionism might serve as a refuge, a "night-shelter" to those in immediate distress or danger. Bruce Saposnik has brilliantly argued that this way of thinking about Zionism – distinctly favourable to the Uganda plan – was embraced most enthusiastically among the Zionists actually living in Palestine.[34] Although there is no need to accept the pious delusions of the early Zionists, it is neverthe-less important to recall that, rather than a naked Jewish/Arab struggle, the greatest obstacles, historically, to the fulfilment of the Zionist project seemed to be the physical environment of Palestine, and the recalci-trant, ultra-Orthodox, anti-Zionist (Jewish) population of the country.[35]

Žižek insinuates that, given a choice between "Zionism" and the annihilation of the Jews, Eichmann – echoing Eichmann himself – would have chosen Zionism. There was, in fact, at least one instance where Eichmann did face precisely that choice. This was presented in the trial in the deposition of Max Merten, one of the Nazis in the Bal-kans,[36] an event that remains to be fully explored by scholars. I would now like to turn to a document that I believe can illustrate what Eich-mann did when he was confronted with a decision between "Zionism" or mass murder. Most of us are aware that Richard Breitman's *Official Secrets* was mainly concerned with illuminating the extent to which the unfolding of genocide, particularly the atrocities of the Einsatzgruppen, were known to the British though their interception and decoding of Nazi secret communications.[37] One of these messages can also help us to understand Eichmann's role in the course of the Holocaust.

Eichmann was complicit and perhaps personally responsible for a decision to quash a deal that would have allowed Jewish women and children in Salonika, and possibly those who had found refuge in Italian territory, to be transferred by boat to Palestine. Between March and August 1943, some 40,000 Jews were deported from Salonika to Auschwitz/Birkenau, where most were killed upon arrival. René Burckhardt of the International Committee of the Red Cross made a plea for the rescue plan, and apparently had made arrangements. This complements the account in *The Red Cross and the Holocaust* by Jean-Claude Favez. Favez writes,

> As the ICRC's assistant delegate in Salonika [Burckhardt] was not content with sending reports and arranging food supplies ... On 13 March [1943], as the first trains left for Auschwitz, he sent to his collaborator, the head of the German administration for food supplies to Macedonia, a telegram for Geneva, which he trusted would be forwarded via the German Red Cross. It read: "Please telegraph the ICRC at Geneva headquarters. Start of deportation of 45,000 Jews from Salonika almost decided. Urgent examination [*sic*] needed with governments involved. Deportation [*sic*] women and children to Palestine indispensable."[38]

The intercepted German communications suggest that Burckhardt had gone even further, actually developing a plan. What is not stated, though, by Favez or any other historian, is that responsibility for the demise of this deal, the pressure to have René Burckhardt replaced – ironically by someone with the same last name, Carl Jacob Burckhardt – had come from Eichmann and Dieter Wisliceny.[39] So when the situation did indeed arise where Eichmann had a choice between Palestine or extermination, he chose the latter. In addition to undermining the humanitarian effort of René Burckhardt, the message shows Eichmann's culpability in neutralizing the attempt of the Archbishop of Greece, Damaskinos Papandreou, to intercede on behalf of the Jews.[40]

To enhance our view of Eichmann's diverse encounters with Zionist matters, I would like to shift the focus back to the prewar period. I wish to draw attention to a period approximately two months before 26 September 1937, a date of historical importance to Žižek. I shall revisit an incident, related by David Cesarani and others, involving Rabbi Joachim Prinz.[41] Prinz is well remembered as a towering intellectual figure in pre-Nazi Germany and a formidable religious leader in the United States. "Toward the end of 1936," Prinz wrote in his memoir, "[Otto] Kuchmann, a Gestapo friend, came to inform me officially, in the name of Adolf Eichmann, that I was herewith expelled from Germany. I would soon learn that the man in charge of the State Police, a certain Dr. Flesch, had the rather strange notion to recruit me to become a spy for the Gestapo after my arrival in America. *I told him what he wished to hear* [emphasis added]: that I would be very happy to write to him from time to time."[42] "On the evening of 26 June 1937," as Allan Nadler recently wrote, "thousands of Berlin Jews packed the city's grand Brüdervereinhaus to bid farewell to Rabbi Joachim Prinz, who had been ordered by the Gestapo to leave Germany immediately or face an almost certain death sentence for political subversion. Prinz had been the most popular, outspoken, and inspirational champion of Jewish national rights and Zionism in the dark years since the Nazis' rise to power, preaching to overflow crowds at Berlin's most important temples about the need to leave Germany and immigrate to Palestine."[43] This complements Michael Brenner's astute analysis of Weimar Jewish culture, in which he describes Prinz as challenging and captivating thousands in his adult education courses and occasional lectures on Jewish historical subjects.[44] "By the summer of 1937, [Prinz] had already been arrested a dozen times by the Gestapo," but because of the express warning from Kuchmann, he decided to make his break. A sponsorship by Rabbi Stephen S. Wise in New York provided the opportunity. "Among the uninvited guests at Prinz's farewell," Nadler reminds us, was Adolf Eichmann. Benno Cohn, who had been an important German Zionist, recalled that "the large hall was packed full. The public thronged to this meeting. Suddenly, as chairman of the event I was called to the door and my office clerk told me, 'Mr Eichmann is here.' I saw this same man, for the first time in civilian clothing, and he shouted at me. 'Who is responsible for order here? This is disorder of the first degree ...' I watched him the entire time from my place in the chair."[45] Prinz later wrote,

> The fact that [Eichmann] attended my last speech became very important. For legal reasons it was necessary to identify Eichmann when he was tried in Israel. Until such identification was made he was only purported to be Adolf Eichmann. My friend Benno Cohn, a judge who had dealings with Eichmann in Berlin, was asked to identify him legally and in the presence of witnesses. Cohn said to Eichmann at the trial, "I am glad to see you here. The last time I saw you was at the farewell speech that Rabbi Fried delivered." This was an attempt to elicit from Eichmann a correction of the name. Eichmann fell for it and said immediately, "This was not Rabbi Fried but Joachim Prinz who delivered the speech." These words legally identified him as Adolf Eichmann.[46]

David Cesarani is generous to Eichmann, giving him the benefit of the doubt, indicating that his brusque treatment of Cohn resulted from him being jostled by the unruly Jewish crowd.[47] My main point, however, is not to quibble about how Eichmann behaved with Jews – even though Tom Segev takes pains to show how polite, or not, he was to Teddy Kollek in Vienna. [48] In general, however, Eichmann "refused 'for ideological reasons' to shake hands with Jewish representatives or even Zionist emissaries. He berated, threatened, and taunted the Jews."[49] I wish to raise the issue of familiarity, or more precisely, imagined familiarity. It is not surprising that Žižek and others choose to see any interaction between Nazis and Zionists as collusion. Scholars such as David Cesarani, Doron Rabinovici, Frank Nocisia, Hans Safrian, Jonathan Steinberg, and others have shown more sophistication in appreciating that dealing with the Nazis often involved play-acting, as Prinz so clearly spells out in his "promise" to be a Nazi spy.[50] Eichmann was at that grand meeting, hoping not be noticed, because he was trying to gain an upper hand – to further immerse himself in Jewish affairs and to hone his supposed expertise. No doubt he became upset when his presence became an issue. The fact that he was the leading Nazi official at this event attended by "several thousand people" became legendary to thousands of others. Although Eichmann may not yet have been a household name, he became notorious in the minds of German and Austrian Zionists. German Jews, as we know well, would play an extraordinarily large role in the hunt for and prosecution of Eichmann. German Jewry often regarded themselves as entitled to full legal prerogatives, and it is no surprise that the Zionists among them ardently sought to bring Eichmann to justice according to what they regarded as proper procedure.

There are two other strange interludes concerning Eichmann and Zionism that bear mention. The first is broached but not actually discussed by Arendt. She writes that Eichmann had "protested against desecrations of Herzl's grave in Vienna, and there are reports of his presence in civilian clothes at the commemoration of the thirty-fifth anniversary of Herzl's death."[51] What we know for certain is that, in his defence, Eichmann tried to show that he took great pains to allow for "the exhumation of the remains of Theodor Herzl" from Vienna to Palestine as requested by Leo Loewenherz, in March 1939.[52] The year before, there was an even more bizarre instance in which Eichmann might have believed that he was somehow taking on Herzl's mantle. David Cesarani, Hans Safrian, and others inform us that Eichmann had planned to establish a Zionist newspaper, the *Zionistische Rundschau*, and in a letter to Herbert Hagen, he stated, "In a sense it will become 'my' paper."[53] (He was, however, probably little more than a censor.) Yet no matter how much Eichmann desired to hasten the emigration of Jews to Palestine, he never had any sense of Herzl's fundamental desire to foster honour for and among Jews. That Eichmann evolved into a murderer meant that he had absolutely no connection with the ideas that men like the newspapermen Herzl or Boehm had ever written or thought about.

There is another Zionist dimension to the historical context of the Eichmann trial that has thus far elicited little attention: the Jewish Agency, the instrument of the Zionist organization that served as a bridge between the Yishuv and the diaspora, sought to establish grounds for prosecuting Nazi war criminals under its own auspices. Through the work of Laura Jockusch, Boaz Cohen, and others, we have learned that almost immediately after the Second World War Jewish organizations struggled to comprehend and deal with the catastrophe that had befallen European Jewry.[54] It is unclear, however, to what extent the activity of the Jewish Agency was subsumed under the umbrella of the Central Historical Commission, a topic taken up by Jockusch.[55] It is not surprising that Jewish organizations were concerned with identifying the Nazis and accomplices responsible for the genocide. Obviously, the Allied powers assumed the major role for apprehending and bringing to justice those deemed war criminals. But Jewish organizations, perhaps earlier than historians have indicated, also became involved in such efforts. The Zionist Organization is not typically seen as significant in this regard.

Although the focus of their work was bringing Jews to Palestine, then under the British Mandate, and to further consolidate its Jewish settlement, the Jewish Agency – as the official body connecting world Jewry to Palestine – also was devoted to documenting the horrors of what would later be termed the Holocaust. As a quasi-governmental body representing world Jewry, early in 1945 the Political Department of the Jewish Agency began collecting material related to the mass murder of Jews. It seems that Jewish Agency officials believed that they would play a leading role in prosecuting Nazi war criminals. Although this is not what happened – as most accused Nazi leaders were brought to trial under the judicial systems of the Allies or successor states, with the exception of Adolf Eichmann – the Jewish Agency had prepared for a different legal reckoning. They assembled a vast amount of material with the intention of substantiating who, and what organizational units, did what to the Jews, and when. In the summer of 1946 the Jewish Historical Commission (Jüdische Historische Kommission), a related body, came under the control of Simon Wiesenthal. The following year Wiesenthal "renamed the commission the Jewish Historical Documentation (Jüdsiche Historische Dokumentation, JHD)." Its principal function was to assist "legal redress for Nazi crimes against Jews."[56] Wiesenthal himself, though, "heard about Eichmann only after the war, and he later recalled precisely from whom he had heard the name and when: from Aharon Hoter-Yishai, an officer in the Jewish Brigade (who had fought against the Axis as part of the British Army) and a well-known attorney in Palestine, in July 1945."[57] Arthur Piernikarz (Asher Ben-Natan) had supplied Wiesenthal "with a preliminary list of war criminals compiled by the Jewish Agency during the war."[58] Perhaps part of the reason why these historically focused bodies have not received pride of place in the work on Eichmann is because of the competition between Towia Frydman (aka Tovie Friedman) and Wiesenthal about who deserved the most credit for tracking him down.

In any event, the Jewish Agency assembled its own "Records of War Criminals" in the Political Department ("S25") of the Jewish Agency, which are now housed in the Central Zionist Archives in Jerusalem. Eichmann's name appears at least five times.[59] These records consist of thirty-nine files with extensive reports from the killing grounds, primarily derived from eyewitness testimony of Jews and non-Jewish bystanders. Although there are problematic aspects to these documents, they are a relatively underappreciated scholarly resource. They are truly striking for their detail and immediacy. One of the most important aspects is that interviewees – victims and perpetrators – were asked to "name names." In particular the Jewish Agency sought to record the names of the specific offices and units that administered Jewish affairs, and to discern precisely who was accountable to whom. For instance, in Lvov normal (apparently Wehrmacht) "German soldiers" had "rounded up Jews ... abused and mistreated them" and often beat them to death. There was no difference in the behaviour of the men of the Gestapo, the Sicherheitsdienst, and the Sicherheitspolizei.[60] Special attention was paid to those who murdered Jews for no apparent reason, or when a pretext was given, it bore no relationship to the punishment. They also wished to underscore those who undermined the efforts of Jews who were, indeed, "productive." In 1946 Dieter Wisliceny expressly detailed Eichmann's activities for this body.[61]

Tom Segev is one of a few historians to note that Eichmann was of particular interest to the Israelis because his name had come up in this collection.[62] Interestingly, one of the workers in the precincts of the Sochnut (Jewish Agency) who may have helped keep Eichmann's name in play was Eva Michaelis Stern. In 1938 she "was summoned to the office of Adolf Eichmann, who accused her of sending anti-German propaganda to countries outside Germany, in the guise of Youth Aliyah publicity." He stopped the program. "Unable to continue her rescue work, Eva Stern emigrated to Palestine together with her fiancé, Dolf (Adolf) Michaelis (1906–1982), a member of the Executive of the Zionist Federation of Germany." There also is a direct link to Arendt: Stern's brother Günther, known better under his pen name "Anders," was the first husband of Hannah Arendt.[63]

Along with offering insight into why the Zionists, and later Israelis, were so keen to apprehend Eichmann, the Jewish Agency documents also may provide insight into the kinds of questions highlighted by the trial, such as attempts at resistance. For example, one of the documents details a bold act that saved many Jewish lives: "At the end of 1942 a train of deported Jews bound for Belzec was held up on the way by Jewish partisans and all detainees were released. This event forced the German authorities to employ other means for the extermination of the Jews." This is but one example of the potential of these documents in bringing to light lesser known, and even totally obscured, aspects of the Holocaust. The same document, however, reveals the tension between cooperation and collaboration: it specifies that in November 1942, "the Jewish Miliz (police) [in Lvov] was ordered every second day to supply 200 Jews, all of them were transported to Belzec."[64]

To conclude, let us return to what Žižek portrays as his rightful appropriation of Hannah Arendt's work, as well as his self-perception as the inheritor of Walter Benjamin's legacy. I think that part of the problem with the way Arendt has been received stems from a problem of in-group and out-group language and behaviour. This is a double or triple irony due to Arendt's own obsession with the dissolution between the public and private spheres. On another note, it is sometimes shocking to students when they read the diaries of Victor Klemperer and discover him associating Theodor Herzl and Adolf Hitler.[65] Klemperer's attack on the Zionists is harsh. But this was his private view, hidden away in his diary. Such rash judgment is, in part, what was behind Arendt's infamous decision to refer to Rabbi Leo Baeck as the "Führer" of the Jews in her original *New Yorker* report.[66] This insensitive, if not sickening, Jewish/Nazi pairing also was revealed in a taped conversation between Henry Kissinger and Richard Nixon in the midst of the Soviet Jewry campaign, when Kissinger pledged that it would not move him even if Russia's Jews were thrown into "gas chambers."[67] Scholars might be more aware of the slippery use and long history of in-group tensions and bitter criticism, not uncommon in Zionist discourse. Chaim Weizmann, after the First World War, accused Louis Brandeis of using "poison gas" against him. This is distasteful, but indicates how Weizmann chose to express himself.[68] We do not have to go as far as Gershom Scholem in his admonishment of Arendt for a paucity of love for the Jewish people. But we might at least hope for our colleagues to be more diligent and dispassionate, rather than glib, in the all-too-automatic twinning of Zionism and Nazism, as often occurs in the guise of a historical or Arendtian rendering of Eichmann. What is conveniently forgotten by Žižek and his ilk is that even Hannah Arendt concurred that in trying Eichmann, and then hanging him, justice was done. This, too, is part of the legacy of his complicated engagement with Zionism.

Žižek is obviously not an antisemite. Of course there was something of a numbers game in play. Certainly there were forms of Jewish ultra-nationalism emerging in the 1930s that did, in some respects, mimic right-wing movements in Europe. This has been brilliantly illuminated in a recent survey by Bernard Wasserstein.[69] Žižek's version, though, is an unreliable guide for analysing how the Arab/Zionist conflict in Palestine developed as it did. Zionism itself was weak and fragmented. Its "Arab policy" did not necessarily correspond to a left/right axis, and it was vague about the persistent question of how it could be implemented. The specific crisis of Viennese Jewry in 1938–9, as we have seen, helped fuel the perception of Eichmann as a midwife to *aliyah*. What Žižek fails to see, though, is that Zionism – as unflattering as it sounds – was fundamentally propelled by antisemitism. Like so many debates about the Holocaust we sometimes lose sight of what is most crucial: the energy and the effort that the Nazis devoted to persecuting and then murdering the Jews. Palestine for Jews was an option, though not necessarily a favoured one. The conflict with the Arabs did not contribute, as Žižek implies, to enthusiasm for Zionism, but more likely detracted from it. There was a decided lack of passion for Zionism among many German Jews who made their way to Palestine through the "transfer agreement." In so many respects it was a bitter-sweet story.

I would argue, finally, that the "Britishness" of the Mandate for Palestine, even as the government's commitment to the Balfour Declaration was deteriorating, was an attractive inducement for Jews to embrace Zionism, rather than an incentive to displace or take up arms against the Arabs. Many sought Palestine as a means of eventually getting to Britain or America. Žižek's "Eichmann to Zionism" conflation is as absurd as the hackneyed "Luther to Hitler" tack, which few scholars take seriously. There remain, however, issues in which Eichmann was central, lurking, or perhaps even fully responsible that merit our scrutiny, whereas in this case he had been far from the prime mover. In large part, that was what he was about.

NOTES

1 Doron Rabinovici, *Eichmann's Jews: The Jewish Administration of Holocaust Vienna, 1938–1945*, trans. Nick Somers (London, 2011); this book was first published as *Instanzen der Ohnmacht, Wien 1938–1945: Der Weg zum Judenrat* (Frankfurt am Main, 2000).
2 I wish to thank my colleague Eric Jacobson for sharing his insights on an earlier version of this essay.
3 See David Engel, *Historians of the Jews and the Holocaust* (Stanford, 2010).
4 See recent works and references in Bettina Stangneth, *Eichmann von Jerusalem: Das unbehellgte Leben eines Massenmörders* (Hamburg, 2011); Deborah Lipstadt, *The Eichmann Trial* (New York, 2011); Hans Safrian, *Eichmann's Men*, trans. Ute Stargardt (New York, 2010); David Cesarani, *Becoming Eichmann: Rethinking the Life, Crimes, and Trial of a "Desk Murderer"* (Cambridge, MA, 2006). The literature on Hannah Arendt's *Eichmann in Jerusalem*, to which these books all relate, is also abundant. Among the significant interpretations occasionally missing from discussions is Stephen Whitfield, *Into the Dark: Hannah Arendt and Totalitarianism* (Philadelphia, 1980). The version of Arendt's work used here is Hannah Arendt, *Eichmann in Jerusalem: A Report on the Banality of Evil*, intro. Amos Elon (New York, 2006).
5 Numerous versions of Herzl's *Judenstaat* might have been available to Eichmann; there are a few different versions of Boehm's book, and Eichmann was probably familiar with one of the abridged versions, like Adolf Boehm, *Die zionistische Bewegung: Eine kurze Darstellung ihrer Entwicklung* (Berlin, 1920–1). Most likely among the reasons for Eichmann's confusion, in addition to the time that had passed, were that Boehm's work, quoting at length from Herzl, was largely about the Herzlian phase of the movement, and was told from a distinctly Zionist perspective; Eichmann might also have confused this book with one of Boehm's many shorter publications. See Arendt, *Eichmann*, 39.
6 Arendt, *Eichmann*, 38.
7 Michael Berkowitz, *The Crime of My Very Existence: Nazism and the Myth of Jewish Criminality* (Berkeley, 2007).
8 Berkowitz, *Crime of My Very Existence*, 112–44.
9 Richard Evans, *In Hitler's Shadow: West German Historians and the Attempt to Escape from the Nazi Past* (New York, 1989).
10 Klaus-Michael Mallmann and Martin Cüppers, *Nazi Palestine: The Plans for the Extermination of the Jews in Palestine*, trans. Krista Smith (New York, 2010).
11 See, for example, Francis R. Nicosia, *The Third Reich and the Palestine Question* (New Brunswick, NJ, 2000); Jeffrey Herf, *Nazi Propaganda for the Arab World* (New Haven, 2009) .

12 Brian Amkraut, *Between Home and Homeland: Youth Aliyah from Nazi Germany* (Tuscaloosa, 2006).

13 "Back to the land: Experiment in Vienna," *Jewish Chronicle*, 12 August 1938, 16: "The movement is known as the 'Emigration Action Siegfried David,' after the man who conceived the idea, and is under the personal direction of Herr Otto Adler, a Viennese engineer, who, after great difficulties, has succeeded in obtaining semi-official recognition of the work."

14 "Palestine immigration from Austria. Negotiations with Nazi authorities," *Jewish Chronicle*, 29 April 1938, 5. Among those who participated were "General Sir Wyndham Deedes of London and Dr [Leo] Lauterbach of Jerusalem, the General Secretary of Zionist Organisation."

15 "Hitler attacks "interference by Britain" – and gibes at Palestine Administration," *Jewish Chronicle*, 14 October 1938, 28. This was, as well, a period of great conflict between Jews and Arabs in Palestine, and it seems that Hitler also may have wished to cause trouble for the British by pushing the Zionist presence in Palestine.

16 Ads in the *Jewish Chronicle*: 2 April 1938, 15; 6 May 1938, 17; 20 May 1938, 17; 27 May 1938, 19.

17 "Manchester: German and Austrian Jewry. Local appeal efforts. Palestine the only hope," *Jewish Chronicle*, 5 May 1938, 38; "Birmingham: Appeal for Austrian Jewry: Inaugurated by Mr. A. de Rothschild," *Jewish Chronicle*, 13 May 1938, 38.

18 Ad: "Austrian Jews in Distress! THE BEST HELP for your relatives and friends is a Remittance of Haavaramarks. FOR FULL PARTICULARS APPLY TO: Dr. Arthur Koenigsberger, 2. Basinghall Avenue, London, E.C. 2, METropolitan 0165," *Jewish Chronicle*, 6 May 1938, 20.

19 "Austrian Jewry. An Appeal," *Jewish Chronicle*, 29 April 1938, 14.

20 "Vienna Jews driven from their homes," *Jewish Chronicle*, 16 September 1938, 27; "Curfew for Vienna Jews. Refuge from Nazi Assaults. Arrests and evictions," *Jewish Chronicle*, 19 August 1938, 19.

21 "Vienna Jews' appalling poverty. Majority dependent on communal relief. Food shortage danger," *Jewish Chronicle*, 5 August 1938, 25; "Vienna community's plight. Without funds and without hope," *Jewish Chronicle*, 8 April 1938; "Austria. 'The Jews must get out quickly. Vienna reign of terror. Wholesale suicides. Jewish Charity funds seized," *Jewish Chronicle*, 1 April 1938, 41; "Jews faced with starvation: Relief funds seized," *Jewish Chronicle*, 25 March 1938, 41.

22 "Austrian Nazis fall out. Herr Buerckle's 'Prussian' methods. Jew-baiting as a safety-valve," *Jewish Chronicle*, 3 June 1938, 21.

23 "More Vienna arrests," *Jewish Chronicle*, 24 June 1938, 34.

24 "Confusion in Austria. Officials at sixes and sevens. Women attack Nazi Jew-baiters. Family of 22 commits suicide," *Jewish Chronicle*, 1 July 1938, 30;

"Nazis quarrel over Jewish victims. Party v. state in Austria," *Jewish Chronicle*, 29 July 1938, 13–14.

25 "Austrian extremists checked? Gauleiter Buerckel's promise. "Aryanisation on legal basis. S.S. partrols to protect Jewish shops," *Jewish Chronicle*, 6 May 1938, 20.

26 "The hell which is Austria," *Jewish Chronicle*, 29 April 1938, 7.

27 Joachim Prinz, "Knights of the Anvil," *Reform Judaism*, 56 (2007): 56.

28 Leni Brenner, "Historian Glosses Over Eichmann-Zionist Collaboration," review of *Becoming Eichmann*, by David Cesarani, www.rense.com/general77 /eich.htm.

29 Tom Segev, *The Seventh Million: The Israelis and the Holocaust*, trans. Haim Watzman (New York, 1993).

30 Slavoj Žižek, *The Parallax View* (Cambridge, MA, 2009), 256.

31 Jonathan Steinberg, *All or Nothing: The Axis and the Holocaust*, 2nd ed. (New York, 2002), 168; Mark Mazower, *Hitler's Empire: How the Nazis Ruled Europe* (New York, 2009), 34–5.

32 "Das 'Land ohne Volk' für 'Volk ohne Land'," *Zionistische Rundschau* 8 (8 July 1938): 7.

33 Michael Berkowitz, *Zionist Culture and West European Jewry before the First World War* (Cambridge, UK, 1993), 147–64.

34 Arieh Bruce Saposnik, *Becoming Hebrew: The Creation of a Jewish National Culture in Ottoman Palestine* (New York, 2008).

35 See Michael Berkowitz, *Zionist Culture*, and Berkowitz, *Western Jewry and the Zionist Project* (Cambridge, 1997).

36 See Safrian, *Eichmann's Men*, 141, 147.

37 Richard Breitman, *Official Secrets: What the Nazis Planned, What the British and Americans Knew* (London, 2000).

38 Jean-Claude Favez, *The Red Cross and the Holocaust*, ed. and trans. John Fletcher and Beryl Fletcher (Cambridge, UK, 1999), 169.

39 National Archives, Kew Gardens, UK, HW 19/271, GC 1188, CX/MSS/2327/ para 11. The entire text reads:

> To Riechsicherhietshauptampt IV B to be shown at once to SS. Oberstrumbannführer EICHMANN from Reichsicherheitshauptamt, Special Detachment, signed WISLICENY, SS. Hauptstrurmführer, dated 21/3
>
> Ref. Official journey to Athens.
>
> On 16/3.43 the undersigned was ordered to visit the German Plenipotentiary, Envoy ALTENBURG at Athens.
>
> The subject of the discussion was the attitude of the International Red Cross (I.R.K.) in SALONICA, Dr. BURCHKARDT, Jews of foreign nationality and the extension of measures against the Jews to Italian territorial area(s).

The Swiss Dr. BURCKHARDT had attempted to interfere since the beginning of the action against the Jews. He proposed in a telegram to the International Red Cross that Jews be transferred from SALONICA to PALESTINE. It was possible to prevent the despatch of the telegram. For this reason BURCKHARDT is being dismissed on the intervention of Envoy ALTENBURG, and is being replaced by a Swede. ALTENBURG stressed that also Jews of Spanish and Italian nationality must disappear from German territorial areas. A corresponding report has been sent to the Foreign Department.

If corresponding pressure is brought to bear in Rome, an extension to the Italian zone of anti-Jewish measures is possible. The Italians are supposed to be waiting for intervention of that type.

At the wish of ALTENBURG, Prime Minister LOGOTHETOPOULOS was given an exposition of anti-Jewish measures. LOGOTHETOPOULOS may have been insufficiently informed by his authorities. From another quarter, political personalities like the Archbishop of GREECE, DAMASKIONOS, had intervened with him against the Jewish emigration. The discussion with LOGOTHETOPOULOS convinced him fully and dispelled his doubts. It is requested that the question of foreign Jews and measures in the Italian zone be taken up with the Foreign Department.

V.G. 13.4.43

40 See Mark Mazower, *Inside Hitler's Greece* (New Haven, 2001), 233; credit usually goes to Walter Blume.

41 Cesarani, *Becoming Eichmann*, 59.

42 Prinz, "Knights of the Anvil," 68.

43 Allan Nadler, "The Plot for America," *Tablet Magazine*, 25 February 2011, http://www.tabletmag.com/news-and-politics/59863/the-plot-for-america/.

44 Michael Brenner, *The Renaissance of Jewish Culture in Weimar Germany* (New Haven, 1996), 218.

45 Benno Cohen [sometimes "Cohn"], in Allan Nadler, 1.

46 Prinz, "Knights of the Anvil," 60.

47 Cesarani, *Becoming Eichmann*, 59.

48 Segev, *The Seventh Million*, 31.

49 Rabinovici, *Eichmann's Jews*, 35.

50 Prinz, "Knights of the Anvil," 60.

51 Arendt, *Eichmann*, 31.

52 "The Trial of Adolf Eichmann, Session 81 (Part 4 of 5), The Nizkor Project, http://www.nizkor.org/hweb/people/e/eichmannadolf/transcripts/Sessions/Session-081-04.html.

53 Safrian, *Eichmann's Men*, 231, note 67; 29.

54 Laura Jockusch, *Collect and Record: Jewish Holocaust Documentation in Early Postwar Europe* (New York, 2012); Boaz Cohen, *Israeli Holocaust Research: Birth and Evolution*, trans. Agnes Vazsonyi (Abington and New York, 2013).

55 Jockusch, *Collect and Record*, 128–9.

56 Ibid., 160.

57 Tom Segev, *Simon Wiesenthal: The Life and Legends*, trans. Ronnie Hope (London, 2010), 15.

58 Jockusch, *Collect and Record*, 150.

59 Segev, *Wiesenthal*, 13n4; 416.

60 Central Zionist Archives, Jerusalem, Jewish Agency for Palestine, Political Department, Records of War Criminals, Reference Material, L/1, "The Extermination of the Jews in Lvov," 5 June 1945.

61 CZA, Z4\14968.

62 Ibid., 13; CZA, S25/7887.

63 Sara Kadosh, "Eva Michaelis Stern," Jewish Women's Archive, http://jwa .org/encyclopedia/article/stern-eva-michaelis [accessed February 2014].

64 CZA, "The Extermination of the Jews in Lvov," 8.

65 Victor Klemperer, *I Will Bear Witness, 1942–1945: A Diary of the Nazi Years*, trans. Martin Chalmers (New York, 1999), 86.

66 Amos Elon, "Introduction," in *Eichmann in Jerusalem*, ix.

67 See Shlomo Shamir, "Kissinger apologizes for comments about gassing Soviet Jews: 'It is hurtful to see an out-of-context remark being taken so contrary to its intentions and my convictions," *Haaretz*, 26 December 2010, www.haaretz.com/print-edition/news/kissinger-apologizes-for-comments -about-gassing-soviet-jews-1.332950.

68 Chaim Weizmann, "Lay Down Your Arms," *New Maccabaean*, 20 May 1921, 23–4; Berkowitz, *Western Jewry and the Zionist Project*, 65.

69 Bernard Wasserstein, *On the Eve: The Jews of Europe before the Second World War* (New York, 2012), 215–18.

PART II

Eichmann and Jurisprudence

4 Prosecuting "Crimes against the Jewish People": The Eichmann Trial and the History of a Legal Concept

LAURA JOCKUSCH

Some contemporary observers of Israel's 1961 trial of Adolf Eichmann linked the proceedings in Jerusalem to the Allied war crime trials that took place in Nuremberg between 1945 and 1949. Israeli Prime Minister David Ben-Gurion called the Eichmann trial the "Nuremberg of the Jewish people,"[1] while the political philosopher Hannah Arendt considered it "the last of the numerous Successor trials which followed the Nuremberg Trials."[2] That both Ben-Gurion and Arendt, whose worldview and overall stance on the Eichmann trial were diametrically opposed, nevertheless saw a direct link between Nuremberg and Jerusalem raises the question: What were the historical ties between the trials and what can be gained from comparing them?

A number of differences immediately come to mind: The "Nuremberg trials" were a series of thirteen military trials of close to 200 top Nazi leaders held by the victorious Allies in occupied Germany, the first lasting from October 1945 to October 1946 before the four-power International Military Tribunal (IMT) and the subsequent twelve trials held before the separate American Nuremberg Military Tribunal (NMT) from December 1946 to April 1949. The Eichmann trial was a criminal trial of one individual for his responsibility in implementing the Nazi mass murder of European Jews; it was held by the government of a state that had not existed at the time of the offences, but which represented itself as the heir of the victims of the Final Solution and a representative of its survivors.

While the trials at Nuremberg and Jerusalem prosecuted both crimes against humanity and war crimes, the Israeli trial also applied the legal category of "crimes against the Jewish people," which is unique to Israeli law.

Although Eichmann was not indicted at Nuremberg – since he was not in Allied custody at the time and was wrongly believed to have committed suicide – testimony of other major Nazis at the IMT implicated him. For example, SS-Hauptsturmführer Dieter Wisliceny – who as Eichmann's aide had played a major role in the deportation of the Jews of Slovakia, Greece, and Hungary and who appeared as a prosecution witness against Ernst Kaltenbrunner – incriminated Eichmann as the organizer of "the planned extermination and destruction of the Jewish race."[3] Similarly, Auschwitz-Birkenau commandant SS-Obersturmbannführer Rudolf Höss, a defence witness for Kaltenbrunner, asserted that it was through Eichmann that Himmler's orders regarding European Jewry's "mass executions through gassing" had been transmitted.[4] Even if only a vague picture of Eichmann's role in the Final Solution emerged from the Nuremberg trials, Eichmann became a person of interest for Jews engaged in hunting Nazis who would eventually track him down. Israeli secret service agents then kidnapped him in Argentina and brought him to Israel in May 1960.[5]

Fifteen years apart, the IMT and Eichmann trials occurred in fundamentally different historical contexts. Crimes against Jews were not the central focus of the prosecutions' cases at Nuremberg, but aggressive war was; victim testimony was relegated to the sidelines while Nazi documents provided the main evidence. The Jerusalem trial, on the other hand, concentrated on the Holocaust as a whole and gave survivor witnesses a central role in the courtroom. Although the Nuremberg trials were instrumental in initiating widespread public awareness of the Nazi genocide of European Jews, only the Eichmann trial provided the details and narratives that would build Holocaust consciousness in Israel and globally. At Nuremberg, Jews had been non-state actors whose voices were not heard; in 1961, they had a sovereign state that sat in judgment over a Nazi war criminal.[6]

These differences nevertheless indicate the intrinsic connections between the trials. As this essay will show, the Eichmann trial emerged as a trial of the Holocaust and its survivors because of the way in which the Allies had previously treated (or failed to treat) Nazi crimes against Jews. Some Jewish observers criticized the IMT and NMT trials at the time and voiced some demands of how the Holocaust should be addressed, which foregrounded and shaped the later proceedings in Jerusalem. Hence the Nuremberg trials provide an illuminating lens for understanding the Eichmann trial with regard to (1) the legal conceptualization and treatment of Nazi crimes against Jews, (2) the question of who could speak in the name of the victims of the Holocaust, and (3) the role of Holocaust survivors and their narratives in the prosecution of Nazi war crimes.

1. The Legal Conceptualization and Treatment of Crimes against Jews

As Michael Marrus has shown, the IMT trial against twenty-two "major war criminals" from the ideological, political, and military leadership of the Nazi regime – including Hermann Göring, Julius Streicher, Ernst Kaltenbrunner, Hans Frank, Albert Speer, Baldur von Schirach, Arthur Rosenberg, Joachim von Ribbentrop, and Rudolf Hess, in addition to Martin Bormann in absentia – played a foundational role in shaping public knowledge of the Holocaust. It was the first comprehensive public presentation of the historical development and death toll of the Nazi genocide of European Jews.[7] But although the IMT explored and condemned crimes against Jews, assisted by the new legal category of crimes against humanity, its proceedings did not constitute a "Holocaust trial" because, as Lawrence Douglas argues, "the prosecution's case was not primarily occupied with trying the defendants for the extermination of the Jews of Europe but instead focused on the accuseds' roles in launching and waging an aggressive war."[8] The category of crimes against humanity, which according to the London Charter of August 1945 included "murder, extermination, enslavement, deportation, and other inhumane acts committed against any civilian population before or during the war, or persecutions on political, racial, or religious grounds,"[9] was a complete novelty in international law. For the first time ever, a sovereign government could be held responsible for mistreating and murdering its own civilians even if domestic law did not criminalize those acts. Yet due to various political considerations the first Nuremberg tribunal restricted the new legal category's progressive attack on state sovereignty by linking it to the other three counts of the indictment. Crimes against humanity were considered only insofar as they related to crimes against peace, war crimes, and the conspiracy to wage a war of aggression. This meant that the crimes of the Final Solution were treated as a subset of Nazi war crime.[10] In the twelve American NMT trials, which tried 185 defendants representing various agencies of the Nazi state – medical doctors, jurists, military and economic leaders, diplomats, and the SS – the nexus between crimes against humanity and war crimes was not required, and the NMT also gave greater weight to crimes against Jews than the IMT.[11] Following the legal strategy of focusing on different Nazi agencies separately, the NMT covered crimes against Jews in all cases but did not treat the Holocaust as a unit in a separate case.[12]

Many contemporary Jewish observers, convinced that the Nazi mass murder of European Jews was a crime *sui generis* given its magnitude and transnational scale, were dissatisfied with this legal strategy. Already during the preparations for the IMT trial, the World Jewish Congress (WJC), a voluntary body of Jewish organizations founded in Geneva in August 1936 to represent the interests and needs of the Jewish collective in the diaspora, asked US Chief Prosecutor Justice Robert H. Jackson for a separate trial dealing only with crimes against Jews.[13] In a meeting with Jackson on 12 June 1945 in New York, a WJC delegation headed by the Lithuanian-born international lawyer Jacob Robinson proposed a separate Jewish indictment on the grounds that "the Jewish people is the greatest sufferer of this war, if not in the absolute number of its casualties (the Soviet Union has a larger total), certainly in relative numbers (the ratio of surviving Jews ... to their pre-war total in some areas). It therefore has a case of its own against the ... Nazi war criminals."[14] As a further point, Robinson argued, "The Nazis have not only exterminated two-thirds of European Jewry, but have infested the continent with anti-Jewish feeling, that makes the life of Jews in liberated Europe insecure. We believe that a specific indictment for the crime committed against our people will clear the atmosphere in Europe and make it easier for the survivors to reestablish themselves there."[15] Jackson immediately rebuffed the idea of a separate Jewish case; with Poles, Sinti, Roma, and other victimized groups without representation, a separate case for the Jews was not an option. Instead, Jackson affirmed that the Jews would have their place within the IMT trial.[16]

During the NMT trials, the WJC pushed US Chief Counsel Telford Taylor to include a separate trial specifically focusing on the deportation and mass murder of Jews from across Nazi-occupied Europe. Yet, these efforts were to no avail, leaving the WJC deeply dissatisfied with Taylor's decision to stick to the legal strategy of focusing on distinct Nazi agencies and to break up the Jewish case over several trials.[17] In the end, the SS-Einsatzgruppen trial, case nine of the NMT trials, which took place from 29 September 1947 through 10 April 1948, came closest to a trial that was solely dedicated to crimes against Jews.[18] However, even it focused only on a very specific aspect of the Nazi Final Solution – the mass shootings of Jews on Soviet territory by mobile SS killing squads.

Many Holocaust survivors in Germany and beyond felt that the Allies did not adequately represent and redress the loss and suffering of the Jewish people when prosecuting Nazi war criminals. The extensive coverage of the Nuremberg trial in the Jewish press shows that the issue of criminal proceedings against Nazi perpetrators deeply concerned the 250,000 East European Jews temporarily living in Germany as Jewish displaced persons, as well as the 15,000–30,000 German Jews who sought to rebuild their communities. Many of the more than 100 periodicals that appeared in Germany in the years 1945–9 had correspondents in the Nuremberg courtroom. Nonetheless, survivors felt marginalized and voiceless, and they worried that their fate had been subsumed under other crimes. For example, twenty days into the IMT trial, one correspondent for a major Yiddish newspaper raised the question, "Where is our ... enormous tragedy at this trial?"; he despaired that "this devastating issue ought not to be touched upon ... Yes, not only we, the survivors, are a disagreeable commodity in the big democratic postwar world, it is not only for us that this world can only spare hollow phrases, also our dead have no better lot. The entire 'Jewish part' of the trial is treated like a step-child, everyone is pushing it around but no one wants to shelter it."[19] While the Jewish DPs tended to think that this marginalization was a sign of the Allies' outright antisemitism, it seems to have been due to the fact that the Allies, seeking to make sense of the Nazi regime's inner workings, failed to grasp the distinct ideological nature of the genocide of European Jews and did not think that treating the Final Solution as a unit served their legal strategy.[20]

In a radical departure from previous trials, Israel's case against Adolf Eichmann was arguably the first "Holocaust trial." It focused on Nazi crimes against European Jews as a whole and Eichmann's personal responsibility for the larger event. In his opening address, Attorney General Gideon Hausner stressed that "the calamity of the Jewish People in this generation was the subject of consideration at a number of the trials conducted in the wake of Germany's defeat in World War II ... But in none of those trials was the tragedy of Jewry as a whole the central concern."[21] Echoing this view, the judgment stated that although the Holocaust had been "dealt with extensively" during the IMT and NMT trials, only "this time it has occupied the central place in the Court proceedings, and it is this fact which has distinguished this trial from those which preceded it."[22] Hausner sought to present the Jewish story of the Final Solution that had been missing from the Nuremberg trials by basing his case on the human stories of the victims and survivors of the genocide.

Hausner's overarching narrative portrayed the Jewish past as a constant struggle against antisemitism, in which Eichmann embodied an archetypical Jew-hater, a modern-day incarnation of Pharaoh, Haman, and Amalek. The constant of suffering in Jewish history, which had ultimately led to the Holocaust, had been broken only when Jews created a sovereign state that could bring the murderers of Jews to justice and speak in the name of the victims.[23] "And lo, in the days of the return of Judah and Jerusalem," Hausner opened his concluding address in quasi-biblical language, "a trial is held here for the violence done to the sons of Judah and for their blood, the blood of the innocents that was spilt, as foreseen by the prophet Joel. And again I ask you, Judges in Israel: Bring in a true and just verdict!"[24] As Lawrence Douglas observed, Hausner integrated past and present by presenting the unprecedented cataclysm of European Jews as "the fulfillment of divine prophecy" and the trial as the "celebration of legal self-sufficiency in which the power both to pass judgment and execute sentence is once again vested in a people left juridically and politically impotent since biblical times."[25] But the prosecution's mission went well beyond establishing and punishing Eichmann's guilt in the framework of Jewish history. It also fulfilled extralegal educational purposes, such as teaching young Israelis and world public opinion a lesson about the Holocaust, one that was, as Hausner put it in his memoirs, "a living record of a gigantic human and national disaster, though it could never be more than a feeble echo of the real events."[26]

Israel's 1950 Nazis and Nazi Collaborators Punishment Law provided the legal basis for judging Eichmann. By 1961, this law had been used to try some two dozen survivors accused of "collaboration" with the Nazis.[27] Along with war crimes and crimes against humanity, the law codified a distinct legal concept of "crimes against the Jewish people," defined as "any of the following acts, committed with intent to destroy the Jewish people in whole or in part: (1) killing Jews; (2) causing serious bodily or mental harm to Jews; (3) placing Jews in living conditions calculated to bring about their physical destruction; (4) imposing measures intended to prevent births among Jews; (5) forcibly transferring Jewish children to another national or religious group; (6) destroying or desecrating Jewish religious or cultural assets or values; (7) inciting to hatred of Jews."[28] Not only did this law make Nazi crimes against Jews justiciable throughout the years 1933–45, but it also declared the murder of Jews to be a distinct kind of crime, indeed the most severe form of crimes against humanity.[29] Accordingly, Eichmann's indictment named the "death of millions of Jews" by implementing "the plan of the Nazis for the physical extermination of the Jews, a plan known by its title 'The Final Solution to the Jewish Question,'"[30] as the gravest of war crimes or other crimes against humanity, thus providing the legal basis for a focus on the Jewish story that had been absent in the IMT and NMT prosecutions.[31]

Hannah Arendt, one of the most outspoken critics of this category of crimes against the Jewish people, believed that to distinguish between the murder of Jews and the murder of other human beings missed the crucial point that the Holocaust had been an onslaught on humanity at large. For her, the core crime of the Holocaust was not that the victims of the Final Solution were *Jews*, but rather that the Holocaust represented the systematic murder of a *kind* of human being, which by destroying the plurality of humankind, made it an attack on humanity itself. Israel was justified in prosecuting these crimes only because antisemitism motivated the choice of the victim. But Israel's Nazis and Nazi Collaborators Punishment Law could not provide an adequate legal basis for this trial, because, for Arendt, the issue was not that the Nazis had singled out the *Jewish* people, but rather that they had singled out *a* people for systematic mass murder.[32] Thus Arendt revived the debates that had surrounded the IMT's use of the new concept of crimes against humanity. Yet, Lawrence Douglas has emphasized the irony of Arendt's critique, because "the Israelis' creation of a separate offense, the crimes against the Jewish people, can be seen as born of the failure of crimes against humanity adequately to name and comprehend the crimes of the Holocaust."[33]

Indeed, Jewish observers of the IMT had taken offence that the Allies failed to acknowledge the distinct ideological motivation that resulted in the disenfranchisement, exploitation, expulsion, incarceration, and ultimately the systematic murder of Jews across the Nazi orbit of power, and that these crimes were given no adequate place in the Allies' treatment of crimes against humanity. Already in late 1942, the WJC approached the European governments-in-exile in London with the claim that Europe's Jews had suffered a distinct kind crime, which must be reflected in the legal frameworks that would be used to bring the Nazis to justice. Although it did not use the term "crimes against the Jewish people," the WJC specifically insisted that the concept of war crimes must be broadened to accommodate the Jewish case. After the war, the group continued this line of argument.[34]

Similarly, Jewish DPs in postwar Germany who followed the proceedings at Nuremberg voiced their belief that just such a separate category of offences should exist. In parallel to the Allied trials, the Jewish DPs created their own legal system inside the DP camps for trying such crimes. While these courts mainly dealt with offences that occurred since the liberation, several dozen of the "rehabilitation cases" investigated the pasts of survivors accused by their fellow-survivors of having collaborated with the Nazis, typically as Jewish council or ghetto police members or as kapos or other prisoner functionaries in the Nazi camp system. These rehabilitation cases applied a legal category of crimes against the Jewish people, and those found guilty of such crimes against other Jews were declared "traitors to the Jewish people."[35] Although these courts had no jurisdiction beyond the DP camps and Jewish communities, they were powerful instruments of social control within Jewish society; those found guilty of having besmirched their hands by collaborating with the murderers of Jews faced excommunication and were prevented from emigrating to Palestine/Israel or elsewhere. Most crucially, these court cases – which also occurred in the Jewish communities of several other European countries – represented the first manifestation of the idea that crimes against Jews (whether committed by Jews or non-Jews) were a distinct kind of crime and that Jewish courts should sit in judgment over them. Thus the concept, which was codified in Israeli law two years after the founding of the State of Israel, actually predated Jewish sovereignty. Moreover, this concept was created by survivors themselves, who had established their own sphere of jurisdiction in the extraterritorial reality of the DP camps in postwar Germany. The Eichmann trial thus answered Jewish demands to recognize and codify in law a distinct legal category: crimes against Jews. It was also the first, and so far only, prosecution where the legal basis created by the Jewish state was applied to a German war criminal.

2. Who Is to Speak in the Name of the Dead?

Closely connected to the role of the Jewish story of the Holocaust at the Eichmann trial was the issue of who represented the Jewish collective and who was entitled to speak in its name. In Nuremberg the World Jewish Congress had pushed for an official Jewish delegation with observer status at the tribunal. As an international voluntary body with member organizations in over thirty states – and in the absence of a Jewish state – the WJC viewed itself as a representative of the Jewish people. The idea of an official status for the WJC and recognition of its delegations as spokespersons for world Jewry predated the IMT. By the fall of 1943, the WJC was attempting to gain a seat on the United Nations War Crimes Commission in order to speak as experts on crimes against Jews.[36] In its self-understanding as a non-state actor and representative of the Jewish collective, the WJS continued its prewar strategies of fact-finding, information-gathering, and lobbying, which it had developed in the 1930s in the fight for Jewish minority rights in the League of Nations.[37]

In late November 1944, the WJC held an emergency conference in Atlantic City, New Jersey, which published a statement on the future treatment of Nazi war criminals. Among other demands, the WJC claimed that the Allied nations should grant it official status at any future war crimes tribunal.[38] The WJC repeated this demand at its meeting with Justice Jackson in June 1945, specifically that the group deserved the status as *amicus curiae* (friend of the court) to ensure independent Jewish participation in the tribunal. In this capacity, rather than as a party to the case, the WJC would lack the power to indict, but could assist the court by providing relevant information in the form of evidence or expert testimony. The WJC sought to convince Jackson that "the Jewish survivors are entitled to have someone represent them at the trials, as the spokesman of those who perished as well as of the living. Such representation would bring to the fore more clearly the moral implications of punishing the conspirators against an entire people."[39] Ultimately, the idea of appearing as a "spokesman for the dead and the living" at Nuremberg and other war crimes tribunals failed, because the Allies did not accept the then daring proposal to include a non-state actor in an international military trial. Ironically, the WJC nevertheless made an impact on the IMT by providing Jackson and his team with statistical and documentary material on the German genocide of European Jews. Moreover, WJC representatives believed they had achieved some success, including toward recognition of the Jewish collective.[40]

The survivors in the DP camps who observed the IMT and NMT proceedings were far more convinced than the WJC that they lacked a voice at Nuremberg. This resulted in part from their strong sense that the victims and survivors of Nazi atrocities were entitled, indeed obligated, to speak in the "name of millions of dead." Their direct experiences with the Nazi regime made them rightful accusers, whose claims, many believed, were more legitimate than those of the Allied judges and prosecutors who lacked their experience of victimhood. Upon the opening of the trial, a survivor reporting for the Yiddish press remarked: "We, the surviving remnant of European Jewry, though we have not been called to the prosecutors' table, are convinced that we are the ones who should point an accusing finger. It is our voice, we know, that should be the first to be lifted against those who stand accused."[41] In a similar vein, another courtroom correspondent urged the IMT judges: "Call upon any one of us who have survived. Ask one of us to unburden our hearts. Give ear to the story of the child, the mother, the father who now struggles through the living death bequeathed to him by those standing at the Bar of Justice. His story is the story of the Jew. Bitterly, in the despair of his great loss in the burning memory of flowing blood, he cries with a heartrendering [*sic*] silence – 'WE ACCUSE!'"[42] As a consequence, Jewish DPs were frustrated that ultimately no one spoke in the name of the dead at Nuremberg; in their eyes, those who had liberated the remnants of European

Jewry from Nazi rule proved to be unreliable and weak advocates for the victims and survivors of the Holocaust.

At the Eichmann trial, a sovereign Jewish state acted as the direct representative of the Holocaust's dead, and even as a representative of world Jewry, although the state had not existed when and where the atrocities being prosecuted had occurred. As Leora Bilsky observed, "The court based its extraterritorial jurisdiction on the doctrine of passive personality, according to which a state acquires jurisdiction over crimes committed outside its territory when it can show special relations to the victim."[43] Thus, the ability to try Nazi war criminals in Israel, even if *ex post facto* and involving an illegal act of kidnapping, constituted an essential aspect of Israel's sovereignty.

Before and during the trial, Prime Minister David Ben-Gurion – whom Hannah Arendt called the "invisible stage manager"[44] of the proceedings – made a strong case for the Jewish state's right to speak in the name of those murdered in the Holocaust since most of the victims were Jews and had been murdered solely because of their Jewishness.[45] Consequently, the prosecution referred to victims of the Holocaust as citizens of Israel involuntarily *in absentia*.[46] In his opening address Hausner claimed to speak in the name of millions of dead:

> When I stand before you here, Judges of Israel, to lead the Prosecution of Adolf Eichmann, I am not standing alone. With me are six million accusers. But they cannot rise to their feet and point an accusing finger towards him who sits in the dock and cry: "I accuse." For their ashes are piled up on the hills of Auschwitz and the fields of Treblinka, and are strewn in the forests of Poland. Their graves are scattered throughout the length and breadth of Europe. Their blood cries out, but their voice is not heard.[47]

Although the state's retroactive advocacy for the victims of the Holocaust answered demands that Jews had voiced in the context of the Nuremberg trials, such a role remained contested at the time of the Eichmann trial. Critics of the trial, most notably Eichmann's German defence attorney, Dr. Robert Servatius (who had defended Fritz Sauckel at the IMT), questioned the legitimacy of the Israeli court – mainly on the grounds that Eichmann's kidnapping violated international law and that the trial's jurisdictional claim was retroactive.[48] It is striking that Jewish circles also expressed some scepticism, in particular regarding Israel's exclusive right to speak for the dead, indeed as the representative of world Jewry. Even committed Zionists such as Nahum Goldmann, then chairman of the executive of the World Zionist Organization, criticized Israel's claim to exclusive jurisdiction over the accused. He suggested that an Israeli chief justice might preside, but that foreign jurists from the countries where Eichmann had committed his crimes should serve on the tribunal.[49] Similar ideas came from American Jews from across the ideological spectrum; the World Jewish Congress, for example, pushed for internationalizing the trial by suggesting, yet again, an official WJC delegation representing diaspora Jewry.[50] This idea resonated with the American Jewish Committee (AJC), which opposed Israel's role as exclusive advocate for world Jewry out of concern that Israel's actions in the trial would hurt the status of diaspora Jews, particularly in the United States. Former AJC president Judge Joseph Proskauer suggested that Eichmann be extradited to West Germany for prosecution and trial.[51] Ben-Gurion rejected all these ideas; limiting Israel's jurisdictional sovereignty was not an option once Jews had their own legal system.[52] "Now it was the Jews themselves who could decide what was best for their position," Gideon Hausner wrote in his memoir: "They could do so because they had their own machinery of justice, their own prosecutors and their own policemen. The trial was thus, in itself, an overwhelming manifestation of the revolution in the position of the Jewish people that had taken place in this generation."[53] As in Nuremberg, the WJC failed to achieve official status as the representative of the Jewish people, just that this time it was denied by the Jewish state exercising its sovereignty.

3. The Role of Holocaust Survivors and Their Narratives

At the IMT in Nuremberg, Jewish victims and witnesses stood on the sidelines, and Jews figured mainly as death statistics. Several survivors gave written affidavits, among them the Hungarian Jewish leader Rudolf Kasztner and the Austrian Jewish émigré psychologist Bruno Bettelheim.[54] But only three witnesses testified in court, two of them for the Soviet prosecution: the Lithuanian-born poet and partisan Avrom Sutzkever, who appeared on 27 February 1946 regarding the Vilna ghetto and the mass shootings of 60,000 Jews at Ponary, and Szmuel Rajzman, a Polish Jewish accountant who described extermination practices at Treblinka and his work in the Sonderkommando. The third Jewish witness, Izrael Eizenberg, a Polish Jew, appeared on 7 August 1946, called as a British prosecution witness to clarify his earlier written affidavit on SS involvement in the murder of the Jewish population of the Lublin District during 1941–2. Sutzkever described holding his baby boy shortly after his murder by the Germans in the infant ward of Vilna's Jewish hospital; Rajzman, who had seen his mother, sister, and two brothers go to the gas chambers, told of finding a photograph of his wife and child among the clothing he sorted; and Eizenberg, questioned about the scar on his cheek, told how he survived a mass execution of some 1,000 Jews in October 1942 in a field near Majdanek.[55] Yet, the human story of Jewish suffering remained marginal to the overall trial.

Some of the most excruciating details on the crimes of the Final Solution came from non-Jewish witnesses, including those by the Nazi perpetrators. Auschwitz-Birkenau commandant Rudolf Höss spoke with pride of the murders of 2.5 million Jews during his term as camp commander in 1940–3, and SS Einsatzgruppen leader Otto Ohlendorf reported that his Einsatzgruppe D had murdered 90,000 Jewish men, women, and children in southern Ukraine and the Crimea in 1941 and 1942.[56] Non-Jewish political prisoners who provided details on the mass murder of European Jews included the Polish Auschwitz inmate Severina Shmaglevskaya, on the murder of Jewish women and children in Auschwitz-Birkenau, and the French journalist and resistance fighter Marie-Claude Vaillant-Couturier, who revealed gruesome details on the medical experiments and gassings of Jewish women and children at Birkenau.[57]

The small number of Jewish witnesses who appeared at the IMT – and the situation was no different at the NMT – was in part the result of the Allies' political concerns over not focusing on Nazi "race crimes" and not giving Jews in particular the centre of the courtroom stage. But this paucity of Jewish witnesses also stemmed from anti-Jewish prejudice that tended to discount the words of survivors, whose subjectivity and alleged vengefulness, it was thought, would make their reports on the fate of their brethren less trustworthy.[58] But most importantly, both the IMT and NMT took place in a legal culture in which *victims* of mass atrocities and their narratives of human drama had no active role. Rather, the Allies who aimed to put the Nazi regime on trial focused on the central figures of the Nazi leadership elites, those whose crimes had no specific location and whose guilt would be established on the basis of the Germans' own documents. The Nuremberg prosecutors and judges clearly attributed a higher value to these contemporaneous records than to the oral and retroactive testimony of individual survivors of the Nazi extermination machinery on the Reich's periphery.[59] The prosecutors even feared that the horrifying details they recounted might be a distraction. Thus, the IMT and NMT proceedings relied primarily on documents, not on witness testimony.[60]

Jewish witnesses had a higher representation at some of the subsequent trials in the Allied occupation zones that focused on particular camps and crimes with a specific location. For example, in the trial against Josef Kramer, the last commandant of Bergen-Belsen, and 44 other defendants from that camp and Auschwitz-Birkenau, conducted at the British Military Tribunal in Lüneburg from 17 September–17 November 1945, a majority of prosecution witnesses – 19 out of 35 who appeared in court – were Jews. In addition, 60 of the 113 affidavits cited were openly identified as from Jews.[61] Several Jewish witnesses also appeared in the 460 trials against 1,676 "minor war criminals" known as the "Dachau series"; most of these trials took place at the site of the former Dachau concentration camp between November 1945 and August 1948. As in the British Belsen trial, the Jewish witnesses spoke out *as Jews*, stressing that they had been persecuted solely because of their ethnic background, whereas prosecutors, seeing these witnesses as Allied nationals, neither treated Jews as a separate group of victims nor attached specific significance to their suffering.[62] However, some of the testimonial tropes that emerged from the Eichmann trial – such as a survivor's fainting in the witness stand when unable to communicate unspeakable horrors, accounts of of miraculous survival in the face of mass exterminations, and even the submission to the court of vestiges from the past – both as material evidence of the witnesses' experiences and as tokens that the survivors had fulfilled their obligations toward the dead – had already occurred in Allied courts during the immediate postwar years.[63]

In the Jerusalem trial, victims commanded the stage, and their narratives made a great impact on Israeli society. Lawrence Douglas has noted that between the IMT and the Eichmann trials a radical shift from "documentary" to "testimonial" occurred in the logic of representation.[64] Gideon Hausner's decision to base his case against Eichmann and the Nazi regime at large on the oral testimony of Jews, most of them direct survivors of Nazi atrocities, radically broke the hierarchy of perpetrator and victim sources that Nuremberg had established. Survivors and their narratives not only held centre stage at the trial, but the prosecution credited their testimony as reliable and even authoritative.[65] While, as Hausner believed, the Allies' preoccupation with documents at Nuremberg had "failed to reach the hearts of men," narrating the history of the Holocaust through the accounts of individual witnesses would prove to leave a lasting impression on the trial's spectators in Israel and throughout the world.[66] For Hausner, doing justice went well beyond establishing the guilt of the accused and finally telling the Jewish story of the Final Solution, which earlier trials had not done. By giving voice to survivors, this trial would change their position in Israeli society, erase the judgmental attitudes under which they had suffered, and teach the Holocaust to a younger generation of Israelis who only had abstract knowledge of the events.[67] As Leora Bilsky has argued,

Hausner's prosecution strategy was motivated by ethical and humanist concerns.[68]

The one hundred survivors who appeared at the Eichmann trial had been chosen by special investigation unit Bureau 06, with help from Rachel Auerbach, herself a survivor and former co-worker of Emanuel Ringelblum in the Warsaw ghetto and now the head of Yad Vashem's oral history department.[69] They were unified in their wish to testify, although it was emotionally taxing for most. Ada Lichtman, a Sobibór survivor from Poland, was the first witness to testify in Yiddish, on 28 April 1961. Many survivors remained standing as they told their stories in the courtroom, thus echoing Avrom Sutzkever's testimony before the IMT when, as he noted in his diary, he had refused an invitation to take a seat by the presiding judge Sir Geoffrey Lawrence: "I spoke standing as if I was saying kaddish for the dead."[70]

Witness Leon Wells described his survival of the *Sonderkommando* at the Janowska camp in Lvov, where he had dug his own grave and, ill with pneumonia, hallucinated about drinking his own blood to still his thirst. Wells further told about his attempted suicide after escaping execution; he had been saved by a relative who convinced him of his moral obligation to live in order to become the agent of all those who would not be able to speak for themselves.[71] Taking the stage of the tribunal was a fulfilment of this mission. This same powerful incentive to live motivated Dov Freiberg, another survivor of Sobibór, who told the court, "We had to inform the world; somebody had to be sent outside, we had to try to escape."[72] And the writer Yechiel Dinur – until then known to the Israeli public only by his pen name, Kazetnik – began his testimony by saying that he had sworn an oath to the dead: "If I am able to stand before you today and relate to the events within that planet [by which he meant Auschwitz-Birkenau], if I, a fall-out of that planet, am able to be here at this time, then I believe with perfect faith that this is due to the oath I swore to them there. They gave me this strength." Seconds later, his strength left him, and uttering the words, "I see them, they are staring at me, I see them, I saw them standing in the queue …,"[73] he collapsed, presenting what Lawrence Douglas termed a "spectacular testimonial failure."[74] Dinur never resumed his testimony.

Survivors who appeared on the stand found meaning in their survival and fulfilled an imperative imparted by those dear to them; they spoke not just for themselves, but also in the name of their now destroyed families, communities, and towns.[75] A number of witnesses seem to have lived in anticipation of precisely the day when they would be able to appear before a court. Witness Adolf Berman, for example, brought a pair of children's shoes as material evidence from the Treblinka death camp and as a transitional object from past to present.[76] Similarly, Avrom Sutzkever had handed a document to the IMT, which he had collected in the Vilna ghetto, proving that the Germans reused the clothing of the dead.[77]

Immediately after the war, the deep sense of duty and obligation to bear witness in the name of the dead became a common trope in the public discourse of survivor communities. This sense of obligation to the dead pervaded the search for legal redress and informed the self-understanding of witnesses as "rightful accusers" and even prosecutors.[78] While this mission had been frustrated by the marginal position of survivors at Nuremberg, the Eichmann trial finally offered its fulfilment. In the words of Leora Bilsky, in the Eichmann trial "the entire Jewish nation (represented by Israel) stood in judgment of one of its worst oppressors, Adolf Eichmann, and by implication, nazism itself. The very structure of the trial symbolically inverted the past by transforming the persecuted victims into the prosecutors."[79] What then was the use and limit of survivor accounts at the Eichmann trial?

Beginning with Lichtman, many witnesses chose to turn from Hebrew to Yiddish, leading the Hebrew poet Natan Alterman to observe, "You shivered on hearing the words of the language of the slaughtered and the burned."[80] The very possibility of bearing witness in Yiddish itself presented an inversion of the IMT. Back then, Sutzkever's determination to testify in Yiddish, "the language of the nation whom the men in the dock tried to extinguish," and which Sutzkever wanted to be heard in the courtroom "as a symbol of our immortality,"[81] was ultimately thwarted by the Allies because the IMT lacked the requisite interpreters.

As Gali Drucker Bar-Am has shown, some of the witnesses in Jerusalem believed that neither the Yiddish language nor Yiddish culture or its institutions and values were accorded appropriate recognition in the trial conducted by the sovereign – and predominantly Hebrew-speaking – Jewish nation. The Yiddish-speaking survivor community of half a million Jews who had arrived in Israel in recent years was particularly dismayed by the fact that the court did not deem it necessary to publish its proceedings in that language.[82]

Clearly, the prosecution's presentation of the Jewish story of the Holocaust followed its own agenda. On the one hand, it carefully avoided the issue of Jewish collaboration, which – as the Kasztner trial had shown – had the potential to arouse sensitivities beyond the legal realm.[83] On the other hand, Hausner sought to create a heroic image of the Jewish tragedy, often by the use of direct questions that encouraged witnesses to expand on the varieties of resistance, while also making connections among survival, anti-Nazi defiance, and Israeli statehood.[84]

In his concluding statement, Hausner referenced the testimony of Rivka Yosselewska. A survivor of mass shootings near Pinsk, Yoselewska had witnessed the murder of her entire family, including her young daughter; but after crawling from the mass grave the Nazis had intended as her fate, Yoselewska rebuilt her life in Israel after the war, establishing a new family as the mother of two children.[85] For Gideon Hausner, Yosselewska embodied

> all that was perpetrated, all that happened to this people. She was shot. She was already amongst the dead in the funeral pit. Everything drew her downwards, to death. Wounded and wretched, with unbelievable strength she arose out of the grave. Her physical wounds healed, but her heart was torn asunder and broken forever. She found asylum in our country, established her home here and built her life anew. She overcame the evil design. They wanted to kill her, but she lives – they wanted to blot out her memory, but she has brought forth new children. The dry bones have been given sinews, flesh has grown upon them and they have taken on skin; they have been infused with the spirit of life. Rivka Yosselewska symbolizes the entire Jewish People.[86]

Despite the victim-focused and narrative-based proceedings, the Jerusalem trial set limits to the role of testimonial evidence in bringing Eichmann to justice, as reflected in continuing tension between the prosecution's urge to focus on the voices of victims and the court's commitment to legal formalism.[87] The court ruled against the defence's argument that the testimonies were not relevant to the case, but it also asked the prosecution to "limit the extent of its evidence" and guide witnesses by using specific questions.[88] In a number of instances, the court showed impatience at individual witnesses who added details to their accounts, often rudely interfering and cutting short their stories, while also acknowledging that such dramatic and horrifying accounts could not be interrupted.[89] In the words of Lawrence Douglas, the court struggled to maintain its "juridical authority against the force of survivor narrative."[90]

Likewise, the court showed ambivalence regarding the juridical value of survivor testimony in establishing the guilt of the accused, since it faced the dilemma that most of the testimonies could not be linked to Eichmann's own deeds. While defence attorney Robert Servatius never doubted that crimes related at the trial had happened, he argued that Eichmann had no personal responsibility for them. Against his objections, the court ruled that testimonies that lacked a direct link to the defendant were nonetheless relevant to the broader historical events that formed the core of this trial.[91] Yet the court faced the dilemma that the most reliable testimonies – in the sense that witnesses could give detailed descriptions of their experiences in ghettos and camps – were least relevant to the case against Eichmann, whereas those that were most relevant – from witnesses who claimed to have seen or interacted with Eichmann – were the least reliable because they were vague and relied on hearsay.[92] With the exception of Joel Brandt, whose negotiations with Eichmann, if successful, could have saved Hungarian Jewry in return for the delivery of material goods behind the German frontlines – most witnesses were too far removed from those with positions of power inside the Nazi regime, not to mention from Eichmann himself.[93]

Ultimately, then, survivor testimony had only a limited impact on the trial's legal outcome. "In the judges' weighing of the evidence," Hanna Yablonka observed, "we see the opposite of what occurred among the Israeli people," who were deeply moved by victim narratives. The court itself, however, "on every count on which the defendant was convicted … chose to rely on documents – except in connection with the forced emigration from Germany and Austria, where it also relied on testimony."[94] Aware of the trial's profound impact on the Israeli public, the judgment emphasized the extrajudicial value of the testimonies. The justices had no doubt that "the testimony given at this trial by survivors of the Holocaust, who poured out their hearts as they stood in the witness box, will provide valuable material for research workers and historians, but as far as this court is concerned they are to be regarded as by-products of the trial."[95] The judges were adamant about that:

> It is the purpose of every criminal trial to clarify whether the charges in the prosecution's indictment against the accused … are true, and if the accused is convicted to mete out due punishment against him. Everything which requires clarification in order that these purposes may be achieved, must be determined at the trial, and everything which is foreign to these purposes must be entirely eliminated from the court procedure.[96]

For the witnesses themselves, as for survivor circles and the broader Israeli public, the trial had tremendous significance and led to a change in public consciousness.[97] Besides evincing sympathy and understanding for survivors, witness stories of horrendous Jewish suffering made room for a more nuanced public discourse on the past, breaking down a polarized version of the Holocaust, one that contrasted Zionist-minded Jewish resistance fighters with passive Jewish victims who had supposedly gone "like sheep to the slaughter."[98] In addition, although survivors had told their individual stories before, they were now listened to and their narratives had a different effect on the public in Israel and around the world.[99]

Conclusion

Long before the Eichmann trial Jewish individuals and organizations demanded that Nazi crimes against Jews be dealt with in separate trials and that these crimes required a distinct legal category – crimes against the Jewish people. They had also demanded the inclusion of a prosecutorial role for a non-state actor in international criminal justice. Lastly, they had called for a more victim-centred judicial process. Although these demands proved futile in the context of the Nuremberg trials, they nevertheless preconditioned the Eichmann trial's later focus on crimes against Jews, the Holocaust as an event *sui generis*, and the experiences and voices of Jews who had survived. Trying Eichmann in Jerusalem was an expression of Jewish sovereignty, a demonstration of the ability of the Jewish state to try the murderers of Jews on its own territory and on the basis of its own legal system.

Eichmann's defence attorney, Servatius, questioned the objectivity of the Israeli judges because of their affinity with the people victimized by the Final Solution. In other words, Jews' emotional preoccupation with the victims prevented their objectivity in judging the murderers of their kin.[100] Israel's kidnapping of Eichmann in violation of international law only seemed to confirm the supposed Jewish penchant for vengeance.[101] Hannah Arendt rightly replied that the magnitude of the crimes justified the kidnapping; moreover, it was the only possible way to get the defendant to court.[102] She further observed that the argument regarding the problematic affinity between the court and the victims of mass atrocities was made selectively in regard to Israel, and not against courts in other nations whose citizens had suffered under the Nazis.[103]

Elaborating on the issue of vengeance and the law, Arendt offers the hypothetical option of shooting Eichmann on the spot, drawing an instructive parallel with two historic examples of minorities that used extralegal means to draw public opinion to the far greater injustices perpetrated against them: the 1921 murder of the former Ottoman Interior Minister Pasha Mehmet Talaat by the Armenian Soghomon Tehlirian and the 1926 murder of the former Ukrainian head of state Simon Petliura by the Ukrainian Jewish watchmaker Sholem Schwartzbard. Each of the assassins belonged to a minority group that had suffered genocidal atrocities that had gone unpunished. Because neither group had a state that could adjudicate the crimes, these men saw no recourse but to take matters into their own hands, thereby breaking the law in the name of a greater good, namely, bringing the atrocities to public consciousness. Arendt sees a parallel between the Schwartzbard and Eichmann trials in that both used evidence compiled in the name of Jewish victims of mass atrocities.[104]

For Arendt, the most crucial link between Nuremberg and Jerusalem was that both trials had misunderstood the unprecedented novelty of the crimes of the Final Solution and its most distinctive variety of perpetrator, as personified in Eichmann. The Allies had developed the concept of crimes against humanity in part as a way to address the unprecedented nature of what had happened to Europe's Jews. But because they had tied it to war crimes and crimes against peace, they had not realized the full potential of this legal innovation. Accordingly, Arendt was dismayed that Israel had made crimes against the Jewish people a separate criminal offence, thus, in her view, presenting the crimes being linked to Eichmann "as not much more than the most horrible pogrom in Jewish history."[105] Just as the Allies before, the Jerusalem court had failed to understand the true meaning of the crimes of the Holocaust, as an onslaught on humanity in the form of the Nazis' attempt to erase a distinct human group from the face of the earth. Thus, in failing to elaborate and use the full potential of the legal category of crimes against humanity, the Jerusalem court had repeated the same mistakes made by the various war crimes trials in postwar Germany. In the end, Arendt believed that only an international court representing humanity at large could rightfully prosecute crimes against humankind, regardless of the national identity of the victims.[106] Until such a court was created with a mandate to prevent the complete elimination of any particular group of humans, no people – the Jews, in particular – would be safe from such a catastrophe.[107]

Finally, it is unfair to judge the Eichmann trial solely by its impact on the legal prosecution and prevention of genocide. The prosecution's decision to focus on the stories of survivors, regardless of their direct relevance to the guilt or innocence of the defendant, had a major impact on the Israeli public, on the increase in Holocaust-consciousness in world opinion, and in creating what Annette Wieviorka has called the "era of the witness."[108] According to Leora Bilsky, the Eichmann trial's "lasting contribution ... to the development of international criminal law" was Hausner's "unique interpretation of the meaning of justice, an interpretation that not only insists on telling the untold story but also acknowledges the importance of who tells it ... The role given to the Jewish victim in the trial carried a universal message about society's commitment to restore the dignity of the victims of the crime through the legal process." The core issue, for Bilsky, is the continuing need "to rethink the role of a courtroom in enhancing the 'recognition' of silenced groups, such as victims of atrocities, as part of the process of 'doing justice.'"[109] In this respect, the Eichmann trial was a crucial step toward the kind of victim-focused criminal justice that some Jewish observers demanded immediately after the war.

NOTES

1 Quoted in Annette Wieviorka, "La construction de la mémoire du génocide en France," *Le Monde Juif* 149 (1993): 30.

2 Hannah Arendt, *Eichmann in Jerusalem: A Report on the Banality of Evil* (New York, 2006), 263.

3 See Wisliceny's testimony of 3 Jan. 1946, in IMT, ed., *Trial of the Major War Criminals before the International Military Tribunal, Nuremberg 14 November 1945–1 October 1946*, 42 vols. (Nuremberg: International Military Tribunal, 1947–9) [hereafter *IMT*], 4: 356, similarly 358.

4 See Höss' testimony of 15 April 1946, in ibid., 11: 419.

5 See, for example, Andrew Nagorski, *The Nazi Hunters* (New York, 2016), 134–85.

6 See, for example, Hanna Yablonka, "As Heard by the Witnesses, the Public, and the Judges: Three Variations on the Testimony in the Eichmann Trial," in David Bankier and Dan Michman, eds., *Holocaust Historiography in Context: Emergence, Challenges, Polemics and Achievements* (Jerusalem, 2008), 567–87; Hanna Yablonka, *The State of Israel vs. Adolf Eichmann* (New York, 2004); Deborah Lipstadt, *The Eichmann Trial* (New York, 2011), xi–xii.

7 The indictment mentioned crimes against Jews under all four counts; the tribunal established the number of 5.7 million Jewish victims, and references to crimes against Jews, illustrated by graphic documentary evidence, permeated the entire proceedings. See Michael R. Marrus, *The Nuremberg War Crimes Trial: A Documentary History* (Boston and New York, 1997), 65, 70; Michael R. Marrus, "The Holocaust at Nuremberg," *Yad Vashem Studies* 26 (1998): 5–41.

8 Lawrence Douglas, *The Memory of Judgment: Making Law and History in the Trials of the Holocaust* (New Haven, 2001), 6.

9 See article 6c of the Charter of the International Military Tribunal, *IMT*, vol. 1.

10 See Donald Bloxham, *Genocide on Trial: War Crimes Trials and the Formation of Holocaust History and Memory* (New York, 2001); Douglas, *The Memory of Judgment*, 38–64; Arie J. Kochavi, "The Role of the Genocide of European

Jewry in the Preparations of the Nuremberg Trials," in David Bankier and Dan Michman, eds., *Holocaust and Justice: Representation and Historiography of the Holocaust in Post-War Trials* (Jerusalem, 2010), 59–80.

11 Kevin Jon Heller, *The Nuremberg Military Tribunals and the Origins of International Criminal Law* (New York, 2011), 236–7.

12 Ibid., 4.

13 On the World Jewish Congress and its lobbying efforts, see Boaz Cohen, "Dr. Jacob Robinson, the Institute of Jewish Affairs, and the Elusive Jewish Voice in Nuremberg," in Bankier and Michman, *Holocaust and Justice*, 81–100; Omry Kaplan-Feuereisen, "Im Dienste der Nation: Jacob Robinson und das Völkerrecht," *Osteuropa* 8–10 (2008): 279–94; Leon Arie Kubowitzki, *Unity in Dispersion: A History of the World Jewish Congress* (New York, 1948); Mark A. Lewis, "The World Jewish Congress and the Institute of Jewish Affairs at Nuremberg: Ideas, Strategies, and Political Goals, 1942–1946," *Yad Vashem Studies* 36, no. 1 (2008): 181–210; Michael R. Marrus, "A Jewish Lobby at Nuremberg: Jacob Robinson and the Institute of Jewish Affairs, 1945–46," *Cardozo Law Review* 27, no. 4 (2006): 1651–65.

14 American Jewish Archives, World Jewish Congress Collection, available at the website of the Truman Library [hereafter AJA, WJC, TL], Minutes of a meeting with Justice Robert H. Jackson, held at the Federal Court House, N.Y.C., Tuesday June 12, 1945, from 10 to 11:30 A.M., 1.

15 Ibid., 5.

16 Ibid., 5–6.

17 On the WJC's efforts to push for the prosecution of some Wannsee conference participants in the Wilhelmstrasse/Ministries case, see Jonathan A. Bush, "The Prehistory of Corporations and Conspiracy in International Law: What Nuremberg Really Said," *Columbia Law Review* 109 (2009): 1187–8, and Bloxham, *Genocide on Trial*, 74–5, and Heller, *The Nuremberg Military Tribunals*, 80–1. See also American Jewish Archives Cincinnati, World Jewish Congress Collection [hereafter AJA, WJC], C125/3, Telford Taylor's letter to Stephen S. Wise, 27 December 1947, 1.

18 Hilary Earl, *The Nuremberg SS-Einsatzgruppen Trial, 1945–1958: Atrocity, Law, and History* (New York, 2009).

19 K. Shabtai [pseudonym for Shabse Klugman also known as Shabtai Keshev], "Makom ha-resha – sham ha-mishpat, no. 5," *Undzer veg*, 14 December 1945.

20 For example, as Telford Taylor admitted when reflecting on his experiences as assistant to Jackson at the IMT and chief prosecutor of the twelve subsequent trials at the American Military tribunal, "I myself did not become aware of the Holocaust until my exposure to the relevant documents and witnesses at Nuremberg." Telford Taylor, *The Anatomy of the Nuremberg Trials* (New York, 1992), 26n.

21 *The Trial of Adolf Eichmann: Record of Proceedings in the District Court of Jerusalem* (Jerusalem, 1992) [hereafter *TAE*], 1: 63.
22 Ibid., 5: 2082.
23 Leora Bilsky, *Transformative Justice: Israeli Identity on Trial* (Ann Arbor, 2004), 97–9, 122.
24 *TAE*, 5: 2043.
25 Douglas, *The Memory of Judgment*, 152
26 Gideon Hausner, *Justice in Jerusalem* (New York, 1968), 291.
27 Interestingly, the Eichmann and Demjanjuk trials were exceptions in that most trials based on this law between 1951 and 1964 concerned Jewish survivors who allegedly had collaborated with the Nazis in their capacities as kapos, members of the Jewish councils or Jewish police in East European ghettos. See Orna Ben-Naftali and Yogev Tuval, "Punishing International Crimes Committed by the Persecuted: The Kapo Trials in Israel (1950s and 1960s)," *Journal of International Criminal Justice* 4 (2006): 128–78.
28 Nazis and Nazi Collaborators Punishment Law, 1 August 1950, see https://mfa.gov.il/mfa/mfa-archive/1950-1959/pages/nazis%20and%20nazi%20collaborators%20-punishment-%20law-%20571.aspx (accessed 18 June 2019); it is striking that the wording of the category of "crimes against Jews" was based on the UN Genocide Convention, just that "group" was replaced with "Jews."
29 Bilsky, *Transformative Justice*, 103.
30 *TAE*, 1:3.
31 Counts 1–4 of the indictment concerned crimes against Jews, see David Cesarani, *Becoming Eichmann: Rethinking the Life, Crimes, and Trial of a "Desk Murderer"* (Rayleigh, 2006), 252–3.
32 Arendt, *Eichmann in Jerusalem*, 268–9, 272.
33 Douglas, *The Memory of Judgment*, 174.
34 Lewis, "The World Jewish Congress and the Institute of Jewish Affairs at Nuremberg," 184–91. See also Laura Jockusch, "Justice at Nuremberg? Jewish Responses to Nazi War Crimes Trials in Allied Occupied Germany," *Jewish Social Studies* 19, no. 1 (Fall 2012): 107–47.
35 See, for example, the case of Regina Szenberg, accused of having mistreated fellow Jews while a *Blockälteste* at Auschwitz-Birkenau; she was found "guilty of sadistic treatment of Jewish women and children, of beating without reason Jewish women, of making their lives miserable, selling food which she stole from rations that belonged to children and women, and has therefore committed a *crime against the Jewish people*. For the abovementioned deeds the accused Regina Szenberg … will be punished by being publicly declared *traitor to the Jewish people*." See YIVO Archives, Displaced Persons Camps and Center in Germany Collection, folder 222.

See also Isaiah Trunk, *Judenrat: The Jewish Councils in Eastern Europe under Nazi Occupation* (New York, 1972), 548–69; Margarete Myers Feinstein, *Holocaust Survivors in Postwar Germany, 1945–1957* (New York, 2010), 238–48; Rivka Brot, "Julius Siegel: A Kapo in Four (Judicial) Acts," *Dapim: Studies on the Shoah* 25 (2011): 65–127. On the Jewish honour court cases in postwar Germany see also Laura Jockusch, "Rehabilitating the Past? Jewish Honor Courts in Allied-Occupied Germany," in Laura Jockusch and Gabriel Finder, eds., *Jewish Honor Courts: Revenge, Retribution, and Reconciliation in Europe and Israel after the Holocaust* (Detroit, 2015), 49–82.

36 See the protocols of the meetings of the World Jewish Congress representatives with General de Baer, a Belgian member of the U.N. War Crimes Commission and Sir Cecil Hurst, its chairman: American Jewish Archives Cincinnati, World Jewish Congress Collection [hereafter AJA, WJC], C118/5, "Minutes of the meeting January 5, 1944"; AJA, WJC, C118/7, "Note of Conversation between Sir Cecil Hurst and a Delegation of the World Jewish Congress," 20 July 1944, and AJA, WJC, C118/7, "Note of Conference between Representatives of the United Nations' Commission for the Investigation of War Crimes and the World Jewish Congress in London," 2 August 1944.

37 Philipp Graf, *Die Bernheim-Petition 1933: Jüdische Politik in der Zwischenkriegszeit* (Göttingen, 2008).

38 AJA, WJC, C125/10, World Jewish Congress, "Statement and Resolution on the Punishment of War Criminals," War Emergency Conference, 26–30 November 1944, 1–3. See the various preparatory drafts: AJA, WJC, C118/2, "Memo to the Members of the Retribution Committee from Dr. Robinson," 13 April 1944; AJA, WJC C118/2, "Memo to the Members of the Office Committee from Dr. Robinson," 22 May 1944; AJA, WJC C118/2, "Statement on Retribution," 2 June 1944; AJA, WJC, C118/2, "Punishment of War Criminals: A Statement by the World Jewish Congress," 14 June 1944; AJA, WJC, C118/7, "Draft of a Letter to Be Sent to the British Section re: War Crimes," 17 August 1944.

39 AJA, WJC, TL, Minutes of a meeting with Robert H. Jackson, 5.

40 The WJC's impact lay in providing the US prosecution team with documentary and statistical evidence and commenting on various drafts of the indictment. In late November, Jacob Robinson visited the IMT to assist William F. Walsh, assistant trial counsel for the United States, in preparing Walsh's mid-December presentation of evidence on the persecution of the Jews mentioned under counts one and four of the indictment. See Walsh's Jewish brief (13–14 December 1945), *IMT*, 3: 519–72; see also AJA, WJC, TL, Report from Jacob Robinson to the World Jewish Congress, 6 December 1945, 7–8, 13; AJA, WJC, TL, Minutes of Office Committee Meeting, World Jewish Congress, 10 December 1945, 5.

41 Zalman Grünberg, "Nürnberg," *Undzer veg*, 20 November 1945.
42 Leivy Salitan, "We Accuse: A Word to the Judges in Nuremberg," *Undzer veg*, 12 October 1945.
43 Bilsky, *Transformative Justice*, 133.
44 Arendt, *Eichmann in Jerusalem*, 5.
45 Cesarani, *Becoming Eichmann*, 239–40; Lipstadt, *The Eichmann Trial*, 29.
46 *TAE*, 1: 36–7, 44, 47.
47 Ibid., 1: 62. See also *6,000,000 Accusers: Israel's Case against Eichmann*, edited by Shabtai Rosenne (Jerusalem, 1961).
48 See Servatius' objections in *TAE*, 1: 8–10. Servatius had served in the German army and was of nationalist conservative opinions, but had not been a member of the Nazi Party; at the time of the Eichmann trial he was practising law in Cologne; after defending Fritz Saukel at the IMT he also defended Dr. Karl Brand at the Doctors Trial and Paul Pleiger at the Ministries Case. See Cesarani, *Becoming Eichmann*, 246–7.
49 Lipstadt, *The Eichmann Trial*, 31.
50 See the following letters in the Central Zionist Archives Jerusalem, C2/4493: Maurice Perlzweig to Nachum Goldman, 6 June 1960, 71–4; Nahum Goldman to Alexander Easterman, 6 June 1960, 68; Maurice Perlzweig to Alexander Easterman, 6 June 1960, 69; and Alexander Easterman to Nachum Goldman, 10 June 1960, 67.
51 Lipstadt, *The Eichmann Trial*, 32–3.
52 See Michael Keren, "Ben Gurion's Theory of Sovereignty: The Trial of Adolf Eichmann," in Ronald W. Zweig, ed., *David Ben Gurion: Politics and Leadership in Israel* (London, 1991), 40–2; Yechiam Weitz, "The Founding Father and the War Criminal's Trial: Ben Gurion and the Eichmann Trial," *Yad Vashem Studies* 36, no. 1 (2008): 211–52.
53 Hausner, *Justice in Jerusalem*, 453.
54 Kasztner's affidavit (Document Number 2605-PS, Exhibit USA-242, cited 13 December 1945, in *IMT*, 3: 501–2) was part of US executive trial counsel Thomas J. Dodd's presentation of a case on concentration camps. Kasztner was a defence witness for SS Obersturmbannfueherer Kurt Becher, who escaped prosecution thanks to Kasztner's testimony on the Budapest negotiations. See Shlomo Aronson, "Israel Kasztner: Rescue in Nazi-Occupied Europe; Prosecutor in Nuremberg and Accused at Home," in Shmuel Almog et al., eds., *The Holocaust. The Unique and the Universal: Essays Presented in Honor of Yehuda Bauer*, 2nd ed. (Jerusalem, 2005), 1–47; Shoshana Barri (Ishoni), "The Question of Kastner's Testimonies on Behalf of Nazi War Criminals," *Journal of Israeli History* 18, nos. 2–3 (1997): 139–65; and Yechiam Weitz, *The Man Who Was Murdered Twice: The Life Trial and Death of Israel Kasztner* (Jerusalem, 2011), 57–67. Bettelheim's use of his experiences in the German camp system

in a doctoral dissertation and scholarly articles came to the attention of
the US military, which sought insights into dealing with former inmates
whom they would encounter while liberating Germany. See especially
Bettelheim's 1943 essay "Individual and Mass Behavior in Extreme
Situations," *Journal of Abnormal and Social Psychology* 38 (1943): 417–52; his
affidavit, given on 10 July 1945, to Jackson's staff is an abridgment of his
1943 essay, L-73 Affidavit of Bruno Bettelheim in United States Office of
Chief of Counsel (ed.), *Nazi Conspiracy and Aggression*, 8 vols., Nuremberg,
1945–6, vol. 7, 818–39. See Kim Wünschann, "The 'Scientification' of the
Concentration Camps: Early Theories of Terror and Their Reception by
American Academia," *Leo Back Institute Yearbook* 58 (2013): 111–26. Other
affidavits came from Franz Wolff, a German Jew and former editor of the
Frankfurter Allgemeine Zeitung, whose affidavit was read on 12 July 1946,
Document PS-3954, Exhibit USA 377; David Wajnapel, on ghetto Radom,
6 August 1946, Document D-953, Exhibit GB-566; Mojzesz Goldberg
on Lemberg, Document D-955, Exhibit GB-565, 6 August 1946; Henri
Monneray, Document PS-2519, Exhibit USA-530, 3 January 1946; Robert
M.W. Kempner, Document PS-3355, Exhibit USA-682, 16 January 1946.

55 Avrom Sutzkever, "Mayn eydes-zogn in nirnberg," *Di goldene keyt* 54
(1966): 6. Szmuel Rajzman in *IMT*, 8: 327. See also his testimony: Yad
Vashem Archives O.3, folder 561. On Izrael Eizenberg's court appearance,
see *IMT*, 20: 484–5; his affidavit, document D-939, exhibit GB-563, was
read in court on 6 August 1946. See also his testimony: Yad Vashem
Archives M.1.E, folder 220.

56 Höss testified on 15 April 1946, in *IMT*, 11: 396–401. Ohlendorf testified
on 3 January 1946, see *IMT*, 4: 311–54; see also Taylor, *Anatomy of the
Nuremberg Trials*, 246–8.

57 Severina Shmaglevskaya in *IMT*, 8: 316–21. She testified on 27 February
1946, in Polish. Marie-Claude Vaillant-Couturier in *IMT*, 6: 202–30. She
testified on 28 January 1946, in French.

58 Bloxham, *Genocide on Trial*, 68; Donald Bloxham, "Jewish Witnesses
in War Crimes Trials of the Postwar Era," in Bankier and Michman,
Holocaust Historiography in Context, 540–2.

59 Bloxham, "Jewish Witnesses," 540; Marrus, "The Holocaust at
Nuremberg," 19. This focus on the perpetrators also dominated academic
Holocaust research for decades. The integration of victim perspectives in
the historical narrative began only at the end of the 1990s. Raul Hilberg's
The Destruction of the European Jews (Chicago, 1961), heavily based on
the IMT archives, is a prominent example of a perpetrator-focused
Holocaust history. Saul Friedländer's *Nazi Germany and the Jews* (vol. 1,
1997, and vol. 2, 2007) exemplifies the recent trend to integrate victim and
perpetrator perspectives and sources into the historical narrative.

60 See Jackson's introduction to Whitney R. Harris, *Tyranny on Trial: The Evidence at Nuremberg* (Dallas, 1999), xxxv–xxxvi.

61 Kramer had served in Auschwitz as Höss' deputy in 1940 and himself as camp commander in 1944. See U.N. War Crimes Commission, ed., *Law Reports of Trials of War Criminals: The Belsen Trial*, vol. 2, (New York, 1983; first published in 1947); Raymond Phillips, ed., *The Trial of Josef Kramer and 44 Others (The Belsen Trial): War Crimes Trial Series*, vol. II (London: 1947); John Cramer, *Belsen Trial 1945: Der Lüneburger Prozess gegen Wachpersonal der Konzentrationslager Auschwitz und Bergen-Belsen* (Göttingen, 2011), 158–74.

62 See Lisa Yavnai, *Military Justice: The U.S. Army War Crimes Trials in Dachau, Germany, 1944–1948* (PhD diss., London School of Economics and Political Science, 2007), especially 189, 204–6; Robert Siegel, *Im Interesse der Gerechtigkeit: Die Dachauer Kriegsverbrecherprozesse, 1945–1948* (Frankfurt/Main, 1992). On the Mauthausen trial of the Dachau series, see Tomaz Jardim, *The Mauthausen Trial: American Military Justice in Germany* (Cambridge, MA, 2012), 141–5.

63 See, for example, the testimony of witnesses at the Belsen trial in Phillips, *The Trial of Josef Kramer*, 79–84; 104; 745–6. See also Devin O. Pendas, Laura Jockusch, and Gabriel Finder, "Auschwitz Trials: The Jewish Dimension," *Yad Vashem Studies* 41, no. 2 (Fall 2013): 12–13.

64 Douglas, *The Memory of Judgment*, 104–5.

65 Bilsky, *Transformative Justice*, 112–13.

66 Hausner, *Justice in Jerusalem*, 291.

67 Douglas, *The Memory of Judgment*, 161–2; Bilsky, *Transformative Justice*, 111.

68 Bilsky, *Transformative Justice*, 88.

69 Auerbach's testimony of 3 May 1961, *TAE*, 1: 421–5. On Auerbach's role in the selection of witnesses see Cesarani, *Becoming Eichmann*, 251; Boaz Cohen, "Rachel Auerbach, Vad Vashem, and Israeli History," in Gabriel Finder et al., eds., *Making Holocaust Memory: Polin*, vol. 20 (Oxford, 2008): 197–221.

70 Sutzkever, "Mayn eydes-zogn in nirnberg," 14.

71 *TAE*, 1: 364.

72 Ibid., 3: 1174.

73 Ibid., 3: 1237.

74 Douglas, *The Memory of Judgment*, 147.

75 Yablonka, "As Heard by the Witnesses, the Public, and the Judges," 571–2.

76 *TAE*, 1: 427.

77 See, *IMT*, 8: 306. The document was later classified as USSR-444.

78 For example, the Jewish Historical Commission in Linz, a body headed by Simon Wiesenthal which busied itself collecting evidence against Nazi war criminals, argued in the context of the IMT that those who had survived

the cataclysm were "standing in front of the judgment of history as living witnesses, as reminders and authorized accusers; today, our former merciless judges – who by mere accident did not execute their verdict against us and who would never have dreamed that fate would play them such a bitter joke – sit in the dock; today, the terrible barbarians stand in front of the people's tribunals throughout the world and the Allied military tribunals and are prosecuted not by feelings of revenge but on the basis of the laws of the democratic nations. For us – this is a reminder of the children marched [to their deaths] like herds of animals, of the most sophisticated murders and mass exterminations, atrocities and robberies, committed by the most bloodthirsty wild hordes and individual bestial creatures in human appearance [...] dressed in swastikas. In the name of the dozens, hundreds and millions of victims who were shot, hanged, burnt alive and gassed; in the name of our children [...], our women, brothers and sisters, fathers and mothers who perished in martyrdom *we fulfil our holiest duty*: we testify – we remind the world and demand justice of humankind, of all peoples! We will not rest as long as the last war scoundrel is still hiding, as long as the last S.S. brute is wearing various disguises and masks, until the last criminal is not given to the hands of the democratic justice of humanity which defeated the horrific enemy – Hitlerism – at the cost of seas of blood and tears, of millions of murdered innocent lives." See YIVO DPA, reel 5, folder 151, frame 0968, Call to the public, U.S. Zone Austria, no date, Yiddish, emphasis in original.

79 Bilsky, *Transitional Justice*, 85.

80 Quoted in Tom Segev, *The Seventh Million: The Israelis and the Holocaust* (New York, 1993), 350.

81 Sutzkever, "Mayn eydes-zogn in nirnberg," 6.

82 Gali Drucker Bar-Am, "The Holy Tongue and the Tongue of the Martyrs: The Eichmann Trial as Reflected in Letste Nayes," *Dapim: Studies on the Shoah* 28, no. 1 (2014): 17–37. See also Rachel Auerbach's testimony, *TAE*, 1: 421–5.

83 Hausner, *Justice in Jerusalem*, 341; Hausner, opening address, *TAE*, 1: 71.

84 See, for example, the testimonies of Avraham Aviel, Moshe Beisky, Hulda Campagnano, Abba Kovner, Rivka Kuper, Zivia Lubetkin, Liona Neumann, Joseph Reznik, and David Wdowinski.

85 *TAE*, 1: 517–18; Douglas, *The Memory of Judgment*, 172–3.

86 *TAE*, 5: 2004.

87 Douglas, *The Memory of Judgment*, 113.

88 *TAE*, 1: 366.

89 See, for example, the testimonies of Abba Kovner, Mordechai Ansbacher, Raya Kagan, Rachel Auerbach, and Rivka Yosselewska in *TAE*, 1: 466; 2: 682; 3: 1279, 1: 425, 1: 517.

90 Douglas, *The Memory of Judgment*, 135.

91 For example in the case of Leon Well's testimony, *TAE*, 1: 366.

92 Douglas, *The Memory of Judgment*, 142.

93 Ibid., 141–2. See, for example, the court's response to the testimony of
Zvi Zimmerman, *TAE*, 3: 1124; Yaakov Friedman, a Majdanek survivor
who claimed to have seen Eichmann at the camp, when cross-examined
by Servatius and Landau (ibid., 3: 1164–6) could not distinguish between
authentic memory and understandings that had been read back into the
past. Landau apologized that he did not mean to belittle the witnesses'
experiences, but that his remarks "referred to the legal weight of certain
statements in this evidence" (ibid., 3: 1127).

94 Yablonka, "As Heard by the Witnesses, the Public and the Judges," 585;
similarly, Douglas, *The Memory of Judgment*, 149. See also *TAE*, 5: 2082, and
5: 2146, for the court's own reflection on its problems with testimonial
evidence.

95 *TAE*, 5: 2083.

96 Ibid., 5: 2082.

97 Yablonka has been particularly outspoken on this influence; see her "The
Development of Holocaust Consciousness in Israel: The Nuremberg,
Kapos, Kastner, und Eichmann Trials," *Israel Studies* 8, no. 3 (Fall 2003):
1–24, and her monograph *The State of Israel vs. Adolf Eichmann* (New York,
2004), esp. 218–35. Other historians have minimized the impact of the
Eichmann trial on Israeli society; see, for example, Dan A. Porat, "From
the Scandal to the Holocaust in Israeli Education," *Journal of Contemporary
History* 36, no. 4 (2004): 619–36, and to a lesser degree Lipstadt, *The
Eichmann Trial*, 188–203.

98 On this polarization in the years from Israel's establishment to the
Eichmann trial, see Orna Kenan, *Between Memory and History: The
Evolution of Israeli Historiography of the Holocaust, 1945–1961* (New York,
2003); Roni Stauber, *The Holocaust in Israeli: Public Debate in the 1950s*
(London, 2007).

99 According to Deborah Lipstadt, "The *telling* may not have been entirely
new, but the *hearing* was"; consequently, the trial evoked a "new hearing
of the history of the Final Solution," in Israel and beyond, which "would
shape our contemporary understanding of this watershed event in human
history." Lipstadt, *The Eichmann Trial*, 193, 194, emphasis in original.

100 *TAE*, 1:8.

101 Rejecting Servatius' claim that it could not conduct a fair trial because
of its affinity to the victims, the court acknowledged that "As for the
Accused's fear concerning the background against which this trial will
be heard we can only repeat the principles which apply to every judicial
system worthy of the name; that indeed while on the bench a judge does

not cease to be flesh and blood, possessed by emotions and impulses. However, he is required by law to subdue emotions and impulses ... it is true that the memory of the Holocaust shocks every Jew to the depth of his being, but when this case is brought before us we are obliged to overcome these emotions while sitting in judgment. This duty we shall fulfil. Those charged with the task of judging are professional judges accustomed to weighing evidence." See *TAE*, 1:60.

102 Arendt, *Eichmann in Jerusalem*, 264–5.
103 Ibid., 259.
104 Ibid., 265–6.
105 Ibid., 267.
106 Ibid., 269–71. Arendt rejected Nahum Goldman's idea of an international court in Jerusalem that comprised judges from countries occupied by the Nazis because it also failed to represent all humankind.
107 Ibid., 272–3.
108 Annette Wieviorka, *The Era of the Witnesses* (Ithaca, 2006).
109 Bilsky, *Transformative Justice*, 114.

5 The Eichmann Trial: Towards a Jurisprudence of Victims as Eyewitnesses to Genocide

LEORA BILSKY

Much has been written about the Eichmann trial by scholars, historians, journalists, and intellectuals as well as by the trial's central players. Some criticized the trial for being a mere "political" or "Jewish" trial; others focused on its narrow contribution to international law.[1] In my view, the Eichmann judgment[2] was overshadowed for many years by the Nuremberg proceedings,[3] considered the more important precedent for international criminal law. Thus, scholarship on Holocaust trials tends to view these two paradigmatic trials as fulfilling distinct functions. The Nuremberg trial, which relied primarily on written documents to convict the defendants, is seen as having contributed to the development of international criminal law. In contrast, the Eichmann trial, in which victim testimonies took centre stage, is seen as having contributed to extralegal goals such as the formation of a collective memory of the Holocaust.

In a groundbreaking article published in 2013, William Schabas argues that the Eichmann judgment is an important precedent for international law, and that the trial's critics at the time were wrong not to see its legal contribution.[4] Yet discussion of a central issue in the Eichmann trial is absent from Schabas' analysis: the status of the victim in atrocities trials, even though this issue has received much attention since the early 1990s in international criminal law. Some scholars continue to uphold the widespread criticism of the Eichmann trial for having provided a stage for the testimony of Holocaust survivors.[5]

I argue that the Eichmann court developed an innovative jurisprudence that confers legal recognition to the testimonies of victims of genocide. I identify three steps that enabled the transformation of the victim-witness role: first, a novel interpretation of "crimes against the Jewish people" as genocide; second, a new theory of modes of liability specific to collective crimes; and third, a new understanding of the social value that is protected by the criminalization of acts that systematically attack the humanity of the victim. I end by arguing that the narrative offered by the court in the Eichmann judgment foreshadows recent developments in the historiography of the Holocaust that call for an integrated history, one that weaves together the perspectives of perpetrators and victims.

Part I. Responsibility for Collective Crimes – Jurisprudential Innovations in the Eichmann Judgment

The difficulty in identifying the Eichmann trial's contribution to the jurisprudence of genocide as later developed by international courts stems from the fact that the indictment was based on the category of "Crimes against the Jewish People" – a category unfamiliar in international law.[6] Historian Donald Bloxham writes that the Allied reticence at Nuremberg to address the race-specific crimes of the Nazis stemmed from a liberal-universalist refusal to single out the treatment of any ethnic group as unique, as well as the fear that centring the trial on the crimes of the Holocaust would distract attention from the crime of aggression (aggressive war), war crimes, and conspiracy that were the focus of the Allies' prosecution at the Nuremberg trial.[7] It can be speculated that the difficulty to adjust the Eichmann trial to the categories of international law has made international law scholars long ignore the Eichmann trial as a precedent for international law.[8] Moreover, criticism made by Arendt and other international writers about the court's reliance on "Crimes against the Jewish People" as articulated by Israeli law, instead of the category of "Crimes against Humanity,"[9] further prevented international legal scholars from seriously engaging the Eichmann judgment as an important precedent for international law.[10]

Law professor Lawrence Douglas proposes that the "atrocity framework," which was marginalized at the International Military Tribunal (IMT) but was central in the Eichmann trial, came to prominence only later, during the 1990s in the ad hoc tribunals of the International Criminal Tribunal for the former Yugoslavia (ICTY) and the International Criminal Tribunal for Rwanda (ICTR).[11] Building on Douglas' historical mapping of the field of international criminal law, I argue that this development has made the Eichmann trial an important precursor to contemporary international criminal law, and that in comparison with the IMT, it is the Eichmann trial that carries the more relevant legacy for its development. Specifically, the Eichmann trial constitutes one of the early moments for the development of the jurisprudence of atrocity, in particular by giving centre stage to atrocity crimes such as "Crimes against Humanity" and genocide.[12] It is against this background that we can begin to understand the legal significance of admitting Holocaust victim testimonies as eyewitnesses to genocide.

The Israeli court had to deal with international criticism, in particular regarding the perceived illegitimacy of the category of "Crimes against the Jewish People." The court responded by pointing out that this category is not an Israeli invention, but an accurate translation of the crime of genocide as defined by the 1951 United Nations Convention on the Prevention and Punishment of the Crime of Genocide.[13] However, unlike the Genocide Convention, which was prospective in effect, the Israeli law was meant to overcome a legal lacuna in relation to the Holocaust and apply retroactively to the crime of genocide committed by the Nazis, hence its focus on Crimes against the Jewish People.[14] Looking beyond the dispute over the particularism of "Crimes against the Jewish People," we see that the Eichmann trial made use of the newly defined international crimes of "Crimes against Humanity" and genocide – as epitomized by the Nazi crimes. Similarly to international criminal trials of recent decades, the Eichmann trial focused on the need to protect victim groups against their own state, and not only on the protection of state sovereignty against aggression by other states, as was the main concern in the IMT in Nuremberg.

An Original Theory of Modes of Participation in Collective Crimes

The Eichmann court grappled with a unique category of criminality – that is, systematic, collective crimes.[15] Such large-scale, highly organized crimes are carried out as part of an officially sanctioned policy; they are based on mobilization of many participants and affect large numbers of victims.[16] This category poses a major legal problem, as domestic criminal law is premised on individual responsibility, or, when it applies to a group of criminals, the ordinary division of responsibility differentiates between the physical perpetrator(s) and accomplice(s). The IMT overcame this difficulty by developing the charge of conspiracy. However, the Israeli court, concerned with the overreach of conspiracy in domestic law, sought a different solution to the problem. The Eichmann court was not satisfied with the legal outcome of the traditional division of responsibility between principal perpetrators and accessories present in Israeli criminal law, so it developed an original theory of responsibility for participation in these collective crimes, akin to the modern doctrine of joint criminal enterprise (JCE). This doctrine extends the mode of participation in a crime by conceiving it as part of a larger enterprise. However, those tribunals involved in developing the JCE in the 1990s, the ICTY and ICTR, and the international law scholars discussing the doctrine, neglected to reference the Eichmann judgment as an early precursor.[17]

To reach perpetrators higher in the ranks of the German bureaucracy, the IMT and the trials under Control Council Law No. 10 relied mainly on the doctrine of criminal conspiracy. The Eichmann court could have had similar recourse to this doctrine given that it had been incorporated into Israeli domestic law from Anglo-American Law.[18] However, the court decided to reject the application of the conspiracy doctrine to the Eichmann case as overreaching and as constituting a threat to individual freedom by undermining the distinction between principal and accessory. This stance taken by the Eichmann court is commendable; despite the need for a doctrine that would allow the court to overcome the difficulties of attributing responsibility in a multi-perpetrator offence, the court chose a higher threshold of proof for Eichmann's guilt. The decision to reject conspiracy led the court to search for an alternative way to bridge the gap between the collective crime and the need to prove individual responsibility.

In order to deal with the difficulty of establishing Eichmann's responsibility, the court proceeded in two directions. First, the court distinguished between the responsibility of an accomplice in a standard criminal trial and the responsibility of those who would have appeared to be accomplices in the Final Solution but were in fact principally responsible for the crimes. Second, it developed a type of JCE responsibility that permitted imposing criminal liability on defendants who did not personally commit the crimes in question if it was proven that they entered a common plan to commit these crimes and participated in a significant way in furthering that plan.

The court analysed the "Crimes against the Jewish People" as compatible with the definition of genocide, and found that it was a collective crime by its nature: both from the perspective of criminal intent, which was not directed toward a specific victim but toward a whole group, and from the perspective of the criminal act, which was dependent upon an apparatus coordinating the actions of a vast number of persons in different places as part of the same extermination mechanism.[19] From the collective nature of the crime the court determined Eichmann's participation as a principal perpetrator. The judgment read: "[W]hoever collaborated in the extermination of Jews, with knowledge of the plan for the 'Final Solution' and for its furtherance, is to be regarded as an accomplice in the extermination of the millions who were destroyed during the years 1941–1945, irrespective of whether his actions extended over the entire extermination front or only over one or more sectors of it. His responsibility is that of a 'principal offender' who has committed the entire crime in conjunction with the others."[20] The concerns animating the Eichmann court in devising a doctrine for the division of responsibility – in particular the dissatisfaction with complicity law – could explain the development of JCE by international criminal tribunals in the 1990s.[21] The solution in both cases is similar: it is a solution based on understanding the collective nature of the crime and taking into account the organization or collectivity as something without which the crime cannot be effectuated.[22]

Part II. Victim Testimonies and the Determination of Guilt

Why did Justice Moshe Landau, who presided at the trial and was known for his formalist jurisprudence, agree to open the door to the testimonies of more than one hundred Holocaust survivors, the majority of which were not "eyewitnesses" in the strict sense? Was this simply a sign of the politicization of the trial? Landau's biographer, attorney Michal Shaked, suggests that his decision in relation to victim-witnesses stands in tension with his legal formalism.[23] I believe, however, that we can find a legal rationale for his decision. The court's novel interpretation of the crimes of the Final Solution as collective crimes, together with its articulation of a JCE type of responsibility, rendered the testimony of victims an integral part of the legal investigation into Eichmann's guilt. Furthermore, the Eichmann judgment's analysis of the collective nature of the crime of genocide, combined with the novel theory of modes of liability, transformed the role of testimony given by victims during the Eichmann trial. In the court's judgment these testimonies were granted a juridical rationale going beyond the didactic goals of clarifying history and constructing collective memory of the Holocaust.

Three principal functions of victim testimony can be found in the court's judgment. The first function was to introduce incriminating information about Eichmann from eyewitnesses who met or saw him. The second was to provide the historical context for the crime of genocide.[24] A third function of witness testimony was to highlight aspects of the Final Solution that could not have been ascertained from Nazi documents alone.[25] The first function of the victim-witness conforms with the traditional view of eyewitness testimonies and warrants no further elaboration. The second function has received extensive attention in the literature on the didactic rationale of the Eichmann trial and its political uses. However, the third function has escaped notice and will be the focus of my examination.

In his criticism of the IMT trial at Nuremberg, historian Donald Bloxham writes, "Crimes that were not documented, or of which no documentation survived, were not likely to emerge at Nuremberg."[26] The Nazi crimes were unique in that they relied on a bureaucratic apparatus and division of labour that created an almost hermetic separation between the planning "head" – the desk murderers such as Adolf Eichmann – and the performing "hand" – the people who shot, gassed, and otherwise killed the victims. Exclusive reliance on the documents of the Nazi perpetrators intensifies this gap by presenting the victims as faceless, storyless statistics.[27] Moreover, the Germans were engaged in a massive effort to conceal any traces of the crime and to create a "crime without witnesses." The Eichmann court attempted to overcome this difficulty by intertwining perpetrators' incriminating documents with victim testimonies to create "post factum" an integrated narrative of the crimes of the Final Solution. In doing so, it offered a novel understanding of this facet of the new crime, which structurally separates victimizer and victim. Crucially, this approach by the court was not taken solely for extralegal, didactic purposes, as might have been the intention of the prosecution, but rather to adapt the law itself to the nature of the collective crimes of the Final Solution. Thus, in the judgment, the testimony given by victims was put to various legal uses, including proving *mens rea* and the systematic pattern of the crimes. Moreover, the relevance of victim testimonies not only signalled changes in the general theory of modes of participation in collective crimes but also reflected an understanding of the social value underlying the new categories of genocide and "Crimes against Humanity" – protection of the humanity and dignity of the victims.

The Judgment's Reliance on Victims' Testimonies

To determine Eichmann's involvement in the first two stages of the persecution of the Jews, from 1933 to September 1939 and September 1939 to mid-1941, the court relied on documents and victims' testimonies, though the latter were usually cited briefly and in passing. At times, the court corroborated a certain testimony with a document and vice-versa. We notice a change when the court turned to examine the period of the Final Solution, particularly the events in Eastern Europe. Here, the court provided more space for victims' testimonies and the judgment quoted verbatim passages from their testimonies.[28] Two examples illustrate this point.

First, Eichmann presented himself as an expert on transportation and testified at length on the conditions of the transportation of Jews to the East. To contradict his testimony of ignorance about the actual conditions of the transports, the court juxtaposed perpetrator documents with the witness testimony: "From the minutes of a meeting (T/1162) which took place in Munkacz between representatives of the Hungarian

gendarmerie and the German Gestapo, we learn about transportation conditions. A Hungarian officer remarks: 'If necessary, even 100
people can be put into a single carriage. They can be packed like salt
herrings, for the Germans need strong people. Those who cannot hold
out will fall. Fashionable ladies are not needed there in Germany.'"[29]
The court continued: "Thus, Veesenmeyer reports on May 25, 1944 on
'the increased exploitation of the railway cars' (*staerkere Belegung der
Waggons*), enabling a much quicker completion of the evacuation pro-
gramme from Carpatho-Russia (T/1193)."[30] The court subsequently
incorporated, by referral, the testimony of a Jewish survivor: "Mr. Ze'ev
Sapir gave evidence about the deportation of Jews from Munkacz. The
whole community of 103 persons were loaded into one freight car without food and without water for the whole three-day journey to Auschwitz (Session 53, Vol. III, pp. 971–2)."[31]

This juxtaposition of document and victims' testimonies breaks
through the Nazi, dehumanizing jargon contained in the perpetrator
documents by conveying the victims' experience and revealing that
one freight car meant the elimination of an entire community. The testimony established the inhuman transportation conditions, namely the
lack of food and water for three days. To reinforce this point and tie it
back to Eichmann's state of mind, the court quoted the testimony given
by Hansi Brand, who directly negotiated with Eichmann about the fate
of the Jews of Hungary. Brand stated that when she and Dr. Kasztner
approached Eichmann "with the news that 100 people had been loaded
into one car, this is how he reacted: 'He told us we were not to worry,
because this only concerned Jews from Carpatho-Russia, whose families
were blessed with many children. These children therefore did not need
so much air and so much room, and nothing would happen to them.'"[32]
The method employed by the court to tie together documents, victims'
testimony, and eyewitness accounts not only determines Eichmann's
link to the actual crime that had been committed against those transported, but also his mental state during its commission. It also brought
to light the way in which the humanity of the victims was undermined
by the crime and the way it was reflected by language.

Second, in relation to murder by gassing, the court first presented the
perpetrator's viewpoint. It cited the following statement by Eichmann:
"Perhaps it was that in Eastern Ministry circles they said to themselves: 'This must be done in a more elegant manner.'"[33] What does the
euphemism "elegant manner" mean? The court turned to examine the
method of murder by gassing, and quoted at length from a testimony
given by a survivor of the Chelmno extermination camp, in which gassing was used extensively and regularly. Holocaust survivor Michael

Podhlebnik was taken to Chelmno at the end of 1941, was locked in a cellar, and reported in his court's testimony:

> A truck was waiting for them on the other side ... The people saw the truck, and did not want to get on, but S.S. men with batons in their hands stood around, they beat them, they hustled them and forced them to get on to the truck ... These vans were of the kind in which the people were locked and then gas was let in ... We heard screams from inside the vans, and when the engine was started, the gas was released. Slowly the screams died down until they could no longer be heard outside.[34]

The contrast between the two worlds, between the inhuman experience of the victims and Eichmann's reference to death by gassing as an "elegant" solution, conveys something important about the nature of this crime. The structure of the crime allowed the planning "head" to be isolated from the terrible reality of the victims and to use language as a further distancing device. Later, Podhlebnik was taken to a forest in which he and other Jews were forced to dig pits for the trucks that arrived from that same building, and he testified to what he saw: "I was working there a few days until ... all the people I knew in town were brought. My wife and two children were there ... I lay down near the bodies of my wife and two children and wanted them to shoot me. An S.S. man came up to me and said: 'You are still strong, you can go on working.' He hit me twice and pushed me on to work again."[35] The court mentions that Jews from the vicinity, especially from the Lodz Ghetto – in which Jews from other countries were assembled – were brought to Chelmno, and that Eichmann and his department were in charge of arranging the transportation of Jews from the Reich to Lodz, according to German documents. The court concludes by quoting from an official Polish report the total number of Jews exterminated in Chelmno.[36]

According to the division of responsibility under regular criminal law, Eichmann – who was in charge of transporting Jews to the Lodz ghetto – would not be accountable for the murder of these Jews in Chelmno. But according to the new JCE-type doctrine, once the court proved that transportation to ghettos as well as murder by gassing were all part of one systematic genocidal plan for a "Final Solution" to the "Jewish Problem" in which Eichmann had an active and central role, he then became liable for the murders as well.[37] Here we also see the link between the doctrine of legal liability and the testimony of Podhlebnik and others. Examining together the points of view of perpetrator and victim, a juxtaposition that did not occur at the time of the events due to the complex bureaucratic apparatus that separated them, created an "integrated history" of the Holocaust. In the judgment, such "integrated history" was masterfully used by the court for legal purposes – to throw light on the new crime that is characterized not only by mass murder, but also by the structural separation of victimizer from his victims. Two more aspects of the bureaucratic apparatus are made apparent by Podhlebnik's testimony and its juxtaposition with perpetrator documents: first, the person who issues the order and the person who acts in its pursuance are geographically separate; second, the victims themselves are implicated in the crime, they dig the graves, and thus reluctantly become part of the deadly apparatus.

By expanding the concept of liability to include the entire plan for the Final Solution, "irrespective of whether [the defendant's] actions extended over the entire extermination front or only over one or more sectors of it,"[38] Podhlebnik's testimony becomes relevant in proving Eichmann's guilt.

The position the court took on the relevance of victim testimonies also sheds light on the protected social value it attached to "Crimes against Humanity" and genocide. While Arendt conceptualized the crime as protecting the universal value of human plurality, the court strove to restore the humanity of the individual victim as the core value protected by the legal prohibition.[39] The court's jurisprudence is meant to go beyond abstract justice. It attempts to reaffirm the humanity of the victim, not merely by bringing to justice the perpetrator, but also by giving voice to the victims and by extending legal recognition to victims' testimonies as integral part of the process of determining the guilt of the defendant. Victims' testimonies, and not only perpetrators' documents, were considered relevant evidence for proving the collective crime of genocide.

Part III. Historiographical Implications: An Integrated History of the Holocaust?

The integration of perpetrator documents with victim testimonies carries significant historiographical implications. In the following I offer a complementary rationale for the Eichmann court's approach, as it relates to the agency of victims in developing a new form of criminal trial that can better respond to the reality of mass victimization. This new approach can be traced back to the historiographical debate that began in the Jewish displaced persons (DP) camps in Germany after the war. In these DP camps, two visions of how history should be written competed: the traditional approach that sees history as the domain of expert historians, and the a more radical "community approach," in which history belonged to the community of victims at large, and each victim can become an agent of collective memory. The community approach won in the DP camps and later made its impression on the prosecution in the Eichmann trial.[40] Here the survivors were not mere eyewitnesses: their testimony was part of a collective effort by the victims' community to write their own history. An early proponent of this approach was Rachel Auerbach – a Holocaust survivor from Warsaw who took part in the clandestine "Oneg Shabbas" archive project, a grassroots effort led by Jewish historian Emanuel Ringelblum to document the crimes of the Nazis by the Jewish victims. After immigrating to Israel, Auerbach became the director of the witnesses unit in Yad Vashem institute – and convinced the lead prosecutor, Gideon Hausner, to invite over 100 Holocaust survivors to give testimony in the trial and to narrate the story of the Holocaust through their individual stories.[41]

How did this revolutionary change in the role of victims in atrocity trials impact the historical narrative of the Eichmann court? What can we say about the weaving together of Nazi documents and survivor testimonies in the judgment of the court. Here I would like to refer to Saul Friedländer's monumental book *Nazi Germany and the Jews*, in which he sought to bridge the gap between historians whose writing is based on perpetrator documents (such as the epic work of Raul Hilberg) and historians whose work is drawn from sources created by the Jewish victims. Friedländer introduced what he termed an "integrated history" of the Holocaust, a history which wove together the perspectives of the perpetrators, the attitudes of the surrounding societies, and the experiences of the victimized Jews. For Friedländer, the anti-Jewish policies initiated from the top could not be understood without the words of the victims on the ground.[42] The voices of the victims should not be understood as an "example" of statistical data or simply as history written from the point of view of the victims. Rather, by integrating victims' voices into the general narrative, Friedländer wishes to preserve the dimension of disbelief and misunderstanding of the crime as it was occurring.[43]

We can detect a similar approach in the Eichmann judgment, although there it stemmed from its legal framework. The court began its historical narrative by referring to two testimonies, that of K-Zetnik (pseudonym of the Holocaust survivor and author Yehiel Dinur) and that of judge Moshe Beiski (Holocaust survivor, at the time of the trial a magistrate court judge and later a Supreme Court justice). At first glance, the testimonies are striking in their differences. K-Zetnik, a survivor from Auschwitz, perhaps the most famous witness in the Eichmann trial, had collapsed on the stand in his failed attempt to bridge the abyss separating the "here" and "there."[44] In contrast, the testimony of Beiski was detailed, analytical, and rationalist in nature until he was confronted with Hausner's question: "15,000 people stood there – and opposite them hundreds of guards. Why didn't you attack then, why didn't you revolt?" The court chose to quote in full Beiski's response: "It is no longer possible even for us – and I admit this – to describe the feeling of terror 18 years later. As I stand before Your Honours, it no longer exists and I do not think it is possible to impart that feeling to anyone ... The conditions existing at the time cannot be conveyed today to the courtroom, not that I think, God forbid, that someone may not understand this, but even I myself cannot do so and I felt it on my own flesh."[45]

The court's choice to begin its judgment with these two legal "low points" – one witness collapsing and the other stumbling for words – points, in my view, to the way in which the court asks us to read the historical narrative presented in the judgment. Despite the analytical and rational order the judgment imposes on the historical narrative of the Holocaust, the frame, or "disclaimer" with which the court opens its narrative, is designed to point to the difficulties and preserve the victims' "shock of disbelief." I see similarity between the court's choice and the approach proposed, many years later, by Friedländer, who writes, "By its very nature, by dint of its humanness and freedom, an individual voice suddenly arising in the course of an ordinary historical narrative of events such as those presented here can tear through seamless interpretation and pierce the (mostly involuntary) smugness of scholarly detachment and 'objectivity' ... it is essential to the historical representation of mass extermination and other sequences of mass suffering that 'business as usual historiography' necessarily domesticates and 'flattens.'"[46] Much like the historian, the judge perpetuates the shock of disbelief by juxtaposing the points of view of perpetrator and victim, first by integrating victims' testimonies alongside perpetrator's documents, and second by preserving the unbridgeable gap between the worlds of the victimizer and victim – the trace of which was to be found in the witness' collapse on the stand.

With this choice of frame, the court implicitly and subtly challenged the narrative of the prosecution that sought to bestow an omnipotent, didactic role to the law. The court's judgment, in contrast, kept at bay the rush to adopt totalizing explanations, by listening to survivors' hesitations, and by proposing that the poet and the historian might be better equipped for this endeavour than the judge. In this sense the court's legal and historical approaches are similar: in both cases, the court introduces reflexivity, challenging our confidence in the epistemic tools available to us to discuss the Holocaust. The willingness of the court to transform the concept of "eyewitness" testimony both in order to do justice to the victims and to better understand the new crimes of the Final

Solution is part of this endeavour. The choice to begin the court's judgment with reference to the testimonies of K-Zetnik and Beiski reminds us that the seemingly rational structure of the historical narrative that the court offers, progressing chronologically and geographically and attempting to provide a comprehensive view of the Shoa by integrating the perspectives of Nazi perpetrators and Jewish victims, might actually be misleading. The judgment's narrative announces itself to be only an approximation, a legal re-presentation that cannot overcome the gap of incomprehensibility separating the court from the lived experiences of the victims of the crimes.

NOTES

1 A version of this chapter was first published as Leora Bilsky, "The *Eichmann Trial: Towards a Jurisprudence of Eyewitness Testimony of Atrocities,"* *Journal of International Criminal Justice* 12 (2014): 27–57. The Israel Science Foundation supported this research under grant No. 1163/19.

2 *A-G of the Govt. of Israel v Eichmann* (Dist. Ct. Jerusalem) (1961), 36 *Int'l L. Rep.* 5, as reprinted in E. Lauterpacht, ed., *The Eichmann Judgments* (London, 1968). Hereinafter "Eichmann Judgment."

3 *Trial of the Major War Criminals before the International Military Tribunal, Nuremberg, 14 November 1945–1 October 1946.* Hereinafter "IMT trial" and "IMT" respectively.

4 William A. Schabas, "The Contribution of the Eichmann Trial to International Law," *Leiden Journal of International Law* 26 (2013): 667–99.

5 For a recent example, see Stephan Landsman, "The Eichmann Case and the Invention of the Witness-Driven Atrocity Trial," *Columbia Journal of Transnational Law* 51 (2012): 69. For elaboration on the contribution of the Eichmann trial to the central role of victim witnesses to genocide, see Annette Wieviorka, *The Era of the Witness* (Ithaca: Cornell University Press, 2006), 56–95.

6 See items 1–4 of the indictment (as read in the District Court, Session 1, 1–3) and the discussion that follows.

7 Donald Bloxham, *Genocide on Trial: War Crimes Trials and the Formation of Holocaust History and Memory* (Oxford: Oxford University Press, 2001), 66.

8 Another obvious reason is that the Eichmann trial was decided by a domestic court and not by an international tribunal. This distinction, however, has been challenged by international law scholars who expose the interplay between domestic and international law. See Naomi Roht Arriaza, *The Pinochet Effect* (Philadelphia: University of Pennsylvania Press, 2005); Harold Hongju Koh, *Transnational Litigation in United States Courts* (New York: Foundation Press, 2008).

9 Hannah Arendt, *Eichmann in Jerusalem: A Report on the Banality of Evil* (New York: Penguin Books, 2006; originally published in 1963), 269–72.

10 For some contemporary writing dealing with international law issues arising out of the trial, as well as the trial's exceptionalism, see J.E.S. Fawcett, "The Eichmann Case," *British Yearbook of International Law* 38 (1962): 181–216; R.K. Woetzel, "The Eichmann Case in International Law," *Criminal Law Review* (1962): 671; H. Silving, "In Re Eichmann: A Dilemma of Law and Morality," *American Journal of International Law* 55 (1961): 307–58.

11 In another article Douglas sees elements of the "atrocity paradigm" in the trials held under Control Council Law 10 at Nuremberg. See Lawrence Douglas, "From IMT to NMT: The Emergence of a Jurisprudence of Atrocity," in Kim C. Priemel and Alexa Stiller, eds., *Reassessing the Nuremberg Military Tribunals* (New York, 2012), 276–95.

12 See Judith N. Shklar, *Legalism* (Cambridge, MA: Harvard University Press, 1964), 154–5; Mark J. Osiel, *Mass Atrocity, Ordinary Evil and Hannah Arendt* (New Haven: Yale University Press, 2001), 61–2. By contrast, compare with Schabas, who throughout his work uses the Eichmann trial as a case dealing with genocide: William A. Schabas, *Genocide in International Law* (Cambridge: Cambridge University Press, 2000), 286. See also Cassese, who mentions that Eichmann was tried for the offence of crimes against the Jewish people, which incorporates all the elements of the definition of genocide. Antonio Cassese, *International Criminal Law* (Oxford: Oxford University Press, 2008), 131.

13 "The 'Crimes against the Jewish People' is defined on the pattern of the crime of genocide defined in the Convention for the Prevention and Punishment of Genocide which was adopted by the United Nations Assembly on 9 December 1948." *Eichmann* Judgment, ¶ 16, 29–30. Article 2 of the *Convention on the Prevention and Punishment of the Crime of Genocide* defines genocide as "acts committed with intent to destroy in whole or in part, a national, ethnic, racial or religious group." Article 1(b) of the Nazis and Nazi Collaborators (Punishment) Law 5710-1950 (Israel) (hereinafter "Nazis Punishment Law") defines crimes against the Jewish people as "acts committed with intent to destroy the *Jewish people* in whole or in part." The Israeli law replaces the general term of a racial or ethnic group with the specific term "Jewish People," but the list of acts that follows is identical in both instruments (apart from the destruction of cultural assets and incitement to hatred of Jews, which was added in the Nazi Punishment Law). As Laura Jockusch has pointed out, the category of crimes against the Jewish people was born several years earlier at Jewish displaced persons (DP) camps, where several trials against Jewish survivors who had collaborated with the Nazis were conducted, in which these persons were accused of committing crimes against the

Jewish people and – if found guilty – were declared "traitors to the Jewish people." See Laura Jockusch, "Prosecuting 'Crimes against the Jewish People': The Eichmann Trial and the History of a Legal Concept," paper submitted to "The Trial of Adolf Eichmann: Retrospect and Prospect" conference, University of Toronto, 9–11 Sept., 2012, 9–10.

14 The court solved this problem by stating that the Nazi Punishment Law had not created any new crime that was not already in existence. The legislation may have been *ex post facto* but it was not retroactive: "Not one of the crimes defined in the Law in question was, in the words of Blackstone, 'an action indifferent in itself' when committed, which the 'legislature then for the first time declared to have been a crime.'" *Eichmann* Judgment, ¶ 7, 22–3. The court distinguished between two functions of the convention: a declaration of the deep conviction of the international community that the crime of genocide is an international crime, and a contractual undertaking by the parties to prevent this crime in the future and to punish its commission. *Eichmann* Judgment, ¶ 21–2, 34–5.

15 I am using the terms "collective crimes" and "bureaucratic crimes" interchangeably in this article, since both were related in Nazi criminality. See Zygmunt Bauman, *Modernity and the Holocaust* (Ithaca: Cornell University Press, 1989). However, there is a distinction between the collective nature of the crimes and their bureaucratic nature which might raise different legal concerns. For example, while collective crimes involve many people, they can still operate on a personal level, while the bureaucratic setting adds a level of estrangement between the actor and the victim and the results of his or her deeds, as well as a division of labour that can significantly influence his or her *mens rea*. Further analysis of this distinction exceeds the limits of this essay. I thank Galia Schneebaum for highlighting this point. For an elaboration of the importance of this distinction for the contemporary work of the ICTY see Harmen Van der Wilt, "Joint Criminal Enterprise and Functional Perpetration," in A. Nollkaemper and H. Van der Wilt, eds., *System Criminality in International Law* (Cambridge, 2009): 158 at pp. 166–70. Van der Wilt argues that while joint criminal enterprise (JCE) can be adequate for collective crimes involving gang crimes or mob violence, it is ill-fit for system criminality in which the bureaucratic apparatus plays a crucial role in distancing and dissociating the perpetrator from victim. I thank an anonymous reader for pointing me to this article.

16 Office of the High Commissioner for Human Rights (OHCHR), *Rule of Law Tools for Post-Conflict States: Prosecution Initiatives* (New York, 2006), 11–12.

17 One of the most recent cases that mentions the *Eichmann* Judgment (in relation to the term "accomplice" in interpreting "complicity in genocide" and not strictly to JCE) is *Prosecutor v. Brđanin,* Judgment, Case No. IT-99–36-T,

1 Sept. 2004, ¶ 725. In legal scholarship the only relevant article seems to be Michael P. Scharf, "Seizing the 'Grotian Moment': Accelerated Formation of Customary International Law in Times of Fundamental Change," *Cornell International Law Journal* 43 (2010): 439–69. Scharf mentions the application of the JCE doctrine by the Eichmann court on page 464–5.

18 "The Attorney General argued that the plan for the 'Final Solution' must be regarded as a criminal conspiracy ... The Accused participated in this criminal conspiracy and therefore must *ipso facto* be held liable for all the offences committed to accomplish the conspiracy, whether or not a particular act ... was committed with his active participation." *Eichmann* Judgment, ¶ 187, 230.

19 *Eichmann* Judgment, ¶¶ 190–4, 242.

20 *Eichmann* Judgment, ¶ 194, 234. To avoid confusion, it should be noted here that the term "accomplice" was not used in the Hebrew original in its legal meaning in terms of modes of participation but more generally as a "partner," who could be a principal offender as well. In relation to this assertion by the court, Schabas points to the concept of co-perpetration as formulated at the ICC Pre-Trial Chamber I: "the concept of co-perpetration is originally rooted in the idea that when the sum of the co-ordinated individual contributions of a plurality of persons results in the realization of all the objective elements of a crime, any person making a contribution can be held vicariously responsible for the contributions of all the others and, as a result, can be considered a principal to the whole crime." Lubanga (ICC-01/04–01/06), Decision on the Confirmation of Charges, 29 Jan. 2007, para. 326 and claims that it "does not seem substantially different from the vision of the District Court of Jerusalem." William A. Schabas, *An Introduction to the International Criminal Court*, 4th edition (Cambridge, 2011), 227.

21 Similar to the Eichmann court, the ICC today is not satisfied with complicity law, as explained by Zahar and Sluiter: "JCE doctrine could generate a much higher level of responsibility ... than the ... straightforward commission of the crimes and of aiding and abetting others to commit them. JCE ... creates a class of equally responsible co-perpetrators of an expanded set of crimes, a set which moreover consists not only of the co-perpetrators' intended crimes, but also of crimes foreseen by them." Alexander Zahar and Göran Sluiter, *International Criminal Law: A Critical Introduction* (New York: Oxford University Press, 2008), 222. JCE thus functions as a multiplier of individual criminal responsibility.

22 Since *Eichmann* was the only case at the time in which an Israeli court dealt directly with the commission of crimes of the Final Solution by a Nazi

perpetrator, the court only cursorily sketched the liability of the distant
perpetrator (such as the centrality of his contribution and the mental
element required for genocide). There were several prosecutions in Israel
in the 1950s and 1960s based on the Nazi Punishment Law. However, these
cases – which for the most part were not published – were directed against
Jewish victims-collaborators and included indictments not based on the
provision relating to crimes against the Jewish people. For elaboration
see Orna Ben-Naftali and Yogev Tuval, "Punishing International Crimes
Committed by the Persecuted," *Journal of International Criminal Justice* 4
(2006): 128–78. In contrast, the JCE jurisprudence of the ICTY and ICTR
has evolved to clarify the scale of the joint criminal enterprise, the type
of contribution required of a distant perpetrator, and the mental state
regarding the common objective, and so on. For instance, in the ICTY's
interpretation of JCE liability we can detect an evolution leading to a
requirement that the contribution of the accused be significant to the
commission of the crimes (though it need not be necessary or substantial).
Van der Wilt, "Joint Criminal Enterprise and Functional Perpetration,"
172–4 n15. For an example, see Brđanin Appeal Judgment, IT-99–36-A, ¶
430 and the declaration of Judge van den Wyngaert.

23 Michal Shaked, *Moshe Landau: Judge* (Hebrew) (Tel Aviv: Sifrey Aliyat
Hagag (Books in the Attic), 2012), 210.

24 See paragraphs 56, 57, 64, 66, 109 of the *Eichmann* Judgment. For example,
the description of the persecutions of Jews in Germany in the first stage is
described, *inter alia*, through the testimonies of Mr. Benno Cohn and Mr.
Zyndel Grynszpan. The purpose of referring to these testimonies was to
demonstrate how these actions were aimed "to deprive the Jews of citizen
rights, to degrade them and to strike fear into their hearts, to separate
them from the rest of the inhabitants, to oust them from the economic and
cultural life of the State, and to close to them the sources of livelihood."
Eichmann Judgment, ¶ 56, 82.

25 For example, see the *Eichmann* Judgment, paragraphs 100, 122–7, 130, 136.

26 Bloxham, *Genocide on Trial*, 63. In this respect it is worth raising questions
about the assumed "objectivity" of Nazi documents vis-à-vis the subjectivity
of victim testimonies. Although for legal purposes, incriminating documents
by the perpetrators are the best way to prove guilt objectively (because
they were authored by the perpetrators at the time of the events), these
documents carry problematic expressive implications that should not be
ignored in trials of atrocities. The ideological aspect of Nazi camera is raised
in a documentary film by Israeli director Yael Harsonski, *A Film Unfinished*
(Oscilloscope Pictures, 2010).

27 One of the prosecutors in the Eichmann trial, Gabriel Bach, who later
became a Supreme Court Justice, exemplified this problem in his

biography. Bach explains that the prosecution encountered difficulties proving the number of murdered Jews in the Holocaust, because a document from Auschwitz indicating the number of inmates had no legal validity. To resolve the problem, Bach suggested that the prosecution call survivors to the witness stand and compare the numbers tattooed on their arms with the numbers in the document, in order to prove that the document was reliable. See Yael Roseman, *Gabriel Bach: Attorney, Judge and Gentleman* (Hebrew) (Tel Aviv: Hemed Books, 2011), 84–5. Here we see a reversal: because the testimony of survivors who were not classic eyewitnesses could not be relied upon as objective evidence, the prosecution wanted to rely on the numbers tattooed on their arms. This anecdote shows how the ordinary rules of evidence can reproduce the dehumanization of the original crime, by reducing the individual from a human being with a name and a story to tell, to statistical number.

28 The judgment noted that "[h]ere and there in our Judgment, we have interspersed verbatim passages from the evidence." *Eichmann* Judgment, ¶ 119, 150.

29 *Eichmann* Judgment, ¶ 112, 139.

30 Ibid.

31 Ibid.

32 Ibid.

33 *Eichmann* Judgment, ¶ 122, 154.

34 Ibid.

35 *Eichmann* Judgment, ¶ 122, 155.

36 Ibid.

37 Although the court did not pose it as a formal requirement to prove the elements of the doctrine, the judgment nevertheless emphasized throughout Eichmann's centrality and the breadth of his operations and rejected his claim of being a simple clerk, mechanically executing the orders he was given.

38 *Eichmann* Judgment, ¶ 194, 234.

39 Different interpretations of the core value protected by "Crimes against Humanity" entail different views about victim participation. Arendt objected to viewing crimes against humanity as cruel "inhuman acts" and instead saw them as protecting the value of human plurality; she therefore objected to using victim testimonies to elaborate on the inhumanity and cruelty of the crime. By contrast, David Luban maintains that "crimes against humanity are simultaneously offenses against humankind and injuries to humanness" and that they assault one specific aspect of human beings, namely their character as political animals. David Luban, "A Theory of Crimes against Humanity," *Yale Journal of International Law* 29 (2004): 85–168, 90.

40 Ada Schein, "'Everyone Can Hold a Pen': The Documentation Project in the DP Camps in Germany," in D. Bankier and D. Michman, eds., *Holocaust Historiography in Context: Emergence, Challenges, Problems, Achievements* (New York: Berghahn Books, 2008) 103; Laura Jockusch, *Collect and Record!: Jewish Holocaust Documentation in Early Postwar Europe* (New York: Oxford University Press, 2012), 121–59.

41 D.E. Lipstadt, *The Eichmann Trial* (New York: Nextbook/Schocken, 2011), 52. Auerbach was also active in the Jewish historical commission in Poland. She testified in the Eichmann trial along with two other witnesses who were active in this commission: Leon Wliczker (Wells) and Ada Lichtman, a founding member of the Jewish Historical Commission in Lublin. See Lawrence Douglas, *The Memory of Judgment: Making Law and History in the Trials of the Holocaust* (New Haven: Yale University Press, 2001), 97–182.

42 Saul Friedländer, *Nazi Germany and the Jews: The Years of Persecution, 1933–1939*, vol. 1 (New York: HarperCollins, 1997), 1–2; and Saul Friedländer, *Nazi Germany and the Jews: The Years of Extermination, 1939–1945*, vol. 2 (New York: HarperCollins, 2007), xv. Jockusch argues that the first to introduce the unique integration between Nazi sources and Jewish sources were the historical commissions created by Jewish survivors after the war. Laura Jockusch, *Collect and Record!*, note 40, 84–120.

43 Friedländer, *Nazi Germany and the Jews*, vol. 2, xxvi. Interestingly, throughout the book, the term "disbelief" is used to describe reactions (sometimes in their own words) of various witnesses to the events, including a soldier who watched executions of Jewish persons, not out of curiosity but out of "disbelief that something of this type could happen" (ibid., 218); the Jewish victims (ibid., 438); a Swedish intelligence agent (ibid., 459), and the inhabitants of Kiev who "had expressed disbelief and then horror when faced with the Babi Yar massacres" (ibid., 537).

44 A video of K-Zetnik's testimony can be found at http://www.youtube.com/watch?v=4PvJWXPFgfI. An English translation of the testimony transcript can be found at https://www.nizkor.org/session-068-01-eichmann-adolf/ (accessed 23 March 2021).

45 *Eichmann* Judgment, ¶ 119, 150.

46 Friedländer, *Nazi Germany and the Jews*, vol. 2, xxv–xxvi. For a critical assessment of the project see Amos Goldberg, "The Holocaust and History: Cut-offs in a Postmodern Era" (Hebrew), *Theory and Criticism* (2012): 121.

6 What Makes a Prosecution an International Landmark Trial? Reflections on the Tensions between Legal Proceedings, Politics, and Historical Facts

RUTH BETTINA BIRN

The Transitional Justice Framework

The scholarly literature on transitional justice provides parameters to assess trials of political crimes. Many of the considerations deemed important in the context of transitional justice are not applicable to the Eichmann trial.[1] This was not a trial in which a formerly untouchable political figure was brought to justice: the Nazi regime had long been overthrown and Eichmann had fled to Argentina, where he lived under a false name. This was not a trial where hitherto untold truths about crimes were made public for the first time. Allied as well as national courts had dealt extensively with Nazi crimes. A substantial body of historical literature existed, and archives were open. This was not a trial that forced a population to confront crimes its own government, army, and elites had committed.

The Eichmann trial belonged to another category of prosecutions of political crimes, one in which a government aims at utilizing past crimes to build support and legitimacy for itself and invites the population to identify with the victims.[2] David Ben-Gurion, the prime minister of Israel, intended to use this trial to remind the world of the Holocaust, to teach the younger generation about the past, and to strengthen Zionist convictions.[3] In order to do so, the whole history of Nazi persecution of Jews was to be displayed in court, with special emphasis on ideologically important episodes involving Jewish resistance and heroism. Many of these historical episodes had nothing to do with Eichmann. While Eichmann was one of the major perpetrators and committed numerous crimes, there were components of the Holocaust in which he was not active. Chief Prosecutor Gideon Hausner, however, followed the politically pre-set script and throughout the trial tried to inflate Eichmann's role. In his oral summary Hausner even alleged that Eichmann had been "more extreme even than that evil man Hitler himself."[4]

History Represented or History Distorted?

A landmark trial should – or, so we might expect – establish the individual criminal responsibilities of an accused in the context of the historical setting in which the crimes were committed, while strictly observing procedural rules. The Eichmann trial is often lauded for having achieved exactly that: for the first time, the Holocaust stood at the centre of a major prosecution and the responsibility of one of the major perpetrators was established in a fair trial. This assessment does not hold up to legal scrutiny. The history of the Holocaust stood at the centre of the trial, but for this very reason Eichmann's role and responsibilities were often distorted. One of the first witnesses, for example, testified about events in 1933 – before Eichmann had even moved from Austria to Germany.[5] Many of the witnesses called by Hausner spoke about terrible acts of persecution they had witnessed or suffered, but the prosecution did not establish that they were linked to Eichmann.

While presenting a comprehensive narrative of the Holocaust through the testimony of witnesses, Hausner encountered increasing resistance from the defence and the presiding judge against introducing evidence not related to Eichmann. Faced with that objection, Hausner took recourse to the concept of a criminal conspiracy.[6] One can trace in the trial record how this argumentation evolved.[7] Hausner even justified calling a witness on Jewish partisans on the following grounds: "I know it is not the Court's wish that we attempt to depict the Holocaust fully, for the Court desires – and, with all due respect, rightly so – to confine the matters brought before it only to the indictment against the Accused. But, in our view, that also relates to the Accused. They fled from these hardships which the Accused brought upon them – they were forced to hide, and everything they underwent came from the Accused, if not directly, at least indirectly."[8] Hausner used this concept to exaggerate Eichmann's historical role and failed to focus on the many crimes he committed. In his final submissions he stated, "Eichmann stands at the center of the conspiracy, and therefore he bears criminal responsibility for the results of the conspiracy in all its stages and in all its manifestations, up to the last of the gunmen of the Einsatzgruppen in Nikolajew and in Smolensk, and wherever else."[9]

The judges did not accept the conspiracy theory argued by Hausner because he had not charged Eichmann with conspiracy. However, they arrived at the same result – that the Holocaust had to be seen as a whole:

> Although we did not accept the Attorney General's argument as put forward by him in his summing up, we are of the opinion that his general approach is correct, viz, that all the acts perpetrated during the implementation of the Final Solution of the Jewish Question are to be regarded as one single whole, and the Accused's criminal responsibility is to be decided upon accordingly. In our opinion, this is to be concluded not from the law of criminal conspiracy, but from the very nature of the "Final Solution," as being a crime against the Jewish people, in accordance with the legal definition of that crime.[10]

The court continued:

> Hence everybody who acted in the extermination of Jews, knowing about the plan for the Final Solution and its advancement, is to be regarded as an accomplice in the annihilation of the millions who were exterminated during the years 1941–1945, irrespective of whether his actions spread over the entire front of the extermination or over only one of more sectors of that front. His responsibility is that of a "principal offender" who perpetrated the entire crime in co-operation with the others.[11]

Despite their own conclusion, the judges "alternatively" examined Eichmann's individual responsibility.[12] The court rejected some of the prosecution's allegations in its judgment and made a narrower and more accurate assessment of Eichmann's criminal responsibility.[13] Nevertheless, for several crimes Eichmann was wrongly found guilty.[14]

In part, this is connected with the documents that the prosecution used as evidence, which had not always been specifically selected for the trial.[15] Many documents came from the holdings of the German Foreign Office – they were available, whereas the Security Police had destroyed a large portion of their own files at the end of the war. This contributed to a distorted view of the situation, as the structure and functioning of the SS and Police apparatus of which Eichmann was a part were not properly understood. One misinterpretation with far-reaching consequences concerns an important document: the protocol of the Wannsee conference, which took place on 20 January 1942. There, Reinhard Heydrich, Head of Security Police and SD (Sicherheitsdienst), informed representatives of Reich ministries and other important government bodies about the planned "Final Solution of the Jewish Question" and solicited their cooperation. Heydrich presented himself as centrally in charge (*federführend*). When sending the protocol to the *Unterstaatsekretär* of the Foreign Office, Martin Luther, Heydrich suggested future meetings between subordinate officials (*Sachbearbeiter*). The contact person for Heydrich's office, the Reichssicherheitshauptamt (RSHA), was Adolf Eichmann (*zuständiger Referent*) in section IVB4.[16]

Hausner interpreted this as a general empowerment of Eichmann, not only in dealings with outside contacts like the Foreign Office, but also within the SS and Police apparatus: "I have proven that the man who was in charge of the implementation of this order was Heydrich, and that Heydrich, for his part, appointed the Accused. This has already been proven. Consequently, the Prosecution maintains that everything that was done as a result of that decision and under that control for the extermination of the Jews is relevant. The accused will be held responsible for all this."[17] This cornerstone of Hausner's argumentation[18] was accepted by the court.[19] (The judges had, of course, nothing but the evidence put in front of them; no expert historian on structures and chains of command of the Nazi machinery of destruction had been called.)

In general, the prosecution mistook knowledge for command responsibility. Whenever Eichmann was informed of something, he was assumed to be in charge. For his part, Eichmann (who claimed only to have carried out orders) wanted to conceal the extent to which he was informed and had helped coordinate the smooth running of the machinery of mass murder, beyond the deportations he organized.[20]

We will discuss the wrongful convictions in the following section, including the evidentiary basis for the court's decisions and also, whenever possible, whether the information used represented the highest level of knowledge Hausner could have obtained in 1961. Apart from historical literature,[21] this often meant information generated through German investigations. The notion that German prosecutors could have assisted their Israeli counterparts runs counter to the widespread belief that the Eichmann trial caused the not very motivated or knowledgeable German authorities to subsequently launch prosecutions of Nazi perpetrators. That this was not the case can easily be demonstrated by a review of the major German investigations of Holocaust crimes. In 1958, a Central Agency for the Prosecution of Nazi Crimes had been set up in Ludwigsburg, which started new cases and developed new investigative techniques. A lot of the information they had compiled was relevant for the case against Eichmann.[22]

Zyklon B

Count I, f 1, of the indictment, referring to Auschwitz, alleges: "The Accused directed the commanders of this camp to use the gas Zyklon B and during the years 1942 and 1944 actually took steps to ensure the supply of a quantity of gas for the purpose of exterminating Jews."[23] In his opening address Hausner claimed that Eichmann's word "put gas chambers into action."[24]

This allegation was based on accounts by two former SS members, both deceased at the time of the trial. Kurt Gerstein, an SS officer with an ambiguous relationship with the Nazi Party, wrote several personal reports because he wanted to alert the world to the fact that Jews were being murdered in gas chambers, as he had seen himself in Belzec. Gerstein worked in the SS-Führungshauptamt, Hygiene-Institut der Waffen-SS,[25] and he was involved in distributing Zyklon B (which could be used for sanitary purposes or mass murder) to the Waffen-SS and concentration camps. According to Gerstein, Eichmann's deputy, Rolf Günther, approached him twice for large quantities of Zyklon B, which were then supplied.[26] The second account comes from Rudolf Höss, former commandant of Auschwitz. Zyklon B was used in Auschwitz for disinfestation purposes. According to Höss, his deputy first used it on an experimental basis for the murder of Russian prisoners. Afterwards, the poison was routinely used for mass killings in Auschwitz. Höss informed Eichmann of this development.[27] The court accepted Gerstein's and Höss' accounts[28] and decided that they proved that Eichmann and his section, IVB4, were involved in the introduction of Zyklon B in Auschwitz.[29]

However, Eichmann's section was not involved in the deliveries of the poison. Zyklon B was initially delivered from the producer directly to the concentration camp system. Later it was distributed by the medical service of the Waffen-SS, which was under the authority of Dr. Joachim Mrugowsky (Gerstein's boss). As supply of the poison was low, its distribution was apportioned and centrally organized.[30] Most of the historical literature agrees that the first mass killing with Zyklon B in Auschwitz took place at the beginning of September 1941.[31] It can be assumed that Höss informed Eichmann about this development during one of his visits. But other sections of the SS and Police, not IVB4, were involved in experiments on killing methods carried out in conjunction with the "Euthanasia" program run by Hitler's Chancellery.[32] Teams of doctors, which were killing sick camp inmates, were active in Auschwitz in 1941 and worked in close cooperation with the camp personnel. Here lies the likely origin of the use of Zyklon B in Auschwitz.[33]

The facts about the production of Zyklon B and its distribution to concentration camps were established in two court cases that had taken place between 1946 and 1955.[34] Gerstein and Höss cannot be considered entirely trustworthy sources. Already in 1953, the editor of the first scholarly edition of the Gerstein reports pointed out that the author's intention to unveil a terrible crime should be appreciated, but many details were not accurate. A critical approach was warranted, in particular as not to give support to Holocaust deniers, who were already exploiting Gerstein's mistakes for their own ends.[35] The same can be said about Höss.[36]

Gas Vans

Eichmann was also found guilty of the introduction of gas vans: "Therefore, we find that the Accused took part in exchanging the system of execution by shooting for execution by means of gas vans."[37] The evidence was exhibit T/308, consisting of several documents written by Dr. Erhard Wetzel, including a letter dated 25 October 1941.[38] At that time Wetzel was in charge of "Jewish affairs" in the Ministry for the Occupied East. The letter dealt with introducing the use of gas for mass murder to the occupied East, Reichskommissariat Ostland.[39] Wetzel had gained the support of Viktor Brack from Hitler's Chancellery for this plan; he also mentioned that Eichmann, from the RSHA, had given his consent.[40]

The court was aware of the use of gas vans in the "Euthanasia" program and afterwards in the occupied East,[41] but obviously not that in the RHSA, the Kriminaltechnisches Institut in Department V and Technical Matters, II D not IVB4, were in charge of the development, deployment, and maintenance of gas vans.[42] Again, Eichmann's role as a point of contact and coordination was misinterpreted as being in charge.[43] Indicative of how much the judges overestimated Eichmann's importance is the link they created between Eichmann's self-confessed revulsion at the sight of a mass killing of Jews in Minsk and the development of alternative methods of murder: "The question of finding a 'cleaner' and more efficient system for mass executions than shooting undoubtedly occupied the attention of the Accused as early as the end of the summer or the beginning of the autumn of 1941."[44] A similar link has been made between Heinrich Himmler's reaction to a mass shooting in Minsk in August 1941 and the search for other killing methods. Leaving aside whether Himmler really had shown revulsion,[45] as Reichsführer SS and Chief of German Police he was in a position to give the necessary orders to department heads in the

RSHA for the development of gas vans for the occupied East, which Eichmann was not.

Bergen-Belsen

As part of its examination of Eichmann's criminal responsibility, the court wrote, "We have also described his rule over the Terezin ghetto (sections 150–2) and over Bergen-Belsen camp (section 153)."[46] This is not correct, as far as Bergen-Belsen is concerned. Bergen-Belsen was under the control of the SS Wirtschafts-Verwaltungshauptamt (WVHA), while the Terezin ghetto was under the Central Office for Jewish Emigration in Prague and, on the higher level, the RSHA.[47] It seems that the court was confused by the fact that a commander of Terezin had been transferred to Bergen-Belsen.[48] Bergen-Belsen was set up for potential exchanges between Jewish inmates and Germans living abroad; both RSHA/IVB4 and Foreign Affairs were involved in the project. WVHA commanders were responsible for the living conditions of the inmates. In fact, the increasingly terrible conditions, which led to mass starvation and death, were counter to the initial purpose of exchanges.[49]

Occupied Poland – The Generalgouvernement

Many of the worst crimes of the Holocaust were committed in occupied Eastern Europe, Poland, and the Soviet Union (including the Baltic states). Hausner allocated a lot of space to events in Poland in his presentation of evidence, calling about twenty witnesses to speak about what they had experienced and suffered.[50] This was disproportionate to Eichmann's role there, which had been quite limited, in particular in the part of Poland named Generalgouvernement. Hausner tried to weave Eichmann into the grand narrative through the oral presentations of his case. In his opening speech he said, "The Accused, as head of the Gestapo Department for Jewish Affairs, as Special Commissioner for the extermination of the Jews, bears direct responsibility as the initiator and implementer of this blood bath. We shall show proof of his initiative and his control over the ghettos, his responsibility and his role in the setting up and the operation of the extermination camps, and the responsibility for the destruction of Polish Jewry."[51]

Many of the survivor witnesses had nothing to say about Eichmann's crimes, but were asked to testify for other reasons. Moshe Beisky talked about atrocities in the Krakow ghetto and Plaszow camp, which were under the command of the Civilian Administration, the local Security Police, and the SS Police Leader Krakau, not Eichmann.[52] Crimes in

Plaszow and Krakow had been under investigation in Germany since 1960, and Beisky later gave a statement in this context.[53] At the Eichmann trial, Beisky had just finished a description of a harrowing scene in Plaszow when Hausner sprung this question on him: Why had the Jewish inmates not revolted? The witness, severely shaken, indicated that the question showed a complete lack of understanding of how terrorized the inmates had been. In his memoirs of the trial Hausner admitted that he asked the question for effect.[54]

Ada Lichtman was asked to testify about the persecution of the Jewish population in her hometown in the early period of the German occupation of Poland.[55] Hausner's promptings show that he had preselected the components of Lichtman's story that he wanted to use.[56] Eichmann was, again, not responsible for the crimes Lichtman described in her testimony.[57] Lichtman could have been, however, an important witness on Sobibor, to where she was later deported. The Central Agency had had her questioned by the Israel Police on 30 March 1960. Eichmann's office was instrumental for deportations from Western Europe to Sobibor and Lichtman could have legitimately spoken about this death camp during the trial, as she did on other occasions.[58] Yet, Hausner did not question her about Sobibor; but tried to generalize the acts of cruelty described by Lichtman in his summing-up: "The mode of operation in the Generalgouvernement ... also bears resemblance, nonetheless, to the system in the West. About this, we know that he supplied the guidance, he showed the way and he gave direction."[59]

Hausner included the Aktion Reinhard in the indictment: in Count 1, f, 3–5, Belzec, Sobibor, and Treblinka are listed among the death camps; in Count 7, b, 5, the Aktion Reinhard is referred to under the heading "plunder of Jewish property."[60] This allegation was justified for the death camps, to which Eichmann's section had deported Jews. However, the Aktion Reinhard was not run by the RSHA, but by the SS and Police Leader Lublin.[61] In 1961, this fact was well established. The Central Agency had reconstructed in several investigations the enormous crimes committed and the complex chain of command for Aktion Reinhard, of which Eichmann was not a part.[62]

Not much remained of Hausner's allegations after a review by the court. The judges realized that "the evidence brought before us in connection with the Generalgouvernement area and the millions of Jews who lived there at the time of the Germans' entry into the area is rather scanty."[63] However, the few points on which they found Eichmann guilty (discussed in the following section) do not stand up to historical scrutiny and hardly warrant the generalizing conclusion: "We find that the Accused and his section were also authorized to deal with matters concerning the Final Solution of the Jewish Question within the area of the Generalgouvernement." The court added, though, that Eichmann's main activity was elsewhere.[64]

One point concerned the deportation of Jews by rail within the Generalgouvernement. IVB4 was not involved. Local commanders of the Security Police and SS and Police dealt directly with the railway authorities.[65] One piece of evidence, an exchange of letters between Karl Wolff, chief of Himmler's personal staff, and the deputy minister of the Ministry of Transport states exactly that.[66] Other evidence about rail transport demonstrates that the recollections of survivors might not be useful when determining the chain of command between German governmental authorities.[67]

Another point demonstrates that here, too, the court's findings are distorted by the notion that Eichmann would have been in charge whenever the RSHA was active. Correspondence with the Foreign Office concerning the fate of Jews of foreign nationality in the Warsaw ghetto shows Eichmann as the contact person dealing with these matters, but it does not show, as the court found, that he "appears as a decision-maker on behalf of the RSHA in matters concerning the Warsaw ghetto and he certainly had authority to carry out his decisions. This is proof of the fact that he implemented the authority which was granted to him as a result of the Wannsee conference."[68] (The Warsaw ghetto, like other ghettos, was under the administration of the German civilian administration.)

As the court did not fully understand the structure of the SS and Police and their interaction with civil and military bodies in the Generalgouvernement,[69] documents were misinterpreted. For example, a letter from the chief of Security Police and SD, marked IVB4, to Himmler's personal staff concerning Jewish workers for the Beskiden-Öl company stands in the context of efforts by the company's management to protect its Jewish workforce and involved the highest levels of the political leadership and the German army.[70] Eichmann was involved in the ensuing correspondence, not in the decision-making.[71]

Occupied Soviet Union, Einsatzgruppen, SK 1005

Another important part of the Holocaust, depicted at length in the trial, had unfolded in the German-occupied Soviet Union.[72] In this region, too, Eichmann's involvement had been minimal. For example, Eichmann was not responsible for the removal of the traces of mass murder by opening the graves and burning the corpses, as claimed by the prosecution. Jewish prisoners were forced to perform this gruesome task, and later at regular intervals they too were killed. The descriptions of some of the few survivors belong to the most heart-rending testimony heard in court. Hausner claimed that Eichmann was the superior of Paul Blobel, the SS officer in charge of the perpetrator unit, Sonderkommando 1005.[73] The Central Agency, as part of a 1959 investigation of a subunit of Sonderkommando 1005, had reconstructed the chain of command and identified the perpetrators. Blobel was directly under Heinrich Müller and Blobel's unit was supported by the local Security Police offices. Eichmann was not in charge.[74] One of the witnesses testifying in Jerusalem had been in this specific subunit; he and other survivors had already been interviewed for the German case.[75]

Presumably the best-known unfounded allegation against Eichmann is that he was responsible for the activities of the Einsatzgruppen mobile task forces. Reference to "Operations Units (Einsatzgruppen)" appears in Count 1, g, of the indictment: "Four Operations Units were organized by the Head Office for Reich Security (RSHA) working in collaboration with the Accused in the extermination of Jews."; in Count 1, h, 1–5, the four Operation Units were listed, together with the number of their victims, ranging in the hundreds of thousands.[76]

Hausner's efforts to support this allegation belong to the least edifying parts of the trial. He called the former judge in Case 9 of the Nuremberg successor trials, Michael Musmanno; Musmanno recounted a lot of hearsay evidence but under cross-examination had to admit that he did not mention Eichmann in his judgment. His testimony shows that he accepted lies told to him by Nuremberg defendants that implicated Eichmann while exculpating themselves.[77] On this point, too, consultation with German prosecutors could have been helpful. The 1958 Ulm trial and several subsequent investigations dealt with Einsatzgruppen.[78] How they operated had been correctly described in an indictment against Otto Bradfisch, dated 19 April 1960 – well before Eichmann had even been kidnapped.[79]

The trial record shows that Hausner considered every death squad an Einsatzkommando. Here again, the level of knowledge in 1961 had gone beyond that supposition. In several investigations it had been detailed which types of units (belonging to Security Police, Order Police, or other organizations) committed mass murder in the occupied East. This can be demonstrated using the example of one of Hausner's witnesses. Rivka Yosselewska told the terrible story of how her whole community in Belarus was led to an execution site and shot; only she managed to escape from the pit alive.[80] Not only Hausner but contemporary literature attributes this mass murder to Eichmann,[81] even though he had nothing to do with it. The actual perpetrator, Alfred Renndorfer, head of the local Security Police outpost, was not under Eichmann's command. The Central Agency started an investigation against him in December 1959 and he was later sentenced, along with other Security Police members, for this very crime.[82] Another earlier mass murder action mentioned by Yosselewska was perpetrated by yet another unit, SS-Kavallerieregiment 2, which stood under the command of the Kommandostab Reichsführer SS, not the RSHA. This crime was part of the allegations against and conviction of the commander of the unit, Franz Magill.[83] However, not only the Hausner prosecution but also the court assumed that the crimes described by Yosselewska and another witness had been committed by Einsatzgruppen.[84]

The court did not consider the evidence sufficient to find Eichmann responsible for the crimes of SK 1005.[85] Regarding the Operations Units, it was established that IVB4 transports went to areas where they were active.[86] Beyond that, the court saw two links connecting Eichmann to the Operations Units. He had been present at a meeting of members of Einsatzgruppen just before the German attack on the Soviet Union and he received their situation reports (*Ereignismeldungen*), in which the numbers of Jews killed were recorded. These links are quite tenuous. It is not explained whether the meeting served any nefarious purpose. A copy of an *Ereignismeldung*, which was a trial exhibit, is marked "65th copy," indicating that Eichmann was just one of many recipients.[87] By the 1950s, it had been established which section in the RSHA compiled, edited, and distributed the situation reports. IVB4 was not involved.[88] This hardly warrants the court's finding that Eichmann had been "participating in directing their activities."[89]

The judges found Eichmann guilty on all counts of the indictment, though they acquitted him of some of the crimes in the counts.[90] This was to be expected. The judges made the following overall assessment: "It appears, therefore, that even if we view each sector of the implementation of the Final Solution separately, there was not one sector wherein the Accused did not act in one way or another, with a varying degree of intensiveness, so that this alternative way would also lead us to find him guilty all along the front of extermination activities."[91] This conclusion was reached on the basis of partially wrong findings, as demonstrated above.

Although the trial court corrected Hausner's depiction considerably, the Supreme Court reconfirmed Hausner's historical narrative.[92] The Supreme Court found that Eichmann "held a powerful, virtually independent status,"[93] that "it was he who was supreme, he was the commander in all that pertains to Jewish affairs,"[94] and that "he carried out his unspeakably horrible crimes with genuine joy and enthusiasm."[95]

It continued: "It is clear that the idea of the Final Solution was not his own, but the Führer's. Yet that idea might not have assumed so satanic and infernal an expression – in the bodies of millions of tortured and martyred Jews – but for the thorough planning, the zeal, the fanatical enthusiasm, and the insatiable bloodthirstiness of the Appellant and those who did his bidding."[96]

Witnesses and Affidavits

At one of the conferences commemorating the fiftieth anniversary of the Eichmann trial, a critic summarized the major flaws of the prosecution: a retroactive law, police interrogations without counsel present, and no witnesses for the defence heard in front of the court.[97] And even the right of the defence to scrutinize the prosecution's evidence was curtailed. This is connected with the prosecution's heavy reliance on perpetrator affidavits obtained by Nuremberg investigators – even if they were evidently exculpatory. All that seems to have mattered is that the affiant strongly denounced Eichmann. (Though researched only in part, it appears that Nuremberg prison was a hotbed for the concoction of defensive strategies. German prosecutors had begun to realize at the end of the 1950s that they had to find a new pool of perpetrator witnesses, beyond those who had been already identified at Nuremberg.) Some of these affiants, such as Rudolf Höss and Dieter Wisliceny, had been executed. The statements of Wisliceny, formerly a member of Eichmann's section, were particularly problematic and influential – he clearly tried to implicate Eichmann while exonerating himself.[98] Section 15 of the Israeli Nazi Collaborator Law allowed the court to set the usual rules of evidence aside and admit such statements. The judges stated, however, that they would not accept statements of dead "accomplices" like Höss without corroborating evidence.[99]

Nevertheless, through their choice of affidavits, the prosecution gave legitimacy to these exculpatory stories of Nazi perpetrators. For example, Hausner argued, "But testimony of this kind, such as that of Wisliceny and Höss, and a few other collaborators, have a probative value of the highest order."[100] Robert Servatius, Eichmann's defence counsel, who had been part of the defence in Nuremberg and was obviously well aware of what had been going on, pointed out the obvious mendaciousness of Wisliceny and that he and Höss had spent time together in Nuremberg jail, where they could concoct a common defence.[101]

Other affiants were still alive. Servatius tried to subject their authors to cross-examination before the Israeli court. Hausner vehemently opposed these witnesses being called and, relying on his double role of lead prosecutor and attorney general of Israel, refused their safe conduct to Israel to testify.[102] The court finally decided to have lists of questions drawn and depositions taken in Germany, Austria, and Italy.[103] This was not an adequate substitute for cross-examination before the Israeli court, which would have permitted Servatius to show self-exonerations, contradictions, and inconsistencies.[104] Servatius made this one of his grounds of appeal.[105]

What was the impact of perpetrator affidavits on the findings of the court?[106]

The impact can be seen on three points: assessing Eichmann's role and importance, defining his attitude toward his deeds, and deciding on the date of a Hitler order to murder all Jews. This informed the court's findings on from what time Eichmann knew about the common plan for the Final Solution and whether Eichmann acted with the intent to destroy the Jewish people. This goes to the heart of the case.

The prosecution considered Eichmann's role in the 1944 deportations from Hungary decisive. In the indictment, the accused is mostly alleged to have acted "together with others"; in the section on Hungary, this addition is missing.[107] While Eichmann had contributed significantly to the destruction of Hungarian Jewry, the allegation leaves out the important role played by the German Plenipotentiary, Edmund Veesenmayer, the Higher SS and Police Leader in Hungary, Otto Winkelmann, and the Hungarian authorities.[108] Four of the six prosecution witnesses had been in Hungary in 1944.[109] Their statements provided a skewed account of responsibilities, putting all the blame on Eichmann while exonerating themselves and their former superiors and colleagues. For example, Hans Jüttner and Kurt Becher reported how outraged not only they but also Winkelmann had been about the forced foot marches of Jews. They claimed to have been powerless against Eichmann – thus creating the image that Eichmann had been a monster even by SS standards.[110] Becher was involved in the SS takeover of a Jewish armament factory in Hungary, but claimed postwar to have always tried to help Jews. His statements were referred to by the prosecution as "trustworthy,"[111] while Servatius commented sarcastically, "This is Mr. Becher, on his knees before Himmler, begging for the Jews."[112] (In 1961, a better understanding of these individuals' criminal responsibilities was possible. The Frankfurt Prosecution Office had Jüttner and Becher included in their investigation of Eichmann's Special Command in Hungary; Winkelmann had been declared co-accused on 3 May 1960.)[113] The Hungarian Jewish leaders who testified in the Eichmann trial compounded this skewed picture by virtue of the fact that they had had contacts with Eichmann and his staff, but not with the higher echelons of the SS and Police. In the chapter on Hungary, the Jerusalem court endorsed the exaggerated image of Eichmann's role and found that he was the "chief stimulating force in implementing the final solution in Hungary" and "frequently acted on his own," while "Veesenmayer only sent in reports."[114]

The influence of perpetrator statements is also visible in the court's assessment of Eichmann's position in the RSHA and of his attitude toward his deeds. That Eichmann had "special powers" in the RSHA is based on statements from Walter Huppenkothen, Wisliceny, Franz Six, and Konrad Morgen.[115] The court concluded, "We find that in the RSHA, which was the central authority dealing with the Final Solution of the Jewish Question, the Accused was at the head of those engaged in carrying out the Final Solution."[116] Statements by Wisliceny, Höss, Horst Grell, and Wilhelm Höttl[117] helped to shape the image of Eichmann as zealously advancing the Holocaust and as an ardent anti-semite: "He believed wholeheartedly in the National Socialists' bogus ideology ... His hatred was cold and calculated, aimed rather against the Jewish people as a whole, than against the individual Jew, and for this very reason, it was so poisonous and destructive in all its manifestations."[118]

The court sought to establish the exact date at which Eichmann had been informed of the plan to destroy the entire Jewish population.[119] Here perpetrator evidence was decisive: an affidavit by Walter Blume, in Case 9 of the Nuremberg Military Tribunal, stating that Heydrich had conveyed Hitler's extermination order to the Einsatzgruppen prior to the attack on the Soviet Union.[120] Eichmann had admitted that he had been at such a meeting. Corroboration was found in Höss' statements; two documents were fitted into this theory.[121] The court thought it safe to take one of these documents, Eichmann's letter to Foreign Affairs, dated 28 August 1941, concerning the end of Jewish emigration, as proof of the definite date.[122] On this basis, the court convicted Eichmann of having knowingly implemented the "plan which was known as the Final Solution of the Jewish Question" from August 1941 onwards.[123]

This is not supported by historical facts, though in 1961 it was accepted wisdom, based on witness testimony in Case 9 (including Blume's) that a general extermination order by Hitler had been given in June 1941. Now it is generally acknowledged that this testimony was part of a defence strategy and no Hitler order was given to the assembled Ein-satzgruppen.[124] Historians have developed different theories about the decision-making leading to the Holocaust, suggesting alternative dates for a final Hitler order.[125]

Law vs Memory

Increasingly, the importance of the Eichmann case is seen in its contribution to memorialization, not law.[126] This is problematic, because of the inherent tension between the two. The justice system is meant to provide a sphere outside the influence of the state or other powerful actors. Memory, in particular public memory, can be influenced, if not outright generated, by governments and the media. The Eichmann trial is a case in point. The live dissemination of the trial by radio and television and the Israeli government's efforts to attract several hundred journalists led to enormous public attention. These circumstances do not necessarily translate into a truthful rendering of history. For instance, media reports from this time period almost automatically linked all newly arrested Nazi perpetrators to Eichmann.[127] These connections were not always valid, showing that the importance of a trial cannot be measured by media coverage. The trial provided space for individual memory and for survivors to speak publicly, but all was carefully choreographed by the prosecution.[128] The trial record shows examples of false memory, some innocent,[129] some less so.[130] On a wider level, one can find examples of genuine memory, when people remembered and reported crimes they witnessed,[131] but also of false memory, when, for example, a perpetrator used the public attention on the Eichmann trial to reconstruct his own past criminal responsibilities.[132]

The great flaw of the Eichmann trial is the prosecution's strategy of displaying a comprehensive history of the Holocaust that went considerably beyond Eichmann's historical role. Hausner, in the presentation of his case, distorted Eichmann's role and responsibility – and, one should add, to a lesser extent, the history of the Holocaust. This was politically inspired and, as has been pointed out above, entirely unnecessary as there was more than enough evidence to convict Eichmann for the crimes he had really committed.[133] As we have seen, the level of information available in 1961 would have allowed, through outreach to German prosecutors, a more accurate assessment. That way, the prosecution could have avoided lending legitimacy to dubious sources, which could be used by Holocaust deniers, and to untruthful perpetrator statements.

To return to our initial question concerning what constitutes a historical landmark trial: legal scholars have to decide to what extent the wrongful convictions and the inequality of arms between prosecution and defence impacts on the legal legacy of the case. To the historian it is evident that the Eichmann trial did not do justice to history.

NOTES

1 As the literature on transitional justice is vast, an authoritative text was used as a yardstick: Neil Kritz, ed., *Transitional Justice: How Emerging Democracies Reckon with Former Regimes*, 3 vols. (Washington, 1995). Volume 1 provides a list of eight considerations, the following of which are not relevant: the political system of Israel was not in transition in 1961; non-criminal sanctions and lustration had been addressed by Allied programs of re-education and denazification in Germany and by similar measures in countries which were Nazi victims; and a program for the compensation of Nazi victims had been launched by the West German government in the 1950s. For similar deliberations, see Gary Bass, "The Adolf Eichmann Case," in Stephen Macedo, ed., *Universal Jurisdiction: National Courts and the Prosecution of Serious Crimes under International Law* (Philadelphia, 2004).

2 See Donald Bloxham, "Beyond 'Realism' and Legalism," in Dirk Moses, ed., *Genocide: Humanitarian Intervention, the Prosecution of Genocide, Trauma and Recovery*, vol. 6 (London, 2010), 87–8.

3 See Hanna Yablonka, *The State of Israel vs Adolf Eichmann* (New York, 2004); Tom Segev, *"The Seventh Million": The Israelis and the Holocaust* (New York, 1993); Ylana N. Miller, "Creating Unity through History: The Eichmann Trial as Transition," *Journal of Modern Jewish Studies* 1, no. 2 (2002): 131–49; Idith Zertal, *Israel's Holocaust and the Politics of Nationhood* (Cambridge, 2011).

4 *The Trial of Adolf Eichmann: Record of Proceedings in the District Court of Jerusalem*, published by the State of Israel, Ministry of Justice, 1992–5 (hereafter *Trial*), vol. V, 2016. Vol. VI contains an index of trial documents and exhibits. Trial documents are available on microfiche in vol. IX.

5 See testimony of witness Benno Cohn, *Trial* I, 210–32.

6 The charge of a criminal conspiracy had limited success in Nuremberg. Although criminal conspiracy is a useful tool for prosecutors when dealing with criminal organizations, its applicability to acts committed within a criminal state is debatable. See Jesse Silverglate, "The Conspiracy Prosecution at the Nuremberg War Crimes Trials," *Revue de Droit International* 50 (1972): 251–67; Raha Wala, "From Guantanamo to Nuremberg and Back: An Analysis of Conspiracy to Commit War Crimes under International Humanitarian Law," *Georgetown Journal of International Law* 41, no. 3 (2010): 683–709; Jens Meierhenrich, "Conspiracy in International law," in Dirk Moses, ed., *Genocide, Humanitarian Intervention: The Prosecution of Genocide, Trauma and Recovery*, vol. 6 (London, 2010).

7 The first mention was in response to the objections of Eichmann's defence counsel, Robert Servatius, against the testimony of witness Leon Wells,

because it had nothing to do with Eichmann. According to Hausner: "Thirdly, we have maintained that there was a criminal conspiracy for the extermination of Jewry between the Accused and others and we accordingly worded the indictment 'together with others.' We shall argue that it was possible to remain in Berlin and to be responsible for the extermination of the Jews of Lvov, if the deed was done by virtue of that conspiracy." *Trial* I, 366. The court ruled against the defence and Wells continued his testimony. A similar argument arose over the testimony of witnesses who were victims of sterilization and the court ruled the same way. *Trial* III, 1195–6.

8 *Trial* III, 1341.

9 Hausner quote: *Trial* V, 1995. Arguments on conspiracy charge: *Trial* V, 1980–98, 2043–5. Hausner wanted Eichmann convicted accordingly: "Your Honour, my request is for a finding that Eichmann was involved in a conspiracy to commit crimes against the Jewish people and against humanity, in each of these stages; that he held a central position in the set-up of this conspiracy during the stage of its execution, and that he is, therefore, responsible for all the probable consequences deriving from the acts committed by him, and by others, as a result of the conspiracy." *Trial* V, 2043.

10 *Trial* V, 2185.

11 *Trial* V, 2186; see also *Trial* V, 2185–7.

12 "… but alternatively we shall continue and examine his responsibility, assuming, contrary to our opinion, that he is responsible only for those actions connected with the Final Solution in which he personally participated." *Trial* V, 2187.

13 "We found that the focus of his activities was within the Reich itself, the Protectorate, and in the countries of Europe to the West, North, South, Southeast and Central Europe." *Trial* V, 2187.

14 In its focus on the judgment this essay is a response to the discussion at the conference titled "The Adolf Eichmann Trial: Retrospect and Prospect," held in Toronto, 8–10 September 2012. Some of the participating jurists stressed how important the verdict was for an assessment of the legacy of the trial. For an overview of unsubstantiated accusations, see Ruth Bettina Birn, "Staatsanwalt Zeug in Jerusalem: Zum Kenntnisstand der Anklagebehörde im Eichmann-Prozess und der Strafverfolgunsbehörden der Bundesrepublik," *Einsicht 05, Bulletin des Fritz Bauer Instituts* (2011).

15 *Trial* I, 117. The prosecution used copies of Foreign Affairs documents, which had been obtained in 1955 by a researcher from the Hebrew University for an unrelated project.

16 Trial document T/186.

17 *Trial* I, 366.

18 Even more pronounced: "But these traces are sufficient since, first of all, he stood at the centre of the entire operation; for it was decided at the Wannsee Conference, with the approval of all these present, that the Head Office for Reich Security – in other words, Eichmann – would be the one to carry out the Final Solution everywhere." *Trial* V, 2000.

19 For example: "But the Wannsee Conference carried a more important meaning also for the Accused personally, for it was there that his position as the authorized Referent of the RSHA in matters connected with the Final Solution of the Jewish Question was confirmed in the presence of representatives of all the other authorities. This much we gather also from a letter sent by Heydrich to Luther (T/186) at the end of February 1942." *Trial* V, 2128 (see also 2155–6). The court listed German organizations other than the Security Police that were responsible for the Holocaust; the SS and the Order Police are missing from this list. *Trial* V, 2204.

20 Eichmann's statements to the police and in court are an odd mix of admissions and denial, depending on the situation in which they were made. An evaluation is complicated; the court did not always distinguish correctly between lies and truth. Caution is also required in respect to his statements made in Argentina, which do not necessarily represent the "real Eichmann." There are many examples of SS men engaged in collective reconstruction of the past in the postwar period.

21 The ground-breaking work by Raul Hilberg, *The Destruction of the European Jews*, appeared in 1961. Hilberg had sent the manuscript to Yad Vashem in 1958 for publication, but director Joseph Melkman refused. See Raul Hilberg, *The Politics of Memory: The Journey of a Holocaust Historian* (Chicago, 1996), 109–12, 148. Hausner received his historical advice from Yad Vashem, and Dr. Melkman was a witness for the prosecution. *Trial* II, 609.

22 The Central Agency worked closely with Yad Vashem and a special unit of the Israel Police, under Eitan Liff, which had been established to interview witnesses for German investigations of Nazi crimes. Yad Vashem advised the prosecution team on historical matters. Links between members of the police unit supporting the Eichmann prosecution and Liff's unit can be established. The Eichmann prosecutors could have easily obtained information about the investigations of the Central Agency

23 *Trial* I, 3.

24 *Trial* I, 62

25 In 1943 the Hygiene-Institut was put under the command of the Reichsarzt SS und Polizei; see Jürgen Schäfer, *Kurt Gerstein –Zeuge des Holocaust: Ein Leben zwischen Bibelkreisen und SS* (Bielefeld, 1999), 155–6.

26 Trial documents T/1306–1315; see also Saul Friedländer, *Kurt Gerstein ou l'ambiguité du bien* (Tournai, 1967); Schäfer, *Gerstein.*

27 Trial document T/90; see also Martin Broszat, ed., *Kommandant in Auschwitz: Autobiographische Aufzeichnungen des Rudolf Höss* (Munich, 1963), 126–7, 157–72.
28 *Trial* V, 2150–1, 2176–8.
29 "We have before us the following material, proving the Accused's part in the introduction of the system of killing by Zyklon B at Auschwitz, and in the supply of this gas to Auschwitz." *Trial* V, 2176–8, 2188.
30 Peter Hayes, *From Cooperation to Complicity: Degussa in the Third Reich* (Cambridge, 2004); Jürgen Kalthoff and Martin Werner, *Die Händler des Zyklon B. Tesch&Stabenow: Eine Firmengeschichte zwischen Hamburg und Auschwitz* (Hamburg, 1996); Eugen Kogon, Hermann Langbehn, and Adalbert Rückerl, eds., *Nationalsozialistische Massentötungen durch Giftgas: Eine Dokumentation* (Frankfurt, 1983), 223–4; CF Rüter, ed., *Justiz und NS-Verbrechen*, vol. 13, no. 415 (Amsterdam, 1975). The SS pharmacy in Auschwitz handled the Zyklon B shipments; see Hayes, *Degussa*, 291–3. Mrugowsky was sentenced to death in the Doctor's Case in Nuremberg.
31 Wolfgang Benz et al., "Auschwitz," in *Der Ort des Terrors: Der Geschichte der nationalsozialistischen Konzentrationslager* 5 (Munich, 2007), 121–2; see also Karin Orth, *Das System der nationalsozialistischen Konzentrationslager: Eine politische Organisationsgeschichte* (Hamburg, 1999), 137–41.
32 There are indications that experiments with Zyklon B were conducted as early as 1939 in Poland. The victims were mentally ill patients, and one of the potential perpetrators was a chemist, who had been deployed by the RSHA, Department VI, to the Kanzlei des Führers (in charge of "Euthanasia"). See Volker Riess, *Die Anfänge der Vernichtung 'lebensunwerten Lebens' in den Reichsgauen Danzig-Westpreussen und Wartheland 1939/40* (Frankfurt, 1995), 273–304.
33 Orth, *Konzentrationslager*, 113–41; an SS pharmacist and a SS doctor were present at the experimental killing. See Kalthoff and Werner, *Zyklon B*, 174–5.
34 The heads of the two vendor companies were on trial. One case was heard in 1946, the other between 1949 and 1955. See Rüter, *NS-Verbrechen*, 102–225.
35 Hans Rothfels, ed., "Augenzeugenbericht zu den Massenvergasungen," *Vierteljahreshefte für Zeitgeschichte* 1 (1953): 177–94. Yad Vashem must have been in possession of the publication, or at least aware of it. But even without additional information, a critical reading of the various versions of Gerstein's account (which were all part of the evidence at the Eichmann trial) shows a number of doubtful points, which should have caused concern. For a critical analysis, see Schäfer, *Gerstein*, 204–38; see also Friedländer, *Gerstein*, 165–7. According to Gerstein, Günther visited him in civilian clothes and demanded a huge supply of poison, enough to kill eight million people. Gerstein assumed that the intention was to kill

a large part of the German people, in particular the clergy. Gerstein also talked about killing Jews in open air with Zyklon B, while it was always used in sealed rooms.

36 Jean-Claude Pressac, *Die Krematorien von Auschwitz: Die Technik des Massenmordes* (Munich, 1994), 136, 173–4; Kogon et al., eds., *Massentötungen*, 207; Christopher Browning, *Fateful Months: Essays on the Emergence of the Final Solution* (New York, 1985), 22–6; Christian Gerlach, "The Eichmann Interrogations in Holocaust Historiography," *Holocaust and Genocide Studies* 15, no. 3 (2001): 429, quoting Karin Orth.

37 *Trial* V, 2176, 2188.

38 Trial documents T /37 (188), marked exhibit T/308.

39 The letter was used at Nuremberg, document NO 365. On this basis, Zeug had started an investigation against Wetzel on 10 July 1959. See Central Agency file number AR-Z 231/59. The investigation did not lead to an indictment – it was stayed by the Prosecutor's Office in Hanover. See file number 2Js 49/61.

40 In English: "May I point out that Sturmbannführer Eichmann, the Referent for Jewish Affairs in the RSHA, has agreed to this procedure." *Trial* V, 2175.

41 *Trial* V, 2174.

42 Riess, *Vernichtung*, 273–355; Mathias Beer, "Die Entwicklung des Gaswagens beim Mord an den Juden," *Vierteljahreshefte für Zeitgeschichte* 35, no. 3 (1987): 403–17; Browning, *Fateful Months*, 57–67, especially 63 for the Wetzel letter; Kogon et al., *Massentötungen*, 81–6.

43 According to the letter, the contact between Reichskommissar Ostland and Hitler's Chancellery had to be established via the Higher SS and Police Leader (HSSPF) in Riga – thus, a chain of command in which Eichmann was not included.

44 *Trial* V, 2174. In order to make this theory work, the court dated the visit to September 1941 "at the latest." *Trial* V, 2175. Eichmann and the defence argued for winter 1941/4; a historical assessment places the visit in March 1942. See Gerlach, *Interrogations*, 436.

45 Riess, *Vernichtung*, 273–81.

46 *Trial* V, 2188; see also *Trial* V, 2166–7.

47 Eberhard Kolb, *Bergen-Belsen 1943 bis 1945: Vom "Aufenthaltslager" zum Konzentrationslager* (Göttingen, 1996); Thomas Rahe, "Bergen-Belsen," in Wolfgang Benz et al., eds., *Der Ort des Terrors: Geschichte der nationalsozialistischen Konzentrationslager*, vol. 7 (Munich, 2008); Orth, *Konzentrationslager*, 262–9; Alexandra Wenck, *Zwischen Menschenhandel und "Endlösung": Das Konzentrationslager Bergen-Belsen* (Paderborn, 2000), 103, mentions that Eichmann explained in an interview with Willem Sassen in Argentina that it was Pohl's job to erect concentration camps like Bergen-Belsen.

48 See *Trial* V, 2166–7.

49 While the exchange program was never implemented as planned, smaller groups of Jews did travel abroad via Bergen-Belsen.

50 *Trial* I, 323–447; *Trial* III, 1122–7. Statements of survivors of death camps followed, shedding light on conditions in the camps to which Eichmann had people deported.

51 *Trial* I, 89. In his summing up, Hausner stated, even more pointedly, "In actual fact, Eichmann dealt with the Jews of the Generalgouvernement in exactly the same way in which he dealt with the Jews of occupied Europe, as had been decided at Wannsee." *Trial* V, 1992. In historical reality, the chain of command could lead from Berlin either via the HSSPF to local SSPF or via the *Befehlshaber der Sicherheitspolizei* to local Security Police units, without Eichmann's section being included.

52 *Trial* I, 343–54; see also Angelina Awtuszewka-Ettrich, "Konzentrationslager Plaszow," in Wolfgang Benz et al., eds., *Der Ort des Terrors, Geschichte der nationalsozialistischen Konzentrationslager*, vol. 8 (Munich, 2008).

53 Central Agency case numbers AR-Z 225/59 and AR-Z 283/60; BArch Ludwigsburg, B 162/1974, statement Dr. Moshe Beiski [*sic*], 8.6.1966. According to Beisky, he was questioned already in 1960, *Trial* I, 347.

54 *Trial* I, 349; see also reference in judgment, *Trial* V, 2146; Gideon Hausner, *Justice in Jerusalem: The Trial of Adolf Eichmann* (London, 1966), 176–7.

55 *Trial* I, 323–6; see also Lawrence Douglas, *The Memory of Judgment: Making Law and History in the Trials of the Holocaust* (New Haven, 2001), 97–122.

56 *Trial* I, 326.

57 Hausner referred to the crimes committed in Poland in 1939, which the witnesses had experienced, during Eichmann's cross-examination: "And you saw the tortures, the butchering, the murders with which the German occupiers carried out upon the Jews of Poland, beginning with the first days of the occupation…" Eichmann's presumably truthful answer ("I saw neither murders nor tortures …") created outrage in the audience. *Trial* IV, 1599.

58 BArch Ludwigsburg, B 162/4425, Zeug to Kermisz/Yad Vashem, 12.1.1960: see also BArch Ludwigsburg, B 162/4431, statement Ada Lichtman, 23.4.1963. See also Barbara Distel, "Vernichtungslager Sobibor," in Wolfgang Benz et al., eds., *Der Ort des Terrors, Geschichte der nationalsozialistischen Konzentrationslager*, vol. 8 (Munich, 2008).

59 *Trial* V, 2000.

60 "The Accused, together with others, perpetrated the extermination of Jews" in Auschwitz, Chelmno, Belzec, Sobibor, Treblinka, and Majdanek death camps. *Trial* I, 3. "The Accused, together with others, caused the plunder of the property of millions of Jews …" *Trial* I, 5–6.

61 Trial observer Zeug, who had spent two years investigating
Aktion Reinhard, immediately spotted a mistake in Count 7 of the
indictment, which mentioned a non-existent perpetrator organization.
Hauptstaatsarchiv Stuttgart (hereafter HStA), EA 4/106, Bü 12, report
11.4.1961. Hausner corrected the mistake a few days later in his opening
address. *Trial* I, 90.

62 Apart from the SSPF Lublin, Hitler's Chancellery played a role. Hausner
had a rather sketchy notion of the chain of command. He assumed,
erroneously, that, as the SS organization responsible for concentration
camps (the Wirtschafts und Verwaltungshauptamt, or WVHA) was
not in charge, this had to mean that it was the RSHA. *Trial* IV, 1727;
Trial V, 2009. Eichmann admitted in his interrogation that he met SSPF
Globocnik in Lublin. *Trial* VII, 170–3, 179–80, 229–31, 239–40. Recently
discovered documents show the extent of contacts between Eichmann
and Globocnik. See Stephen Tyas, "Der britische Nachrichtendienst:
Entschlüsselte Funkmeldungen aus dem Generalgouvernement," in
Bogdan Musial, ed., *"Aktion Reinhardt": Der Völkermord an den Juden im
Generalgouvernement 1941–1944* (Osnabrück, 2004).

63 *Trial* V, 2156.

64 *Trial* V, 2158. The quote ended with the remark that "whilst in the
Generalgouvernement area there existed other channels of command,
wherein the Accused had no part," which indicates that the court did not
realize that this was true for other areas as well.

65 Raul Hilberg, *Sonderzüge nach Auschwitz* (Mainz, 1981), 57; Robert
Seidel, *Deutsche Besatzungspolitik in Polen: Der Distrikt Radom 1939–1945*
(Paderborn, 2006), 292–3; Dieter Pohl, *Nationalsozialistische Judenverfolgung
in Ostgalizien 1941–1944* (Munich, 1996), 292.

66 Trial document T/251; *Trial* V, 2158; see also Hilberg, *Sonderzüge*, 82–4,
177. The Central Agency had commenced in 1959 an investigation
concerning the same matter. Central Agency case number AR-Z 203/59.

67 Rivka Kuper testified about the arrival of transports from the
Generalgouvernement to Auschwitz. *Trial* I, 430–4. Ludwig Rajewski, in a
statement for the Höss trial in Poland, had mentioned that an IVB4 rubber
stamp existed in Auschwitz for Jews from the Generalgouvernement and
Bialystok. *Trial* III, 1321. These statements do not indicate who organized
the rail transports; see *Trial* V, 2158.

68 *Trial* V, 2157.

69 In particular, the court did not understand the important role HSSPF and
SSPF played in the Holocaust in the Generalgouvernement.

70 Trial document T/266. See also *Trial* V, 2156–8. For background see
Pohl, *Ostgalizien*, 237; Thomas Sandkühler, *"Endlösung" in Galizien:
Der Judenmord in Ostpolen und die Retttungsinitiative von Berthold Beitz*

1941–1944 (Bonn, 1996), 334–48, with reference to the letter on 532n142. Sandkühler's account is not entirely accurate.

71 The court erroneously stated, "It appears that these orders were given by the Accused's section and hence this is further confirmation that this Section was authorized to decide the fate of Jews in the Generalgouvernement area whenever the necessity for such special instructions arose." *Trial* V, 2158. According to the court, the document was signed by Müller; in the presently available reproduction, the signature is not readable.

72 See witness statements in *Trial* I, 447–525.

73 *Trial* I, 366. According to Rachel Auerbach, head of the "Collection of Testimony Department" of Yad Vashem, this special command was "led by one of Eichmann's helpers, SS Standartenfuehrer Blobel. I have been working for years on the documentation of unit No 1005 ..." See "Witnesses and Testimony in the Eichmann Trial," in *After the Eichmann Trial*, ed. Nathan Eck, *Yad Vashem Bulletin* (April/May 1962), 48.

74 Central Agency case number 8 AR-Z 395/59; BArch Ludwigsburg, B 162/4973, Zeug, final report, 2.4.1960, and KdS Lemberg to HSSPF Krakau, 28.5.1944. Eichmann had admitted that he was in charge of organizing supplies for Blobel's unit and that it was housed in an adjacent building, when it was in Berlin. *Trial* VII, 264–5; *Trial* IV, 1556–7.

75 Testimony by Joseph Reznik, *Trial* III, 1159–62. The statements by Reznik and others had been sent by the Israel Police to Germany 27.7.1960; see BArch Ludwigsburg, B 162/4976, Landsberg to Liff, 14.9.1961. Rohlfing, the head of this subunit of SK 1005, had been identified in March 1960.

76 *Trial* I, 3–4.

77 *Trial* II, 704–29; see also HStA, EA 4/106, Bü 12, Zeug report, 29.5.1961. Another trial observer, historian Wolfgang Scheffler, was equally critical in his view. See BArch Koblenz, B 305/965, Scheffler to Raab, 5.6.1961.

78 After the Ulmer Einsatzgruppenprozess (concerning the German-Lithuanian border area), the newly established Central Agency opened between 1958 and 1960 investigations against all Einsatzgruppen in the occupied Soviet Union.

79 BArch Ludwigsburg, B 162/3177, indictment of Otto Bradfisch et al., 19.4.1960. Bradfisch had been in interrogative custody (*Untersuchungshaft*) since 21 April 1958.

80 *Trial* I, 514–18.

81 Yablonka, *State*, 3.

82 Central Agency case number 202 AR-Z 94/59. See also case record in BArch Ludwigsburg, B 162/3407–3420, and judgment in BArch Ludwigsburg, B 162/4197.

83 Central Agency case number AR-Z 296/60. See also case record in BArch Ludwigsburg, B 162/2324–29, and judgment in BArch Ludwigsburg, B 162/14299.

84 *Trial* V, 2003–4, 2146–7. The other witness, Avraham Aviel, described
   mass shootings in May 1942, near Lida in Belarus. They were presumably
   committed by local Security Police commandos. *Trial* I, 495–9. See
   also Christian Gerlach, *Kalkulierte Morde: Die deutsche Wirtschafts- und
   Vernichtungspolitik in Weißrußland 1941–45* (Hamburg, 1999), 695–7.

85 *Trial* V, 2164.

86 *Trial* V, 2147.

87 Trial document T/305, *Ereignismeldung* 151, dated 5.1.1942. There is no
   indication whether the court had been influenced by the statement of
   a former SS general, Erich von dem Bach-Zelewski, who had said that
   if Eichmann received the Situation Reports, this would mean that his
   section was important. *Trial* V, 1959–63.

88 Helmut Krausnick and Hans-Heinrich Wilhelm, *Die Truppe des
   Weltanschauungskrieges: Die Einsatzgruppen der Sicherheitspolizei und des SD
   1938–1942* (Stuttgart, 1981), 337–41.

89 *Trial* V, 2188. In an earlier summary, the court wrote: "Accordingly, we
   find that the Accused was in contact with the Operations Units from the
   commencement of their activities. From the spring of 1942, the Accused
   began to be active in connection with the issue of operational directives to
   these Units by collecting the material relating to the extermination of Jews
   and preparing summaries thereof." *Trial* V, 2160. These summaries, the
   court found, were intended to assist decisions about the "continuation of
   the activities of the Operations Units."

90 Eichmann was acquitted of the following allegations: crimes against the
   Jewish people before August 1941 (Count 1, 3); all allegations in Count
   4, apart from preventing births in Terezin; and membership in a hostile
   organization before May 1940 (Counts 13, 14, 15). The court did not
   see it as proven that the Accused knew about the fate of the Gypsies he
   deported and that he had murdered the children of Lidice. *Trial* V, 2205–6.
   A few other assessments in the judgment are historically questionable,
   like the plunder of property or Eichmann's relationship with the Mufti.
   However, this concerns minor points or questions on which no direct
   evidence exists.

91 *Trial* V, 2188.

92 *Trial* V, 2360–9.

93 *Trial* V, 2362. The full quote reads: "We have dealt thus far on the status
   of the Appellant in relation to those serving under him. What was his
   status in relation to those above him, the persons and authorities who
   were his superiors? The reply to this question, in all brevity, is that
   he held a powerful, virtually independent status. To be sure, he was
   formally subordinate to Müller, and Müller to Heydrich (Kaltenbrunner),
   but in effect and in actual fact those Big Two left to the appellant all
   affairs regarding Jews, the plunder of their possessions, their emigration

and evacuation, and with very few and isolated exceptions – for
considerations of high policy or other important considerations – they
neither interfered in his acts of persecution of Jews, nor 'deflected' him
from them."

94 *Trial* V, 2368.

95 *Trial* V, 2369.

96 *Trial* V, 2368.

97 Christian Gerlach, "Final Commentary" (paper presented at the
conference "Eichmann nach Jerusalem: Hintergründe, Be-Deutungen
und Folgen des Prozesses," Vienna, 26 September 2013), provided in an
e-mail by Dr. Gerlach to author. Stephan Landsman provides a detailed
assessment of the procedural shortcomings of the Eichmann prosecution
in *Crimes of the Holocaust: The Law Confronts Hard Cases* (Philadelphia,
2005), 56–109.

98 Wisliceny made statements in Nuremberg and in Bratislava. Servatius
read into the court record the parts – omitted by Hausner – which
indicated best Wisliceny's motives for incriminating his former boss. *Trial*
I, 195, 238–9. Several of Hausner's unfounded allegations are based on
Wisliceny's testimonies.

99 *Trial* V, 2163.

100 *Trial* I, 204.

101 *Trial* I, 206. Hausner had claimed that the statements by Höttl, Höss, and
Wisliceny had been made "without contact between them," to increase
their credibility. *Trial* I, 204.

102 Of the six prosecution witnesses, Wilhelm Höttl, Walter Huppenkothen,
Kurt Becher, and Hans Jüttner had been SS officers, and Eberhard von
Thadden and Horst Grell were with the Foreign Office. *Trial* I, 245–51,
256–60, 305–8; *Trial* II, 730–5. Hausner did not know much about his
witnesses. When he submitted statements by Höttl and Huppenkothen, he
suggested himself that the defence might want to call them and that they
could come to Israel. *Trial* I, 245, 259. (Trial observer Zeug pointed out that
Huppenkothen had been *Kommandeur der Sicherheitspolizei* in Lublin from
1940 to 1941 and, therefore, heavily involved in the persecution of Jews
in the Lublin district. See HStA Stuttgart, EA 4/106, Bü 12, Zeug report,
7.5.1961.) Only after Servatius explained that Thadden had worked in the
Section on Jewish Matters in Foreign Affairs, Hausner stated that he would
indict Thadden if he were to come to Israel, and tried to distance himself
from his own witnesses: "I shall not accept von Thadden as my witness –
not in any circumstances." *Trial* I, 259, discussion on Thadden 250–1.

103 Servatius added the names of other former perpetrators to the witness list
in order to counter the affidavits the prosecution had introduced. *Trial* I,
384–6, 500–2.

104 Text of the depositions taken abroad: *Trial* V, 1874–1972.

105 *Trial* I, 247; *Trial* V, 2056–7, 2222.

106 This question was taken up in William Schabas, "The Contribution of the Eichmann Trial to International Law," *Leiden Journal of International Law* 26 (2013): 694.

107 "The Accused caused the deaths of approximately half a million of the Jews of Hungary by means of their mass deportation to the extermination camp at Auschwitz and other places during the period between 19 March 1944 and 24 December 1944 when he was serving as Head of the 'Eichmann Special Command Unit' (Sondereinsatz-Kommando Eichmann) in Budapest." See Count 1, l, *Trial* I, 4.

108 The prosecution had a 1948 affidavit by Winkelmann on their list of evidence: Trial document T/37 (253). Servatius added Veesenmayer and Winkelmann to his witness list. See *Trial* V, 1943–7, 1952–8.

109 Höttl, Becher, and Jüttner were in the SS and Police, and Grell was with the Foreign Office. Gabriel Bach introduced this evidence (apart from Höttl's) when the prosecution's case turned to Hungary. *Trial* II, 730–3.

110 For more detail, see Ruth Bettina Birn, "Fifty Years After: A Critical Look at the Eichmann Trial," *Case Western Reserve Journal of International Law* 44, nos. 1–2 (2011): 443–73. The court followed Jüttner's account on the foot marches. *Trial* V, 2142–3.

111 Prosecutor Gabriel Bach: "We shall ask the court to consider Becher's statement to be trustworthy" – even as he was regarded as a "criminal offender against the Jewish people." *Trial* II, 730–1.

112 *Trial* IV, 1533. Becher actually described such a scene, where he was imploring Himmler to stop foot marches out of Budapest. Servatius pointed out in appeal that Winkelmann wanted to create the impression that he was "insignificant when compared to the accused," while in reality he and Veesenmayer were mainly responsible for the deportations: "Becher tried to create the impression that even Reichsführer-SS Himmler was afraid of the Accused. The witness Veesenmayer, Reich Plenipotentiary, and the SS Generals in Hungary, Winkelmann and Geschke, alleged that they were insignificant compared with the Accused, who was subordinate to them, and that they had nothing whatsoever to do with his actions in the persecution of the Jews." *Trial* V, 2247, 2334–6. Hausner, undeterred, read out parts of Winkelmann's affidavit at the Supreme Court, in which he claimed that Eichmann had not been subordinate to him. *Trial* V, 2283.

113 BArch Ludwigsburg, B 162/5351, Decision Oberlandesgericht Frankfurt, 21.8.1961. Becher and Jüttner were included in the Frankfurt investigation of *Sonderkommando* Eichmann in Hungary 1944. See Central Agency case number AR-Z 150/59.

114 As far as Winkelmann and the Commander of Security Police and SD in
Hungary, Hans-Ulrich Geschke, were concerned, the court assumed that
"some formal connection" with Eichmann's Special Command existed,
but no evidence showed that Eichmann had "received any substantive
instructions" from them. *Trial* V, 2145–6. The judges pointed out that
they had arrived at this conclusion without having recourse to the
statements by Veesenmayer and Winkelmann themselves. Documents
on Winkelmann's activities in Hungary exist, but they had not been
included in the evidence the prosecution presented. See Ruth Bettina
Birn, *Die Höheren SS und Polizeiführer. Himmlers Vertreter im Reich und in
den besetzten Gebieten* (Düsseldorf, 1986), 177–9, 297–304.

115 *Trial* V, 2178–83, quote on 2180. Six and Morgen were witnesses for the
defence. Other information mentioned comes from a Dutch witness,
Eichmann's own statements and interviews with the journalist Willem
Sassen in Argentina, and German administrative regulations.

116 *Trial* V, 2182.

117 *Trial* V, 2202–3, and 2195–204 (as part of a larger assessment of Eichmann's
attitude toward his deeds). Eichmann's own statements and interviews
with Sassen are also quoted.

118 *Trial* V, 2203

119 "First, let us elucidate the date at which the Accused was informed
that an order for complete extermination had been given by Hitler, for
clearly we can place upon him responsibility for participating in the
implementation of the Final Solution of the Jewish question only from the
moment when he began to act in the full knowledge that the signal had
been given for carrying out the Final Solution." *Trial* V, 2172–3.

120 Trial document T/306. Blume had been leader of Einsatzkommando 7a,
until September 1941.

121 The court corrected Höss' estimate of when he was informed of an order
by Hitler, as well as Eichmann's estimate, in light of Blume's affidavit. See
Trial V, 2172–4. The two documents: Trial document T/179, Göring's letter
to Heydrich, dated 31.7.1941; Trial document T /683, Eichmann's letter to
Foreign Affairs, dated 28.8.1941.

122 *Trial* V, 2183. The court assumed, though, that "The Accused was privy of
the extermination secret, as from June 1941." *Trial* V, 2187.

123 *Trial* V, 2205. Eichmann was acquitted for the period until August 1941.

124 Alfred Streim, "Zur Eröffnung des allgemeinen
Judenvernichtungsbefehls gegenüber den Einsatzgruppen," in Eberhard
Jäckel and Jürgen Rohwer, eds., *Der Mord an den Juden im Zweiten
Weltkrieg. Entschlussbildung und Verwirklichung* (Stuttgart, 1985).

125 Depending on which theory a historian adheres to, Eichmann's letter
to Foreign Affairs, dated 28 August 1941, would be given a different
interpretation.

126 See Douglas, *Memory*; Shoshana Felman, "'Theaters of Justice': Arendt in Jerusalem, the Eichmann trial and the Redefinition of Legal Meaning in the Wake of the Holocaust," in Gerry Simpson, ed., *War Crimes Law*, vol. 2 (Farnham, 2004); Anita Shapira, "The Eichmann Trial: Changing Perspectives," in David Cesarani, ed., *After Eichmann: Collective Memory and the Holocaust since 1961* (London, 2005); Mark Osiel, "In Defense of Liberal Show Trials – Nuremberg and Beyond," in Guenael Mettraux, ed., *Perspectives on the Nuremberg Trial* (Oxford, 2008). For a critical view see Kristen Rundle, "Julius Stone and the Eichmann Trial: A Duty to Learn?" in Helen Irving, Jacqueline Mowbray, and Kevin Walton, eds., *Julius Stone: A Study in Influence* (Alexandria, NSW, 2010).

127 Politisches Archiv des Auswärtigen Amts, B 83/743, Raab/Zentrale Rechtsschutzstelle, memo to file 2.3.1961; BArch Ludwigsburg, B 162/1698, clippings of newspaper reports on Michalsen, 537–49; BArch Ludwigsburg, B 162/1699, clippings of newspaper reports, 670; BArch Koblenz, B 305/960 Bd. 1, Zentrale Rechtsschutzstelle to Ministry of Justice, 29.4.1951; Zentrale Stelle der Landesjustizverwaltungen Ludwigsburg, Generalakten III-44, Zeug to Schüle, 6.7.1961.

128 See a 2012 opinion piece by Moshe Arens, complaining that the role of the Jewish Military Organization in the Warsaw Ghetto uprising has been "deliberately erased from the pages of history" by letting only members of a rival underground organization testify at the Eichmann trial. Thus, the Labour Party "influenced the formation of collective memory." Moshe Arens, "A Holocaust Hero Who Should Be in the History Books," *Haaretz*, 27 March 2012.

129 See testimony of Moshe Bahir, *Trial* III, 1178–82, 1188, 1219–20, 1341.

130 See testimony of Zvi Zimmermann, Member of Knesseth, who talked at length about his heroic deeds in the Krakow ghetto. Upon questioning from the bench about how this was relevant, Zimmermann added some "general rumour" about Eichmann. The ensuing exchange became quite acerbic and demonstrates the difficulties the presiding judge had in narrowing the flow of recollections of survivors to what was relevant to the case. *Trial* III, 1122–7. The testimony of Abba Kovner in respect of Eichmann is based on hearsay and difficult to reconcile with historical knowledge. *Trial* I, 455–66.

131 BArch Ludwigsburg, B162/95, Müller to Generalstaatsanwaltschaft Hamburg, 21.6.1960. The Eichmann prosecutors received several letters from Germany with information, which they handed back to the Central Agency. Zentrale Stelle der Landesjustizverwaltungen Ludwigsburg, Generalakten III-44, Zeug to Schüle, 13.8.1961, and Zeug to Mainz Prosecution Office, 13.8.1961.

132 BArch Ludwigsburg, B 162/5801, Statement by Wilhelm Rasp, 18.12.1961. Rasp, the head of a Security Police outpost in Pinsk, was deeply involved

in the mass murder of the Jewish population of his district. He claimed to have received an order by Eichmann, but Rasp's deputy contradicts that claim. BArch Ludwigsburg, B 162/5801, Statement Heinrich Geigenscheder, 20.12.1961. The chain of command from the RSHA to Rasp did not include Eichmann.

133 In a critical pretrial article, Telford Taylor suggested an alternative way forward: an Israeli inquest of the facts, giving voice to the victims, coupled with an international trial. Telford Taylor, "Large Questions in the Eichmann Case," *New York Times*, 22 January 1961. Taylor's warnings against a national trial were justified by several incidents that reflected Israeli political interests and the influence of the government: biased judges who remained on the bench, special laws passed by the Knesset, and interference of the government with the work of prosecution and police.

Eichmann and Geopolitics

7 The Eichmann Trial's Impact Reconsidered

BOAZ COHEN

It is commonly held that the Eichmann trial was responsible for a drastic change in the attitudes in Israel toward the Holocaust and its survivors. This essay maintains, conversely, that the Holocaust and its survivors had a vocal and visible presence within Israeli society long before the trial, and that the formidable public impact of the trial was not a sign of a long period of silence coming to its end. It was, rather, the manifestation of the very strong presence of the Holocaust in Israeli public discourse from the early post-Holocaust years and up to the trial itself.[1] Moreover, the centrality of survivor testimonies in the trial was the fruit of many years of work by survivor historians and activists, especially Rachel Auerbach.

This essay makes two intertwined claims, both pertaining to the presence and visibility of the Holocaust in pre-Eichmann trial Israel. The first is that the Holocaust and its commemoration were ingrained in Israeli public discourse from the early 1950s and had a visibility that no newspaper reader or radio listener could ignore. The second is that survivors were a major element of the new Israeli society, and they ensured the emergence of an Israeli Holocaust consciousness not only through their existence and personal pain but also through the work of survivor memory activists and survivor historians.[2]

I begin with an overview of the discussions and representations of the Holocaust in the early Israeli public sphere: in legislation, politics, the courts, and the media.[3] I then continue with a discussion of the place of the survivor public in the young Israeli state. This serves as an introduction to the issues of commemoration, research, and the role of survivor historians in public debates on the subject. The specific contribution of survivor historians to the Eichmann trial, especially that of Rachel Auerbach, is covered in the last part of the essay.

Re-reading Israeli Holocaust Consciousness

The re-evaluation of the place of the Holocaust in early Israeli public life is apparent in the work of several Israeli researchers, including myself. Together, this new research adds up to a reconsideration of early Israeli society in general, and the development of Holocaust consciousness and commemoration in that society in particular.

Research into the omnipresence of the Holocaust in early Israeli society has been led by Hanna Yablonka, who has shown the interplay between the public profile of the Holocaust and the agency of Holocaust survivors in Israeli society.[4] Her work paved the way for the next generation of researchers, who are working to uncover "the silence that never was." These new researchers show that Israelis encountered the Holocaust in many facets of their everyday life and that Holocaust representation vis-à-vis the Israeli public was much more nuanced and varied than we have been led to believe. Research by Sharon Geva, for example, demonstrates how Israeli women's magazines such as *La'isha* frequently published stories on women Holocaust survivors and their heroism in resisting the Nazis. Readers of this type of magazine were thus given a personal, non-political image of the Holocaust and its survivorsunlikethe one that was purported to be the standard Israeli worldview.[5] Michal Shaul shows the centrality of Holocaust memory to the ultra-orthodox Haredi community and to its phoenix-like reconstitution and growth after the Holocaust.[6] New research by Gali Drucker Bar-Am on the Yiddish press discusses the establishment of a survivor public identity.[7] Another avenue of research considers the "microhistory of commemoration" of specific communities. Ada Gebel's work on Holocaust survivors in Kibbutz Hafetz Haim and Michal Glater's research on the survivor village of Yesodot are contributions to this emerging area of study.[8]

The Israeli citizen of the pre-Eichmann trial years encountered the Holocaust in many spheres of social, national, and cultural life: in Knesset legislation, in widely publicized trials, on the pages of newspapers, in memorial services and assemblies, on bookshelves, and on the theatrical stage. Debates about the Holocaust and its consequences – some of them very powerful, even violent – demonstrate that the memory of the Holocaust and the attitude toward it had a central place in Israeli consciousness and public discourse at the time.

Legislating the Holocaust

Israel's first decade was a whirlwind of nation-building as myriad laws were enacted in the establishment of the nascent state. Disagreements on major political and ideological issues broke up coalitions and toppled governments. During this time the Knesset passed several laws that shaped the nascent Israeli state's Holocaust commemoration and its approach to Holocaust-related issues. In 1950 it passed the Law for Bringing the Nazis and Their Helpers to Justice; in 1951 the Knesset declared the date of 27 Nissan (according to the Jewish Calendar) as the Holocaust and the Ghetto Uprising Commemoration Day, without mandating how to mark the day; in 1953 the Knesset passed the Holocaust and Heroism Commemoration Law, establishing Yad Vashem as the national authority for the commemoration of the Holocaust and heroism, and defining its tasks and the issues to be commemorated by it; in 1954 the Knesset accepted the Disabled Veterans of the War against the Nazis Law; and in 1959 it enacted the Memorial Day of the Holocaust and Heroism Law, defining the public profile and state rituals of the day.

The Knesset legislation was impacted by the survivor public. Holocaust survivors served as members of the Knesset and were active in passing this legislation. One of them was Avraham Adolf Berman, a former activist in the Warsaw ghetto, who served for the duration of the Second Knesset. Most prominent was Rabbi Mordechai Nurock of the Mizrachi and a representative of the United Religious Front in the Knesset.[9] He was a candidate for the state presidency in 1952, and at the end of that year served as Minister of Postal Services. Nurock, formerly of Riga, who lost his wife and two sons in the Holocaust, throughout the 1950s spearheaded legislation related to the Holocaust. Knesset members accepted that Nurock, as a survivor, was an authority on Holocaust commemoration, and he led several Knesset committees on the subject.

Some of the laws enacted in Israel's first decade were initiated by survivors who lobbied the Knesset. Pressure from survivors for legislation to bring to trial collaborators with the Nazis, such as kapos, culminated in the 1950 Law for Bringing the Nazis and their Helpers to Justice. In 1954, years of lobbying by a disabled veterans of World War II organization brought about the Disabled Veterans of the War against the Nazis Law. The most visible lobbying by survivors aimed to redefine the nature of Holocaust Memorial Day. The Council of Organizations for Setting the Character of Holocaust Memorial Day (a survivor umbrella organization comprising, as its organizers claimed, a hundred survivor organizations and *Landsmanschaften*) petitioned the Knesset to enact mandatory public mourning practices for the Holocaust. It claimed that the day, as designated by law in 1951, was not adequately observed in the Israeli streets, school system, and public institutions. The council took on the role of guardian of memory and approached the Knesset "in the name of organizations working for the commemoration of the holy martyrs of the Holocaust and the heroes of the uprising, of the sons of these communities who are representing the heritage of Jewish communities uprooted by the Nazis."[10] The Knesset accepted their petition, though in a watered-down version, and on 8 April 1959 passed the Holocaust and Heroism Memorial Day Law. This episode clearly shows that survivors had articulated a distinct public voice and ideology, playing the political game (or field), and were being heard by the press and state institutions.

Holocaust Politics

The above-mentioned legislation did not lack a political agenda. During debates and assemblies Israeli legislators tied the Holocaust to burning issues of Israel's identity and foreign policy. In particular they considered the East-West divide and the question of whether Israel should align itself with the Western or Eastern blocs. While Israel's ruling party, Mapai, decided to align with the West, its left opposition parties, Mapam and the Communist Party, fought vehemently against any collusion with the "imperialists and fascists." The "German Question" was central in this debate. Should Israel have relations with West Germany? Should it demand reparations for the damages of the Holocaust, conduct negotiations, and sign agreements with the West German government on reparations? It was obvious to both sides that a reparations agreement would pave West Germany's path to legitimacy and its inclusion in the Western bloc.

Israel's relations with Germany were constantly debated in the public and the political spheres. The issue was, on the surface, a political one, but it also had ethical and emotional implications. It involved obtaining compensation for Jewish property looted by the Germans, establishing diplomatic and cultural relations with Germany, and brokering Israeli-German weapon deals. Vehement debates took place within the government and in the Knesset, but also publicly in the press and in the streets. For instance, when the Knesset debated the question of reparations in early January 1952, a violent demonstration took place outside the Knesset: the building was stoned, police clashed with demonstrators, and hundreds of people were injured or arrested.[11] The debate on reparations revealed the strong emotions the Holocaust stirred up in the Israeli public, and the proposal was barely accepted by a vote of 61 Knesset members out of 120. The two poles of the Israeli political spectrum, Mapam on the Zionist left and Herut (Freedom Party) on the right, headed by Menachem Begin, agitated and voted against the agreement, although they did not act in tandem.

The issue of Israeli-German relations brought down the government in 1957 and again in 1959.[12] In December 1957, Prime Minister David Ben-Gurion resigned, bringing the seventh government to an end, following a leak about the planned visit to Germany by Chief of Staff Moshe Dayan to discuss weapon sales. In July 1959 opposition by Ahdut ha-Avoda (United Labour, the Zionist left) to weapon sales to Germany brought about Ben-Gurion's resignation and the fall of Israel's eighth government. From the first debates in 1952 to the struggle in 1964 against the acceptance of the proposed statute of limitations on war crimes in Germany, Holocaust survivor organizations led opposition to government policy on relations with Germany through public assemblies and demonstrations.

The Holocaust in Court

The Law for Bringing the Nazis and Their Helpers to Justice was aimed at the "helpers" more than at the "Nazis." Its importance for the survivor public can be seen in the more than 200 complaints against alleged Jewish collaborators with the Nazis. These complaints brought about thirty-three trials in the 1950s, some of which resulted in convictions ranging from short prison sentences to the death penalty (though this sentence was never implemented). In general, Israeli judges were reluctant to pass judgment on Holocaust survivors. [13] Hanna Yablonka claims that the trials did not receive much publicity and remain only as personal narratives within the lives of survivors.[14] Nevertheless, one of the trials became an event of central importance in the history of Israel in the 1950s: the Kastner trial. Israel Kastner was the deputy president of the Rescue Committee of the Zionist movements in Hungary. During the last phases of the war he conducted negotiations with the Nazi authorities aimed at saving Hungarian Jews who were, in 1944, being sent to their death in Auschwitz. He succeeded in saving a group of 1,684 Jews on the "Kastner Train" and claimed to be influential in saving others as well.

The trial, which took place between 1 January and 22 June 1954, began as a libel case against an elderly activist, Malkiel Grunwald, who accused Kastner of colluding with the Germans during the Holocaust. It quickly metamorphosed into a trial against Kastner himself and the activities, or rather the inactivity, of the Zionist movement during the Holocaust, especially Israel's ruling party, Mapai. Supported by a vehement campaign by the weekly tabloid *Ha-Olam Ha-Zeh* (This World), edited by Uri Avneri, Grunwald's attorney, Shmuel Tamir, raised a public storm over the alleged collaboration by individuals and institutions within Mapai and the Zionist establishment. The court determined that Kastner bore direct responsibility for the tragic fate of Hungarian Jewry during the Holocaust. Judge Benjamin Halevy's ruling that Kastner "sold his soul to the devil," Kastner's murder in 1957, and the overturning of Halevy's sentence by the Supreme Court in 1958, occupied the Israeli public and raised painful questions concerning the reactions of Jewish, Zionist, and Yishuv leadership to the Holocaust.[15] It also led to a discussion of broader Jewish responses during the Holocaust albeit in black and white moral tones. The legal dispute boiled over into a venomous political and public debate, with repercussions that could be felt in the years to come.[16]

Culture: Literature and Theatre

The Holocaust and its survivors were prominent in the Israeli artistic and literary realms in work by survivors and non-survivor writers. By the mid-1950s, novels by young survivors were appearing in Hebrew, including works by Uri Orlev, Aharon Appelfeld, Benzion Tomer, Shamai Golan, and Itamar Yaoz-Keszt. Israeli literary scholar Avner Holtzman has written of the "empathy, appreciation, and sometimes even a feeling of inferiority in the face of the Holocaust survivors" apparent in the literature of the first generation of native-born Israeli writers. He claims that these writers were critical of the "wrongs and the injustices in the attitude that was displayed toward survivors" and aspired "to make them part of the Zionist enterprise."[17] Any claim of indifference by non-survivor Israeli writers to the Holocaust and its survivors was, in the words of writer Hanoch Bartov, "a wicked slander."[18]

Israeli audiences were treated to plays about the Holocaust beginning in the early 1950s. Plays such as Leah Goldberg's *The Lady of the Castle* and Nathan Shacham's *New Reckoning* were highly successful and played to full houses. These plays and others tackled sensitive issues of survival and collaboration, and questioned the wisdom of passing judgment on choices made during the Holocaust and its aftermath.[19]

"Survivor-land": A Society of Survivors

The Holocaust was a personal and painful living memory for hundreds of thousands of Israelis. Holocaust survivors amounted to a quarter of the population of the budding Israeli state (approximately 500,000 out of 2,000,000 in 1960). Hundreds of thousands of other Israelis who emigrated from Eastern Europe and Germany before the war also lost family members in the Holocaust. Holocaust-related loss was thus manifest in the homes and families of a very large segment of Israeli society. The phrase "Israeli society and Holocaust survivors" is misleading: not only were Holocaust survivors a major component of Israeli society, but many others were indirect victims of the Holocaust. Most Israelis immigrated there before the Holocaust or after it, so the difference between "Israelis" and "survivors" rested in their date of immigration as well as their experiences during the years 1939–45. There were native Israelis – "sabras" – but they were few. For example, in the 1948 war – Israel's war of independence – only 22 per cent of soldiers (approximately 20,000 men) in the young Israeli army were born in Israel.[20]

The survivors, many of whom were young and of working age,[21] were not passive spectators to the emerging Israeli state but were active participants in its development. In the Israeli War of Independence survivors comprised 50 per cent of the young Israeli army. Survivors then took part in building the young state in the private and public sectors. They were not immigrants in an established state with an exsisting infrastructure and culture but were instead taking part in its creation. Many survivors identified with the Israeli experience, seeing their own success tied to that of the state.

Even though survivors were busy rebuilding their lives and becoming integrated into society, a survivor public identity began to emerge in "Survivor-land," a term coined by Meir Dworzecki, a survivor activist, historian, and leader. As Gali Drucker Bar-Am has shown, a major site for survivor identity-building was the flourishing Yiddish press and publishing industry in 1950s Israel. She writes that the destruction of the mother culture in Eastern Europe and the migration of the majority of the survivors to Israel brought about a boom in Yiddish newspapers and books. Thirty Yiddish language newspapers and weeklies were printed in Israel by survivors, who also established three new Yiddish publishing houses. "From the outset," writes Drucker Bar-Am, "the Yiddish press persistently and extensively engaged with the Holocaust and its memory in great detail on a daily basis ... Furthermore, it was through this press that the survivors were able to conduct their civil campaigns ... for the perpetuation of Holocaust memory, for the rights of the survivors in Israel."[22]

The survivor public established associations and organizational infrastructure. A great deal of survivor activities took place in the smaller circle of communal *Landmanschaften* and immigrant associations that organized commemoration events, built memorials, and published memorial books. Many survivor organizations tied their commemoration work to the Zionist ethos of building the land. Survivors built new neighbourhoods or other projects, answering their need for a home and commemorating their destroyed communities. Such neighbourhoods were, in the words of the survivor press, a "living commemoration," not dwelling on the pain but looking to a better future.[23] At the same time some of these organizations and activists were also working to integrate Holocaust memory into the Israeli life experience and society as a whole.

The Survivor Historians

Central to the development of Israeli Holocaust consciousness and to the emergence of Holocaust research, prior to the Eichmann trial and following it, were the survivor historians. These were East European Jewish intellectuals who survived the Holocaust under Nazi rule or as refugees in the Soviet Union. They lost most of their family members and witnessed the destruction of the Jewish community in Poland. Survivor historians drew on the modern East European Jewish tradition of writing history as a national project – a *folksarbeit*, whereby the public took part in the endeavour of writing the nation's history through collection and documentation. This method facilitated the telling of the Jewish narrative of the Holocaust. Following liberation, these intellectuals established historical commissions that collected testimonies, documents, and materials from survivors. The commissions published much of the collected material, as well as research guides, document collections, and monographs.[24]

Members of the historical commissions saw their work as "a holy mission and also an obligation" and were driven by the feeling that they had "a historical mission."[25] They believed, in the words of Nathan Eck, that "the group of people who experienced the terrors on their own flesh … has a special mission in this investigation."[26] They worked under the premise that they constituted the only authorized source capable of understanding and recording what had happened. Future researchers and the wider public need the "evaluation and processing of this material by people who witnessed and personally experienced the events themselves," wrote Eck.[27] By the late 1940s the historical commissions in Europe wound down and many of their principal activists immigrated to Israel. Prominent among them were Joseph Kermish, Nachman Blumental, and Rachel Auerbach (Roykhel Oyerbuch), who were joined there by Meir (Mark) Dworzecki and Nathan Eck, formerly active in East European survivor circles in Paris. This was a vocal group in Israeli public discourse. In the public eye they were accepted as authorities on the Holocaust – the torchbearers of its research and commemoration – and were considered the "Jeremiahs of our generation."[28]

The Battle for Yad Vashem

During the years 1957–9, the recently established Yad Vashem found itself in the centre of a public debate regarding its purpose and activities. Internal tensions at the institution found their way into the press and resulted in an open confrontation between the Yad Vashem chairman, erstwhile historian Ben-Zion Dinur, and his associates on one hand, and the survivor historians on the other. Survivor organizations also joined in: the Organization of Disabled Veterans of the War against the Nazis, for example, held a sit-down strike at the Yad Vashem offices, protesting its lack of interest in Jewish combat and resistance during the Holocaust. The Fourth International Council of Yad Vashem, convening to discuss the institution's budget, turned into a battlefield between proponents and opponents of Dinur's policies. At its conclusion Dinur resigned his post as head of Yad Vashem.

The debate over Yad Vashem played out as two connected conflicts. One was the mounting divergence of aims inside Yad Vashem between survivor historians working at the institution and Dinur at its head. Dinur envisioned a historical research institute that would investigate the long history of each of the destroyed communities from its origin to its end during the Holocaust. In order to achieve this aim, Dinur staffed Yad Vashem with his students from the Hebrew University of Jerusalem, trained as historians in the German tradition. The collection of archival sources was outsourced to the Israeli Historical Society and a joint research institute was established: the Hebrew University and Yad Vashem Institute for Research into the Destruction of European Jewry and Its History in the Last Generation.[29]

In contrast, survivor historians wanted to research the Holocaust per se, which they considered to be the burning need of their generation. They regarded the Holocaust as a national trauma whose wounds needed healing through the work of survivor historians. "The purpose of Holocaust research at Yad Vashem," Nathan Eck stated, "is to provide scholarly answers to diverse issues and problems that have come up in the context of the Holocaust and have been gnawing at our world." The Holocaust elicited existential questions about national and human solidarity and "many problems, some of which are not always expressed and put into words, but rather erode and bore away at the recesses of the psyche."[30]

According to survivor historians, the Yad Vashem leadership tried to silence their voices and stifle their influence in the institution. A growing sense of marginalization forced their hand. The second aspect of the debate over Yad Vashem consisted of public opposition to Dinur's research-oriented policies by survivor organizations and their supporters. These organizations protested the lack of Holocaust commemoration in Yad Vashem, which at the time had only one building serving the administration, the library, and the archive, and no venue for commemoration.

In manifestos, press articles, and testimonies before Yad Vashem's International Council and its subcommittees, survivor historians and their supporters argued that Dinur's long-term research policy came at the expense of the study and commemoration of the Holocaust. "The heads of Yad Vashem have inflicted a stinging defeat on this institution," they charged, listing Holocaust research and commemoration as prime among the directorate's "failures."[31] Dinur was shocked by the vehemence of the opposition as manifested in the press. "Now I see that it cannot go on anymore. The situation here is much more serious. It is an organized response. They are organizing a smear campaign against us in the press," he told the members of Yad Vashem directorate.[32]

Yet, directorate members, well aware of the public status of survivor historians, accepted that they were the "founding generation" of Holocaust research. "This group is made up of those who laid the foundations of this literature. Already in Poland they had published dozens of books in this topic, some of which has not been translated into Hebrew yet,"[33] said Moshe Kol. Directorate members concurred with Kol's claim that survivor historians were people with vision and mission, "who have the Holocaust running in their veins," therefore "they should not be considered as ordinary employees ... because they are dedicated to the matter and to this sacred idea, and they want to see this institute become perfect." This support for the survivor historians coupled with a similar spirit in the discussions of the Fourth International Council of Yad Vashem brought about Dinur's resignation. Thus, the survivors won a public victory.

The battle over Yad Vashem displays the visibility and prominence of Holocaust survivors in the evolution of Israel's public Holocaust memory. The survivors' campaign had wide press coverage, which showed that criticism by survivors – especially the survivor historians – was powerful and that the Yad Vashem leadership had to bow to their demands. The survivor organizations' above-mentioned campaign in the Knesset in 1959 should be seen in this context.

Survivor historians and activists, emboldened by their success with Yad Vashem, strove to make a major change in Israeli Holocaust commemoration.

Rachel Auerbach and the Eichmann Trial Testimonies

Survivor historians were not only involved in debates about the path of Holocaust research and the character of Yad Vashem: their work contributed directly to the evolution of the Eichmann trial and its role as a major memory event. Rachel Auerbach, a writer, journalist, and survivor of the Warsaw Ghetto, established and directed the Department for the Collection of Testimonies at Yad Vashem, and played a key role in this development.[34] Auerbach, a former contributor to the clandestine *Oneg Shabbat* archives in the Warsaw ghetto and a founding member of the postwar Central Historical Commission in Poland, was strongly committed to testimony collection. Dinur and his students in Yad Vashem looked deprecatingly at Auerbach's work. Professional historians trained in the German historical tradition saw little appeal in these oral histories collected from laypersons by laypersons. Yet, Auerbach continued with her work, developing the department's methodology and philosophy as the work progressed.

Auerbach regarded testifying as an expression of a broad popular movement, as recording history "of the people and for the people." The roots of this movement began during the Holocaust, when "an entire people clutching pens, in ghettos, in hiding places, in the face of gas chambers and machine gun muzzles, found the strength to write – for the sole reason that at some time the world should know, so that these things should be known to their brethren."[35] Auerbach drew parallels between giving testimony and the publication of community memorial (*Yizkor*) books. The grassroots nature of memorial books appealed to her as an expression of a "collective, spontaneous effort, stemming from the depths of the spirit of the people."[36] Although Auerbach's department was not involved in publishing, she believed that Yad Vashem should contribute support and tools to this popular movement: "All of our organized activity is nothing but an instrument for this movement; everyone involved needs to understand this. In this lies the secret of our existence."[37]

As work began building the case against Eichmann, Auerbach was concerned that it would become a regular, "dry" trial. She observed that the team preparing the trial "wanted only official documents that could serve as direct proof of his guilt. Witnesses, if any, would only be those who could produce direct evidence as to his culpability."[38] Auerbach was convinced that this "unique opportunity" should be used to tell the world about "the character and dimensions of the genocide attempted upon the Jews of Europe."[39] Auerbach considered survivor testimony as one of the central pillars in the evolving historiography of the Holocaust: she outlined three principal reasons for its importance, which she put forth in several lectures and articles.

The first reason was that the Jewish history of the Holocaust needed to be told. In Auerbach's opinion, as in that of other survivor historians, the commonly accepted picture of the Holocaust was distorted because it relied on "a large number of official documents, the majority of which originated from German sources." These documents told only the story of the murderers, but not of the murdered. A Jewish researcher wanting to describe Jewish life during the Holocaust, wrote Auerbach, ought not "to disregard the material of remembrance that constitutes the majority of the documents of Jewish origin." These Jewish sources "give us a picture of reality, which it is possible to use to fill in the already built framework based on official sources," she stated.[40]

The second reason was that the testimonies play a part in psychological healing. Auerbach saw the act of testifying as a "popular psycho-hygienic enterprise." "I am convinced," she proclaimed, "that the confessions, called giving testimony, from the era of the Holocaust have a calming and healing influence and help free them [the survivors] from the horrors." She further noted that "according to the opinions and the experiences of psychologists, the healing is painful – to the recorder no less that the witness – but, nonetheless, it is known to us that denial and the suppression of sorrow cause much greater damage." She added, "We know that psychological complexes are diminished by exposure and divulgence and sharing with other people." However, this endeavour meant not only relief but also a measure of overcoming "the destruction and the death" and building for the future "with the help of the spiritual effort" required in giving testimony. The "creative catharsis" involved in giving testimonies allowed survivors to find the strength to "rise above the mass graves."[41] Therefore, claimed Auerbach, collecting testimony is not only a historical project but also a mission of "societal and national healing." The therapeutic aspect of taking testimony necessitated, according to her, "including the maximum numbers of survivors."[42]

The third reason was that the testimonies would provide historical materials for a future period in which the Jewish voice could be heard on the stage of history. "In no [war crime] trial has it been permitted us, the Jewish people, who suffered the hardest oppression, to be present as an interested party," she wrote, while Jews' participation as witnesses at trials had been "weak and incomplete." Moreover, the testimonies collected up to that point had been presented and put together for publication in an "impoverished, minimized, and sometimes also distorted" fashion. It was imperative to "prepare Jewish testimony that will give voice to our sorrow and our fury also at the hour when we will no longer be in the world," before "the court of history." Thus, already in the mid-1950s, Auerbach prepared the ground, unknowingly, for the inclusion of survivor testimonies in the Eichmann trial, for which she fought vigorously a few years later.[43]

Auerbach was not content with transferring witness lists and survivor testimonies to the prosecution. She also suggested a conceptual division of topics for which witnesses should be brought forward. She was convinced that the destruction of the Jews should be covered at the trial using "three aspects: geographic, chronological and phenomenological." She suggested presenting "phenomena and methods of extermination" in four subject matters: "preparation, execution, atrocities, spoliation following murder."[44]

Auerbach's assertion that survivor testimonies must be integrated in the trial was accepted by the prosecutor, Gideon Hausner, who shared her views concerning the historical significance of the trial, as well as its importance for public relations. Indeed, many witnesses were involved in the trial, and dozens of them were contacted by the prosecution through the Yad Vashem staff. Hausner "turned to us many times with requests for 'coverage' on one subject or another," wrote Auerbach.[45]

The involvement of the survivor historians in facilitating the survivor testimonies of the Eichmann trial underlines the work done by these survivors during the 1950s. Their belief in the need to record and express the voice of the survivors and the Israeli establishment's willingness to give a place of honour to this voice ensured the Eichmann trial's powerful impact on its generation and on those to come.

Conclusion

The Eichmann trial marked a new stage in Holocaust awareness in the Israeli public sphere and greatly influenced the future development of Holocaust memory. Radio, film, and press coverage all contributed to the trial's impact. Yet, as was shown in this essay, it was not a radical turning point in the course of Israel's Holocaust memory. Nor was it a watershed moment, preceded by alienation toward survivors and rejection of the Jewish experience in the Holocaust and followed by acceptance, identification, and the centralization of the Holocaust and its survivors in Israeli national consciousness. It was indeed a leap ahead, though in an ongoing process of commemoration and working through of Holocaust memory. Its impact was not due to the shock of encountering the Holocaust and breaking the silence surrounding it, but rather to the strong foundations of private and public Holocaust awareness that preceded it.

The Israeli public arena was strongly imbued with Holocaust memory, and Holocaust-related issues were constantly debated in politics and the courts, and in the press, in literature, and onstage. Israelis, be they veterans or new immigrants, survivors or those who were not "there," encountered and enacted the memory of the Holocaust in many ways. Holocaust survivors were an integral part of Israeli society but were also developing a survivor-Israeli identity. As such they were active in communal commemorations but also were striving to influence the Israeli commemoration of the Holocaust. Most prominent in this endeavour were the survivor historians and memory activists who saw themselves as wards of Holocaust memory and were seen as such by Israeli society. They were successful in utilizing the press and public opinion to effect a change in Yad Vashem and its commemoration policies. It was through the work of one of them, Rachel Auerbach, that the voices of survivors were heard in the Eichmann trial.

NOTES

1 For a wider discussion of many of the issues explored here, see Boaz Cohen, *Israeli Holocaust Research: Birth and Evolution* (London, 2013).

2 Ibid., 26–35; Boaz Cohen and Tom Lawson, eds., *Holocaust Studies: A Journal of Culture and History*, special issue, *Survivor Historians* (forthcoming).

3 On public discourse see Roni Stauber, *The Holocaust in Israeli Public Debate in the 1950s* (London, 2007).

4 Hanna Yablonka, *The State of Israel vs. Adolf Eichmann*, trans. Ora Cummings and David Herman (New York, 2004); Hanna Yablonka, "Oriental Jewry and the Holocaust: A Tri-Generational Perspective," *Israel Studies* 14 (2009): 94–122.

5 Sharon Geva, *To the Unknown Sister: Holocaust Heroines in Israeli Society* (Hebrew) (Tel Aviv, 2010).

6 See, among others, Michal Shaul, "Holocaust Memory in Ultra-Orthodox Society in Israel: Is It a 'Counter-memory'?" *Journal of Israeli History* 32 (2013): 219–39.

7 Gali Drucker Bar-Am, "May the Makom Comfort You – Place, Holocaust Remembrance and the Creation of a National Identity in the Israeli Yiddish Press, 1948– 1961," *Yad Vashem Studies* 42, no. 2 (2014): 155–95

8 Ada Gebel, "Kibbutz Chafetz Chaim in the Face of the Holocaust" (MA rhesis, Ben-Gurion University of the Negev, 2007); Michal Glater, "The Prayer Shawl and the Sickle: Yesodot – Haredi Pioneer Settlement in the Soreq Valley, 1945–1953" (MA equivalence thesis, Bar-Ilan University, 2013).

9 Although two out of 120 members of the Knesset make up less than 2 per cent of the legislature, it is important to remember that the survivor community was an immigrant community of mainly young people, so its integration into the political system was not easy and took time.

10 Press release by the Council of Organizations for Setting the Character of Holocaust Memorial Day.

11 The Knesset debates about reparations and the accompanying demonstrations took place 7–9 January 1952.

12 Neima Barzel, "Dignity, Hatred and Memory – Reparations from Germany: The Debates in the 1950s," *Yad Vashem Studies* 24 (1994): 247–80.

13 Rivka Brot, "There Wasn't a Righteous Person among Them: The Gray Zone of Collaboration in the Israeli Courtroom," in Gabriel Finder and Laura Jockusch, eds., *Jewish Honor Courts: Revenge, Retribution, and Reconciliation in Europe and Israel after the Holocaust* (Detroit, 2015), 327–60.

14 Hanna Yablonka, "The Development of Holocaust Consciousness in Israel: The Nuremberg, Kapos, Kastner, and Eichmann Trials," *Israel Studies* 8 (2003): 1–24.

15 Boaz Cohen, "The Difficulties of Creating a Holocaust Archive: Yad Vashem and Israel Kastner, 1947–1948," *Journal of Jewish Culture and History* 15 no. 3 (2014): 173–87.

16 Yehiam Weitz, "The Holocaust on Trial: The Impact of the Kastner and Eichmann Trials on Israeli Society," *Israel Studies* 1 (1996): 1–26. Also see Michael Berkowitz's contribution to this volume.

17 Avner Holtzman, "'They Are Different People': Holocaust Survivors as Reflected in the Fiction of the Generation of 1948," *Yad Vashem Studies* 30 (2002): 368.

18 Hanoch Bartov, "The Wicked Slander about Our Indifference to the Holocaust," in *I Am Not the Mythological Sabra* (Hebrew) (Tel Aviv, 1995), 26–36.

19 Ben-Ami Feingold, *The Theme of the Holocaust in Hebrew Drama* (Tel Aviv, 2012).

20 Oz Almog, *The Sabra – A Profile* (Hebrew) (Tel Aviv, 1997), 14n7.

21 Fifty-three per cent of immigrants from Europe were between the ages of 15 and 44.

22 Gali Drucker Bar-Am, "The Holy Tongue and the Tongue of the Martyrs: The Eichmann Trial as Reflected in *Letste Nayes*," *Dapim: Studies on the Holocaust* 28 (2014): 20, 21–2.

23 Gali Drucker Bar-Am, *"Am I your Dust"? Representations of the Israeli Experience in Yiddish Prose in Israel, 1948–1968* (PhD diss., Hebrew University of Jerusalem, 2013), 174–85.

24 Laura Jockusch, *"Kurban Forshung*: Jewish Historical Commissions in Europe 1943–1949," *Simon Dubnow Institute Year Book* 6 (2007): 441–73; Boaz Cohen, "Holocaust Survivors and the Genesis of Holocaust Research," in Johannes-Steinert Dieter and Weber-Newth Inge, eds., *Beyond Camps and Forced Labour: Current International Research on Survivors of Nazi Persecution* (Osnabrück, 2005), 290–300.

25 Meir Dworzecki, *Bein Ha'btarim* [Between the Parts] (Jerusalem, 1956), 79.

26 Nathan Eck, "Bring Relief to the Soul of the Generation" (Hebrew), *Dapim la-Heker ha-Shoaveha-Mered* 1 (1951): 203–4.

27 Ibid.

28 David Lazar, "What Did You Do at Yad Vashem?" (Hebrew), *Maariv*, 9 May 1958.

29 Boaz Cohen, "The Birth Pangs of Holocaust Research in Israel," *Yad Vashem Studies* 33 (2005): 203–43.

30 Hebrew University in Jerusalem Archives (HUJA), 1954/8, Nathan Eck, "Testimony before the Permanent Committee," 17 July 1958.

31 Yad Vashem Archives (YVA), AM1/364, "Yad Vashem Loyalists to Members of Yad Vashem Council," 17 June 1958.

32 YVA, AM2, Dinur, Meeting of the Yad Vashem Directorate, 22 May 1958. Melkman (director of Yad Vashem, a survivor from the Netherlands) maintained that it was a "defamation campaign in the media ... organized by Auerbach."

33 YVA, AM2, Meeting of the Yad Vashem Directorate, 22 May 1958.

34 Boaz Cohen, "Rachel Auerbach, Yad Vashem and Israeli Holocaust Memory," *Polin: Studies in Polish Jewry* 20 (2008): 121–97.

35 Rachel Auerbach, "What Is the Struggle in Yad Vashem All About," (Hebrew) *Davar*, 7 October 1958.

36 Rachel Auerbach, "Yizkor Books: A Grassroots Movement" (Hebrew) *Davar*, 4 April 1958; Rachel Auerbach, "Sifrei zikaron" (Hebrew), *Davar*, 12 January 1958.

37 YVA, P16/41, Rachel Auerbach, "Lecture Highlights for the Eliyahu Club, Haifa," 24 June 1960.

38 YVA, P16/41, Rachel Auerbach, "Witnesses and Testimony in the Eichmann Trial," 45–54.

39 Ibid.

40 Auerbach, "Lecture Highlights."

41 Ibid.

42 Rachel Auerbach, "Testimonies: Follow-ups to Yad Vashem's Activities" (Hebrew) *Davar*, 4 November 1955.

43 Ibid.

44 Auerbach, "Witnesses and Testimony."

45 Ibid.

8 The Eichmann Trial and the Relations between the Federal Republic of Germany and Israel: A Positive or Negative Influence?

DOMINIQUE TRIMBUR

When Adolf Eichmann was kidnapped and put on trial, the Federal Republic of Germany (FRG) and Israel had no diplomatic relations with each other, despite having close contacts since the 1952 reparations agreement.[1] The announcement of the abduction of the former SS (Schutzstaffel) officer, on 23 May 1960, took place only a few months after a series of antisemitic incidents across West Germany and a short time after the first and very promising encounter between Chancellor Konrad Adenauer and Prime Minister David Ben-Gurion. The trial's searing revelations of a very recent past in which the actors were still alive and active – some in positions close to the German chancellor – threatened to endanger the pragmatic and delicate relationship between Israel and the FRG.

How did the Eichmann trial influence German-Israeli relations at the official level and within each society? Did its impact change over the years? Did the trial constitute a halt, a step backwards, or a step forwards in the rapprochement between the two countries?

Before the Trial

At the beginning of 1960, the context of German-Israeli relations was tense and quiet. On one side were the antisemitic incidents in Cologne and elsewhere;[2] on the other was the first encounter between Adenauer and Ben-Gurion in New York on 12 March 1960,[3] a meeting which revitalized the rapprochement initiated by the famous reparations agreement.[4] The news of Eichmann's kidnapping was a surprise for the FRG. In an awkward coincidence, Theodor Heuss, the former president of the Federal Republic, found himself on a private journey to Israel just as the news was announced.[5] Yet, some people in Bonn may have known about the possibility of Eichmann's capture.[6] The reaction of the West

German Foreign Office (the Auswärtiges Amt) is surprising. The relevant people in the legal section of the Foreign Office considered the idea of extraditing Eichmann from Israel to West Germany just one day after the announcement of the kidnapping. The resulting report enumerates the obstacles that could hinder such a procedure: no diplomatic relations with Israel, no extradition agreement between the two countries, and no hope for the success of such a request. Moreover, the FRG was not willing to request an extradition.[7]

The Federal Republic opposed Eichmann's extradition to its own territory or to a country in Eastern Europe. The latter possibility arose when the Polish government contemplated such a move. In the context of the Cold War, many assumed that a trial in Warsaw would be used against the FRG and key West German figures.[8] The Foreign Office wanted to avoid any risk of the kind and felt that if an extradition of Eichmann was to be permitted by Israel (for instance, to Argentina), the FRG should get priority ranking on the list of countries to which he would be sent; Bonn could then promote the conclusion of an extradition agreement between the two countries.[9]

The Foreign Office also considered its responsibility for Eichmann's legal counsel. Should it engage to his benefit the services of the Zentrale Rechtsschutzstelle (ZRS), an agency within the Foreign Office that helped West German citizens prosecuted abroad?[10] Should the Federal Republic designate a West German counsel to defend Eichmann? And if it did, what were the risks of defending a former Nazi criminal? The Foreign Office continued to worry when Cologne lawyer Robert Servatius offered to serve as Eichmann's lawyer. The Foreign Office anxiously awaited the Israeli answer: if it accepted the proposal, everything would be fine; if not, the German Democratic Republic (GDR) might propose a lawyer, risking harm to Bonn's position.[11] Fortunately, Israel and Eichmann's family accepted the appointment of Servatius. However, the FRG refused to cover the costs of the defence.[12] Afterwards, Bonn once again had to address the extradition topic. Servatius requested extradition, invoking ZRS procedures and the lack of diplomatic relations: according to him, the FRG could not cooperate with the Israeli judiciary, the latter being in no legal position to prosecute Eichmann.[13] The legal section of the Foreign Office rejected Servatius' request, based on an agreement between West Germany and Israel, signed on 13 July 1957, which provided legal assistance to West German citizens prosecuted by the Israeli judiciary.[14] The FRG's refusal to extradite Eichmann was based not only on a legal technicality but also a strong desire to not revoke the Nazi memory in what many West Germans felt was a "mastered past." The FRG was not willing to have a trial on its soil, for, according to Chancellor Adenauer, "old matters" and suffering would be remembered. Fearing it would lead to turmoil – especially after having reached a degree of political and economic stability – the FRG firmly opposed Eichmann's extradition.

The end of the matter is well known: to the detriment of Servatius, the extradition never took place. This procedure would have saved Eichmann's life (for there was no death penalty in West Germany, unlike in Israel) according to Eugen Gerstenmaier, then the Christian Democrat head of the Bundestag, and a politically engaged Protestant who was close to the 20 July Plot circles.[15]

The West German authorities considered their options in how to respond to Eichmann's capture. The general atmosphere was one of detachment as well as resignation: Bonn was used to attacks, notably those directed against Hans Globke, the closest associate of Chancellor Adenauer. Since the mid-1950s, Globke was regularly denounced for having held a high position within the Third Reich's inner ministry, specifically dealing with anti-Jewish legislation.[16] Regardless of these attacks, the protocols of West German government meetings show that the Eichmann topic was hardly discussed by the cabinet.[17]

The impression of calmness on the West German side does not mean that nothing was done.[18] In the months devoted to the preparation of the trial, Bonn installed what can be characterized as a public relations campaign, using every possible and available means to promote the FRG's image throughout the world. This campaign was a standard feature of German-Israeli relations,[19] and became more necessary because of the antisemitic episodes and the potential for unpleasant disclosures during the trial – a trial that might underline silences, continuities,[20] or even complacence linked to the persistence of what Raphael Gross has called the "Nazi morale."[21] West Germany was particularly concerned with its image in the United States and Israel.

Adenauer was personally invested in West Germany's reputation in the United States, and he visited Washington at the beginning of the trial. The image of a federal Germany addressing its past was then indispensable for Adenauer, the same way it had been during the spring of 1953 when he had moved forward the ratification process of the reparations agreement before his official journey to the United States.[22] Other prominent Germans considered making similar trips, including Willy Brandt, the Social Democrat mayor of Berlin, who was willing to demonstrate that Germany was mastering its past,[23] and Hendrik van Dam, general secretary of the Central Council of Jews in Germany, the representative body of the small but very symbolic Jewish community in the FRG.

Regarding Israel, Bonn feared the worst based on several difficult moments that had affected German-Israeli relations in recent years.[24] Taking this into consideration, Bonn acted cautiously; for instance, it ordered that trips to Israel by West German figures be avoided for the duration of the trial, to avoid the animosity of a sensitive Israeli population.[25] In contrast to the mistrust of the Israeli population, leading Israeli politicians had a benevolent attitude toward West Germany. Prime Minister Ben-Gurion had regularly expressed his own faith in the "new Germany" as embodied by Adenauer.[26] As well, the head of the Israeli mission in Cologne,[27] Felix Shinnar, often repeated that nothing would happen to harm the FRG: the Eichmann trial would deal with the Third Reich and nothing else.[28]

In connection to its public relations campaign, Bonn made material available to discourage suspicions that the FRG had not done enough to punish war criminals on its soil.[29] The Federal Press Office provided the West German diplomatic representations throughout the world and other bodies with a range of documentation.[30] By establishing this inventory, the FRG showed that its preoccupation was not the trial itself; rather it was concerned with the ways that Eastern European countries might use the trial to tarnish its reputation. As the tenth anniversary of the reparations agreement drew near, the FRG showcased its achievements benefiting the Jews and Israel, and set itself in contrast to the GDR. Social Democrat parliamentarian Fritz Erler emphasized in January 1961 the importance of demonstrating that the "new," "other" Germany was not merely a façade.[31] In the same way, in April 1961, Gerstenmaier drew attention to the absence of antisemitic campaigns in West Germany following the decision to prosecute Eichmann.[32]

Prior to the trial, relations between Israeli and West German authorities were harmonious, to say the least, and West Germany was willing to provide archival documentation to strengthen the file against Eichmann.[33] Shinnar in Cologne/Bonn was the man in charge of the coordination of efforts, being the contact person between both governments. Ben-Gurion asked state prosecutor Gideon Hausner, in charge of the indictment against Eichmann, to avoid any mention during the trial of the activities of former Nazis appointed to West German governing bodies,[34] and to focus the proceedings on Nazi Germany, not Germany generally speaking.[35] Menachem Begin of the Herut party denounced this decision in a logical continuity of his hostility to any rapprochement between Bonn and Tel Aviv.[36] On the eve of the trial, Adenauer made a televised declaration in which he called on viewers not to conflate Eichmann with all Germans, and he expressed confidence that the trial would result in justice.

During the Trial

In concrete terms, what did the FRG do during the trial? Lacking diplomatic relations with Israel, the FRG had no local representatives on hand to attend the trial and report on the debates. Instead it sent a West German delegation to Israel for the duration of the trial.[37] This idea was supported by Julius Klein, an American Jewish lobbyist based in Chicago, and a promoter of German-Israeli rapprochement.[38] In an early 1961 memo to Adenauer, Foreign Minister von Brentano, and Globke, Klein nominated Franz Böhm as head of the delegation. Böhm, a Christian Democrat parliamentarian, had led the West German delegation during the reparations agreement negotiations in 1952. He was a figure above all suspicion, and seen as particularly benevolent toward Israel. Klein argued that Böhm would use this position to prevent any damage to the FRG by countering Eastern European activities.[39]

Simultaneously, the Foreign Office considered the idea of sending a delegation. In a context deeply marked by the severe competition between both Germanys – on the eve of the building of the Berlin Wall – the Foreign Office noted a potential legal obstacle: if it sent a delegation, the GDR might respond in kind, which would require the application of the Hallstein Doctrine. If Israel recognized the GDR delegation, the FRG (which denied the legal existence of the GDR) would have to break off ties to Israel.[40] This move also raised a political obstacle: sending such a mission ran the risk of being asked about Bonn's motivations in the matter.

Nevertheless, the delegation was sent, under the strict control of the political division of the Foreign Office. Ordered to refrain from any political statements, the mission was indeed no diplomatic representation. It was established under the chairmanship of Gerhard von Preuschen, a lawyer from the same *Bundesland* as Fritz Bauer – the prosecutor whose investigations had assisted in Eichmann's capture.[41] Having been part of the July Plot against Hitler and having been jailed for that reason, von Preuschen was furthermore a personal friend of Foreign Minister Brentano.[42] Assisting him in his task[43] were a representative of the Federal Press Office, Hans Stercken; a historian, Wolfgang Scheffler, the author of a study on Nazi antisemitic policy that just had been published in the FRG;[44] and finally *Deutsche Zeitung* journalist Rolf Vogel, who was a promoter of German-Israeli relations, a "half Jew," and a close friend of Adenauer.[45] In addition, prosecutor Dietrich Zeug was sent to Jerusalem in order to represent the Ludwigsburg Zentrale Stelle, the central bureau collecting the information for future trials against Nazi criminals.

The delegation's main role was to report on the trial; it was above all interested in any comments about the "other Germany" during the Third Reich. For instance, the delegation highlighted discussion of the German diplomat Georg-Ferdinand Duckwitz in Copenhagen; he had contributed to the rescue of the Danish Jews in 1943, shortly before a roundup that would have meant their deportation and extermination.[46] The delegation also noted mention of Pastor Heinrich Grüber, whose rescue activity for converted Jews provided the opportunity to highlight German rescuers at this key moment.[47]

One of the delegation's tasks was to gather information to use against former Nazi criminals in Germany.[48] It also aimed to collect information of a more general kind. Coded telegrams communicated back to Bonn[49] relayed the Israeli mood, which was more German-friendly than previously feared. At the climax of the trial the delegation even considered a visit to Israel by West German president Karl Heinrich Lübke, even if such a trip had been discouraged shortly before.[50] From time to time the delegation noted that former German Jews who had settled in Israel felt a kind of "*Hassliebe*" toward their former homeland.[51] The delegation wanted to cultivate goodwill toward West Germany, and emphasize the difference between West Germany and Nazi Germany by making direct contacts with high Israeli officials, mostly diplomats,[52] or with the local press whose sensitivity regarding German topics became well known to the West German delegates. Through a public relations campaign directed at the Israelis, the delegation aimed to maintain a good climate toward the FRG during the trial, in contrast with the campaign operating at the same time by the GDR. As the first official West German group sent to Israel, the delegation presented the possibility of collecting first-hand information on the country: beyond information linked to the trial, the telegrams sent from Jerusalem contained many details on day-to-day life in Israel. Furthermore, the delegation gained the opportunity to disseminate in Israel information about the FRG.

The Trial's Impact on German-Israeli Relations

On the one hand, the trial had a negative impact. FRG authorities and their Israeli counterparts perceived intense concern regarding the anti-FRG activities of Eastern European countries, specifically the GDR, aimed again and again at Staatssekretär Hans Globke.[53] These activities had some influence, underlining historical revelations or reminders about delicate issues connected with the proceedings. Many people, among them Chancellor Adenauer, wished to avoid such a situation. On 14 December 1961, during a break between the two parts of the trial,

Adenauer stated, "This Eichmann trial has heavily damaged us, even if people do not claim it loudly."[54] It was indeed a painful moment for the FRG. West German leaders secretly hoped that the Eichmann trial would preclude the need for similar trials in the future.[55] But, to the contrary, the trial was in no way an end to such reckoning; rather, it was a starting point for West German society and leaders to deal with a past that until then had not caused much disturbance.[56]

The trial affected West Germany's relations with the Jewish diaspora. For instance, American Jews remained suspicious of Germany, even if the trial was channelled by the American Zionist leader Nahum Goldmann, whose benevolence toward West Germany was well known.[57] The trial also had some negative consequences for German-Israeli relations. For instance, in the January 1962 debate about a vote in the Knesset dealing with cultural relations between the two countries, West Germany perceived the issue as a step backwards because it imposed obstacles on trips to West Germany by groups of Israeli youngsters by denying them official approval.[58]

Regarding German-Arab relations, the Arab states were disappointed at the FRG's attitude toward the trial. As confirmed by West German diplomats in those states, in the eyes of the Arabs Bonn had conceded too much during the Eichmann trial,[59] regardless of the fact that the proceedings set West Germany at a disadvantage. Arab states assumed that Israel was using the trial to exert pressure on the FRG to offer more material concessions. And, the Arab states warned, they would not allow this outcome, having already been upset by the March 1960 encounter between Adenauer and Ben-Gurion in New York.[60] According to Gilbert Achcar,[61] the Arab reception was complex: in fact, some Arab voices emphasized that the activity of certain communist countries against Eichmann and the FRG constituted a de facto acknowledgment of the State of Israel;[62] though the FRG was constrained by American pressure to act the way it did, it continued not to formally acknowledge the State of Israel, which should be put to its credit.[63]

On the other hand, the trial had a positive influence on German-Israeli relations, even as it maintained the status quo from the years before the trial: excellent de facto relations, but still no de jure relations. Regarding de facto relations, the trial provided a good opportunity for intense exchanges between the Foreign Office and the Israeli mission based in Cologne, between the West German delegation in Jerusalem and the Israeli administration, and perhaps even between the Zentrale Stelle and Yad Vashem.[64] In summer 1961 this may have been perceived as a favourable turning point in the relations between both countries, especially in terms of West Germany's attitude. Indeed it was interpreted this way by the actors themselves. Von Preuschen wrote on 22 September 1961, "The trial has led to something like a purification of the atmosphere in the relations with the Federal Republic."[65] Contemporary journalists and historians writing later offered the same interpretation.[66] In conformity with Ben-Gurion's prior commitment, nothing was said during the trial that could have harmed the image of the "new Germany," which had been a major concern for him.

Economic relations between the two countries were enhanced immediately after the first part of the Eichmann trial in August 1961. The improvement was a logical continuation of Adenauer's promise to Ben-Gurion dating back their March 1960 encounter in New York, meaning that this improvement took place before the end of the reparations agreement.[67] Furthermore, in June 1962, the two countries reached an agreement dealing with huge military deliveries benefiting Israel.[68] Immediately after the end of the trial, some high-ranking West German figures travelled to Israel for official visits, including Eugen Gerstenmaier, the Christian Democrat speaker of the Bundestag,[69] and Thomas Dehler, the former minister of justice and a Liberal politician. After leaving power, Theodor Heuss returned on a private basis in 1963,[70] as did Konrad Adenauer in 1966.[71]

Important individuals and bodies hoped that the trial would have positive impacts on de jure relations. This part of West German civil society had sought a formalization of relations following a convergence of efforts dating back the end of the 1950s. Pastor Heinrich Grüber, for instance, the only German witness at the Eichmann trial to testify against the accused, gave many speeches with that purpose,[72] as did Social Democrat politicians in the opposition.[73] Within the Christian Democratic Party, Franz Böhm also favoured a formalization of the relations to take place after the trial. The West German Jewish community supported this opinion and was willing to express itself as an integrated part of the FRG and of the diaspora, specifically in the aftermath of the antisemitic incidents in Cologne.[74] Other Jewish communities abroad expressed the wish to develop relationships with West German diplomats, signalling a new era in German-Jewish relations.[75]

The trial ushered in a new era by overcoming the obstacles that prevailed since the middle of the 1950s, and it followed regular calls for a formalization of relations, which for the time being remained on a de facto level.[76] With the presence of West German officials in Israel for the first time, the FRG government noted the possibility of transforming the West German delegation into a permanent representation. One of its members, Wolfgang Scheffler (who was present in Jerusalem during the first part of the trial), wrote a memorandum describing the type of person who could fit the position of an "official observer." Philosemitism was insufficient; the position called for an awareness of the delicate Israeli context and a deep understanding of the past.[77] The same idea was expressed by Israeli leaders. For instance, the general director of the Israeli Foreign Office, Haim Yahil, considered that the Eichmann trial created an atmosphere favourable to moving forward.[78] Nevertheless, this transition from the status of a provisional delegation to a permanent mission was rejected: beyond the classic reluctance linked to the Hallstein Doctrine, some West German diplomats like Duckwitz considered such a move disgraceful.[79] The strongest rejection stemmed from the Israelis, who did not accept an in-between, unsatisfying solution; the choice was between everything (meaning full relations) or nothing.[80] Paradoxically, Israel profited from this situation because the FRG was more helpful without diplomatic relations.[81]

Among the positive impacts of the Eichmann trial on German-Israeli relations are its effects on Holocaust consciousness. The matter is complex, and Raphael Gross[82] and Bettina Stangneth[83] have observed the awakening of this consciousness during the trial, a phenomenon which should be interpreted as the return of the *refoulé*, the past which had been until then repressed. Adenauer expressed this feeling: "The Eichmann trial has been a very bad thing; indeed, it has brought back memories. There I heard things I did not know – horrors."[84] Adenauer's statement raises the issue of German involvement in the Nazi past, or what Raphael Gross explains with his concept of the "non-guilty guilty," which allowed the majority of Germans to go on with the *refoulement*, the denial of their own involvement in the Nazi crimes.[85] In contrast to Adenauer's secret hopes and the disillusioned conclusion of Israeli philosopher Yeshayahu Leibowitz, the Eichmann trial brought the Holocaust as a topic to be reckoned with into West German society.[86] This was especially true within the West German legal system, even though the Ludwigsburg Zentrale Stelle had already been active before the Eichmann trial:[87] during the following years the Auschwitz trials took place,[88] as well as debates on the federal indemnification law and its developments, and the renewal of the debate regarding the statutory limitation on Nazi crimes.[89] From the trial onwards, new interrogations were carried out regarding the involvement of particular institutions in Nazi crimes and the continued presence of individuals associated with the Nazi regime in the current West German civil service.[90] Reflections within West German society also took place. For instance, Grüber launched a pro-Israel association in October 1961.[91] Rolf Hochhuth's 1963 play, *The Deputy*, was an indictment of the Catholic Church's role during the Holocaust. During the trial itself, German bishops encouraged prayers in memory of the victims, and hoped to learn lessons from what was revealed in the Jerusalem courtroom.[92]

In Israel, the Eichmann trial also marked a "before" and an "after" in society's Holocaust consciousness.[93] The head of the Israeli press office stated on 16 November 1961, "The inner confrontation with the 'Eichmann' problem has constituted, for the German people as well as for the Israeli one, a curative process."[94] According to Teddy Kollek, then a close collaborator of Ben-Gurion, the file was closed.[95] But this very political statement was made too quickly, as shown by the evolution of the debate afterwards.[96]

Conclusion

As early as December 1960, the Foreign Office was eager to believe that the Eichmann trial would not have any impact on German-Israeli relations. This was confirmed by Golda Meir on a trip in Iceland in May 1961,[97] and by Ben-Gurion at the end of March 1961.[98] In fact, German-Israeli relations did not register any change, conserving their former status: de jure relations stalled, and de facto relations improved following the New York encounter and the development in those years of youth exchanges and city partnerships. This was indeed a victory of pragmatism over morale.[99]

Two of the great actors of German-Israeli relations – and of the Eichmann trial – retired in 1963: Ben-Gurion left power in June and Adenauer in October, for reasons of age and of domestic politics. Tensions remained between the two states. For example, the presence of German ballistic specialists in Egypt in 1962–3 was interpreted in Israel as an alliance between the Nazis of the past and the "Nazis" of the present day.[100] Tension was also apparent with the "Near East crisis" (Nahostkrise) in 1963–4, when the West German press revealed the German-Israeli military secret agreements of 1962, provoking the fury of the Arab states and indecision and panic in Bonn.[101]

Finally, diplomatic relations were established between West Germany and Israel in 1965. Some might interpret this as a "demonstration of reconciliation"[102] resulting, in part, from the Eichmann trial. It is more likely that the current political circumstances, independent of the consequences of the Eichmann trial, prevailed, and at last joined "morale" and "realpolitik."

NOTES

1 Niels Hansen, *Aus dem Schatten der Katastrophe: Die deutsch-israelischen Beziehungen in der Ära Adenauer und David Ben-Gurion; ein dokumentierter Bericht* (Düsseldorf, 2002); Yeshayahu A. Jelinek, *Deutschland und Israel 1945–1965: Ein neurotisches Verhältnis* (Munich, 2004). See also Yeshayahu A. Jelinek, ed., *Zwischen Moral und Realpolitik: Deutsch-israelische Beziehungen 1945–1965: Eine Dokumentensammlung* (Gerlingen, 1997).

2 The incidents were all the more shocking in that they began with the desecration of the synagogue in Cologne, one of the oldest Jewish communities in Germany. In September 1959, twenty-one years after the destruction of the original synagogue during the Reichskristallnacht, a new one was inaugurated in the presence of Konrad Adenauer, then federal chancellor and the former mayor of the city.

3 Yeshayahu Jelinek and Rainer Blasius, "Ben-Gurion und Adenauer im Waldorf Astoria- Gesprächsaufzeichnungen vom israelisch-deutschen Gipfeltreffen in New York am 14. März 1960," *Vierteljahrshefte für Zeitgeschichte* 45 (1997): 309–44.

4 Yaakov Sharett, ed., *The Reparations Controversy: The Jewish State and German Money in the Shadow of the Holocaust, 1951–1952* (Berlin and Boston, 2011).

5 Jelinek, *Deutschland und Israel 1945–1965*, 340.

6 The fiftieth anniversary of the trial has led to several revelations or reminders, including the fact that the West German authorities more or less knew about the fate and location of Adolf Eichmann before his abduction. See "Deutscher Geheimdienst kannte Eichmann-Versteck schon 1952," *Der Spiegel*, 8 January 2011; Klaus Wiegrefe, "Triumph der Gerechtigkeit," *Der Spiegel*, 28 March 2011; "Der Fluch der bösen Tat," *Der Spiegel*, 11 April 2011.

7 Archives of the (West) German Foreign Ministry, Berlin (hereafter PA/ AA): files of the Law Department, (Abteilung V, L4), Note (503.88 8086), 24 May 1960, Marmann; files of the Oriental Department (Ostabteilung, Abteilung VII), circular letter from the AA (503.88.80.86) to numerous representations abroad, 14 July 1960, Janz.

8 PA/AA, Abt. VII, Bd. 1038, Eichmann, confidential note (503.88.80.86), 27 April 1961, Raab.

9 Ibid.

10 PA/AA, L4, Bd. 1 Eichmann-Prozess, note (Abt V ZRS E 553/60), 29 June 1960, Raab. Also see Christina Grosse, *Der Eichmann-Prozess zwischen Recht und Politik* (Frankfurt, 1995), 50–118. Previously this agency procedure had mostly benefited war criminals. In the end, the ZRS did not provide Eichmann with juridical assistance.

11 PA/AA, L4, Bd. 1 Eichmann-Prozess, note (Abt V ZRS E 553/60), 25
    November 1960.

12 Regarding the voluminous exchange between Servatius and the West
    German authorities dealing with his own remuneration see Grosse, *Der
    Eichmann-Prozess*.

13 PA/AA, Abt. VII, Bd 1037, Eichmann, letter by Servatius to the AA, 5
    February 1961.

14 PA/AA, Abt. VII, Bd 1037, note (503.88.80.86), 3 March 1961, Janz; letter
    from to AA to Servatius, 6 March 1961, von Brentano.

15 Markus A. Weingardt, *Deutsche Israel- und Nahost-Politik: Die Geschichte
    einer Gratwanderung seit 1949* (Frankfurt, 2002), 135n236.

16 *Kabinettsprotokolle der Bundesregierung*, Bd. 14, 1961, Munich, Oldenbourg,
    2004, meeting of 18 January 1961, 65–6. Concerning Globke, see the latest
    biography that establishes, with some success, a balanced portrait of the
    figure: Erik Lommatzsch, *Hans Globke (1898–1973); Beamter im Dritten
    Reich und Staatssekretär Adenauers* (Frankfurt, 2009).

17 The published version of the protocols mention only that an observer
    was sent to the trial: *Kabinettsprotokolle der Bundesregierung*, Bd. 14, 1961,
    Munich, Oldenbourg, 2004, meeting on 22 March 1961, 134.

18 According to the Berlin lawyer Reiner Geulen, this impression is
    misleading and panic is a better description of the West German attitude.
    See Reiner Geulen, "Die Geheimhaltung der Eichmann-Akten durch den
    Bundesnachrichtendienst," *Recht und Politik – Vierteljahreshefte für Rechts-
    und Verwaltungspolitik* (2011): 171–6; Reiner Geulen, "Eichmann-Prozess
    löste Panik in Adenauers Regierung aus," *Der Spiegel*, 27 March 2011. The
    author does not mention his sources in support of this assertion.

19 While negotiating the reparations agreement, and after its conclusion,
    the FRG did much to improve its image, foregrounding its own
    accomplishments and setting itself in contrast with the Third Reich.

20 Norbert Frei, ed., *Hitlers Eliten nach 1945* (Munich, 2003).

21 Raphael Gross, "Zum Fortwirken der NS-Moral: Adolf Eichmann und die
    deutsche Gesellschaft," in Raphael Gross and Yfaat Weiss, eds., *Jüdische
    Geschichte als allgemeine Geschichte. Festschrift für Dan Diner zum 60.
    Geburtstag* (Göttingen, 2006), 212–34; Raphael Gross, *Anständig geblieben:
    Nationalsozialistische Moral* (Frankfurt, 2010).

22 The parliament took some time to ratify the September 1952 agreement,
    especially due to objections emanating from the ranks of Adenauer's majority
    government (the CDU and above all the CSU). After facilitating the relaunch
    of stalled negotiations in April–May 1952, Adenauer again expedited the
    ratification of the agreement in March 1953. Thus, when he departed shortly
    afterwards to the United States he had this "certificate of good behaviour" in
    his pocket, a useful tool for improving the image of Germany. See Dominique

Trimbur, "American Influence on the Federal Republic of Germany's Israel Policy, 1951–1956," in Haim Goren, ed., *Germany and the Middle East, Past, Present, and Future* (Jerusalem, 2003), 263–89.

23 A trip was contemplated for spring 1960 but never took place. The prospective trip was intended to combine the efforts by Brandt and Adenauer to improve the image of West Germany; later this cooperation did take place, with Brandt's journey to the US in March 1961, just weeks before Adenauer's trip. See Judith Michel, *Willy Brandts Amerikabild und -politik 1933–1992* (Göttingen, 2010), 141–8.

24 German-Israeli relations have been paved with periods of crisis: in 1952 around the negotiations for the reparations agreement, in 1957 and 1959 around military deliveries, and in 1959–60 around the antisemitic incidents in Cologne.

25 PA/AA, L4, Bd. 1 Eichmann-Prozess, letter from the West German embassy in Nicosia (433/60) to the AA, 7 December 1960, Koenig.

26 Ben-Gurion, along with Moshe Sharett, made these statements to justify his own rapprochement policy toward West Germany. See Dominique Trimbur, *De la Shoah à la réconciliation? – La question des relations RFA/Israël (1949–1956)* (Paris, 2000); Roni Stauber, "Realpolitik and the Burden of the Past: Israeli Diplomacy and the 'Other Germany,'" *Israel Studies* 8 (2003): 100–122; Yechiam Weitz, "Ben-Gurions Weg zum 'Anderen Deutschland' 1952–1963," *Vierteljahrshefte für Zeitgeschichte* 48 (2000): 255–79; Lily Gardner Feldman, *Germany's Foreign Policy of Reconciliation: From Enmity to Amity* (Lanham, 2012), 133–200.

27 This was an Israeli purchasing mission based in Cologne established to negotiate with the West German authorities according to the clauses of the reparations agreement; this delegation quickly became an unofficial Israeli representation with consular competence, and it was expected to end with the expiration of the agreement.

28 PA/AA, L4, Bd. 1 Eichmann-Prozess, note (503.88.80.86), 5 January 1961, Janz.

29 PA/AA, L4, Bd. 1 Eichmann-Prozess, note by the press section of the AA, 20 January 1961, Hille. Regarding the slow start to Nazi war criminal trials in the FRG, see Annette Weinke, *Eine Gesellschaft ermittelt gegen sich selbst – Die Geschichte der Zentralen Stelle Ludwigsburg 1958–2008* (Darmstadt, 2008). The permeation of the West German justice system by judges who had served in the Third Reich is well known, as is the similar process in the criminal police system, which was supposed to investigate and deliver to justice people involved in such crimes. See Bundeskriminalamt, ed., *Das Bundeskriminalamt stellt seiner Geschichte* (Cologne, 2008).

30 PA/AA, L4, Bd. 1 Eichmann-Prozess, circular letter (200.80.03 508/61), 3 March 1961, von Brentano: Informationsmappe zum Eichmann-Prozeß.

31 Archives of the German Social Democracy, Friedrich Ebert Stiftung, Bonn, private papers of F. Erler, Bd. 17, RIAS, 24 January 1961, "MdB F. Erler: Über seine Eindrücke in Israel."

32 Archives of the German Christian Democracy, Konrad Adenauer Stiftung, Bonn, private papers of E. Gerstenmaier, Bd. 085/3, *Bulletin*, Nr 66, 8 April 1961, 635, "Zum Eichmann-Prozeß-Ein Interview mit dem Präsidenten des Deutschen Bundestags," ABC.

33 PA/AA, L4, Bd. 1 Eichmann-Prozess, note by the press section of the AA, 20 January 1961, Hille.

34 Yechiam Weitz, "The Founding Father and the War Criminal's Trial: Ben-Gurion and the Eichmann Trial," *Yad Vashem Studies* 36 (2008): 211–52.

35 Willi Winkler, "Adolf Eichmann und seine Verteidiger – Ein kleiner Nachtrag zur Rechtsgeschichte," *Einsicht 05 – Bulletin des Fritz Bauer Instituts*, special issue *Adolf Eichmann vor Gericht – Der Prozess in Jerusalem* (2011): 38–40. According to Hausner, even though Globke's past was known, no document existed to establish a link to Eichmann or to lead to an accusation against him. See Gideon Hausner, *Justice in Jerusalem – The Trial of Adolf Eichmann* (London, 1967), 466. During the examination for discovery conducted by Avner Less, Eichmann told the policeman that he had never heard of Globke. See Avner Werner Less and Bettina Stangneth, *Lüge! Alles Lüge – Aufzeichnungen des Eichmann-Verhörers* (Zurich, 2012), 169–70. According to some authors, the German-Israeli entente also dealt with the Israeli refusal to let East German lawyer Friedrich-Karl Kaul argue against Eichmann on behalf of civil parties located in the GDR. This decision, understood by these authors as the result of West German pressure and as a break with procedure, in fact illustrates for the most part a legal prescription, one that excluded civil parties in a procedure which could end in the death penalty and maintained Jerusalem's wish to preserve the monopoly over accusations against Eichmann. See Geulen, "Die Geheimhaltung der Eichmann-Akten"; Hausner, *Justice in Jerusalem*.

36 "Will the People Come to Thoughts on a Turnaround?" *Herut*, 15 March 1961.

37 Dominique Trimbur, "Eine deutsche Präsenz in Israel – Die bundesdeutsche Beobachtermission anlässlich des Eichmann-Prozesses in Jerusalem," in José Brunner, ed., *Deutsche(s) in Palästina und Israel: Alltag, Kultur, Politik. Tel Aviver Jahrbuch für deutsche Geschichte* 41 (Göttingen, 2013): 229–52.

38 Julius Klein was head of a public relations company hired by West Germany (commercial companies and the state) to improve the image of the FRG in the United States. See Shlomo Shafir, *Ambiguous Relations: The American Jewish Community and Germany since 1945* (Detroit, 1999), 186–8; Lommatzsch, *Hans Globke*, 184–5; S. Jonathan Wiesen, "Germany's PR Man: Julius Klein and the Making of Transatlantic Memory," in Philipp Gassert

and Alan E. Steinweis, eds., *Coping with the Nazi Past: West German Debates on Nazism and Generational Conflict, 1955–1975* (New York, 2006), 294–308.

39 PA/AA, archives of the minister's office, Bd. 147 Julius Klein Public Relations Sammlung, "Confidential Memo" addressed by Klein to Adenauer, von Brentano, and Globke, no date (beginning of 1961). On Franz Böhm see Niels Hansen, *Franz Böhm mit Ricarda Huch: Zwei wahre Patrioten* (Düsseldorf, 2009).

40 PA/AA, Abt. VII, Bd. 1037 Eichmann, document (503.88.80.86), 12 January 1961, Marmann. The 1955 Hallstein Doctrine was a regulation within the West German Foreign Ministry, named after its then state secretary Walter Hallstein. It stipulated that the FRG should break off any relations with states that established diplomatic relations with the GDR because their doing so represented an official recognition of the other Germany, the existence of which Bonn denied.

41 Irmtrud Wojak, *Fritz Bauer: 1903–1968; eine Biographie* (Munich, 2009); Ronen Steinke, *Fritz Bauer, oder Auschwitz vor Gericht* (Munich, 2013).

42 Christina Grosse elaborates on von Preuschen's designation, personality, and profile. See Grosse, *Der Eichmann-Prozess.*

43 As well as those of a coordinating body of the West German efforts, established shortly before in Bonn. See Grosse, *Der Eichmann-Prozess.*

44 Wolfgang Scheffler, *Die nationalsozialistische Judenpolitik: Unterlagen für den Unterricht in Politik und Zeitgeschichte* (Berlin, 1960).

45 In connection with the fiftieth anniversary of the Eichmann trial, the weekly publication *Der Spiegel* revealed that, under the cover of his activities as a journalist, Vogel was sent by the West German intelligence service (the BND) to search East German lawyer Friedrich-Karl Kaul's hotel room in order to seize any documents that would be compromising for West German figures, including Globke. Klaus Wiegrefe, "Aktenklau für die Adenauer-Republik," *Der Spiegel*, 2 September 2010. Vogel is well known for his pro-Israel activities in the FRG, illustrated by collections of documents regarding the West German–Israeli rapprochement. See *Deutschlands Weg nach Israel: Eine Dokumentation* (Stuttgart, 1967); *Der deutsch-israelische Dialog: Dokumentation eines erregenden Kapitels deutscher Aussenpolitik*, 8 vols. (Munich, 1987–90).

46 PA/AA, Abt. VII, Bd. 1038 Eichmann, telegram from the West German delegation in Jerusalem (137) to the AA, 10 May 1961, von Preuschen. For more on Duckwitz, see *Georg Ferdinand Duckwitz in Dänemark: 1943–1945* (Bonn, 1992); Leni Yahil, *The Rescue of Danish Jewry: Test of a Democracy* (Philadelphia, 1969). In recognition of his rescue activities, Duckwitz was honoured as "Righteous among the Nations" by Yad Vashem in 1971. See Arno Lustiger, *Rettungswiderstand: Über die Judenretter in Europa während der NS-Zeit* (Göttingen, 2011), 250, 254.

47 Grüber was one of the first Germans to be honoured as "Righteous among the Nations" in 1964. See Lustiger, *Rettungswiderstand*, 41.

48 The representative of the Zentrale Stelle realized that the Israelis had fewer documents than the Germans, as well as insufficient knowledge of the Nazi apparatus, and that therefore they were not well prepared for the trial. See Ruth Bettina Birn, "Staatsanwalt Zeug in Jerusalem – Zum Kenntnisstand der Anklagebehörde im Eichmann-Prozess und der Strafverfolgungsbehörden der Bundesrepublik," *Einsicht 05 – Bulletin des Fritz Bauer Instituts* (2011): 26–32; a revised version of this paper has been published in Werner Renz, ed., *Interessen um Eichmann – Israelische Justiz, deutsche Strafverfolgung und alte Kameradschaften* (Frankfurt, 2012), 93–117.

49 Grosse, *Der Eichmann-Prozess*.

50 PA/AA, Abt. VII, Bd. 1038 Eichmann, telegram from the West German delegation in Jerusalem (308) to the AA, 5 July 1961, von Preuschen, with extracts from *Ma'ariv*, July 5, 1961.

51 PA/AA, Abt. VII, Bd. 1039 Eichmann, note (ZRS Isr b 689/61), 22 September 1961, Gawlik.

52 Specifically Haim Yahil, general director of the Israeli Foreign Ministry. See PA/AA, Abt. VII, Bd. 1039 Eichmann, note [ZRS Isr b 689/61], 22 September 1961, Gawlik. Haim Hoffmann (later Yahil) had previously been a member of the Israeli representations in the West German territory – the Munich consulate accredited to the occupying powers and the Cologne Israeli mission. A pragmatic man, and a friend of Ben-Gurion, he remained close to his German cultural world. His wife, Leni Yahil, was an Israeli historian; while her husband was stationed as Israeli ambassador to Copenhagen, she became well acquainted with the issue of the rescue of Danish Jews during the Shoah. See note 46 above.

53 PA/AA, L4, Bd. 2 Eichmann-Prozess, telegram from the West German delegation in Jerusalem (288) to the AA, 28 June 1961, von Preuschen. The incredible affair involving the documents stolen from the East German lawyer in Jerusalem shows the trial in light of confrontation between both Germanys. The intensity of East German attacks was easily countered by the FRG since the GDR never undertook any kind of indemnification process with the Jews and remained very aggressive toward the State of Israel. Regarding the attacks against Globke, see the report published by Kaul once he was back in East Berlin: Friedrich-Karl Kaul, *Der Fall Eichmann* (Berlin [GDR], 1963). For more information on the attacks on Globke, see Ausschuss für deutsche Einheit, ed., *Globke und die Ausrottung der Juden – über die verbrecherische Vergangenheit des Staatssekretärs im Amt des Bundeskanzlers Adenauer* (Berlin [GDR], 1960). About the East German campaigns against Bonn, see Michael Lemke, "Kampagnen gegen Bonn: Die Systemkrise der DDR und die West-Propaganda der

SED. 1960 – 1963," *Vierteljahrshefte für Zeitgeschichte* 41 (1993): 153–74; Annette Leo, "Eichmann, Globke und die DDR," in *"Das hat's bei uns nicht gegeben!" – Antisemitismus in der DDR – Das Buch zur Ausstellung der Amadeu Antonio Siftung* (Berlin, 2010), 20–30; Henry Leide, *NS-Verbrecher und Staatssicherheit: Die geheime Vergangenheitspolitik der DDR* (Göttingen, 2005), 80.

54 Hans-Peter Mensing, ed., *Teegespräche 1961–1963* (Berlin, 1992), 48 (entry of 14 December 1961), 117 (similar wording on 20 February 1962).

55 *Akten zur Außenpolitik der Bundesrepublik Deutschland 1963*, Munich, Oldenbourg, 1994, Bd. 1, document Nr 182, meeting between Chancellor Adenauer and the head of the Israeli mission, Shinnar (StS 1267/63 secret), 28 May 1963, 593–6.

56 Norbert Frei, *Vergangenheitspolitik: die Anfänge der Bundesrepublik und die NS-Vergangenheit* (Munich, 1996).

57 Shafir, *Ambiguous Relations*, 219–37; Shlomo Shafir, "Nahum Goldmann and Germany after World War II," in Mark A. Raider, ed., *Nahum Goldmann: Statesman without a State* (Albany, 2009), 207–31; Ronald W. Zweig, "'Reparations made me': Nahum Goldmann, German Reparations and the Jewish World," in Raider, *Nahum Goldmann*, 233–53.

58 Note from the Cologne Israeli mission to the AA, 5 February 1962, Shinnar, in Jelinek, *Zwischen Moral und Realpolitik*, 586–93.

59 For instance, see PA/AA, Abt. VII, Bd. 1038 Eichmann, letter from the West German embassy in Beirut (B 708.82 92.19 393/61) to the AA, 17 April 1961, Scharzmann.

60 PA/AA, Abt. VII, Bd. 1026, note (708.82.07 92.19 562/60), 16 March 1960, Northe.

61 Gilbert Achcar, *The Arabs and the Holocaust: The Arab-Israeli War of Narratives* (New York, 2010).

62 PA/AA, Abt VII, Bd. 171 Eichmann, telegram from the West German embassy in Baghdad (126) to the AA, 2 May 1961, Bargen.

63 PA/AA, Abt VII, Bd. 171 Eichmann, telegram from the West German embassy in Baghdad (90) to the AA, 12 April 1961, Bargen.

64 PA/AA, Abt. VII, Bd. 1717, telegram from the West German delegation in Jerusalem (202) to the AA, 30 May 1961, Vogel.

65 PA/AA, Abt. VII, Bd. 1039 Eichmann, document (ZRS Isr b 689/61), 22 September 1961, Gawlik. Same content in PA/AA, Abt. VII, Bd. 1038 Eichmann, document (ZRS E 553/60 A), 2 July 1962, "Der Prozeßverlauf im Eichmann Prozeß-Urteilsverkündung in der Revisioninstanz (Schlußbericht)," von Preuschen.

66 Peter Krause, *Der Eichmann-Prozess in der deutschen Presse* (Frankfurt, 2002). The Israeli journalist Haim Gouri noted that the West German journalists were among the few correspondents remaining in Jerusalem

for a long while. See Haim Gouri, *Facing the Glass Booth: The Jerusalem Trial of Adolf Eichmann* (Detroit, 2004); Jelinek, *Deutschland und Israel 1945–1965*, 335–56.

67 The improvement took place as early as June 1961, after the settlement on West German economic assistance promised by Adenauer to Ben-Gurion during their New York meeting in March 1960, which entered into force by the end of the same year. See *Akten zur Außenpolitik der Bundesrepublik Deutschland, 1965*, Munich, Oldenbourg, 1996, Bd. 1, document Nr 1, 6–8. Some authors interpret this new step in the economic relations after the first phase of the trial as a reward for Israel, which controlled the debates and protected West Germany's reputation; others propose that economic assistance was a way to exert pressure on Israel for the same purpose. See Bettina Stangneth, *Eichmann vor Jerusalem, das unbehelligte Leben eines Massenmörders* (Zurich and Hamburg, 2011), 448, 453; Geulen, *Die Geheimhaltung der Eichmann-Akten*. Nevertheless, the protocols of the meeting do not confirm what should be considered as unfounded conjecture. See Jelinek and Blasius, "Ben-Gurion und Adenauer im Waldorf Astoria." As a matter of fact, the delay between the promise and the agreement's entry into force has much more to do with the difficulty of transforming an oral commitment into an international act; all in all, and in contrast to the authors cited above, the whole affair should be seen as an act of Israeli pressure on the FRG. See State of Israel, Israel State Archives [B. Gilead, ed.], *Documents on the Foreign Policy of Israel – Volume 14 1960*, Jerusalem 1997, doc. Nr 227, letter from Ben-Gurion to Adenauer, 27 September 1960; Asher Ben-Natan, *Die Chuzpe zu leben – Stationen meines Lebens* (Düsseldorf, 2003), 136. Initially set at 500 million dollars, the settlement ran from 1961 to 1968 and amounted to 2 billion dollars.

68 *Niels Hansen*, "Geheimvorhaben 'Frank/Kol'. Zur deutsch-israelischen Rüstungszusammenarbeit 1957 bis 1965," *Historisch-politische Mitteilungen* 6 (1999): 229–64.

69 Archives of the German Christian Democracy, Konrad Adenauer Stiftung, Bonn, private papers of E. Gerstenmaier, Bd. 086/1, WDR, 24 November 1962, "Bundestagspräsident Eugen Gerstenmaier über Erfahrungen aus seiner Israelreise."

70 Federal Archive, Coblence, private papers of Th. Heuss, Bd. 62.

71 Dominique Trimbur, "Verplichtung und Pragmatismus – Adenauer und Israel," in Hanns Jürgen Küsters, ed., *Konrad Adenauer, Israel und das Judentum* (Bonn, 2004), 55–81; Hans-Peter Mensing, ed., *Adenauer – Rhöndorfer Ausgabe, Die letzten Lebensjahre 1963–1967*, Bd. II (Paderborn, 2009), 210–45.

72 Heinrich Grüber, *Erinnerungen aus sieben Jahrzehnten* (Cologne, 1968).

73 This includes political leaders such as Carlo Schmid, Erich Ollenhauer, and Jakob Altmaier, or trade union leaders like Ludwig Rosenberg, as well as intellectuals like Walter Dirks.

74 Dominique Trimbur, "L'attitude des Juifs ouest-allemands à l'égard des relations RFA-Israël 1949–1965," *Tsafon-Revue d'études juives du Nord* 42 (2001–2): 55–102; Anthony Kauders, *Unmögliche Heimat – Eine deutsch-jüdische Geschichte der Bundesrepublik* (Munich, 2007), 126–60.

75 PA/AA, Abt. VII, Bd. 1037 Eichmann, letter from the West German consulate in New York (Pr 200.80.03 121/61) to the AA, 3 February 1961, Federer.

76 In 1956 the Israelis proposed a formalization of relations with the FRG, aiming at the establishment of diplomatic relations. After some months of consultation, Bonn refused on behalf of the above-described Hallstein Doctrine: if the FRG officially acknowledged Israel, the Arab states would reply with a recognition of the GDR, which would make the division of Germany permanent and lead the FRG to break off any relations with the Arab states. Therefore Bonn suggested remaining at the level of de facto relations, a situation Tel Aviv could live with in the end. An Israeli politician later stated that military deliveries by the FRG were far more efficient at securing borders than diplomats. Each time this topic arose in the following years, the FRG claimed that it was willing to establish diplomatic relations in principle, but that the moment was not appropriate.

77 PA/AA, Abt. VII, Bd. 1020 Israel, note "Beobachtungen und Betrachtungen zu den deutsch-israelischen Beziehungen, vornehmlich zu offiziellen Kontakten zwischen deutschen und israelischen Vertretern," Berlin, 10 March 1962.

78 Jelinek, *Zwischen Moral und Realpolitik*, protocol of a meeting at the Israel Foreign Ministry, dealing with Germany, 10 February 1961, 546–8.

79 Hansen, *Aus dem Schatten der Katastrophe*, 578.

80 Jelinek, *Zwischen Moral und Realpolitik*, report by Max Varon, Israeli Foreign Ministry, West European department, to Shinnar, 25 May 1961, 566–9; report by Shinnar to Varon, 31 May 1961, 569–71; PA/AA, Abt. VII, Bd. 1020, note "dealing with the question of the relations between the Federal Republic and Israel" (708.82.00 92.19), no date or signature.

81 Jelinek, *Zwischen Moral und Realpolitik*, memo by Sh. Bendor, Foreign Ministry, head of the West European Department, to the general director, regarding the relations to the FRG, 18 July 1961, 573–5.

82 Gross, *Anständig geblieben*.

83 Stangneth, *Eichmann vor Jerusalem*.

84 *Teegespräche 1961–1963*, 146 (entry of 2 March 1963).

85 Gross, "Zum Fortwirken der NS-Moral …"

86 "I think it was a conspiracy between Adenauer and Ben-Gurion to clear
the name of the German people. In return, they paid us millions." Quoted
by Hannah Yablonka, *The State of Israel vs. Adolf Eichmann* (New York,
2004), 245.

87 Weinke, *Eine Gesellschaft*. The Zentrale Stelle was founded in 1958 as
a combination of the efforts of local *Länder* justice systems, and as a
continuation of the 1958 Ulm trial conducted against former SS men who
had perpetrated massacres in Lithuania in July 1941.

88 Marc von Miquel, *Ahnden oder amnestieren?: Westdeutsche Justiz und
Vergangenheitspolitik in den sechziger Jahren* (Göttingen, 2004).

89 After several parliamentary debates in the 1960s and the extension of
the legal statutory limitation (*Verjährung*), Nazi crimes were declared
as being not subject to a statute of limitations in 1979. See Peter Reichel,
*Vergangenheitsbewältigung in Deutschland: Die Auseinandersetzung mit der
NS-Diktatur von 1945 bis heute* (Munich, 2001), 182–98.

90 Foreign minister von Brentano, in that position until the end of 1962,
progressively put an end to the ZRS for being too complacent toward
former Nazi criminals.

91 PA/AA, Abt. VII, Bd. 2010, "Worauf wir warten-Vortrag in einer
Jugendkundgebung zur Forderung der Anerkennung des Staates
Israel durch die Bundesrepublik," Probst Grüber, sent to the AA by the
Secretary of the State at the Chancellor's Office, 31 August 1962; Heinrich
Grüber, *Zeuge pro Israel* (Berlin, 1963).

92 Dominique Trimbur, "Après la Shoah: Le rapport des chrétiens ouest-
allemands à la destruction des Juifs d'Europe, à leurs compatriotes
juifs et à l'Etat d'Israël, 1945–1965," in Bruno Béthouart and Pierre-
Yves Kirschleger, eds., *Juifs et chrétiens à travers l'histoire – Entre conflits
et filiations* (XIXème université d'été du carrefour d'histoire religieuse
contemporaine), *Les Cahiers du Littoral* 2 (2011): 135–52.

93 Idith Zerthal, "Les vagues du procès Eichmann – Le procès Eichmann
et la révélation de la Shoah," in *Israël – De Moïse aux accords d'Oslo*
(Paris, 1998), 479–85. Claude Klein even writes about an "Israeli place of
memory." Claude Klein, *Le cas Eichmann, vu de Jérusalem* (Paris, 2012), 136.

94 PA/AA, L4, Bd. 33, letter from the West German embassy in London
(ZRS e 1/61) to the AA, 16 November 1961, von Etzdorf.

95 *Akten zur Außenpolitik der Bundesrepublik Deutschland, 1962*, Munich,
Oldenbourg, 2010, Bd. 2, document Nr 218, telegram by Vogel (114-
5457/62, confidential, then in Nicosia) to the AA, 22 May 1962, 981.

96 As for Israeli society, see Idith Zertal, *Israel's Holocaust and the Politics of
Nationhood* (Cambridge, 2005).

97 PA/AA, Abt. VII, Bd. 1048, letter from the West German embassy in
Reykjavik (Pol 203.83 312/61) to the AA, 25 May 1961, Rowold.

98 PA/AA, Abt. VII, Bd. 1037 Eichmann, telegram from the West German delegation in Jerusalem (31) to the AA, 14 April 1961, Stercken, with an extract from the Israeli daily *Jedioth Achronoth*, 31 March 1961.

99 To use the dichotomy included in Jelinek's title, balancing between "morale" and "realpolitik." This observation is strengthened by the contemporary development of a far less visible aspect of German-Israeli relations – the military ones. See *Hansen*, "Geheimvorhaben 'Frank/Kol'..."

100 Consider the effort made during the Eichmann trial to establish the role played by the Grand Mufti of Jerusalem in the Holocaust by demonstrating, in vain, connections between him and Eichmann, in order to establish a straight line between the Nazi exterminatory policy against the Jews and the destructive Arab policy against Israel. See Hausner, *Justice in Jerusalem*, 345–6; David Cesarani, *Eichmann – His Life and Crimes* (London, 2005), 53–6, 255, 278.

101 Rainer A. Blasius, "Geschäftsfreundschaft statt diplomatischer Beziehungen – Zur Israel-Politik 1962–1963," in Rainer A. Blasius. ed., *Von Adenauer zu Erhard – Studien zur auswärtigen Politik der Bundesrepublik Deutschland 1963* (Munich, 1994), 154–210.

102 Hannfried von Hindenburg, *Demonstrating Reconciliation – State and Society in West German Foreign Policy toward Israel, 1952–1965* (New York, 2007).

9 The Impact of the Eichmann Trial on Relations between Israel and the Federal Republic of Germany

RONI STAUBER

In early spring 1961, Harvard political scientist Henry Kissinger met with Chancellor Konrad Adenauer during a short visit to West Germany. It was not their first meeting and there was already mutual respect between them. In early February, Kissinger, who had earned a reputation for the brilliant political analysis in his book *Nuclear Weapons and Foreign Policy*, was nominated as special adviser to the US National Security Council, his first official post in the US administration. Upon his return from Germany in early April, Kissinger composed a memorandum to President Kennedy titled "A Meeting with Chancellor Adenauer, the Psychological Aspects." It was written to prepare the young president for his upcoming meeting with the old chancellor, scheduled for mid-April in Washington, DC.[1]

The chancellor's apprehensions regarding the new Kennedy administration's policy toward the Federal Republic of Germany (FRG) were well known in Washington. Herbert Blankenhorn, a leading figure in FRG diplomacy and a close adviser to Adenauer, had written a special memorandum to the FRG foreign office "in order to investigate the possibilities of preserving whatever goodwill the Germans have in Washington."[2] Kissinger, who had nurtured contacts with Adenauer, was one of the messengers of the new administration sent to Bonn to assure the chancellor, in his mother tongue, that the new administration would not adopt a policy that countered the interests of West Germany.[3]

The FRG's concern about its image, particularly among its former opponents in the North Atlantic Treaty Organization (NATO), is pertinent to this essay, which analyses the impact of the Eichmann trial on relations between Israel and the FRG. Kissinger's memorandum explained that the German public and its leadership felt ongoing mistrust and resentment directed toward them from countries that had experienced the horrors of the war. FRG leaders feared that these sentiments could prevent them from gaining the support of Western public opinion against possible concessions to the Soviet Union that would harm FRG interests.[4]

Collective Memories and Diplomatic Considerations

West Germany's concerns regarding its negative image fifteen years after the end of the war were not baseless. For example, at the end of 1958 reports in the world press described British resentment toward Germany. The occasion was the historic visit of FRG president Theodor Heuss to London, the first made by a German head of state in fifty years, and the cool welcome that he and his delegates received: "The quietness on the pavements [as the processions clattered by] was especially noticeable. [The British] couldn't pretend to rejoice," wrote the London *Times*.[5] The British press also criticized the queen for emphasizing the German family connections of the British royal family. "Reactions to the West German President's visit have shown that to many Britons, and influential sections of the press, Germany still is in the doghouse," wrote the *New York Times*.[6] Historian A.J.P. Taylor noted that the British could not be expected to be friendly toward the Germans since many of them had served Hitler and were responsible for horrific crimes. It was, however, mainly the German press that reported intensively on the perceived cold reception. The reportage recorded and magnified any seemingly unfriendly gestures and apparent rudeness, occasionally exaggerating expressions of indifference and restraint shown by the British public during Huess' historic visit, which it interpreted as a clear sign of resentment toward Germany.[7]

Mistrust and antipathy toward the FRG, influenced by the memories and experiences of the Second World War and the Third Reich, were shared by leading Western politicians and officials. One of the most prominent of these was British prime minister Harold Macmillan. In a November 1959 memo to British foreign minister Selwyn Lloyd, Macmillan expressed concern about arming the Bundeswehr with nuclear weapons, explaining that "no-one knows at the moment, how many former ex-Nazis are employed in the [FRG] army, public administration and judiciary."[8] The shadow of the Second World War and the suffering the Germans had inflicted still hovered over Europe. Leaders of the FRG, first and foremost Adenauer, made every effort to show that the Germans had turned their backs on their Nazi heritage, and that the "new Germany" was a critical Western democratic ally in the fight against Soviet totalitarianism.

It is against this background that Kissinger's April 1961 memorandum must be considered. Significantly, he mentioned the Eichmann trial as well as William Shirer's book *The Rise and Fall of the Third Reich*. "There is a feeling that the success [the considerable public interest] of the Shirer book and the Eichmann Trial are not accidents," he wrote. "They are thought to reflect lower valuation of Germany as a nation and of German interests. Many Germans, including Adenauer, fear that we will make unwarranted (from the German point of view) concessions on the Oder-Neisse line and on Berlin."[9]

Shirer's book was published in the United States in October 1960 and immediately became a bestseller there and in Europe. Millions of copies were sold in its first year and in March 1961 it won the US National Book Award. In the FRG, however, it aroused anger and harsh criticism. The chancellor himself publicly criticized the book, while politicians and intellectuals labelled it an anti-German manifesto because it identified a supposed "German character" and Germany's unique historical path as substantial reasons for the rise of National Socialism and the horrors of the Second World War. Moreover, Shirer refused to accept the distinction made by German leaders, notably Adenauer, between the German people and the allegedly quite small group of Nazi criminals who took over Germany and committed crimes against the will of the German people. Since many people of the generation who supported Hitler still lived in Germany, Shirer, like Taylor and Macmillan, hinted that the Western world should remain cautious regarding the "German nature," and its commitment to peace and democracy.[10]

It was understandable that Shirer's book sparked concern among West German leaders. Their sensitivity about Germany's image in the West and especially in the United States should be understood in the context of the escalating inter-bloc conflict toward the end of the 1950s, particularly over the political status of the divided city of Berlin. The FRG perceived that the Western powers might be willing to reach an agreement with the Soviets over the unresolved status of that city. Toward the end of 1958 Soviet leader Nikita Khrushchev delivered an ultimatum to the Western Allies demanding that they end their presence in West Berlin within six months and that West Berlin be transformed into a demilitarized "free city." The ultimatum, which exacerbated the conflict between the Soviet Union and the Western powers, especially the United States, lasted until 1963.[11] Other major issues concerned the Germans as well, notably the Oder-Neisse line, which West Germany refused to accept as the final border between itself and Poland, and recognition of East Germany as a legitimate state. The FRG's principal goal, as part of its persistent campaign to delegitimize and completely isolate its communist neighbour, was to prevent any international recognition of the division of Germany as a permanent geopolitical fact.

Shirer's book was published at a time when the American public was becoming increasingly aware of the tensions among the superpowers. As a result, West Germany, the former enemy and current ally, returned to the focus of American and European consciousness as a country that might trigger a conflagration. Shirer reminded them, much to the dismay of West German leaders, who the Germans were and what crimes the Third Reich had committed, insinuating that they should be treated with suspicion. "The book should make clear that a good many people, even in allied states, have not forgotten," wrote *Frankfurter Allgemeine Zeitung* in early November 1960.[12] Central Intelligence Agency (CIA) "Information Reports" referred frequently to FRG leaders' angst about the country's poor image due to its Nazi past. For example, a February 1961 CIA report from Frankfurt addressed Adenauer's misgivings about the appointment of Edward Murrow, the well-known, highly respected American broadcaster, as head of the United States Information Agency. Adenauer may have known that Murrow and Shirer were old acquaintances. It was Murrow who had recruited Shirer as a CBS radio broadcaster based in Vienna and Berlin in the late 1930s and early 1940s, during which time Shirer made a name for himself as an outstanding correspondent. "Chancellor Konrad Adenauer is very upset by this appointment …West German worries concerning the new American administration which had been largely dispelled, are now growing again … since he [Adenauer] believes that Murrow is anti-German and makes no distinction between Nazis and Germans," wrote the CIA correspondent from Frankfurt.[13]

The Eichmann Trial, the International Arena, and Israeli-German Relations

News of the capture of Adolf Eichmann and the upcoming trial constituted an additional component in this mix of collective memories, historiography, and diplomatic considerations, adding to West German concerns. Mention of the trial in Kissinger's report to President Kennedy was only one example of references to the case that can be found in US diplomatic documents concerning the FRG, as well as in CIA intelligence documents released a decade ago under the Nazi War Crimes Disclosure Act. They illustrate the considerable diplomatic interest that the trial aroused in the international arena. One of the most comprehensive reports on possible implications of the Eichmann trial was composed by the Yale history professor Sherman Kent, also head of the CIA's Office of National Estimates, and one of the most respected CIA analysts. Like Kissinger, Kent emphasized the linkage between the success of Shirer's book and deep German concern about the Eichmann trial. Kent wrote, "The West Germans have followed the Eichmann case development and the impending trial with growing apprehension, sometimes bordering on hysteria. The unarticulated though widely-held concern among Germans is that Eichmann's revelations might implicate West Germans now prominent in business, cultural, political and above all governmental life. They are concerned that the publicity resulted from the trial will give new impetus to what they regard as an already existing anti-German trend, both popular and official in the Western world, particularly in the US and UK."[14] Indeed, the first and last sessions of the trial, in particular, were widely covered by the world media. Before the trial, major newspapers published articles on the abduction and Israeli preparations for the hearings, and speculated about the imminent proceedings. Hundreds of journalists from around the world came to Israel to cover the trial. Footage documenting the trial was broadcast by major television networks in the United States and in Europe, including Germany, France, and Britain.[15]

This begs the question as to whether Israeli policy-makers, notably Prime Minister David Ben-Gurion, foresaw the international reverberations of the trial and their possible impact on Israel's international standing, particularly with regard to its gradual rapprochement with the FRG. The minutes of Israeli government meetings held immediately after Eichmann's abduction, as well as documents from the Israeli and German foreign ministries, provide an unequivocal answer to this question. These documents show that the Israeli prime minister and officials in the Foreign Ministry discussed the impact the trial might have on the international arena, particularly in regard to relations with West Germany, and considered how to use the trial to strengthen international support for Israel's security and prosperity.

Ben-Gurion's decision to uncover the entire story of the Final Solution and the Jewish tragedy through the trial of Adolf Eichmann marked a significant change in his attitude toward commemoration of the Holocaust. In previous studies I have demonstrated that, during the state's formative years, Ben-Gurion did not favour the idea of extensive commemoration of the horrors of the Holocaust. He believed that the entire State of Israel was a memorial to the slaughtered. The new society, he claimed, should focus on the ethos of building the country, planting forests, and founding new settlements, and refrain from dwelling on past destruction and exile.[16]

Nevertheless, from the outset of his career Ben-Gurion's leadership was characterized by his ability to make ideological adjustments, and even dramatic conceptual shifts, which led to new political directions. Analysing the change in Ben-Gurion's approach to the Zionist Organization in the 1950s, Yosef Gorny wrote that it "reveals fascinating personality and leadership traits: changing direction while maintaining continuity of the main lines."[17]

I argue that Gorny's assessment fits the transformation in Ben-Gurion's attitude to the centrality of the Holocaust, too. The objectives presented to the government by Ben-Gurion in the government meeting of 29 May 1960 (the first after Ben-Gurion's announcement that Eichmann had been brought to Israel) related to the possible impact of the trial on Israeli society, particularly on the younger generation, and to its potential effect on Israel's international standing. In both, one can clearly see a blend of change and continuity. In contrast to the claim that has been made repeatedly in studies on the Eichmann trial, the minutes of the May government meeting prove that from the outset Ben-Gurion had grasped its deep historical significance. Moreover, the minutes clearly demonstrate that Ben-Gurion had already made up his mind before the decision to hold the historic trial was brought before the government.[18]

For the purposes of this essay, I will focus on Ben-Gurion's second goal, related to Israel's international standing, and I will show how this attitude was reflected in Israel's relations with the FRG. In the international arena, Ben-Gurion sought to use the trial to emphasize the moral obligation of the world community, particularly Europeans, to support the State of Israel as the home of many Holocaust survivors. To Ben-Gurion, this trial was a historic opportunity to explain to the world the unique tragedy of the Jewish people. At the Nuremberg trials, in contrast, the murder of Jews had not been a central issue. "The world wants to forget it, has gotten tired of talking about it … we need to reopen the entire issue again," Ben-Gurion told his ministers.[19]

Referring to international interest in the trial, historian David Cesarani supports Ben-Gurion's assessment that the trial provided a unique opportunity to remind the world of the magnitude of the Jewish tragedy.[20]

Beyond practical considerations regarding international commitment to support Israel, Ben-Gurion's position reflected a deep moral conviction that he shared with his government, which he termed "historical justice." Through the Eichmann trial, the Jewish people, who had gained sovereignty after a prolonged struggle, would finally be able to present in full the idea of the Final Solution. It was a chance to emphasize the process of deliberate destruction and the helplessness of the Jews as a scattered nation. The Israeli prime minister told the ministers, "We will not limit ourselves to Eichmann's deeds alone but we should tell the whole story. It requires thorough preparation and order to provide the Jewish people and the world with a complete picture of everything that happened to the Jews of Europe at that time ... This is 'historical justice,' that the criminal, one of the top criminals, will be judged by the same sovereign people against whom the sin was committed."[21]

Here, one can discern the evolution of Ben-Gurion's perception of the role of Holocaust memory in Israel's diplomacy, in parallel with his conceptual continuum. The Reparations Agreement between Israel and West Germany, signed in September 1952, stressed a model of Israeli diplomacy aimed at gaining support for the Jewish state from countries where Jews had been persecuted in the not-so-distant past; it emphasized, aside from realpolitik, their moral obligation to the Jewish state. During the fierce debate over opening negotiations with the FRG on material reparations in January 1952, Ben-Gurion and leading members of the ruling Mapai party stressed that the main lesson to be learned from the Holocaust was the tragic helplessness of the Jewish people. Thus, it was necessary to build and strengthen the State of Israel with any help that the country could get. They accused those that opposed the negotiations of having a "diaspora mindset," rendering them incapable of understanding the meaning of realpolitik and the political challenges Israel was facing.[22]

Ben-Gurion was cautious about utilizing memory of the Holocaust in relations between Israel and other nations. He argued that repeatedly highlighting the tragedy would only arouse antipathy and even contempt toward Israel and the Jewish people. "What we have to say, the things they did – we'll say if we have to say them ... and we should not say it too much because it would only arouse contempt. If a new Jeremiah appears he will talk ... but if you repeat it too often you will cause loathing among the nations," stated Ben-Gurion.[23]

Nevertheless, toward the end of the 1950s, with the strengthening of ties with West Germany, Ben-Gurion began to refer more frequently to memory of the Holocaust as a key issue in Israeli foreign policy, a carefully thought-out and wise strategy to achieve his political goals. Ben-Gurion believed that the trial would help reinforce support for Israel in Europe, particularly in Germany. Ben-Gurion took this approach in meetings with Adenauer and President Eisenhower in New York two months before the abduction of Eichmann. It is even possible that Ben-Gurion, who knew that disclosure of the nuclear reactor that Israel had built in Dimona was imminent, sought to highlight through the Eichmann trial the duty of Israeli leaders to prevent another Holocaust.[24]

German diplomats demonstrated ambivalence about the trial during their meetings with delegates of the Israeli Foreign Ministry. On the one hand, they expressed their support for the decision to hold the trial in Israel. Thus, for example, Israel's ambassador to France, Walter Eytan, reported to Jerusalem that Blankenhorn had conveyed unreserved satisfaction at Eichmann's capture, adding that the trial in Israel could make an important educational contribution to German society. Similarly, Ludwig Erhard, FRG minister of economics and future chancellor, sent a personal message of support to the Israeli government via the head of the Israel Purchasing Mission, Felix Shinnar.[25] At the same time, however, FRG decision-makers expressed deep concern that the trial might strengthen the negative image of Germans when they needed Western public sympathy in relation to the Berlin crisis. Although the meeting of the heads of the Four Powers in Paris in May 1960 collapsed in the wake of the Soviet downing of an American U-2 spy plane and Eisenhower's refusal to accept Khrushchev's demand for an apology, Adenauer continued to be vigilant lest Soviet pressure on the West lead to concessions at the expense of the FRG. "There is an atmosphere of hysteria [in the FRG], a fear of being left alone or sold out," wrote Kissinger to Kennedy.[26]

About two months before Eichmann's abduction, the FRG witnessed a wave of antisemitic incidents, known as the "swastika epidemic," which triggered expressions of hostility and condemnation of the FRG in Europe and the United States. Criticism was directed against the integration of former Nazi Party members and functionaries of the Third Reich into the FRG administration (especially the Foreign Office, the judiciary, and the education system) as well as in German industry. Another issue highlighted in newspapers around the world was the failure of the West German education system to deal with Germany's Nazi past. Many writers stressed that it strengthened the so-called wall of silence (*Mauer Des Schweigen*) that had been built around the Nazi period under Adenauer's leadership. They further claimed that the FRG legal system had not worked systematically to bring war criminals to justice.[27]

Moreover, the Eichmann trial boosted the Eastern bloc; it encouraged, in particular, East German propaganda against its Western neighbour, which over the past decade had conducted a worldwide campaign to delegitimize the former's existence. East German propaganda sought to galvanize criticism that already existed in the West. For instance, it stressed that while Eichmann was standing trial, many Nazis who bore direct or indirect responsibility for war crimes were employed by the FRG government, including some senior officials. American intelligence reports, composed toward the beginning of the trial, testify to the efforts made by Western intelligence and foreign policy experts to evaluate the potential damage that the Eichmann trial might do to the FRG image. They also reveal that German and American intelligence experts cooperated in obtaining reliable information on Eastern bloc plans in this regard.[28]

In their reports, CIA experts emphasized that the "legal and moral aspects of the case do not concern us here. What is of intelligence interest, however, are the political and propaganda implications of the trial." By the end of January 1961 they noted, for example, that the Poles and the Czechs were working together with the Soviets, compiling documents to be presented at the beginning of the trial in order to embarrass the FRG government, particularly in regard to the role that Hans Globke, Adenauer's closest adviser, played in preparing what Eastern bloc propaganda termed "the legal basis for the extermination of the Jews." CIA analysts referred to a Soviet global plan aimed at exploiting the trial. As one information report stated, "The Soviets anticipate that the Eichmann trial will reawaken anti-German feelings throughout the world ... the Soviet aim is to embarrass seriously the Adenauer government and to cause a loss of faith in Germany on the part of her Western allies. While the attack will be concentrated on Globke, others, including persons in West German Foreign Office, will also be involved .... the USSR will furnish the material to the East German Government which they believe to be the logical and the most effective instrument."[29]

Against this background, Israeli ambassadors were asked by their West German counterparts in various capitals to help them highlight the distinction between Nazi Germany and the "new Germany," and the latter's commitment to democratic values. For example, a few days before the opening of the Eichmann trial, Israel's ambassador to the Netherlands reported on a conversation he had with the German ambassador. "The Germans know that the trial will again stir up feelings of hatred in all countries that suffered from the Nazis," said the German ambassador, adding that "the Dutch resent the entire German people." He then asked the Israeli ambassador to advise him on how to improve his meetings with the Dutch press because "the only positive reactions to FRG repentance are coming from Israeli Prime Minister Ben-Gurion."[30]

The paradox here is breathtaking: German ambassadors were asking Israel for assistance in the FRG's effort to overcome the widespread perception that Germany had been far too slow in confronting its Nazi past. In Jerusalem the heads of the foreign ministry were well aware of the anxiety of West German diplomats on the eve of the Eichmann trial and the importance they attributed to connections with Israeli delegates and the attitude of Israeli leaders. Reports in this regard highlighted the sympathy felt by German diplomats toward their Israeli colleagues worldwide, particularly during official ceremonies and diplomatic receptions. In order to demonstrate friendly bilateral relations, the German Foreign Office, advised by an American public relations firm, asked Israel to arrange mutual visits of journalists and publicity experts. Internal correspondence of Israel's Foreign Ministry stated that "the reason for all this [the German request] is German concern about their international standing – particularly in the United States – in light of [expected] revelations in the Eichmann trial." A positive statement from Ben-Gurion, not only as an Israeli leader but especially as a Jewish leader, was considered a significant show of moral support.[31]

When referring to the question of West German–Israeli relations during the Eichmann trial, the common tendency is to concentrate on the case of Hans Globke. Adenauer feared that his closest adviser and other German public figures and officials might be named during the trial as war criminals. Indeed, East Germany ran a major campaign to highlight Globke's activities during the Third Reich.[32]

Without reducing the importance of this matter, it appears that for Adenauer and the FRG leadership, Ben-Gurion's attitude toward the "other Germany" aroused deep appreciation and a sense of indebtedness. Ben-Gurion presented a historiographic and ethical approach that stood in contrast to that taken by Shirer's book, which had aroused such opposition and anger in the FRG.

Adenauer emphasized the importance of Ben-Gurion's position at a press conference held in the Bundestag in early March 1961. Openly expressing his fear concerning the negative impact that the trial would have on his country's image, Adenauer repeated his belief that the Germans did not bear direct responsibility, let alone guilt, for Nazi crimes. Moreover, Adenauer claimed that, like other people in Europe, the Germans should also be considered victims of the Nazi regime, and that most people who could have done so had helped their Jewish compatriots. The way that Adenauer chose to end his speech is particularly significant: he stressed the favourable attitude of Ben-Gurion, "who has the authority to represent the interests of Judaism" to the Germans, and the moral distinction made by the prime minister between the new democratic Germany and Nazi Germany.[33]

In what ways did the Israeli prime minister show moral support to West Germany? A few days after the end of the trial, *Deutsche Zeitung* journalist Rolf Vogel asked Ben-Gurion whether he had changed his attitude toward the FRG. The prime minister replied firmly that his opinion remained as solid as in the past; that is, he made a clear and sharp distinction between Nazi Germany and the FRG. "Nazi Germany does not exist anymore," he asserted, adding a moral argument from Deuteronomy: "Parents are not to be put to death for their children, nor children put to death for their parents; each will die for their own sin."[34]

Ben-Gurion had begun to consolidate his policy relating to the "other Germany," especially the far-reaching idea to make the FRG a strategic ally and major arms supplier, in early 1957 when the FRG demonstrated support for Israel during the difficult diplomatic battle surrounding the withdrawal from the Sinai.[35] Between 1957 and 1960, at first only in closed meetings but later publicly, Ben-Gurion gradually revealed his ambition to build a close relationship with the FRG. In order to reinforce this policy, which was widely criticized in Israel, Ben-Gurion raised not only practical but moral arguments as well.[36] He had used moral arguments in earlier diplomatic negotiations. For instance, during the dramatic debate over reparations in 1952, Ben-Gurion repeatedly claimed that the demand for reparations from Germany was mainly a moral obligation in accordance with the biblical phrase, "Not only have you killed, but you have also taken possession?"[37] Similarly, in early 1960 his claims were not only practical. "I reject the title 'murderous people' when speaking about the present German people. That would indeed be subscribing to a race theory ... of course, there is still antisemitism in Germany but in other countries as well ... but most of the new generation in Germany are pacifists," he told members of the Knesset in early 1960. Ben-Gurion's words appeared prominently on the front pages of newspapers in Germany. Some Germans, including members of the younger generation, wrote to Ben-Gurion thanking him for his speech.[38]

Officials of the Israeli Foreign Ministry thought that Israel should adopt a much more assertive policy toward West Germany. Ideally, such a policy would serve Israel's diplomatic goals by utilizing the anxiety in the FRG about its image. The diplomats were frustrated and angry at the prolonged failure to convince FRG leaders – who feared that the Arab states would recognize East Germany – to establish diplomatic relations with Israel. Referring to Ben-Gurion's interview with Vogel about the trial, a senior official in the Western Europe department of the Israeli Foreign Ministry wrote that "the prime minister was again praising Adenauer and contemporary Germany and that similar statements he had made previously served to whitewash the Germans in the eyes of the world."[39] These officials expected that the Eichmann trial, and growing criticism of the FRG's failure to confront its Nazi past, would drive West Germany to establish official ties.

Ben-Gurion objected to exploiting the trial in order to put pressure on the FRG in this regard. On the contrary, he saw the trial as an opportunity to reinforce the trust that he had already created between himself and Adenauer and to strengthen Israel's economic and military relations with West Germany. For him, establishing diplomatic ties was secondary to the extensive economic and military aid he had managed to elicit from Adenauer, following their March 1960 meeting in the United States. The agreement to supply weapons to Israel was initially concealed from the Americans, since it violated an agreement between Germany and the United States prohibiting arms sales to a third country without prior permission from the latter. While Adenauer agreed in principle to supply weapons to Israel, mainly in order to compensate Israel for the lack of official ties, details were worked out and executed during and after the Eichmann trial. In this regard, a report composed by senior US Defense Department official William Bundy on arms supplies from the FRG to Israel is instructive. Bundy, who was assigned by the Pentagon and the State Department to investigate the matter of the Israeli-German agreement, met with FRG officials, who gave him complete details about the pact. Bundy reported to his superiors that the Germans used the phrase "lend lease" in order to clarify that the weapons were being given gratis and that he understood from them that the Eichmann trial had influenced their decision to finalize the terms of the secret agreement.[40]

Conclusions

In the highly charged atmosphere of the Eichmann trial, Ben-Gurion emphasized his concept of the "other Germany," with the aim of creating the groundwork for a "political friendship" between strategic allies. His assessment of the diplomatic importance of the trial proved to be correct. The trial highlighted the FRG's moral obligation to Israel, especially given that Adenauer was about to retire from his historic role as the first chancellor.

Ben-Gurion was unwavering in his adherence to the political and the moral stance he had adopted. He distinguished the new democratic Germany from the Nazi totalitarian state; he opposed the biased attitude of some Israeli politicians toward the Germans, an attitude that he did not hesitate to describe as racist; and he objected to the idea of Germany's unique historic path (*Sonderweg*). Thus, he strengthened the trust and friendship between himself and the West German leadership, leading to increased practical support for Israel.

During the Eichmann trial, the behaviour of Ben-Gurion toward West Germany demonstrated a continuation of the trust that he had established with Adenauer, particularly at their meeting in March 1960 in New York. At the end of that historic discussion, the chancellor told Ben-Gurion, "I want to thank you for not identifying the German people today with Hitler and with what they did."[41]

Ben-Gurion's position concerning the notion of the "other Germany" provoked sharp controversy in Israel. It was rightly argued that the Israeli prime minister was contributing to Adenauer's efforts to shape the myth of a clear distinction between Nazis and Germans – a myth that was viewed as whitewashing the moral responsibility of German society for the persecution of the Jewish population. Leading public figures such as the poet Natan Alterman; Gershom Schocken, editor of the daily *Haaretz*; and Yitzhak Tabenkin, leader of *Hakibbutz Hameuchad*, harshly criticized Ben-Gurion's call for friendly relations with West Germany. They claimed that, a mere fifteen years after the end of the Second World War and the Holocaust, the time had not come yet for rapprochement. They did not object to Germany's economic and military support but opposed any reciprocal social and cultural relations.[42]

Other critics of Ben-Gurion included, for example, Ya'akov Hazan and Yigal Alon, the leaders of the left-Zionist parties Hashomer Hatzair and Achdut Haavoda; Menachem Begin, the leader of the extreme-right opposition party Herut; and Yitzhak (Antek) Zuckerman and the poet Abba Kovner, well-known leaders among the underground ghetto movements and the partisan units. These critics argued that the sharp distinction made by Ben-Gurion between the "two Germanys" did not reflect the reality of West German society. They claimed that the backbone of contemporary German society was, in fact, made up of the same Germans who supported Hitler, most of whom had shown no mercy toward the Jews. Moreover, officials who had been part of the Nazi bureaucracy and had been responsible for the anti-Jewish policy had been reinstated in the public service, and many perpetrators were still living a peaceful life. [43]

Even in Mapai there were leading members who criticized the moral validity of Ben-Gurion's "other Germany" concept. Notable among these critics were Golda Meir, the foreign minister, and Zalman Aran, the minister of education in the second half of the 1950s. In a meeting of the leadership of Mapi, Meir stated that "I know the importance of what Germany does [for Israel] and what she might do for us. I do not think, however, that for that we should give her rehabilitation." From a moral perspective, both Meir and Aran, as well as many leading figures and intellectuals in Israel at the beginnig of 1960s, questioned Ben-Gurion's right to announce in the name of Israel that West Germany and Nazi Germany were now two completely distinct entities .

NOTES

1 Kennedy Library, President's Office files, countries, 117A, Memorandum from Henry Kissinger to Kennedy, 6 April 1961.

2 National Archives at College Park, Maryland (NA), RG 263/A1-86/15, *Information Report*, CIA, Germany, Frankfurt, 1 February 1961.

3 Peter Schwartz, *Konrad Adenauer* (Providence and Oxford, 1997), 516; Felix Von Eckardt, *Ein Unordentliches Leben* (Düsseldorf-Wien, 1967), 623–5; Daniel Kosthorst, *Brentano und die deutsche Einheit* (Düsseldorf, 1993), 360–1; Kissinger, Memorandum, 6 April 1961.

4 Kissinger, Memorandum, 6 April 1961. On the FRG diplomatic campaign to delegitimize the GDR in the 1950s, see William Glenn Gray, *Germany's Cold War: The Global Campaign to Isolate East Germany, 1949–1969* (Chapel Hill, 2003), 1–115.

5 *The Times*, 24 October 1958.

6 *New York Times*, 24 October 1958.

7 Frieder Günther, *Heuss auf Reisen: Die auswärtige Repräsentation der Bundesrepublik durch den ersten Bundespräsidenten* (Munich 2006), 147–60; *New York Times*, 24 October 1958; *Davar*, 7 November 1958.

8 Schwartz, *Adenauer*, 516, 434; Dennis L. Bark and David R. Gress, *From Shadow to Substance* (Oxford, 1989), 439.

9 Kissinger, Memorandum, 6 April 1961.

10 Gavriel D. Rosenfeld, "The Reception of William L. Shirer's 'The Rise and Fall of the Third Reich' in the United States and West Germany, 1960–62," *Journal of Contemporary History* 29 (1994): 95–128.

11 Peter Eisemann, *Aussenpolitik der Bundesrepublik Deutschland* (Krefeld, 1982), 74–97; Hans Buchheim, *Deutschlandpolitik 1949–1972* (Stuttgart, 1984), 7–104; Henry Kissinger, *Diplomacy* (New York, 1994), 568–93

12 Quoted in Rosenfeld, "The Reception," 119.

13 NA, RG 263/A1-86/15, "Information Report," CIA, Germany, Frankfurt, 1 February 1961.

14 NA, RG 263/A1-85/15, Office of National Estimates, 28 March 1961.

15 David Cesarani, *Becoming Eichmann: Rethinking the Life, Crimes, and Trial of a "Desk Murderer"* (New York, 2007), 324–9; Jeffrey Shandler, *While America Watches: Televising the Holocaust* (New York, 1999), 91–107; Liat Benhabib, "From 2-Inch to YouTube: The Audio-Visual Documentation

and the Broadcast of the Eichmann Trial," Paper presented at the "Trial of Adolf Eichmann: Retrospect and Prospect" conference, Toronto, 8–10 September 2012.

16 See, for example, Roni Stauber, *The Holocaust in the Israeli Public Debate in the 1950s* (London: 2007), 50–6.

17 Yosef Gorny, *The Quest for Collective Identity* (Hebrew) (Tel Aviv, 1996), 80.

18 Israel State Archives, Jerusalem (ISA), MFA, 10/2968, Minutes of the Israel Government meeting, 29 May 1960, These records from late May contradict, in my opinion, the argument raised by Hanna Yablonka in her book *The State of Israel vs. Adolf Eichmann* (Hebrew) (Tel Aviv, 2001), 59–67, that "at least in regard to the capture of Adolf Eichmann and his prosecution in Israel, it was not the same Ben-Gurion who plans ahead, considers and decides, but a Ben-Gurion who to a certain degree, followed events or rather was dragged along by them." Accordingly, Ben-Gurion began to grasp the historical significance of the trial and particularly its potential impact on Israeli society only after it began. In contrast, I argue that Ben-Gurion emphasized during government meetings the importance of the trial both to Israel's younger generation and to Israel's international standing. Yablonka's claim was reiterated by other scholars as well: see, for example, Deborah E. Lipstadt, *The Eichmann Trial* (New York, 2001), 13. Compare with Tom Segev, *The Seventh Million* (Hebrew) (Tel Aviv, 1991), 310–11; Yehiam Vaits, "The Founding Father and the War Criminal's Trial: Ben Gurion and the Eichmann Trial," *Yad Vashem Studies* 36 (2008): 211–52. Unlike Yablonka, both Segev and Vaitz argue that Ben-Gurion's instruction to kidnap Eichmann in order to try him in Israel was a foresighted idea aimed at achieving national, political, and educational goals.

19 Minutes of the Israel Government meeting, 29 May 1960

20 Cesarani, *Becoming Eichmann*, 324–9.

21 Minutes of the Israel Government meeting, 29 May 1960.

22 Yaakov Sharett, ed., *Moshe Sharett and the German Reparations Controversy* (Hebrew) (Tel Aviv, 2007), 236–41, 347, 413.

23 Ibid., 239.

24 Zaki Shalom, *Between Dimona and Washington* (Hebrew) (Tel Aviv, 2004), 43–6.

25 ISA, MFA, 300/8, Shinar to Europe Department, Israel Foreign Office, 28 June 1960.

26 Kissinger, Memorandum, 6 April 1961.

27 Weissbuch und Erklärung der Bundesregierung, *Die antisemitischen und nazistischen Vorfälle* (Bonn, 1960); Politisches Archive des Auswartigen Amts Berlin, B11, B12/101, Correspondence between Bonn and FRG delegates worldwide, beginning 1960; see also Roni Stauber, "Realpolitik and the Burden of the Past: Israeli Diplomacy and the 'Other' Germany," *Israel Studies* 8 (2003): 102–5.

28 See, for example, NA, RG 263/A1-86/15, To the Director from Munich (A. Eichmann), 22 February 1961.

29 NA, RG 263/A1-86/15, CIA, Office of National Estimates, (A. Eichmann), 28 March 1961; Information Report, 23 January 1961.

30 ISA, MFA, 330913, Israel's Ambassador to the Netherlands to Europe Department, Israel Foreign Office, 10 April1961.

31 ISA, MFA, 3309/13, Israel's Ambassadors to the Netherlands and to Switzerland to West Europe Department, Israel Foreign Office, 29 March 10 April 1961; "Journalists Exchange" (memorandum), 7 March 1961.

32 A special messenger sent by Adenauer to Ben-Gurion made it clear that Globke's name should not be mentioned during the trial. This issue was discussed by Ben-Gurion and the Attorney General, Gideon Hausner. On one occasion, Ben-Gurion tried to convince Hausner to avoid bringing to court an important document that confirmed, among other things, Globke's involvement in the deportation of the Jews from Germany and in the confiscation of their property. Hausner refused Ben-Gurion's request, and did present the document. Later, however, Hausner did accept another of Ben-Gurion's demands by objecting to allowing into court certain notes about Globke that Eichmann had written in his cell. Ernst Pipper, "Adolf Eichmann und der BND," *Der Tagesspiegel*, 17 May 2011, http://www .tagesspiegel.de/kultur/kriegsverbrecherprozess-adolf-eichmann-und -der-bnd/4134500.html ;Interview with Hausner, Ben-Gurion Archives, Sde Boker, audio-visual section, interviews, box 84.

33 Ben-Gurion Archives, Sde Boker, Protocols Section, Protocol of press conference, 10 March 1961; *Davar*, 12 March 1961.

34 Ben-Gurion Archive, Sde Boker, 661/5324, Protocols Section, 13 August 1961, Answers to questions presented by Vogel. In fact, Vogel was an agent of Germany's Federal Intelligence Service (BND). He was sent directly by Adenauer with a letter of recommendation for a meeting with Prime Minister Ben-Gurion. Vogel sought to find out whether Eichmann intend to testify against German public figures and leading officials, particularly Globke. See Ben-Gurion Archives, 660/2238, Correspondence file, 1961, Adenauer to Ben-Gurion, 8 February 1961; Klaus Wiegrefe, "West Germany's Efforts to Influence the Eichmann Trial," *Spiegel On Line*, 15 April 2011, http://www.spiegel.de/international/world/the-holocaust -in-the-dock-west-germany-s-efforts-to-influence-the-eichmann-trial -a-756915.html.

35 Roni Stauber, "The Impact of the Sinai Campaign on Relations between Israel and West Germany," *Modern Judaism* 33 (2013): 235–59.

36 See, for example, Minutes of the Israel Government meeting, 7 April 1957; *Proceedings of the Knesset*, 1 July 1959, Knesset on-line proceedings, http:// fs.knesset.gov.il//3/Plenum/3_ptm_251590.pdf.

37 Sharett, *Moshe Sharett and the German Reparations Controversy*, 310.

38 *Proceedings of the Knesset*, 1 July 1959.

39 ISA, MAFA, 3309/13.

40 Kennedy Library, President's Office files, countries, 117A, William Bundy to Ural Alexis Johnson, 16 November 1963; Hannfried von Hindenberg, *Demonstrating Reconciliation* (New York and Oxford, 2007), 52–4; Dominique Trimbur, "Verpflichtung und Pragmatismus: Adenauer und Israel 1961–1967," in Hanns Jürgen Küsters, ed., *Adenauer, Israel und das Judentum* (Bonn, 2004), 55–81.

41 Zaki Shalom, "Document: David Ben-Gurion and Chancellor Adenauer at the Waldorf Astoria on 14 March 1960," *Israel Studies* 2, no. 1 (1997), 67.

42 See, for example, *Haaretz*, 26, 28 June 1959; *Mibefnim* 20, no. 3 (January 1958); Natan Alterman, *Hatur hashvi'i* (The Seventh Column) (Hebrew) (Tel Aviv, 1981), vol. 2.

43 See, for example, *Proceedings of the Knesset*, 29, 30 June 1959; *Mibefnim*, vol. 22, no. 1; *Al Hamishmar*, 5 July 1959.

10 The Impact of the Eichmann Affair on Arab Holocaust Discourse

ESTHER WEBMAN

Immediately after the execution of Adolf Eichmann on 31 May 1962, Lebanese commentator Basil Daqqaq summarized the lessons of the trial from the Arab point of view, highlighting what he termed as two "historical truths": first, the affair would always remain "a symbol in history of the triumph of politics over justice," regardless of the executioners' success "in arousing the sympathy of the world for the hundreds of thousands of Jewish victims during the Nazi era"; and second, it would serve "as a precedent related, as far as the Arabs were concerned, to the chain of murders and expulsion of the Palestinians ... on the altar of the Jewish state."[1] Reviewing the trial forty years later, Israeli Holocaust scholar Hanna Yablonka wrote that at the Eichmann trial, "there was a meeting between the two most important chapters in modern Jewish history: the Holocaust and the founding of the State of Israel."[2] Moreover, the trial, unlike the Nuremberg trials, turned "information" about the Holocaust into "knowledge," and became an important determinant in the transformation of Holocaust consciousness into a central trait of Western cultural discourse.[3] The two conclusions epitomize the different, contradictory meanings that the trial, the Holocaust, and the establishment of the State of Israel have in Arab and Western discourses. The linkage between the Holocaust and the founding of the state had occupied Arab public discourse since the end of the Second World War. Following the trial, awareness of the Holocaust heightened in Arab countries, but whereas the Israeli and Western societies underwent processes of internalizing the Holocaust and its lessons, Arab societies developed a growing sense of alienation toward it.

The Eichmann affair took place at a time when the Arab-Israeli conflict was prominent on the Arab public agenda, and pan-Arabism propagated by the charismatic Egyptian president Jamal ʿAbd al-Nasser was at its peak. At first glance, the Eichmann affair was an internal Jewish matter. It raised historical, legal, philosophical, and ethical questions which had nothing to do with the Arabs, and seemed only to have given the Jewish people a forum to settle accounts with its executioners. Why, then, were the Arab media so keen to pursue it? Which issues and themes were raised in the public debate? Was it influenced by the worldwide discussion of the trial, and if so, how? What was its impact on the representation of the Holocaust in subsequent Arab public discourse?

This essay addresses these questions and examines the Arab public debate over the affair, challenging the erroneous and one-dimensional depiction of the Arab representation of the trial in Israeli and Western research literature. It will contend that:

a. The debate had a significant impact on the development of the Holocaust discourse in the Arab world. It focused on three themes – the alleged Zionist-Nazi collaboration; the equation of Zionism and Nazism, implying a comparison between the Holocaust and the *nakba*, or between Jewish suffering and Palestinian suffering; and the accusation that Israel and Zionism were exploiting the Holocaust while fostering feelings of guilt among the Germans for material and political gains.
b. Arab media were aware of and attentive to Western publications and arguments about the trial, and particularly to the discourse on the Holocaust in Israel.
c. The Holocaust discourse was subordinated to the political struggle against Israel and Zionism, and intertwined in proliferating antisemitic perceptions.

Instrumentalizing the Trial in an Orchestrated Campaign against Israel and Zionism

The Arab debate on the trial stemmed from the premise that the Holocaust did not directly concern the Arabs but they had to address what was perceived as its possible detrimental political ramifications for the Arab cause and its exploitation by Israel. However, since Israel was quickly forgiven for Eichmann's kidnapping following a U.N. Security Council resolution, and the affair seemed to be playing into Israel's hands, Arab governments and media embarked on a smear campaign to discredit the trial and Israel and minimize their propaganda gains. Eichmann's abduction from sovereign Argentinian soil provided a legitimate opportunity to attack Israel, and an appropriate occasion to call world attention to the alleged crimes committed in Palestine and to expose "the ugly face" of Zionism.[4] The widespread reporting of the affair was not the result of any particular interest in the Holocaust and did not reflect a coherent approach toward it. On the contrary, it reflected a prevailing unease, and, therefore, the main emphasis of the discussion was diverted to political aspects which could be used to attack Israel and Zionism. However, the Arab discourse was attentive to other discourses, and was particularly responsive to the development of the discourse on the Holocaust in Israel.

The Arab press' position on the Holocaust during the trial revealed a wide spectrum of motifs, many of which were not new in the evolving discourse on the Holocaust. These included aspects of denial, the exploitation of the Holocaust by Israel, the equation between Zionism and Nazism and between the Holocaust and the Palestinian *nakba*. Two additional themes emerged in the wake of the affair: alleged Zionist-Nazi collaboration, attention to which had been negligible until then, and the creation of a causal linkage between the Holocaust and the establishment of the State of Israel.

A particular piece that the captured spirit of the Arab media coverage was a lengthy anonymous article about the entire Eichmann affair published in the leading Egyptian daily, *al-Ahram*, shortly before the trial began. Describing the affair as "the most profitable robbery," it listed Israel's goals: presenting itself as judge on behalf of all the Jews of the world; planting fear in the hearts of the Nazis holding important positions in every country, including Germany; embarrassing Adenauer's government by presenting Germany as a country unable to protect its citizens; convincing world public opinion that Arab nationalism is a racist movement similar to Nazism, by trying to show that the Arabs collaborated with the Nazis during the war and continued after it with the employment of ex-Nazi German experts; and enlisting world compassion "for the myth of the persecuted Jewish people," in preparation for a new round of fundraising "that would save their country from collapse."[5]

Attitudes in the Arab press toward Eichmann varied, from pity for the individual, identification with him and understanding for his deeds, to reservations about him and about what he symbolized. Eichmann was viewed as "an old friend of Israel," who had visited Palestine in 1938 as "a guest of the Hagana"; he had signed an agreement with world Zionism in which he committed himself to expelling the Jews from Germany and the Zionists committed themselves to receiving them in Palestine. "If it weren't for the myth of Nazi persecution" Israel would not exist.[6] Eichmann's alleged visit to Palestine and the Jewish contacts with him served as evidence for the claim of Zionist-Nazi collaboration. That claim was also used by the only Egyptian official who referred to the trial. Deputy Foreign Minister Husayn Dhu al-Faqqar, declared in his address to the Security Council in May 1961 that Hitler "was a victim of the Zionists" and that they had forced him to carry out crimes which in the end were supposed to bring about the establishment of the State of Israel.[7]

Although Eichmann was not the most senior Nazi official still alive, Arab writers contended that he was the official with the most close contacts, particularly those related to the Hungarian Jew Israel Reszoe (Rudolf) Kasztner, a representative of the Zionist movement in Hungary who headed the Aid and Rescue Committee in Budapest in 1944.[8] The first time Kasztner's name was mentioned in connection with the Eichmann affair was in a report of the Egyptian weekly *Ruz al-Yusuf*, quoting an interview with Ben-Gurion in *Le Monde*. He was asked about attempts made by political figures in Israel to prevent the trial from taking place in order to avoid revelations on the negotiations the accused had held with Kasztner regarding the rescue of Hungarian Jewry.[9] The above-mentioned article in *al-Ahram* also raised this set of circumstances, specifically referring to the trucks deal that Kasztner sought to close with Eichmann. According to the article, in return for 10,000 trucks and other merchandise, one million Jews would be released from the camps. Moreover, Kasztner agreed to calm Hungarian Jews and encourage them to comply with the Nazi instructions. However, the deal fell through because the representative of the Jewish organization (Joel Brand) was arrested and imprisoned in Egypt by the British, who staunchly rejected the deal.[10] Eichmann was therefore abducted in order to prevent him from publishing the incriminating material on Zionism, and his trial enabled the Zionist leaders to divert attention from the negative political impact of the Kasztner affair, and many of his secrets were buried with him following his speedy execution, the article maintains.

The allegation of Zionist collaboration with the Nazis was not only an attempt to repel and contradict the Israeli claim of Arab-Nazi collaboration. It also reinforced the themes of the equation between Zionism and Nazism and the connection between the Holocaust and the establishment of the State of Israel. Zionism was represented as striving to realize one goal: the establishment of a Jewish state, and the end justified the means. The British historian Arnold Toynbee contributed his share to the equation and was often quoted by the Arab press.[11] Hajj Amin al-Husayni, whose name as a collaborator with the Nazis was raised several times during the trial, also raised that point at a press conference in March 1961. The traces of the Nazis' actions against the Jews had already been erased and now belonged to the past, while Zionist aggression was continuing, he said, and it was no less ugly than the Nazis', "as admitted by Prof. Toynbee and large, neutral international circles." He also stated that the Palestinians had decided to pass a law "for bringing to trial the Zionists responsible for the crimes committed in Palestine, like the law according to which the Nuremberg trials were held and the Zionists themselves were trying Eichmann."[12]

Inspired by the Soviet perception of Zionism and Nazism, Egyptian leftist intellectual Lutfi al-Khuli viewed Zionism as "an aggressive colonial movement which fed on racism," although he recognized the Holocaust but saw no difference between Eichmann's deeds and those of Ben-Gurion. Erasing the differences between the Jewish and Arab tragedies, al-Khuli concludes, "The crime is of the same kind in both cases … it is insignificant to compare the amount of blood spilled in Nazi Germany and the amount spilled in Zionist Israel. Killing one man is like killing a thousand." He was of the opinion that Eichmann should be tried by an international court as a Nazi and an international war criminal, and that Israel feared an objective trial because it was liable to expose Zionist crimes "as a continuation of Nazi crimes." He also anticipated that Zionist leaders would be tried not only for crimes against Arabs but also against Jews, whom they "seduced with the slogan of the national homeland and undermined their stability and security all over the world."[13] Al-Khuli reiterated the equation between Zionism and Nazism in another article, in which he tried to prove that the Zionist hostility to the Arabs and the acts of slaughter carried out against them were the result of Zionism's fanatical, racist worldview.[14]

Columnist Mazin al-Bunduk stressed in the Egyptian weekly *Akhir Sa^ca* that the Arab viewpoint did not reflect an inclination toward Nazism or pity for Eichmann. He contended that it was the Arabs' bad luck that Hitler and Nazism had come to power, because they pushed many Jews into the ranks of Zionism. He denied the numbers of the victims, a theme which had not been prominent until then. Israel, he said, was interested in painting a "horrifying and exaggerated picture of the Jewish victims of Nazism." Its claim that six million Jews had been killed was "entirely untrue." Moreover, the number of non-Jewish victims in the European countries under Nazi occupation was far greater than that of Jewish victims. In addition he added two other objectives that Israel hoped to gain from the trial: to place the responsibility for the persecution of the Jews squarely on the conscience of the West, so that the only way of dealing with the past would be to offer aid to Israel, and to prove to the Jews that they would have peace only by emigrating to Israel and supporting its existence.[15]

The theme of Israel's exploitation of the trial for the realization of material goals appeared in several articles. Israel was accused of terrorizing West Germany, which "was very sensitive to its history of Nazism," to wring additional reparations out of it. Another article in *Akhir Sa'a* indicated that Germany had decided to give Israel more reparations "to prove to the world that Nazism was a thing of the past," and remove their guilt for Nazism.[16] Habib Jamati, in the Egyptian weekly *al-Musawwar*, linked the Holocaust and the establishment of the State of Israel by saying that the persecution of the Jews in "yesterday's" Germany was one of the factors which brought about the conquest of Palestine as a safe haven for the persecuted, and attacked Israel's attempt to involve the Arabs by force in "that filthy affair" as participants in the annihilation of the Jews. It was doing so, it claimed, to cover up its extermination policy against the Arabs of Palestine.[17]

Egyptian intellectual and staunch opponent to Nazism 'Abbas Mahmud al-'Aqqad expressed a different viewpoint, attacking other aspects of the Eichmann affair. What would Zionism say about Eichmann in another thousand years, and which of its many myths would it foster about its sworn enemy, "who was worthy of its malice, as it was worth of his," he wondered. It was reasonable to assume, he stated, that it would be said that the God of Zion had come down to earth and taken Eichmann to Tel Aviv as "a present for the Chosen People and a tasty sacrifice for the feast of the Exodus from Egypt." He also claimed that Eichmann looked Jewish and had been insulted because of it. 'Aqqad was amazed at the interest Eichmann had shown in the people he would come to annihilate, and "why he bothered to learn their language, the Talmud and Jewish history."[18] In 'Aqqad's indirect reference to the affair, he recognized the fact that the Holocaust had occurred, but did not hide his antipathy for the Jewish victims, and that perhaps there was a hint of justification in the assertion that they deserved the hatred they aroused in their enemies. However, 'Aqqad was consistent in his hostility to Nazism as well.

In another column, entitled "When the Enemies of Humanity Speak about Humanity," 'Aqqad rejected the legitimacy of the Israeli court and focused on the mentality of groups who viewed themselves as chosen people. The Aryans thought they were the people most entitled to "purify humanity from this scheming gang," he said. If the Nazis wanted support for their claims, they could find them in the Zionists' faith, because they also believed they were the chosen people. While Jews were God's chosen people in antiquity, the Nazis were the chosen people in modern times. Since Eichmann was denied the basic right of calling witnesses for the defence, 'that admits to one thing: that he was a gentile, and as such then three billion people on earth would share his crime. Thus the Zionist court would have to explain the difference between his enmity for humanity and the Zionist enmity for humanity. 'Aqqad, like many other Arab commentators, claimed that Zionism aspired to the idea of Jewish nationalism from its perception of the Jews as the chosen people, and often did not make the distinction between Jews and Zionists.[19]

Since the early 1960s, Eichmann has been occasionally invoked in Arab newspaper articles to magnify Israel's offences against the Palestinians and to reinforce the equation between its deeds and the Nazi deeds. Those references to Eichmann reveal a striking continuation in the themes and perceptions of the Holocaust. In response to the Israeli operation Cast Lead in Gaza,[20] for example, Layla al-Humud wrote an article entitled "From the Nazi Eichmann to Israel's Leadership Now" in the Jordanian daily *al-Ra'y*. The affair preoccupied the Arab media. It was a fascinating revenge story, she admitted, complicated by the fact that the abductors did not realize that their leaders would also be subjected to charges and face prosecution. "There is no difference between Eichmann and Israel's masters. They both violated human rights and exploited the war to realize racist goals by horrifying massacres." However, al-Humud asserted, Eichmann fulfilled orders whereas the Israeli leadership had given the orders, and whereas Eichmann was abducted, sedated, and brought to trial, the Israeli leaders would be brought to justice awake and conscious.[21]

In March 2010, a Kuwaiti journalist, 'Isam 'Abd al-Latif al-Fulayj, claimed in an article in the Kuwaiti paper *al-Watan* that the Jews understand nothing but force and are ungrateful toward those who try to help them, raising Eichmann's treatment during his trial as proof. Eichmann tried to help the Jews during Hitler's mass murders, and smuggled out thousands in order to save them from death, he contended, allegedly quoting Eichmann as saying, "The fact that cuts me to the heart is that I helped to save you [Jews] from Hitler's crematoria and dealt with you humanely, while you dogs showed me the greatest villainy. The soil of Palestine is not your heritage or your land. You are no more than a gang of terrorists, murderers, and suckers of the blood of the nations. Nothing suits you better than to burn in Hitler's crematoria, so that the Earth will be liberated from your wickedness and your corruption." Al-Fulayj concluded that Eichmann, who purportedly predicted the rise of an Arab Hitler that would utterly exterminate the Jews, so enraged the Jews that they hanged him, burned his corpse, and cast his ashes in the sea.[22] The resort to the justification of the Holocaust, which occasionally appeared in the Arab writings during the Eichmann affair, has not been a recurrent theme in Arab Holocaust discourse since the 1970s.

The Affair in History Books and Arab Anti-Zionist Literature

The polemical literature published about Zionism, both in the first years after the trial and up to the present, has fixated on the same claims and themes which had appeared in the public debate during the trial. Even before it had ended, the trial was mentioned in a book by Najm Halumi and Ahmad Muhammad Saqr called *Zionism Past and Present*.[23] The book, which was part of the series of books on political and national topics published by the Egyptian Ministry of Information, did not deny Eichmann's crimes, but attacked Israel for kidnapping him, for its actions against the Arabs, and for its political use of the trial. *The Terror State* also stressed the kidnapping and arguments against the trial. It quoted Arnold Toynbee, Charles Whitman, Jewish historian Oscar Handlin, and other Jews who denounced the trial. Israel was using the trial, concluded the authors, to warn the entire world that anyone who opposed Zionism could be subject to a fate like Eichmann's. The book, which was published close to the end of the trial, had no significant insights other than those appearing in the press.[24]

Three years after the trial, Egyptian leftist Ahmad Baha' al-Din published a book which included a chapter dealing with the trial, based on Moshe Perlman's book about the kidnapping.[25] Baha' al-Din's discussion of the power of world Zionism led him to the Eichmann trial, where he saw proof of Israel's exploitation of diaspora Jews. As far as he was concerned, the trial was illegal and an unjustified act of revenge. He discussed the connections between the Nazis and representatives of the Zionist movement, and the negotiations for the truck deal, but the chapter's main insight was his assessment that the clash between Zionism and the German racist movement, or Nazism, was natural and unavoidable.[26] The two movements had the same foundations, and hence they were rivals and hostile to one another, claimed Baha' al-Din. Zionism had been founded before Nazism, he explained, and the Nazis were those who slaughtered the Jews and not the other way around, yet that was not because the Zionists were good and the Nazis evil, but because the German Nazis were much stronger and more numerous than the Jews.[27]

Baha' al-Din's thesis was further developed in the writings of 'Abd al-Wahhab al-Masiri, an Egyptian scholar and specialist in Jewish and Zionist studies, who during the 1970s became known for his Islamist tendencies. In 1997 he published a book called *Zionism, Nazism and the*

End of History.[28] He devoted only a very short chapter to the Eichmann affair. Reading between the lines it was obvious that he based it on Arendt's book, but where she wondered, he drew definite conclusions. He noted, for example, that Eichmann had studied Yiddish, Hebrew, and Judaism, while Arendt made it clear that that was a lie Eichmann liked to tell to impress his colleagues and Jewish victims.[29] Al-Masiri adopted the erroneous belief that Eichmann's arrived in Palestine at the invitation of the "Jewish settlers" to learn about the Zionist experiment there.[30] The fact that Eichmann had read Theodor Herzl's book and was supposedly enchanted by Zionist ideology suited al-Masiri's thesis. Eichmann's views and those of the Zionist movement were no different from one another, al-Masiri claimed. They both believed the Jews should immigrate to a special country, since they were a historically displaced people. Eichmann was influenced by Zionist thought and especially by Martin Buber, asserted al-Masiri, who referred to Servatius' reflections as to whether there was something in the character of the Jewish people that led to its persecution and displacement everywhere, quoting him in an ostensibly neutral way: "Is it not possible that this people is responsible for the evil inflicted upon it?"[31]

While Arendt viewed such statements as manifestations of antisemitism along the lines of *The Protocols of the Elders of Zion*, al-Masiri left them as an open question for the reader. He was bothered more by the behaviour of the victims and the functioning of the Jewish councils in the ghettos, the *Judenrate*. The lack of Jewish revolt, he asserted, was the result of Zionist-Nazi collaboration. Without the aid and support of Zionist Jews in Hungary, the Nazis, whose numbers were small, would not have been able to carry out their deeds. The Jews' Zionist representatives, like Kasztner, encouraged and convinced the members of the various Jewish communities to go to the Nazi camps in exchange for the emigration of a few "who had the best biological material," as Eichmann defined them during his interrogation.[32] Those claims were compatible with al-Masiri's basic premise, the leitmotif of the book, which assumed that the treatment of people in the racist Nazi doctrine and Zionism was dictated by the criterion of the benefit they bring, and that both were simply the natural offspring of Western civilization.

Several Palestinian writers also dealt with the alleged ideological affinity between the two movements, "representing a worldview and conduct rooted in the Torah."[33] They attributed Kasztner's activities to his Zionist ideology, repeating the allegation that he sought to save the fittest Zionists for immigration to Israel, and helped the Germans to transfer hundreds of thousands of others to Auschwitz.[34] Issa Nakhle, a Palestinian lawyer residing in the United States, highlights in the *Palestinian Encyclopedia* the "mutual admiration" between Nazis and Zionists, and "cites" Eichmann as saying that had he been Jewish, he would have become an ardent Zionist. The "Zionist-Nazi collaboration," he concludes, assumed the shape of the "worst dangerous devilish alliance between the two most racist and brutal movements in modern time."[35]

Al-Masiri and Mamduh ʿAli al-Shaykh turned Kasztner into an agent of the Hungarian and Nazi espionage services even before the war, whereas Muhammad ʿAli Sirhan had Eichmann escaping to the Middle East together with several other high-ranking Nazi officers, who were all privy to the alleged secret Zionist-Nazi collaboration, fearing that Begin and Shamir would kill them in order to bury the secret. The conspiracy theory about the Zionists found its logical conclusion, and the "plot," which had started during the 1930s, ended by 1962.[36]

Rafiq Shakir Natshe, who had flatly denied the extermination of the Jews in one part of his book on colonialism and Palestine, points to the Kasztner affair as the ultimate proof of the Zionist-Fascist alliance. He describes Eichmann's proposal to the Allies to spare some Jews in exchange for trucks and other commodities as a pro-Zionist scheme to enable the immigration of wealthy Jews and members of the Zionist youth organizations. In return, Kasztner was supposed to guarantee Jewish compliance in the detention camps in Hungary before the Jews were taken to Auschwitz.[37]

The Kasztner–Eichmann deal was even featured in the Syrian *al-Shatat* TV series in 2003, which showed Kasztner making the proposal to Eichmann and promising to mislead Hungarian Jews about the true German intentions behind their deportation to Auschwitz in exchange for Eichmann allowing the emigration of 2,000 Jews "among our best biological specimens." He also proposed to his "friend" Eichmann that in exchange for the Zionists helping the Nazis to "annihilate the Jews of Hungary," the Zionists would benefit from the substantial financial assets which those Jews had hidden in Switzerland, while the Germans would "benefit from the annihilation of the Hungarian Jews."[38]

Arendt served as a source for background on the Eichmann trial in another study on Zionism and racism prepared by three Egyptian scholars: Shihab al-Din Mufid, head of the department of international jurisprudence at Cairo University; al-Sayyid Yasin, then the director of al-Ahram Centre for Strategic Studies; and Yunan Labib Rizq, a historian. The study was carried out after the adoption in 1975 of the U.N. resolution which labelled Zionism as a type of racism. Like other studies, it indicated that Israel had exploited the trial and the Holocaust but for a different purpose – the construction of an Israeli identity or personality.

They claimed that the efforts of Israel's ruling elite were based on a racist perception, preaching suspicion of and hatred for non-Jews, especially Arabs, on the one hand, and on the belief that Jews were superior because they were the chosen people, on the other. The trial's objective had not been to judge Eichmann as a man but rather as a symbol, not only of the Nazi regime but of antisemitic ideology throughout history, in order to display the Jewish tragedy before the world, to rouse guilt feelings among nations, to show Israelis what it means to live as a minority in the diaspora, and to convince them of the justice of the Zionist solution. In addition, the trial attempted to reinforce Jewish identity among Israelis and to strengthen the bond between them and diaspora Jews out of the Zionist belief that antisemitism was a perpetual threat.[39] Notwithstanding the basic accusation in the authors' analysis, they stressed the most important implications of the trial, that is, the changes in the relations between Israel and the diaspora and the place of the Holocaust in Jewish and Israeli identity.

Historian Wajih 'Atiq referred to the Eichmann affair in his study on German-Egyptian relations between 1952 and 1965, in which he emphasized Germany's commitment to support Israel, yet despite his scholarly approach he adopted the narrative that Israel's policy was aimed at plundering Germany by exploiting its guilt feelings toward the Jews. He pointed to the personal motive that played a central role in Germany's relationship to Israel following the affair, namely, fear of the exposure of wanted Nazis who had become key figures in the federal government, such as Hans Globke, one of Adenauer's close advisers, who took part in drafting the Nuremberg Laws in 1935. In return for not "looking too closely at the past of German government members," Israel received military aid. Thus 'Atiq reinforced the claim that the Nazi past was effectively used by Israel as a means of extortion.[40]

On the occasion of the trial's fiftieth anniversary, the US Holocaust Memorial Museum and the German Topography of Terror Foundation jointly organized a symposium in Berlin in May 2011, in which Lebanese London-based scholar Gilbert Achcar submitted a paper on Egyptian responses to the Eichmann Affair. The paper, published later in *Arab Studies Journal*,[41] is one of the few accounts on the Eichmann affair by an Arab scholar, but unfortunately it does not demonstrate a balanced academic approach. Achcar's book *The Arabs and the Holocaust: The Arab-Israeli War of Narratives* includes a short reference to the trial, mainly emphasizing the Arabs' irritation with Israel's political exploitation of the affair.[42]

Achcar's more detailed article examines the coverage of the Eichmann affair in *al-Ahram*, and explores "the whole gamut of expressions about, and attitudes toward, the former Nazi official" as well as toward Israel, Jews, and Nazism during 1960–2 in order to find out "whether hostility to Israel – then Egypt's main national enemy – transcended national sentiment into anti-Semitism and Nazi sympathy."[43] His underlying assumption is that the distortion of the historical record by Israeli and Western scholars and politicians created misconceptions of the Arabs' attitudes toward the Holocaust and Nazism in general in the West and among Arabs themselves. Hence, his work aims at exposing the distortions and setting the record straight. He introduces the historical context: the aftermath of "the ethnic cleansing of Palestine known as the *nakba*"[44] and the 1956 Suez War, the Cold War and the decolonization process, the developments in Nasser's Egypt, the limited knowledge about the Holocaust, and "the staging of the Eichmann trial itself."[45] However, Achcar's position is problematic from the outset in terms of his article's goals. There was no shortage of knowledge about the Holocaust, at least in Arab intellectual circles, as shown in previous works.[46] The blocking of information about the Holocaust and the its distorted representation years after the war indeed created ignorance, but those who participated in the public debate in the 1960s were better informed. The terms "ethnic cleansing" and "staging of the trial" are controversial terms and reflect the author's own biases.

Achcar seeks to prove that for the Israeli leadership a key purpose of the trial was its instrumental value in the conflict with their Arab neighbours, meaning first and foremost to "Nazify" the Arabs in general and the Palestinians in particular, which had been, according to him, a central feature of Zionist ideology and propaganda since the Second World War. He detects three key propaganda devices used since then by Israel to portray Arabs and Palestinians as heirs to Nazism: (1) to claim that Nazis had a direct hand in the Palestinian Arab revolt of 1936–9; (2) to exaggerate Hajj Amin al-Husayni's deeds during the Nazi genocide; and (3) to prove that thousands of Nazi officials fled after the war to Arab states and were integrated into their anti-Israeli and propaganda activities. He challenges these claims, but uses the wrong source to refute them, since he asserts that "*al-Ahram* ignored completely and purposely the aforementioned aspects of the trial, refraining from engaging directly with what was perceived as anti-Arab propaganda" and even from mentioning the Mufti.[47]

Achcar is correct in criticizing the representation of the trial in the Arab media in Israeli research literature and hence in Israel's public awareness. Indeed, it was a one-dimensional representation, based on a small number of articles and cartoons repeatedly quoted, and on Arab propaganda against the trial. That distortion was amplified by the preoccupation with Hajj Amin al-Husayni's connections with the Nazi regime and his influence on them, as Achcar claims in his article. Moreover, the political and ideological use of the trial by Israel also fanned the fires of its instrumentalization by Egypt and other Arab states.

Achcar details chronologically the reports, feature articles, and editorials which appeared in the paper since the kidnapping, and introduces their content, focusing on a few which best suited his views. One of these was the editorial of Lutfi al-Khuli mentioned above, "Eichmann between Nazism and Zionism," published on the first day of the trial.[48] Al-Khuli indeed rejected the notion that Arab condemnation of the kidnapping stemmed from a defence of Eichmann: "by virtue of our revolutionary opinions regarding colonialism and racism, we would never defend Eichmann and Nazism because of their hostile and racist position on the Jews." Moreover, he noted, "we are hostile to all the inhuman principles and views Eichmann and Nazism symbolize." In Arab history, claimed al-Khuli, there were no cases of racist persecution of Jews, and it did not link their fate to Zionism in the 1948 war or during the "triple aggression" in 1956. Achcar is fascinated by al-Khuli for his anti-racist views, and agrees with his perception of Zionism and its equation with Nazism. Indeed, al-Khuli represented a leftist Arab approach which clearly identified with anti-fascist and anti-Nazi forces, but by adopting the equation between Nazism and Zionism – also reflecting the Soviet stand toward Zionism – to delegitimize the state of Israel, he remained in the confines of the consensual Arab discourse on the Holocaust.

Achcar also proved to be an apologist for unsettling statements. In one case, an article published on 12 June 1960, quoting the *New York Herald Tribune*, put two exclamation marks in the subtitle "he caused the extermination of many of *bani isra'il!!*" Achcar chooses to translate *bani isra'il* as "Israel's children" and interprets the exclamation marks as "meant to emphasize the absurdity of this claim in light of Israel not being yet born at the time of Eichmann's crimes"[49] – an absurd interpretation by itself that coincides with his theory that there were no manifestations of Holocaust denial in *al-Ahram*.[50] In fact, the term *bani isra'il* is a common term for "the children of Israel" or Israelites, meaning Jews, which has nothing to do with Israel, and the exclamation marks convey scepticism in the cited fact.[51]

Another example in the same vein is an article by Sami Mansur.[52] The article means to expose the goals of the trial, namely "to win the world's sympathy with the *myth* [emphasis mine] of the oppressed Jewish people," in order to gain more subsidies. Achcar explains that "the argument could be interpreted as a veiled form of denial of the Holocaust. Such an interpretation is not warranted, however, as nowhere in the very long article is there any form of denial of the Holocaust."[53] However, in a note, he speculates that it is highly likely that Muhammad Hassanein Heikal, the editor-in-chief of *al-Ahram*, who "has always had affinities with 'milder' forms of Holocaust denial," played a role in writing the article.[54] In fact, the use of the term "myth" was not accidental in an article which sought to prove the instrumentalization of the Holocaust by the Jews. And as for Heikal, his affinity to denial is so "mild" that he wrote the preface to the Arabic translation of Roger Garaudy's *The Founding Myths of Israeli Politics*.[55]

Achcar feels a similar uneasiness with respect to an article by Salah Disuqi on the *Protocols of the Elders of Zion*.[56] Achcar finds the article by Disuqi, who was a nationalist former police officer and then Cairo's governor, "extremely poor and might not have been published had its author not been a high-ranking official," because it is "at odds with Nasser's official ideology that was displayed much more frequently in *al-Ahram*."[57] He admits that the questionable article was published in Cairo in 1956, but he fails to mention that it was published under the title "International Zionism," as part of an official indoctrination series called "We Chose for You." An Egyptian intellectual and staunch opponent to Nazism, 'Abbas Mahmud al-'Aqqad, wrote it. But this was not the first edition of the *Protocols* in Egypt. It was preceded by an annotated translation in 1951. In fact, Nasser was fascinated by the book and recommended it to an Indian journalist in the mid-1960s, whereas his brother wrote an introduction to the ninth edition, published during Nasser years. [58]

The coverage of the Eichmann affair in *al-Ahram*, concludes Achcar, provided an interesting view of the political ideology of Nasserism, and showed that it was "a combination of radical and firmly grounded opposition to Zionism, a repudiation of racism under all its forms, including Nazism, and a clear repudiation of anti-Semitism."[59] Indeed, one could find a wide spectrum of political and intellectual attitudes toward the Holocaust.[60] But it seems that he is not particularly interested in the discourse on the Holocaust, as was the case with most of the discussions in the course of the affair and after. He does not deviate from a common tendency in the Arab literature to circumvent the issue. Despite the value of *al-Ahram* as a source, it cannot represent by itself the discourse on the affair, the Holocaust, Zionism, Nazism, and the Jews. Achcar does not qualify his conclusions, and he clearly strives to exonerate Nasser and Arab nationalism from any proclivity to Nazism, and by being so eager to prove his thesis, he leans into polemic and ignores the diversity of the discourse on the Holocaust.

Achcar's work, nevertheless, is part of two new welcome phenomena in academic research. One is a wave of studies on Arab responses to Nazism and fascism by Western, Israeli and Arab scholars.[61] The other is a trend among Arab scholars to engage in the study of the Holocaust and related aspects, albeit in a limited way. Egyptian historian Ramsis 'Awad's *Between Acknowledgment and Denial* in 2000, and one of the chapters dealt with Deborah Lipstadt's *Denying the Holocaust*.[62] Egyptian scholar Haggag Ali reviewed Yehuda Bauer's book *Rethinking the Holocaust*, and compares Zygmunt Bauman's *Modernity and the Holocaust* with the work of 'Abd al-Wahhab al-Masiri.[63] Another Egyptian based in Germany, Omar Kamil, is involved in the study of the Holocaust in Arab memory.[64]

Conclusion

"The Eichmann trial was useful to the Arab side during the psychological battles of the 1960s as a way of exposing Israeli callousness to the Arabs, and not especially as an attempt to acquaint Arab readers with details of the Jewish experience," explained Palestinian intellectual Edward Said. Indeed, his remarks support the findings of this essay that the Holocaust was not the focus of the Arab public discourse regarding the trial. The newspaper reports and commentaries recognized the Holocaust as a crime against humanity, but counterbalanced it with the Palestinian tragedy, perceived as a crime no less serious and perhaps even more grievous. Said quoted the findings of a study on the Egyptian and Lebanese press coverage of the trial carried out by Usama Maqdisi, which confirmed that conclusion, but determined that there was no attempt to compare the Holocaust and the Palestinian tragedy, but rather to view them as "two great, despicable crimes."[65] Putting both events on the same plane diminishes the Holocaust and denies its uniqueness. That is not to deny the Palestinian tragedy, but in human history the events of the Holocaust defy comparison.

Some Jewish and Israeli scholars who have dealt with the trial have claimed that the themes of sympathy for Eichmann and regret that the annihilation had not been complete have been particularly characteristic of Arab discourse. Yehoshafat Harkabi gave the example of a cartoon appearing in the Lebanese paper *al-Anwar* which showed Ben-Gurion and Eichmann facing one another and shouting. Ben-Gurion says, "You deserve the death penalty for having killed six million Jews," and Eichmann answers, "There are a lot of people who claim that I deserve the death penalty for not finishing the job."[66] Historian of antisemitism Robert Wistrich wrote that the Arab reactions were "not feelings of regret for the Jewish Holocaust but rather sorrow that the Germans had not managed to finish the job."[67] Bernard Lewis, a historian of Islam and the Middle East, referred to a headline in a Saudi paper, "The capture of Eichmann, who had the honour of killing five million Jews,"[68] as being typical of Arab writing, whereas Hannah Arendt asserted that the Arabs did not conceal their sympathy for Eichmann.[69] The Israeli Foreign Ministry briefings on the Arab press reinforced those evaluations and gave prominence to the Arab claim that the trial was morally a form of torture for Eichmann, reminiscent of trials held under Stalin and Hitler.[70] Those evaluations were based on what had been written, but were far from reflecting the entire scope and nuances in the wider responses to the trial and the Holocaust.

The justification of the Holocaust and regret that the annihilation had not been complete were marginal themes or even absent in Egyptian and Lebanese writing on the trial. The implied identification with Eichmann stemmed primarily from a desire to strike a blow to Israel and Zionism, and not necessarily from censure of his past actions. References to Eichmann as a small cog and a clerk, merely following orders, were not the exclusive province of Arab discourse. Those arguments were part of an intensive international public debate over the trial. Intellectuals such as Egyptian leftists Lutfi al-Khuli and Ihsan 'Abd al-Qudus explicitly noted that their criticism of the trial and Israel did not arise from a desire to defend Eichmann or his deeds.[71]

The Eichmann trial, which served as a watershed event in shaping the attitudes of Israelis and Westerners toward the Holocaust, had a parallel, though opposite effect, on the Arab world, prompting Arab writers to intensify their efforts to either deny the Holocaust or accuse the Zionists of collaboration in the extermination of the Jews. References to the Holocaust as a Jewish tragedy or genocide became scarce.[72] Instead, the Holocaust was deprived of its uniqueness with its equation with the *nakba*; the victims were turned into perpetrators or were even held responsible for their destruction. The exacerbation of the Arab-Israeli conflict after 1967, and the growing movement of Western Holocaust deniers since the late 1970s, boosted Arab interest in the Holocaust. In addition to the rising volume of denial literature, and the growing sophistication of the argumentation, greater effort was made by pseudo-academic publications to "prove" Zionist-Nazi collaboration and the resemblance between the two movements.

The debate over the Holocaust remained dominated by the politics of the Arab-Israeli conflict and by the political realities of the Middle

East. The fact that the Holocaust continues to generate both sympathy and international support for Israel is a deep cause of Arab frustration. There has been a strong correlation between the growing role of the Holocaust in the Israeli and Jewish identity and collective memory and the frequency of Arab reference to it as a means to attack Israel and Zionism. The more central it has become in Jewish consciousness, the more antagonism it has aroused among Arabs and Muslims. Similarly, it seems that the intensified international interest in the Holocaust in the wake of the new millennium has elicited an increase in adversarial positions in Arab and Muslim debate.

NOTES

1 *Al-Hayat*, 2 June 1962.
2 Hanna Yablonka, "The Eichmann Trial and Israelis, 40 years Later," *Bi-Shvil Ha-Zikaron*, no. 41 (April–May 2001, Hebrew): 24.
3 Hanna Yablonka, "The Development of Holocaust Consciousness in Israel: The Nuremberg, Kapos, Kastner and Eichmann Trials," *Israel Studies* 8, no. 3 (Fall 2003): 1–24.
4 *Al-Musawwar*, 17 June 1960.
5 *Al-Ahram*, 6 April 1961.
6 *Al-Jumhuriyya* as quoted in *Middle East Report* 2 (1961): 187; *Arab Observer*, 4 June 1962, 13.
7 *Al-Jumhuriyya*, 3 May 1961; *al-Hayat*, 4 May 1961; Hannah Arendt, *Eichmann in Jerusalem: A Report on the Banality of Evil* (New York, 1963), 17. Eichmann's son, Klaus, had reportedly accused the Jewish leaders of giving the instructions for the killings. *Al-Ahram*, 15–18 December, 2, 3 June 1961; *al-Hayat*, 9 July 1961. The Jewish German newspaper *Deutsche Rundschau* regarded the statement as a result of the influence of former Nazi Johann von Leers, who had settled in Egypt and served as a propaganda adviser. *Wiener Library Bulletin* 15, no. 3 (1961): 48.
8 For a discussion of the annihilation of Hungarian Jews, see Yehuda Bauer, *Jews for Sale? Nazi-Jewish Negotiations, 1933–1945* (New Haven, 1994), 145–71.
9 *Ruz-al Yusuf*, 4 July 1960.
10 *Al-Ahram*, 6 April 1961. *Al-Hayat* gave a factual report about the deal when it was brought up during the trial. *Al-Hayat*, 13 June 1961. At a press conference in March 1961, the Mufti Hajj Amin al-Husayni also referred to it, noting that the Zionists had refused to accept old people, women, and children, and insisted, because of their military calculations, on only young people. "That truth shows how much the Zionists were willing to

sacrifice … for the sake of building up their military force in Palestine."
  Al-Hayat, 5 March 1961.

11 *Al-Hayat*, 7 February 1961.

12 *Al-Hayat*, 5 March 1961.

13 *Al-Ahram*, 12 April 1961. The claim that killing one person is the same
  as killing a million became more common later on, especially in Islamist
  discourse on the Holocaust, and was presented as an Islamic moral
  precept.

14 *Al-Ahram*, 18 May 1961.

15 *Akhir Saᶜa*, 12 April 1961. See also *al-Akhbar*, 14 April 1961.

16 *Akhir Saᶜa*, 26 April 1961. See also *Arab Observer*, 5 February 1962, 18.

17 *Al-Musawwar*, 21 April 1961.

18 *Al-Akhbar*, 12 April 1961. He referred to the Talmud and the books on
  Jewish history as "Zioniyyat," deriving it from "Isra'iliyyat," the term
  for the forged narratives from Jewish sources believed to be implanted
  in Islamic sources. For the significance of the "Isra'iliyyat," see Ronald
  L. Nettler, "Early Islam, Modern Islam and Judaism: The Isra'iliyyat in
  Modern Islamic Thought," in Ronald L. Nettler and Suha Taji-Faruki
  (eds.), *Muslim-Jewish Encounters: Intellectual Traditions and Modern Politics*
  (Amsterdam, 1998), 1–14.

19 *Al-Akhbar*, 26 April 1961. Also see Habib Jamati's article in *al-Musawwar*,
  21 April 1961.

20 An Israeli operation (27 December 2008–18 January 2009) launched in
  retaliation to rocket attacks on Israel by Palestinian militants in Gaza.

21 *Al-Ra'y*, 2 February 2009. In the same vein see http://www.aljazeera.net
  /programs/pages/432ceaee-6a44–4b96-ba56–5667a32c97f4;http://www
  .aljazeera.net/programs/pages/2228ef73–8888–4cf2–86b6–33adca106a4b.

22 *Al-Watan* (Kuwait), 8 March 2010, as quoted in Memri, *Special Dispatch*,
  no. 2891, 6 April 2010.

23 Muhammad Najm Halumi and Ahmad Muhammad Saqr, *Zionism, Past
  and Present* (Arabic) (Cairo, 1961), 51–60. See also Muhammad Nimr al-
  Madani, *Were the Jews Burnt in Gas Ovens?* (in Arabic) (Damascus, 1996),
  41–50.

24 'Ali and 'Abd al-Hadi, *The Terror State* (In Arabic), 71–80. See also 'Abd
  al-Munsif Mahmud, *The Jews and the Crime* (Arabic) (Cairo, 1967), 92–100.

25 Moshe Perlman, *How Eichmann Was Caught* (Tel Aviv, 1961).

26 Ahmad Baha' al-Din, *Isra'iliyyat* (Arabic) (Cairo, 1965), 168.

27 Ibid., 170.

28 ᶜAbd al-Wahhab al-Masiri, *Zionism, Nazism and the End of History* (Arabic)
  (Cairo, 1997).

29 Al-Masiri, *Zionism*, 120; Arendt, *Eichmann in Jerusalem*, 25.

30 Arendt, *Eichmann in Jerusalem*, 57.

31 Al-Masiri, *Zionism*, 121.

32 Al-Masiri, *Zionism*, 122; Arendt, *Eichmann in Jerusalem*, 16–17.

33 *The Palestinian Encyclopedia* (Arabic) (Damascus, 1974), vol. 4, 434; ᶜAbd al-Wahhab al-Masiri, "The Arab Propaganda and the Issue of Collaboration between the Nazis and the Zionists" (Arabic), http://www.elmessiri.com /ar/modules.php?name=News&file=article&sid=16.

34 *The Palestinian Encyclopedia*, vol. 4, 432–3; Kamal Saᶜfan, *The Jews: History and Religion* (Arabic) (Cairo, 1988), 105; Issa Nakhle, *Encyclopaedia of the Palestinian Problem* (New York, 1991), vol. 2, 875; Mahmud ᶜAbbas, *The Other Face: The Secret Relations between Nazism and Zionism* (Arabic) (Amman, 1984), 59; *al-Hurriyya*, 28 January 1990; Hayat al-Huwayk ᶜAtiyya, "The Zionist-Nazi Relation, 1933–1941" (Arabic), http://www .ssnp.info/thenews/daily/Makalat/Hayat/Hayat_5–12–05.htm.

35 Nakhle, *Encyclopaedia*, vol. 2, 873–4.

36 Al-Masiri, *Zionism*, 172–3; Mamduh al-Shaykh ᶜAli, "On a New Arab Reading of the Holocaust" (Arabic), http://www.islamdaily.net/AR /Contents.aspx?AID=2115. Muhammad ᶜAli Sirhan, "Who Monopolizes the Freedom of Opinion and Truth in the West" (Arabic), http://www.baath -party.org/monadel/no-339/almonadil339_8.htm.

37 Rafiq Shakir Natshe, *Colonialism and Palestine: Israel a Colonial Project* (Arabic) (Amman, 1984), 150–1. See also *al-Safir*, 15–21 November 1988.

38 Memri, *Special Dispatch Series*, no. 627, 12 December 2003, www.Memritv .org Clip. 896, 21 October 005. *Al-Shatat* described in 23 instalments the Jewish conspiracy to take over the world based on the *Protocols of the Elders of Zion*. It was first aired on Hizbullah's *Al-Manar* TV during Ramadan 2003, on two Iranian channels during Ramadan 2004, and on the Jordanian *al-Mamnuc* TV channel during Ramadan 2005.

39 Shihab al-Din Mufid, Al-Sayyid Yasin, and Yunan Labib Rizq, *Zionism and Racism: Zionism as One of the Methods of Racial Discrimination* (Arabic) (Cairo, 1977), 69–72.

40 Wajih 'Atiq 'Abd al-Sadiq, *International Policy and the Covert Egyptian-German Relations*, 1952–1965 (Arabic) (Cairo, 1991), 108–10.

41 Gilbert Achcar, "Eichmann in Cairo: The Eichmann Affair in Nasser's Egypt," *Arab Studies Journal* 20, no. 1 (Spring 2012): 74–103.

42 Gilbert Achcar, *The Arabs and the Holocaust: The Arab-Israeli War of Narratives* (London, 2010), 201–5.

43 Achcar, "Eichmann in Cairo," 74–5.

44 Ibid., 76.

45 Ibid., 77.

46 See Meir Litvak and Esther Webman, *From Empathy to Denial: Arab Responses to the Holocaust* (London and New York, 2009).

47 Ibid., 81.

48 Ibid., 89–91; *Al-Aram*, 12 April 1961. See also notes 13 and 14 above.

49 Achcar, "Eichmann in Cairo," 83–4.

50 Ibid., 77.

51 Litvak and Webman, *From Empathy to Denial*, 100.

52 *Al-Ahram*, 8 April 1961.

53 Achcar, "Eichmann in Cairo," 88.

54 Ibid., 102n47.

55 Roger Garaudy, *The Founding Myths of Israeli Politics* (Arabic) (Cairo, 1998).

56 *Al-Ahram*, 25 November 1960.

57 Achcar, "Eichmann in Cairo," 86–7.

58 Esther Webman, "Adoption of the Protocols in the Arab Discourse on the Arab-Israeli Conflict, Zionism, and the Jews," in *The Global Impact of the "Protocols of the Elders of Zion": A Century-Old myth*, ed. Esther Webman (London, 2011), 176–7.

59 Achcar, "Eichmann in Cairo," 99.

60 Litvak and Webman, *From Empathy to Denial*, 93–130.

61 See, for example, Gerhard Höpp, Peter Wien, and René Wildangel (eds.), *Blind für die Geschichte? Arabische Begegnungen mit dem Nationalsozialismus* (Berlin, 2004); Peter Wien, *Iraqi Arab Nationalism: Authoritarian, Totalitarian and Pro-Fascist Inclinations, 1932–1941* (London, 2006); René Wildangel, *Studie Zwischen Achse und Mandatsmacht: Palästina und der Nationalsozialismus* (Berlin, 2007); Jeffrey Herf, *Nazi Propaganda for the Arab World* (New Haven, 2009); Götz Nordbruch, *Nazism in Syria and Lebanon: The Ambivalence of the German Option, 1933–1945* (London, 2009); Israel Gershoni (ed.), *Arab Responses on Fascism and Nazism, 1933–1945: Attraction and Repulsion* (Austin, 2014).

62 Ramsis 'Awad, *Between Denial and Acknowledgment* (Arabic) (Cairo, 2000); Ramsis 'Awad, *The Nazi Concentration Camp in Occupied Poland: Treblinka* (Arabic) (Cairo, 2012).

63 Ali Haggag, "Modernity in the Discourse of Abdelwahab Elmessiri," *Intellectual Discourse* 19 (2011): 71–96.

64 Omar Kamil, *Der Holocaust im arabischen Gedächtnis: Eine Diskursgeschichte 1945–1967* (Leipzig, 2012).

65 *Al-Hayat*, 5 November 1997. The article appeared in English in *Al-Ahram Weekly* on 6 November 1997.

66 Yehoshafat Harkabi, *Arab Attitudes toward Israel* (Jerusalem, 1972), 257.

67 Robert Wistrich, *Anti-Zionism and Anti-Semitism in Our Time* (Hebrew) (Jerusalem, 1985), 14.

68 Bernard Lewis, *Semites and Anti-Semites: An Inquiry into Conflict and Prejudice* (London, 1997), 162.

69 Arendt, *Eichmann in Jerusalem*, 8–10.

70 HZ3757/12, Loya to Ouman, A memorandum about "the position of Arab broadcasts and the Arab press concerning the Eichmann trial," 16 April 1961.
71 See note 50 above; *Ruz al-Yusuf*, 13 June 1960.
72 Such an approach toward the Holocaust was evinced shortly after the end of the Second World War. See Litvak and Webman, *From Empathy to Denial*, 23–57.

PART IV

Representing Eichmann

11 Remaking Eichmann: Memories of Mass Murder and the Transatlantic Student Movements of the 1960s

THOMAS PEGELOW KAPLAN

The 1961–2 Eichmann trial brought about fundamental shifts in the ways in which West German and American societies commemorated the Hitler regime's genocidal crimes. The Jerusalem-based trial established, as Y. Michal Bodemann has argued, these crimes as a "national narrative" in postwar Germany – albeit in ways that largely denationalized the proceedings' defendant. Peter Krause has described the trial as an "important 'building block' for the German 'coming to terms with the past' [*Vergangenheitsbewältigung*]."[1] In the United States, the Eichmann trial also prompted profound transformations of the country's memory cultures. The extermination of the European Jews firmly emerged as a "unique event with its own proper name." As Americans began to conceive of European Jews as the Nazi regime's primary victims, the destruction of this minority population was no longer a mere "aspect of World War II." At the same time, the public and media discourses about the trial remained saturated with moral and universalizing messages that responded to Cold War constraints and further aided an "Americanization of the Holocaust."[2]

Trials like the one in Jerusalem or the subsequent Auschwitz trials in Frankfurt/Main were far from being the only causes for the growing societal willingness to confront recent mass crimes. Studies have also identified the student and youth revolts of the 1960s as a key factor. In their much-noted perpetrator focus, student protesters in the Bonn Republic and United States alike constructed continuities between Nazi mass murderers and leading West German and American political and military figures. Charles DeBenedetti and Charles Chatfield have stipulated that American student and anti-Vietnam War protesters increasingly used the "analogue of Nazi Germany," because it allowed them to "reaffir[m] the Nuremberg doctrine of personal responsibility to resist evil" and undercut the US government's invoking of the failed 1930 appeasement policies. Yet, by constructing a "moral yardstick" based on Holocaust imagery that served their political needs, American activists also marginalized Jewish victimhood and undermined the crimes' conceptualization as a particularistic act against the Jewish people.[3] Reviving polemics and distinctly politicized debates of the 1960s, a number of works on the West German protests, most prominently by Götz Aly, went as far as characterizing leftist activists' use of analogies and perpetrator focus as an "escap[e]" from an emerging societal discussion of Nazi crimes, while increasingly subscribing to antisemitism.[4]

Neither the societal commemorations of mass crimes nor the 1960s student protests, however, can be adequately explained by limiting the analysis to national frameworks. Transnational and increasingly global exchanges shaped collective memories, protest practices, and even the imagery and words available to individuals in countries such as West Germany and the United States to depict these phenomena. On the one hand, much of the recent literature on transnational memories of genocide, including the influential work by Daniel Levy and Natan Sznaider, has strikingly downplayed or ignored the role of leftist protest movements. Studies on the global dimensions of these protests, on the other hand, still devote little space to the examination of the activists' impact on emerging transnational memories of mass crimes.[5]

My essay brings together these two vibrant strands of research, the emergence of Holocaust memory and the role of 1960s student radicalism, by focusing on West German and American student protesters' appropriation and remaking of depictions of Adolf Eichmann. Re-examining key debates, it contributes to our understanding of the crucial transnational dimensions of how concepts and memories of genocide, victimhood, and perpetration evolved in the postwar period. More so than any other Nazi perpetrator, Eichmann occupied the minds of early 1960s student activists. In the course of the decade, he emerged, especially among US protesters, as the archetypal perpetrator of twentieth-century mass crimes. These activists on and off university campuses were hardly the first to turn to the figure of this Nazi perpetrator. More often than not, they appropriated Eichmann imagery precisely because it became so widely recognized in their respective societies at the time of his arrest and trial in the early 1960s. As the protesters participated in giving "iconographic status" to the Nazi regime's genocidal crimes, especially against the Jews, and turning them into a basis of a new "moral standard,"[6] they were keenly aware of the symbolic and political power of naming, comparing, or equating past and present perpetrators with Eichmann. In some cases, there also was a genuine fear of past and surviving Nazi mass murderers.[7] While specific national, regional, and even local factors remain crucial to understand how and why student protesters appropriated Eichmann imagery, these young men and women's political and cultural practices, like the Eichmann trial and its broader reception, evolved as increasingly transnational phenomena. By the mid-1960s, transatlantic ties between West German and American protesters played an essential role in developing their perpetrator imagery and remained important for the impact of the groups' activism on their countries' collective memories.

No trial – or protest – could "by itself," as the late David Cesarani has rightfully pointed out, create broad awareness of a mass crime or what became known as the Holocaust. Like the student protests, the Eichmann trial and its coverage operated in the framework of pre-existing concepts and discourses.[8] Yet, both the trial and the ways in which student protesters continued to invoke and remake its defendant introduced new formats, reiterated specific imagery over other depictions, and triggered individual and collective memories that altered West German and American memory cultures.

How then did student organizers in the Federal Republic of Germany and the United States of America depict Adolf Eichmann? How did they interact, transfer, and translate these images? To what extent was their evolving remaking of Eichmann related to the movements' ongoing radicalization? What, finally, was the impact of the protesters' portrayals of Eichmann on the broader societal memory cultures, perpetrator imagery, and processes of "coming to terms" with genocide?

The Eichmann Trial and the Voices of Student Activists

In West Germany and the United States alike, the print media and television news featured the Eichmann trial in thousands of articles, reports, and editorials.[9] Among the more than 700 journalists who attended the trial's opening in Jerusalem in April 1961, there were sizable contingents of American and West German reporters. Initially, newspaper readers and television audiences confronted images and printed descriptions of Eichmann on a daily basis. According to a May 1961 Gallup poll, 88 per cent of all Americans were "very" or "fairly" interested in the trial. A stunning 80 per cent of young Americans in and after school kept up with the news coverage.[10] At German universities, many students, too, followed the trial. Activists in university-based German-Israeli Study Groups (Deutsch-Israelische Studiengruppen, DIS), predominantly centre-left Israel solidarity organizations founded in the late 1950s, eagerly discussed the proceedings, the accused, and his role in the mass extermination of European Jewry. Heinz Wewer of the DIS chapter at the Free University (FU) of Berlin even convinced West Berlin's Senator of the Interior Joachim Lipschitz to fund his travels to Israel.[11] He spent several months in Jerusalem, observed the proceedings, and reported extensively on the defendant. Wewer did not only share his reflections with fellow students by publishing them in the German-Israeli Study Groups' journal *DISkussion*. With the help of Hanns-Peter Herz, the first editor-in-chief of RIAS Berlin whom the Nazi regime had persecuted as a "Jewish *Mischling*," the DIS activist also reported on the Eichmann trial on the radio. His eleven short features on RIAS, the popular US-founded radio station in the American sector of the divided city, reached a considerably broader audience than any speeches or student group publications.[12]

In his contributions for *DISkussion*'s May 1961 issue, the twenty-six-year-old Wewer presented an image of Eichmann as the "ruthless tool of a merciless machinery of murder." Merging the defendant's courtroom behaviour with his past genocidal practice, Wewer emphasized Eichmann's "habitus of a subject [*Untertanen*]" that was marked by his willingness to "execute his 'duty' assiduously and with cold perfectionism." He "personally saw to it that six million human beings had been killed on time and in proper form [*ordnungsgemäss*]." Yet, with his "lack of individuality" and "inconspicuous" motions in his "glass cell," Eichmann represented, Wewer noted, the "image of a petty bourgeois par excellence." A similar version of Wewer's May 1961 essay had already been aired by RIAS Berlin on 19 April. Even more so than in the *DISkussion* contribution, Wewer used the longer broadcast to unquestionably identify Eichmann as a "German" and, even more chilling for German radio audiences, "one of us." The former SS officer "shockingly" differed from the prevalent societal "cliché of a mass murderer" which, as the DIS activist implied, was in need of revision.[13]

Wewer's construction of a petty bourgeois public servant of mass murder was typical of the early Eichmann imagery by centre-leftist West German student papers and activists. In its June 1961 issue, the Frankfurt/Main-based *Diskus*, one of the country's most prominent student newspapers, for instance, likewise presented Eichmann as a "recipient of orders" (*Befehlsempfänger*), a "dutiful public servant," and someone who carried out his "duty – for the fatherland."[14] This imagery drew on Eichmann portrayals in the mainstream media, which student activists and editors followed closely. Although these students attacked the yellow press, especially the Springer Publishing House's tabloid *Bild*, for commercializing the Eichmann "boom," "demonizing" the defendant, and constructing a "welcome scapegoat," they also reiterated key media depictions such as those of a "public servant of murder"

(*Mordbeamter*), who acted "without hatred," from centrist publications such as *Die Zeit* and *Der Stern*.[15] *Diskus*, known for its biting attacks on institutions of the Federal Republic, even reviewed the Eichmann book by mainstream journalist Robert Pendorf in a favourable light. Pendorf had been among the first to peddle the concept of *Mordbeamter*.[16] All in all, student newspaper editors and activists hardly initiated, but supported and strengthened, an ongoing shift in the dominant mass murder imagery of West German collective memories, from sadistic "concentration camp brute" (*Unmensch*) and "henchman" to "desk murderer" and "desk perpetrator" (*Schreibtischtäter*). No figure was more associated with this new imagery than the defendant in the Jerusalem courtroom.[17]

In the early 1960s, the vast majority of students – not unlike many adult journalists – showed a very limited understanding of the Nazi genocide and its perpetration. Yet, student activists hardly approached the Eichmann trial unprepared. They were able to draw on memory-triggering images, narratives, and concepts that fellow activists had already tested. In July 1959, the delegates' conference of the German Socialist Student Union (Sozialistischer Deutscher Studentenbund, SDS) had endorsed the exhibition "Unredeemed Nazi Justice" spearheaded by the West Berlin–based Reinhard Strecker, who was an active member of both the FU's SDS and DIS chapters. Running in various West German cities until 1962 and, in a revised version, in 1967–8, the exhibit mainly targeted former Nazi jurists who had been involved in prosecuting the regime's alleged enemies and were again serving in West German courts.[18] In the eyes of the SDS, these former Nazis were only the tip of the iceberg and represented a renewed rise of fascism.

In contrast to mainstream media discourses and the Federal Republic's hegemonic memory cultures, activists in and beyond SDS and DIS chapters consistently situated the petty bourgeois desk perpetrator Eichmann among "tens of thousands" of "self-proclaimed members of the master race [*Herrenmenschen*]." As Heinz Wewer reminded RIAS listeners in one of his features from the Jerusalem trial, there were many "Eichmanns invisibly sitting next to" the defendant.[19] Regardless of their involvement in mass murder, many of these men had managed to regain influential positions in the West German ministerial bureaucracy and court system. While some West German newspaper editors and memory makers spoke of other *Eichmänner* who still needed to be brought to justice, they rarely went as far as radicalized student activists like Strecker. To merely remake notions of mass murderers was not sufficient. "Purely scientific research" with its, as Strecker understood it, obligation not to reveal the names of living perpetrators was not enough. Instead, the SDS activist concluded in a contribution to the

Eichmann trial coverage of the prominent leftist journal *Das Argument*, "a purification of our public life from the criminals of the Nazi period and their accomplices ... was not possible without naming names."[20]

Appearing in the year of the Eichmann trial, Strecker's book on Hans Globke, an impressive compilation of documents on the author of an influential legal commentary on the 1935 Nuremberg Laws and former Interior Ministry division head, revealed names along with new imagery of perpetrators and mass crimes. Strecker drew multiple connections between Eichmann and Globke, whose postwar career had culminated in the position of state secretary in the Office of the Federal Chancellery. First, Globke, like Eichmann, emerged as a desk perpetrator. "From a desk," Strecker quoted one of the Nazi state's victims, Globke laid "the foundations ... to outlaw the Jews so that they could be murdered ... by the millions." Second, Strecker related direct contacts between Eichmann and Globke in 1943, when the latter allegedly prevented the rescue of thousands of Greek Jews.[21] The Eichmann trial in Jerusalem also shed light on Globke's role in the regime's mass crimes. In West Germany, however, media attention surrounding Chancellor Adenauer's confidant soon died down again after Globke had brought lawsuits.[22] For centre-leftist student activists like Strecker, meanwhile, the need to name perpetrators and identify crimes persisted. Time and again, they presented images of Eichmann as exemplary of "subject types and petit bourgeois without moral antenna." In fact, he appeared as their very "progenitor [*Stammvater*]." Further universalizing perpetrator imagery, these protesters had little doubt that future "brutes" (*Un-Menschen*) would "carry out Führer orders even more literally." They would "plead superior orders ... the new form of crimes that courts accepted."[23]

All too eagerly, West German activists charged members of the older generations with attempts to "render the past taboo and eliminate it from memory." "Foreign countries," Gerhard Schoenberner wrote in *Das Argument*'s Eichmann coverage, "ke[pt] a much sharper memory of these years."[24] Even a cursory look at collective memories of white Christian Americans at the beginning of the 1960s demonstrates the need to qualify this claim. Outside of American-Jewish temples and homes, the Nazi regime's genocidal practices barely played a role in Americans' communicative memories.[25] If at all, white Christian Americans associated genocidal perpetrators with memories of Stalinist mass crimes, reflecting the escalating Cold War. Few non-Jewish college students connected their veteran relatives with the Holocaust – be it as camp liberators or passive bystanders.[26] Confronted with the Eichmann trial and the massive media attention, American students, like their West German counterparts, turned to press and television news to grasp the enormity of the crimes and nature of their perpetration. Student newspaper authors and activists were no exception.

In a three-part series published in the *Daily Tar Heel*, the University of North Carolina at Chapel Hill's student daily, Wade Wellman depicted Eichmann as "one of the biggest cogs in the whole disgusting apparatus." Writing in January 1961, Wellman presented an all-powerful Eichmann who had personally ordered Jews to be gassed and was "purportedly responsible for the slaughtering of some six million Jews under Hitler's Third Reich." Eichmann had, the articles claimed, displayed "fanatical dedication" to "carr[ying] out his tasks," was committed to an "ugly, sadistic plight," and unwilling to "repent in any way."[27] This representation owed a lot to prevalent pre-Eichmann trial depictions of Nazi perpetrators as sadists and psychopathic individuals in the mainstream American press that helped shape readers' memories of these crimes.

Wellman's depiction of Eichmann did not limit the Nazi perpetrator to mass crimes against Jews. His refusal to connect Eichmann to a particularistic anti-Jewish act already constituted one step in the direction of the universal perpetrator imagery of mid-to-late 1960s student activists. The court's designation of "crimes against the Jewish people," he wrote, was an "unrealistic wording," since the "overall design" of Eichmann's crimes "was to eliminate or reduce all population groups that did not meet Nazi racial standards." Still, Wellman was well aware of the implications of a more universal imagery. For once, he argued against its broad applicability to other crimes. His hypothetical reference to the Congolese Republic's taking "jurisdiction in the persecution of Negro minorities in the United States" serves as a case in point. His ardent rejection of this imagined scenario also underpinned his questioning of the Israeli government's right to try Eichmann – an issue much debated in the American press. Furthermore, Wellman also stayed clear, as did the American news media in general, of what contemporary American-Jewish publications described as the "failures of the free world" that "had contributed to the catastrophe" for European Jewry.[28]

Wellman represents but one voice among the growing cacophony of utterances by American student editors and activists who tackled the Eichmann trial and its implications. In its reiteration of older Nazi perpetrator imagery and drive to defend rather than criticize US government policies, his contribution is representative of many moderate student views and voices at the beginning of the decade and during the trial preparation. *The Skirl*, the student newspaper of Flora MacDonald College in North Carolina, captured and privileged views of

classmates who talked of "6,000,000 people … unmercifully slaughtered" and Eichmann as the "murderer" whom "the world kn[ew]."
They sharply contrasted their own world of "freedom-loving people"
with Eichmann's "barbaric cruelties." On the campus of the University
of Southern California, students talked about how "mentally deranged"
Eichmann must have been.[29]

As the trial continued, some student activists and editors began to
adjust their image of Eichmann and Nazi perpetrators. In a 27 June
1961 editorial, University of Michigan student Peter Steinberger explicitly rejected "perverted ambition" or "greed" as motivations for Eichmann's actions. Instead, the *Michigan Daily* editor presented him as an
"efficient organizer" and someone who was about to be "punished only
for doing his duty, for doing a good job." Steinberger pushed the image
even further. "The Germans" were "our allies" now, he continued, and
Americans bore a "little guilt" for not having taken in "Jewish refugees
before the Germans killed them."[30] Steinberger's rejection of the claim
that "it c[ould] not happen here" and his refusal to acknowledge a "difference in kind" between Eichmann and Americans prompted an out-
cry among student readers. In letters to the editor, they challenged the
image of Eichmann as a man of "entirely normal ambition." Students
also called Steinberger too "immature" for the position of editor and
refuted the claim that he expressed the views of Ann Arbor students
and "many millions of Americans."[31]

Finally, contributions by authors like Wellman and Steinberger do
not reveal any discernible impact of exchanges with foreign student
activists on American students' early Eichmann constructions. And yet,
like most student activists' take on the Eichmann imagery evoked by
Steinberger, this lack of impact was soon to change.

The Radicalization of Student Protests and Reconstruction
of Eichmann Imagery

In the early 1960s, an increasing number of students from universities
across the United States joined the civil rights struggles taking place
across the South. Radicalized in the often-violent confrontations with
white Southern racists, these young men and women also stepped up
the socio-political engagement at their home institutions. The much-
discussed Free Speech Movement (FSM) that started at the University
of California, Berkeley, in the fall of 1964 to defend the right to political
activism on campus was all but the most prominent example. In their
struggle against the university bureaucracy and police that soon aimed
at higher education reform and social change, movement leaders and

the rank and file eagerly searched for explanations for the status quo and the behaviour of their opponents, soon connecting their reflections to broader perpetrator imageries.[32] The 2 October 1964 car-top speech of Mario Savio, an eloquent philosophy major, son of Catholic Italian immigrants, and prominent FSM leader, illustrates this dynamic.

When Savio made his way through the crowd surrounding the campus police car that held arrested civil rights veteran Jack Weinberg, he addressed his fellow students with a commanding "Let me tell you what's going on, folks!" After a brief comment on the university administration, Savio, now standing on top of the car, turned to the subject of the police: "We must really feel very, very sorry for these poor policemen here … Good men, they're family men, you know. They have a job to do. That's right, they have a job to do. It's very like, you know, Adolf Eichmann. He had a job to do: He fed them to the machinery."[33]

Not known to many, Savio's Eichmann comparison, first, had a personal dimension. Memories of the war and mass murder in Europe were highly significant for the speaker. His father Joseph had fought in the US Army during the first three years of Savio's life. At this time, his maternal grandfather, a self-proclaimed fascist and Benito Mussolini admirer, acted as the head of their Manhattan-based household. Second, and even less acknowledged, Savio's mention of Eichmann in his mockery of campus police was prompted by a fellow student's shout of "Just like Eichmann."[34] This interjection and Savio's readiness to incorporate it in his speech exemplified the lasting impact of the Eichmann trial and the prevalence of new frames of reference in which the SS officer figured prominently. This prominence, finally, also has to be tied to Hannah Arendt's *Eichmann in Jerusalem* that first appeared as a five-part series in *The New Yorker* in early 1963.[35]

Arendt's interpretation of Eichmann had become, as Sidra DeKoven Ezrahi aptly phrased it, "the filter through which most Americans" had been "able to conceptualize what was otherwise a morass of indigestible, unintegrable facts" – a "filter" embraced by most American college students.[36] FSM rank-and-file activists in Berkeley repeatedly pointed to the lessons of the mass crimes of Nazi Germany and Eichmann in particular, alluding to Arendt's work. A history graduate student, for example, cited Arendt's writings and the image of Eichmann as the "classic obedient man." Unlike Eichmann, most FSM activists had clearly understood the "perils of silent obedience." This awareness had, the Berkeley student further stressed, enabled them to get involved in "one the great moral issues of our century."[37]

Arendt's reading of Eichmann appealed to many student audiences in- and outside the FSM because it subjected the Nazi perpetrator to a

profound universalization and detached him from the historical referent of the Holocaust. As Arendt put it, Eichmann had to be seen as a
"new type of criminal ... who commits his crimes under circumstances
that make it well-nigh impossible for him to know or feel that he is
doing wrong." The "banality of evil" was rooted in the absence of "evil
instinct" or fanaticism from Eichmann's actions. Instead, his deeds
were the results of the "sheer thoughtlessness" of a mediocre bureaucrat with "no motivations" other than serving a totalitarian state.[38] As
Arendt sought to clarify in a fall 1964 German radio interview with
Joachim Fest, Eichmann displayed an "outrageous stupidity." His
"banality" had "no profundity" and could also not be equated with the
"everyday." In fact, she stressed, "Eichmann is not ... in each of us."
Still, Arendt had turned Eichmann into a "personal, moral," and, one
might add, ahistorical "problem."[39]

In their emphasis on notions of a "recipient of orders" and dutiful,
petty bourgeois public servant, West German student activists and editors had already anticipated components of Arendt's depiction in their
1961 reflections on the trial. Some had been familiar with Arendt's work,
especially her studies of totalitarianism, prior to the trial. Heinz Wewer,
who later launched the *DISkussion* in West Berlin, had even met with
Arendt during her time as a visiting professor at Princeton University,
where Wewer was a graduate student in the late 1950s. He encountered
her again among the observers of the court proceedings in Jerusalem.
In his more recent autobiographical reflections, Wewer takes issue with
Arendt's analysis of the Eichmann trial, especially her dictum of the
"banality of evil." "Evil" has too much of a "religious" connotation,
Wewer stresses, and might at best serve as "one of many metaphors ...
because the unspeakable cannot be adequately named." "Pale, bourgeois characters like ... Eichmann," he admits, "were certainly banal."
By alluding to the "bureaucratic routine" of the "desk component"
of the murderous practices, Wewer's characterization comes closer to
his early 1960s observations on Eichmann. In one of his RIAS features
of May 1961, Wewer, for example, found some credibility in Arendt's
claim that Eichmann was plagued not by "shame," but by "his incomplete success as an official of extermination [*Ausrottungsfunktionär*]."[40]

Like many West German student activists and editors, Wewer found
confirmation for his 1960s Eichmann imagery in Arendt's work, which
had appeared in a German translation in 1964 and could ignore later
clarifications, as in her interview with Fest. The circumstance that a considerable number of German academics rejected Arendt's reading must
have also increased her appeal among some student radicals.[41] Wolfgang
Kraushaar's claim that student movement activists principally ignored

the German-Jewish émigré academic is in need of more nuance.[42] Even if New Leftists found little common ground owing to Arendt's hostility to Marxist thought, West German and American student protesters of all stripes borrowed from her Eichmann imagery. Some, like Daniel Cohn-Bendit and Hans-Jürgen Benedict, a doctoral student at Bochum University, corresponded with the New School–based political philosopher in 1967–8. In a letter of 27 June 1968, Arendt directly supported Cohn-Bendit's political activism and analysis in France and West Germany. For his part, Benedict particularly pushed the universalism of Arendt's writings on Eichmann further and readily introduced Auschwitz-Vietnam comparisons.[43]

German and American student activists did not only share indirect connections in their reading of Arendt's Eichmann treatise. They also increasingly interacted directly, coined transnational protest languages, and engaged in multidirectional transfers in which naming practices and Eichmann imagery played a considerable role. Bernardine Dohrn, who rose to the position of interorganizational secretary in the American leftist organization Students for a Democratic Society (SDS) and travelled extensively to meet with German activists in Frankfurt/Main and other European cities, had watched the Eichmann coverage on US television in 1961 and continued to be moved by the image of the Gestapo officer in the glass box.[44] The employment of this imagery was explicitly linked to transformations – partially triggered by the Eichmann trial – in public discourses and memory cultures in both the United States and West Germany that identified the Holocaust as a distinct genocidal crime against the Jewish people. As a result, American and West German student activists could rely on a considerable overlap in the "interpretative repertoire" and in the very terminology used to address mass crimes and their perpetration.[45] Moreover, protesters from both societies were keenly aware of the highly charged nature of any Holocaust reference. Given their privileged position of speaking at their countries' often revered institutions of higher learning, their protest practices and Eichmann imagery, in turn, enforced and reiterated these transformations.

West German and American student activists also increasingly took advantage of academic exchange programs between universities in the two countries that had accompanied the integration of the Federal Republic into the US-dominated Western military and political alliance system. Among the participants in UC Berkeley's Free Speech Movement in 1964–5 were some West German exchange students. They conveyed protest narratives that deliberately integrated the communicative memories of past Nazi crimes and reinstated perpetrators, while simultaneously absorbing American protesters' perpetrator and Eichmann imagery. One moderate German FSMer readily conveyed to his comrades the practices of Nazi officials at German universities during the "Third Reich," including the "aboli[tion of] traditional freedom," which had motivated him to participate in the Berkeley protests. Yet, the student stopped short of equating the current situation on the California campus with Germany's universities under Hitler.[46] Other German students who spent time at American universities voiced more radical positions. Günther Amendt, a member of the SDS Frankfurt/Main chapter, eagerly analysed Berkeley protest practices and narratives, including Savio's car-top speech, for his West German comrades in the SDS journal *Neue Kritik*. Discussing calls for violence by Black activists, "always the victims" of the other side's "violence and brutality," Amendt drew on Holocaust references to find support for this break with the FSM's commitment to nonviolence. His use of "Mississippi's concentration camp prisons" fused the protest lingos of West German and US student radicals. Amendt communicated these concepts and memories of Nazism to his counterparts in the American SDS. As the German and American SDS intensified their contacts and collaboration during the second half of the decade, they also frequently exchanged speakers and movement periodicals that cited and blended their Eichmann and perpetrator imageries.[47]

The escalating American War in Vietnam drastically altered the protest practices and projects of student activists in the United States and West Germany. Swiftly, the war moved to the centre of the activists' work and turned small groups into mass movements that received international attention. With the enforcement of the Selective Service Act on American university campuses and a rising death toll on all sides, the conflict in Southeast Asia created an ever-greater sense of urgency for American activists. Published in the SDS *New Left Notes* in early 1967, Ralph Schoenman's "Eichmann and Everyman" captured these sentiments. Schoenman placed Eichmann on one side of "the barricades of a moral divide." "'We,' said Eichmann, 'only provided the lorries.'" On the opposing side, the author presented the Cuban revolutionary leader José Martí: "He who witnesses a crime in silence, commits it." For Schoenman, there was no middle ground "between Marti and Eichmann." "There are only those who move from passivity, in the face of horror, to resistance, and those who shrink from resistance no matter what camouflage they contrive," he continued.[48]

In the language of Schoenman and many radicalized SDSers, Eichmann had taken on new relevance. The students' Eichmann imagery was still part of an Arendtian moral problem, now in its New Leftist rendition of a "morality play" in which the Gestapo officer constituted the "epitome of the bureaucratic functionary apathetic to his own complicity in a monstrous wrong."[49] Yet, the stakes had shifted considerably from allegedly Eichmann-like police officers enforcing a crackdown on a politically active campus to Eichmann-like military bureaucrats and perpetrators involved in an imperialist war of aggression. Moreover, the Eichmann imagery now firmly appeared in a Marxist analysis that partially returned to the Old Left's crude categories of anti-imperialism. Currently, Schoenman continued, the "Vietnamese [we]re carrying the whole burden for the cause of oppressed peoples in the world ... As many fronts against American imperialism as possible" were needed to escape being "crush[ed]" by it.[50]

Finally, the SDS editors employed the widely understood Eichmann reference as a blatant justification for political action by the New Left, including the SDS' 1966–7 policy shift "from," in SDS national secretary Greg Calvert's words, "protest to resistance."[51] The range and form of "resistance," meanwhile, remained vague. In light of the unfathomable crime of Nazi genocide, even violence against persons seemed justified. Still, to interpret the SDS' Eichmann references as mere street propaganda amounts to a distortedly narrow view. Instead, in many of the more radical SDS activists' communicative memories, the threats of Eichmann-like perpetrators were all too real. Mark Rudd, typical of other SDSers from Jewish-American families who were raised in communities with many Holocaust survivors, believed American racism to be "akin to German racism towards Jews." As in the case of the New Left's universalized Eichmann, "killing Vietnamese en masse was of no moral consequence to American war planners," Rudd contended.[52] In this sense, Eichmann imagery as part of activists' collective memories helped to propel them into action and radicalized their protests. Many came to operate in what Hannah Arendt observed as a "peculiar desperation" that was in no small part rooted in a perceived lack of allies, even among mainstream liberals. As SDS President Carl Oglesby had phrased it at the large 27 November 1965 anti-war rally in Washington, DC, "the men who now engineer that war – those who study maps, give the commands, push the buttons ... McNamara, Rusk ... the President himself. They are not moral monsters. They are all honorable men. They are all liberals." Without directly invoking Eichmann, Oglesby's wording attributed components of the SDS' Nazi perpetrator imagery to the United States' top leadership.[53] His remarks raised the stakes in a morally charged struggle and propelled student and other protesters to radicalize their activism.

Urged by activists returning from the United States, like Günther Amendt and K.D. Wolff, the 1967–8 SDS chair, student protesters in West Germany read the publications of their fellow American activists, absorbed their perpetrator imagery, and followed the calls for "insurgent actions."[54] American SDSers who travelled to Germany, in turn, encountered their West German counterparts' narratives and imagery of Eichmann-like figures in the country of the Nazi murderers. When Patty Lee Parmalee and Susan Klonsky of the American SDS, for example, participated in the International Vietnam Congress at the Technical University of Berlin in February 1968, they did not only confront this imagery in conversations with German leftists. They also made out its manifestations in the nameless counterdemonstrators and police officers during the street protests that followed the conference. The twenty-one-year-old Klonsky, who had only recently learned about the Germans' murder of many members of her extended Jewish family in early 1940s Poland and Latvia, discussed at length her political work with West German SDSers such as K.D. Wolff. Like Parmalee, she addressed the Vietnam Congress, tackling the American War in Vietnam and American perpetrators, and spoke at smaller gatherings of leftist activists in the Federal Republic. Upon her return to Los Angeles, where she worked at the SDS Regional Office, Klonsky had words of warning for the participants of an anti-war rally. She reported seeing "Nazis … alive and well and living in Germany and . . in other places," incorporating impressions and imageries she had shared and developed with her West German comrades.[55]

For leftist West German and American activists alike, these transnational transfers of knowledge and verbiage were in need of translation. The protesters had to render them intelligible and applicable to the specific politico-cultural contexts of their struggles on both sides of the Atlantic. American activists increasingly employed imagery of an ever more universalized Eichmann. In its final renditions by leading Yippies and anti-Vietnam war activists like Abbie Hoffman, these constructs were devoid of any elements that linked the SS officer to the Nazi genocide or even German fascism. As "a careerist," "Eichmann lives by the rules," Hoffman wrote in 1968, but "there are no rules, only images" and revolutionary "practice." In contrast to the German SDSers whom he met at the September 1968 International Assembly of Revolutionary Student Movements at Columbia University, Hoffman was not well-versed in Marxist theory, but endorsed political theatre as a revolutionary strategy that indeed required some translation.[56]

While American students like Parmalee, Klonsky, and Hoffman – also prodded by their encounters with West German activists – stepped up their references to Eichmann as the widely recognizable archetypal perpetrator of genocide, their West German counterparts increasingly let him fade into the background. Still, Eichmann remained a reference point. Gerd Koenen of the Tübingen SDS, for instance, shocked an auditorium with a largely non-student audience with the claim that any "brave bourgeois and dachshund owner" could be a "pale desk murderer of the Eichmann type."[57] Unlike their American comrades, many German activists, however, had former Nazis in their extended families and saw themselves constantly surrounded by them at home and in the streets. They consequently carried Strecker's naming practices further. Following the June 1967 death of the student Benno Ohnesorg at the anti-Shah rally, activists focused on Hans-Ulrich Werner, the commander of West Berlin's uniformed police who had been in charge of police operations during this protest. Eight months after Ohnesorg's death, the site of the Vietnam Congress at the Technical University of Berlin was inundated with posters depicting the police officer as "SS-Werner" responsible for "mass executions" in the German-occupied Soviet Union in 1942. In the communicative memory of German student activists, the situation had reached a new urgency as the former perpetrators of genocidal crimes had begun to strike and kill once more.[58]

Perceiving themselves as likely future victims of old and new Nazis, leftist German students increasingly identified with often brutalized African American Black Power activists or slaughtered Vietnamese. This framing strengthened the appeal of the more universal Eichmann perpetrator imagery of US activists and their call for resistance. While German student radicals waged their "resistance" against the "Auschwitz generation" at home, they also joined their American counterparts in their alleged struggles against the Eichmann-like murderers abroad. Continually claiming the moral high ground, cohorts of the American and West German New Leftists even felt justified to apply their Eichmann imagery to Israel after the Six-Day War, the very country that had tried the Gestapo officer in the first place.[59]

Student Revolts, Eichmann Imageries, and Transformations of Societal Memory Cultures

The student activists' naming practices and remaking of Eichmann representations in the aftermath of the Jerusalem-based trial had a profound and lasting impact on collective memories in West Germany and the United States. First and foremost, these practices reshaped communicative memories of the student activists and their sympathizers in the broader New Left subcultures themselves. By the end of the 1960s, these groups numbered several hundred thousand in the United States alone. With varying degrees of intensity, these activists used Eichmann imagery to raise their awareness of a violent past, explain a deeply troubling present, and reassure themselves of their protest identities. In a talk at the Free University of Berlin in May 1965, Reinhard Strecker reminded his student audience of the "pogrom atmosphere" that had characterized public responses to his exhibition, the death threats levelled against him, and the law professor who had discussed the exhibition in a lecture to illustrate the offence of treason.[60] Like Globke, Franz Six, and Otto Ambros,[61] Eichmann was more than a figurehead; evoking his name and the associated memories had real consequences. During the second half of the 1960s, the increased interaction between American and West German protesters and its impact on the remaking of Eichmann imagery further altered their communicative memories. The reimported, increasingly denationalized, and universalized Eichmann of US radicals allowed younger cohorts of West German protesters to detach their memories from historic events specific to Nazism and imagine themselves as anti-fascist crusaders surrounded by capitalist-imperialist foes.

Second, even if markedly difficult to determine, the New Left's naming and protest practices also reshaped the broader American and West German memory cultures. Wilfried Mausbach has argued that the protesters' Vietnam-Holocaust comparisons in which Eichmann imagery figured prominently "failed to shatter the self-image of mainstream America" and alter its memory cultures in ways imagined by student radicals.[62] Evidence from mainstream newspaper coverage and letters to the editor calls this broad claim into question. Speaking to a *New York Times* reporter in Vietnam in late 1968, American Green Berets, for example, readily remembered the SS officer. Reflecting the growing loss of confidence in the war, one sergeant eerily "side[d] with Eichmann." His actions had been "inhuman and ruthless – but he had his orders." The men remembered the Nazi perpetrator in light of their own army's court-martialling of eight soldiers who had murdered an alleged Vietnamese spy.[63] American student and peace activists pushed the Eichmann-Vietnam comparisons harder than any other group to depict conflicts at home and abroad. Even if the Berets sought to construct the following of orders as something positive, they nonetheless revealed a striking overlap with the leftist students' Eichmann-Vietnam equation. The protest practices did indeed trigger, and even begin to reshape, collective memories of Americans far beyond the movement.

In the United States and West Germany, broader collective memories of mass crimes remained constantly contested. By the end of the decade, the radicalization of student and anti-war protests increasingly prompted memories among middle-class German onlookers that turned the protesters' use of Eichmann imagery on its head. In a letter to the *Stuttgarter Zeitung* during the "Easter Riots" of April 1968, an older male reader – representative of many – emphasized that the violence and rhetoric of student radicals brought back "memories" of "SA thugs."[64] Similar claims appeared in letters published in other dailies. An already-imprisoned Ulrike Meinhof, whose transition from anti-fascist columnist to left-wing terrorist exemplified the extreme response to the perceived threat of old and new Nazis, illustrated this dynamic during her appearance at Horst Mahler's trial in December 1972. When the presiding judge threatened to transfer an uncooperative Meinhof to the courtroom's special plate glass box, the witness exploded, "You threaten me with your Eichmann box, you fascist, you pig. You want to lock anti-fascists into that box in which Genscher belongs."[65] Her statement captured the broader public sentiments and memories that tied the Red Army Faction (RAF) to Nazi perpetrators like Eichmann, thus reasserting the student movement's resistance narrative. In the eyes of the hostile wider public, the use of this narrative and its Eichmann depictions by a RAF member responsible for bombings and deaths, however, only undermined it further.

And still, even the employment of the Eichmann imagery by Ulrike Meinhof triggered collective memories of past and present mass murders among the broader public. On these occasions, few West Germans still defended Eichmann and most confirmed their rejection of Nazi mass crimes. Moreover, like Meinhof's imagery and protest verbiage – her reference to "fascist ... pig," for instance, also reiterated the global protest language of the Black Panther Party[66] – the broader societal memories of Nazi mass crimes and perpetrators had become increasingly subject to transnational processes and exchanges. In these processes, the transnational student protest languages, especially parts of the universalized Eichmann imagery of West German and American activists, entered the broader memory cultures. Their exculpatory dimensions, undoubtedly, aided these developments. The imagery's *Eichmänner*, after all, seemed to exist everywhere. Indeed, in the analysis of the collective memories of mass murder and depictions of Eichmann in West Germany and the United States during the long 1960s, the transnational voices and practices of leftist student activists played a significant role and require renewed scholarly attention.

NOTES

Research for this article was made possible by fellowships from the Alexander von Humboldt Foundation and the German Historical Institute, Washington, DC, a Davidson College Faculty Study and Research Project Grant, and funds from the professional development budget of the Leon Levine Distinguished Professorship in Judaic, Holocaust, and Peace Studies, Appalachian State University.

1 Y. Michal Bodemann, *In den Wogen der Erinnerung: Jüdische Existenz in Deutschland* (Munich, 2002), 67–8; Peter Krause, *Der Eichmann-Prozess in der deutschen Presse* (Frankfurt am Main, 2002), 302.

2 Daniel Levy and Natan Sznaider, *The Holocaust and Memory in the Global Age* (Philadelphia, 2006), 109; Jeffrey Shandler, *While America Watches: Televising the Holocaust* (New York, 1999), 107.

3 Charles DeBenedetti and Charles Chatfield, *An American Ordeal: The Antiwar Movement of the Vietnam Era* (Syracuse, NY, 1990), 127–8; Edward Tabor Linenthal, *Preserving Memory: The Struggle to Create America's Holocaust Museum* (New York, 1995), 10–11.

4 Götz Aly, *Unser Kampf. 1968 – Ein irritierter Blick zurück* (Bonn, 2008), 148–50.

5 Levy and Sznaider, *Holocaust and Memory*, passim. For more recent exceptions see Jenny Wüstenberg, *Civil Society and Memory in Postwar Germany* (Cambridge, 2017) and Berthold Molden, "Vietnam, the New Left and the Holocaust: How the Cold War Changed Discourse on Genocide," in Aleida Assmann and Sebastian Conrad, eds., *Memory in a Global Age: Discourses, Practices and Trajectories* (Basingstoke, 2010), 79–96.

6 Levy and Sznaider, *Holocaust and Memory*, 17; Thomas Pegelow Kaplan, "The Universalization of the Holocaust as a Moral Standard," in Thomas Pegelow Kaplan, Jürgen Matthäus, and Mark W. Hornburg, eds., *Beyond "Ordinary Men": Christopher R. Browning and Holocaust Historiography* (Paderborn, 2019), 157–75.

7 Jim Miller, interview by author, Washington. DC, 23 June 2014.

8 David Cesarani, ed., *After Eichmann: Collective Memory and the Holocaust since 1961* (London, 2005), 3.

9 Shandler, *While America Watches*, 83–4, 95; George Salomon, "America's Response," *American Jewish Yearbook* 63 (1962): 86; Hans Lamm, *Der Eichmann-Prozess in der deutschen öffentlichen Meinung: Eine Dokumentensammlung* (Frankfurt am Main, 1961), 71.

10 David Cesarani, *Becoming Eichmann: Rethinking the Life, Crimes, and Trial of a "Desk Murderer"* (Cambridge, 2006), 325, 336; Salomon, "America's Response," 101.

11 APO Archiv, Freie Universität Berlin, Ordner "DIS. Deutsch-Israelische Studiengr," "Deutsch-Israelische Studiengruppe an der Freien Universität

Berlin: Grundsätze und Ziele," June 1957; Martin Kloke, *Israel und die deutsche Linke: Zur Geschichte eines schwierigen Verhältnisses*, 2nd ed. (Frankfurt/Main, 1994), 88–92.

12 Heinz Wewer, interview by author, Berlin, Germany, 18 May 2013; James F. Tent, *Im Schatten des Holocaust: Schicksale deutsch-jüdischer "Mischlinge" im Dritten Reich* (Cologne, 2007), 279.

13 Heinz Wewer, "Kleinbürger Eichmann vor seinen Richtern," DISkussion, May 1961, 5–6; Heinz Wever, "Kleinbürger Eichmann vor seinen Richtern. Jerusalem, 15. April 1961," RIAS, 19 April 1961, private archive of Heinz Wewer, Berlin. A copy of the text of this broadcast is in the possession of the author.

14 MJR, "Mörder und Ermordete," *Diskus*, June 1961, 4; Klaus Wagenbach, "Ein Redakteur wird kaltgestellt," *Die Zeit*, 30 March 1962.

15 "Aus der Anklagerede des Generalstaatsanwalts Gideon Hausner," *DISkussion*, May 1961, 3; Karl Jürgen Beutel, "In Sachen Eichmann und andere," *DISkussion*, July 1961, 2–3; Gerhard Schoenberner, "Eichmann und die Deutschen," *Das Argument*, December 1961/January 1962, 206; Robert Pendorf, "Ich war ein beseelter SS-Mann," *Die Zeit*, 21 April 1961, 41.

16 MJR, "Mörder und Ermordete," 4.

17 Thorsten Eitz and Georg Stötzel, eds., *Wörterbuch der "Vergangenheitsbewältigung": Die NS-Vergangenheit im öffentlichen Sprachgebrauch* (Hildesheim, 2007), 545–8.

18 Reinhard Strecker, interview by author, Berlin, Germany, 30 March 2010; Stephan Alexander Glienke, *Die Ausstellung "Ungesühnte Nazijustiz" (1959–1962): Zur Geschichte der Aufarbeitung nationalsozialistischer Justizverbrechen* (Baden-Baden, 2008).

19 Heinz Wewer, "Symptome," *DISkussion*, July 1961, 2; Wewer, "Vor seinen Richtern. Jerusalem."

20 Reinhard Strecker, "Die Namen nennen," *Das Argument*, December 1961/ January 1962, 201–2; Krause, *Eichmann-Prozess*, 298.

21 Reinhard Strecker, ed., *Dr. Hans Globke: Aktenauszüge, Dokumente* (Hamburg, 1961), 5, 260, 258.

22 Krause, *Eichmann-Prozess*, 208.

23 [Heinz Wewer?], "Eichmann," *DISkussion*, February 1962, 3.

24 Schoenberner, "Eichmann und die Deutschen," 204–5.

25 On the concept of communicative memory see Jan Assmann, *Das kulturelle Gedächtnis* (Munich, 2007), 36, 39, 50.

26 Harold Marcuse, "The Revival of Holocaust Awareness in West Germany, Israel, and the United States," in Carole Fink et al., *1968, the World Transformed* (Cambridge, 1998), 432.

27 Wade Wellman, "The Ugly Sadistic Plight of Adolph Otto Eichmann," *The Daily Tar Heel*, 5 January 1961, 2; Wade Wellman, "Eichmann's Case: A Study in Vengeance," *The Daily Tar Heel*, 6 January 1961, 2.

28 Wellman, "The Ugly Sadistic Plight," 2; Wellman, "Eichmann's Case," 2; Salomon, "America's Response," 93.

29 "FMC Students Express Opinions on Crucial World Questions of Today," *The Skirl*, April 1961, 4; "Interview Reveals Majority Opinion in Disapproval over Eichmann Trial," *Daily Trojan*, 18 April 1961, 1.

30 Peter Steinberger, "Israeli Justice and U.S. Morality," *The Michigan Daily*, 27 June 1961, 4.

31 "Letters to the Editor: Eichmann …," *The Michigan Daily*, 29 June 1961, 2.

32 See, for example, David L. Goines, *The Free Speech Movement: Coming of Age in the 1960s* (Berkeley: Ten Speed Press, 1993); Robert Cohen and Reginald E. Zelnik, eds., *The Free Speech Movement: Reflections on Berkeley in the 1960s* (Berkeley, 2002).

33 Cohen and Zelnik, *The Free Speech Movement*, 6; "Car Top Rally, 2 October 1964 (Part 1)," *Free Speech Movement, UC Berkeley Online Audio Recordings – Transcripts*, accessed 30 June 2012, http://www.lib.berkeley.edu/MRC /FSM/fsmtranscripts.html.

34 Robert Cohen, *Freedom's Orator: Mario Savio and the Radical Legacy of the 1960s* (Oxford, 2009), 19, 102.

35 For the first part see Hannah Arendt, "Eichmann in Jerusalem," *The New Yorker*, 16 February 1963, 40–113.

36 Sidra DeKoven Ezrahi, *By Words Alone: The Holocaust in Literature* (Chicago, 1980), 205.

37 Cohen and Zelnik, *Free Speech Movement*, 238.

38 Hannah Arendt, *Eichmann in Jerusalem: A Report on the Banality of Evil* (New York, 1964), 253; Hannah Arendt, *Eichmann in Jerusalem: Ein Bericht von der Banalität des Bösen* (Munich, 1986), 16; Hannah Arendt and Joachim C. Fest, *Eichmann war von empörender Dummheit: Gespräche und Briefe*, ed. Ursula Ludz and Thomas Wild (Munich, 2013); Gary Smith, ed., *Hannah Arendt Revisited: "Eichmann in Jerusalem" und die Folgen* (Frankfurt am Main, 2000), 8.

39 Cesarani, *Becoming Eichmann*, 346.

40 Heinz Wewer, "Der Prozess normalisiert sich, 27. April 1961," *RIAS*, 29 May 1961 and "Erlebtes, Erinnertes," February 2014, 37–8, private archive of Heinz Wewer, Berlin. Copies of these texts are in the possession of the author.

41 Hans Mommsen, "Hannah Arendt und der Prozess gegen Adolf Eichmann," in *Arendt, Eichmann in Jerusalem: Ein Bericht*, xxiv.

42 Wolfgang Kraushaar, "Hannah Arendt und die Studentenbewegung," *Mittelweg 36* (2008): 9–13.

43 Ibid.; Library of Congress, Manuscript Division, Hannah Arendt Papers, Box 9, "General, 1938–1976," Hannah Arendt to Daniel Cohn-Bendit, 27 June 1968.

44 Bernardine Dohrn, interview by author, Chicago, 5 November 2012.

45 Wilfried Mausbach, "America's Vietnam in Germany – Germany in America's Vietnam," in Belinda J. Davis et al., eds., *Changing the World, Changing Oneself: Political Protest and Collective Identities in West Germany and the U.S. in the 1960s and 1970s* (New York, 2010), 51.
46 Cohen and Zelnik, *Free Speech Movement*, 260.
47 Günter Amendt, "Die Studentenrevolte in Berkeley," *Neue Kritik* 28 (1965), 7; Martin Klimke, *The Other Alliance: Student Protest in West Germany and the United States in the Global Sixties* (Princeton, 2010), 52.
48 Ralph Schoenman, "Eichmann and Everyman: The Moral Challenge of Vietnam," *New Left Notes*, 20 January 1967, 2.
49 James J. Farrell, *The Spirit of the Sixties: Making Postwar Radicalism* (New York, 1997), 144.
50 Schoenman, "Eichmann and Everyman," 2.
51 Michael S. Foley, *Confronting the War Machine: Draft Resistance During the Vietnam War* (Chapel Hill, 2003), 58; "National Secretary's Report: From Protest to Resistance," *New Left Notes*, 13 January 1967, 1.
52 Mark Rudd, "Why Were There So Many Jews in the SDS? Or, the Ordeal of Civility," *Fast Capitalism* 1 no. 2 (2005), accessed 30 June 2012, http://www.uta.edu/huma/agger/fastcapitalism/1_2/rudd.html.
53 Hannah Arendt, *Macht und Gewalt* (Munich, 1970), 112; Paul Jacobs and Saul Landau, *The New Radicals: A Report with Documents* (New York, 1966), 258.
54 K.D. Wolff, interview by author, Frankfurt/Main, Germany, 10 May 2010.
55 Susan Klonsky, interview by author, Chicago, 14 February 2014; Patty Lee Parmalee, "1968: SDS und SDS: Eine Amerikanerin in Ost und West," *Beiträge zur Geschichte der Arbeiterbewegung* 43 (2001): 93–5; Klimke, *Other Alliance*, 113–14.
56 Abbie Hoffman, *Revolution for the Hell of It* (New York, 1968), 11; Marty Jezer, *Abbie Hoffman: American Rebel* (New Brunswick, NJ, 1992), 172–3.
57 Gerd Koenen, *Das rote Jahrzehnt: Unsere kleine deutsche Kulturrevolution, 1967–1977* (Cologne, 2001), 97.
58 Landesarchiv Berlin, Photo Archive, 1 Dem 18. Februar – 21 Februar 1968, Inventar-Nr. 125469, "Demonstration gegen den Vietnam-Krieg."
59 Hans Kundnani, *Utopia or Auschwitz? Germany's 1968 Generation and the Holocaust* (New York, 2009), 113.
60 University Archive, Free University of Berlin, TON 1049, "Politisches Forum Asta, Vortrag Reinhard Strecker mit Diskussion," 17 May 1965.
61 Franz Six was the first head of Department II (Gegnerforschung) at the Reich Security Main Office (RSHA) in Berlin in 1939. He later took over the RSHA's Department VII (Weltanschauliche Forschung). In 1941, he was in command of Einsatzgruppe B's Advanced Command (Vorkommando) Moscow and was directly involved in the mass murder of Jews in the Soviet Union. Otto Ambros served as executive board member of I.G.

Farben and played a critical role in the conglomerate's development of chemical weapons. He also headed I.G. Farben's Buna Commission and supported the construction of a massive Buna plant near Auschwitz. Ambros took over numerous offices in the Nazi state's war industry, among others in the Reich Ministry for Armament and Ammunition. Both men were tried after the war and convicted, but served only short prison sentences. Like Globke, they continued their careers in West Germany after the war. See Gideon Botsch, "Politische Wissenschaft," in *Zweiten Weltkrieg: Die "Deutschen Auslandswissenschaften" im Einsatz 1940–1945* (Paderborn, 2006); Lutz Hachmeister, *Der Gegnerforscher: Die Karriere des SS-Führers Franz Alfred Six* (Munich, 1998); Peter Hayes, *Industry and Ideology: IG Farben in the Nazi Era* (Cambridge, 1987).

62 Mausbach, "America's Vietnam in Germany," 55.

63 Henry Kamm, "Berets in Vietnam Still Resentful and Suspicious," *New York Times*, 8 November 1968, 9.

64 "Briefe an den Herausgeber," *Stuttgarter Zeitung*, 17 April 1968, 40.

65 Peter Jochen Winters, "Ulrike Meinhof lässt sich nur Stichworte geben," *Frankfurter Allgemeine Zeitung*, 15 December 1972, 6.

66 "Pig – An International Language," *The Black Panther*, 27 December, 1969, 9.

12 From 2-Inch to YouTube: The Audiovisual Documentation and Broadcast of the Eichmann Trial

LIAT BENHABIB

TRANSLATED BY MIMI ASH

Ari Avneri, director of the news department at Kol Yisrael radio station, in an interview described the dramatic revelations made on 23 May 1960: "Yitzhak Navon, the personal secretary of David Ben-Gurion, telephoned me because he has something to say that he doesn't want to say over the phone. I made it to the office. We sat on a bench in the hallway, and he told me that Eichmann had been caught and that David Ben-Gurion was going to announce that day at four o'clock in the afternoon at the Knesset about Eichmann's capture ... I handled the details for a live broadcast from the Knesset."[1]

Of course, Avneri was talking about live broadcast radio. Today we remember the announcement of Eichmann's capture as adapted for television years later as the iconic primary source of the time. However, many people who were living in Israel at the time mention primarily the live radio broadcast as their formative memory of the trial, more so than what appeared in the print media or the newsreels screened before commercial films in cinemas. And it is not by chance, since this was a seminal live broadcast on Israeli radio, which had been founded twenty-five years previously during the British Mandate. This broadcast was the most important mass communications event in Israel since the live radio broadcast of the declaration of independence.[2]

At the time of the Eichmann trial, television broadcasting existed in some parts of the world, sometimes even in colour, but not in Israel (David Ben-Gurion's opposition to television is well known). Although the first Israeli television broadcast was made by Educational Television in March 1966, it was the founding of the Israel Broadcasting Authority Channel One (then called "general television") that is etched into the collective memory – in particular, the Israel Defence Forces parade on Israeli Independence Day 1968, a television event referred to as "the victory march" after the Six-Day War.

Although Kol Yisrael was government radio, its directors, Chanoch Givton and Nakdimon Rogel, fought with those in charge of the trial for consent to record the trial and control the logistics. But the trial's organizers from the Police Department, headed by Major General Yekutiel Keren, were most concerned with facilitating coverage by foreign journalists, especially from the print media. According to the trial organizers, the role of Israel Radio Kol Yisrael during the preparations was to take care of the logistics that would enable the foreign journalists to do their job, and they vetoed allowing microphones or film cameras into the courtroom in the main hall. The radio managers set up a technical system allowing for one microphone in the main hall, which served all of the recording systems of the foreign correspondents in the outer hall. The staff of Kol Yisrael, dedicated to the professional standards of public journalism according to the British model of the BBC as it was perceived in Israel, promoted the idea of the public interest, and wanted "to prove to the free world that Israel was capable of setting up a technologically up-to-date system that would serve the foreign journalists, and to make sure that the correspondents had free access to information, so that there would be no suspicion of censorship."[3] We will return to the various factors that affected video documentation, which led to decisions, sometimes fateful, about what would be recorded and preserved for coming generations. Ora Herman has studied the protocols of meetings concerning the media coverage of the trial and concluded that "until a late stage, no one mentioned the listening public in Israel, or was concerned with its needs. The concern was for the foreign press, and the need to record the trial was justified by the need to preserve an audio recording for historical purposes."[4]

Two months before the opening of the trial, Teddy Kollek, the general director of the Prime Minister's Office, tried in a letter to convince Yekutiel Keren to authorize a continuous sound recording of the proceedings: "It seems to me that we need to make sure this is done, especially since it does not involve large sums; Kol Yisrael is ready to undertake the recording for free, and the entire cost will be for the acquisition of about a thousand audio reels. I hope that you will find the necessary budget for this."[5] At the same time, arrangements were being made for a video recording of the trial by contracting a small American company, Capital Cities. Less than two months before the beginning of the trial, it turned out that the agreement signed with Capital Cities did not include the requirement of a continuous audio recording of the trial, or even full and continuous video coverage. Only then did Keren and representatives of the Police Department and the Ministry of Justice reluctantly agree to allow audio recording of the trial; the pressure applied by Kollek also played a role in this decision. The radio directors were victorious in their fight to document the trial on audio reels.

Keren was placated, though he made no secret of his dissatisfaction, claiming that he did not see the benefit of the recording. Yet, he authorized it in a way that made his position in the hierarchy clear and highlighted his ability to set the terms of the documentation. In effect, the directors of Kol Yisrael determined the way the audio coverage would be done. Just before the opening of the trial, and lacking an official permit in writing, Nakdimon Rogel, the director of the Operations Department of Kol Yisrael, decided on a live radio broadcast of the opening session of the trial, in addition to reportage in newscasts and evening magazine reports summarizing the events of the day.

The success of the first live radio broadcast brought about a decision, pushed by Gideon Hausner, to provide live radio broadcasts of additional sessions. Actually, only about twelve sessions, including the opening session and the announcement of the verdict, were broadcast live in Israel.[6] This situation arguably reflects attitudes of the state and the organizers of the trial toward public relations and broadcasting; decisions were likely the result of misunderstandings rather than faulty planning.[7]

The video tapings are a saga in themselves, again shedding light on the doubts and the difficulties regarding the decision to utilize audiovisual coverage and documentation, as expressed by the Israeli establishment. Notable figures include Teddy Kollek, Foreign Minister Golda Meir, officials in the Ministry of Justice and the Police Department, the director of the Government Press Office David Landor, and members of the local media mentioned above. The "international stars" of the saga are the three large American networks (NBC, CBS, and ABC), European broadcasting authorities, including the BBC, and even a Japanese television network that offered a substantial sum in return for the recording and broadcasting rights. After the efforts of the foreign networks to influence those close to the prime minister and the foreign minister failed over and over again, legal action was threatened.

But the underdog who achieved fame was Capital Cities, an unknown company owned by an Israeli then living in the United States, Milton Fruchtman. Fruchtman was married to Chava Sternberg, the niece of Minister of Justice Pinchas Rosen.[8]

Threats of legal suits, letters to the minister of justice, the PMO, and to the Israeli ambassador in the United States all complicated the issue of the filmic documentation of the trial, while the "local players," people in power, and the directors of the trial in Israel were busy determining the conditions of foreign news coverage. Instead of dealing with the filming of the trial, those in power were focusing on publishing a book[9] and fantasizing about producing an official documentary film about the trial (which, by the way, was never produced as such).[10]

The greatest fear of the trial organizers was that foreign and professional television networks would assume control over television documentation. As a result, they chose a company that would be subject to their authority in the most direct way, but they failed to understand the technical aspects and the requirements necessary for true television coverage and complete video documentation of the event. Their main worry was that the trial would receive *too much* coverage, negatively impacting the credibility of the criminal legal process, which, at any rate, was controversial in the eyes of the world at the time, and was regarded sceptically by Eichmann's defence.[11] Trial organizers also feared that television coverage would affect the outcome of the trial.

The official arguments, according to Hanoch Givton, director of the Israel Broadcasting Service responsible for Kol Yisrael,[12] revealed the following: the Ministry of Justice forbade having more than one camera in the main hall, the Israel Broadcasting Service did not have the necessary equipment, and, in order to avoid competition between the three major networks, a decision was made to hire the services of Capital Cities as the representative of the Israel Broadcasting Service. The general directors of the American networks united in an unprecedented move, and tried desperately to find alternatives.[13] Attempts were made to organize a "pool" of foreign networks, which was common in the American and European television industries, and to turn over the videotaping and broadcasting at a financial loss to the video unit of the European Broadcasting Authority as a subcontractor of Capital Cities. Both of these initiatives were rejected, although Capital Cities lacked the necessary personnel, as well as equipment, right up to the beginning of the trial.

Film industry representatives in Israel also opposed the decision to grant the rights to Capital Cities. The local newsreel production companies, including Geva Films, headed by Yitzhak Agadati (brother of the renowned Israeli filmmaker Baruch Agadati – one of the pioneers of Israeli cinema, known for the one of the first Hebrew films from 1935, titled *Zot Hi Ha'aretz*), and Mordecai Navon, together with Margot Klausner of Israel Film Studios, which later became Herzliya Studios, turned to Teddy Kollek with their demands. They asked to be allowed to film the trial and distribute the films in Israel: "If an Israeli team was able to capture Eichmann, an Israel team directs his investigation, and the Israeli government rejected every attempt to allow others to judge him – then certainly it is fitting that the matter of the filming of the trial should be left in Israeli hands."[14] One week before the opening of the trial, the Union of Film Employees in Israel, headed by Zvi Assaf, complained vociferously to Minister Abba Eban about the decision to use foreign teams instead of local ones, but their complaints did not achieve the desired results.

At the same time, attempts were made, primarily by NBC and by the European media companies, to use video documentation of the trial to assist them in convincing the Israeli government to set up an Israeli TV channel. These companies used a moral argument – the possibility that in Tel Aviv as well as in Europe and America, a TV newscast summary of the events of the day in the courtroom would be broadcast every day in public places. This would enable Israelis to *see* the trial in real time, or almost in real time, not only in newsreels edited and screened one week after the events in cinemas. As mentioned before, this initiative was a complete failure.

Capital Cities was chosen without a tender and the fee was set at half a million dollars. In return, Capital Cities committed itself to contributing to charity all profits from the sales of the recordings to all broadcast networks worldwide, and Capital Cities would receive only its labour and production costs, in return for supplying the tapes to the State of Israel. At the same time, as Jeffrey Shandler points out, the American news networks paid $50,000 in exchange for a daily one hour of unedited footage throughout the course of the proceedings, until the last session on 14 August 1961.[15]

The organizers of the trial adhered to their decision of January 1961 not to allow filming for distribution in cinemas, but to allow the filmed documentation to be broadcast on closed-circuit television in a nearby hall, so that members of the public unable to find a seat in Beit Ha'am, the trial venue, would be able to watch the proceedings. A special council was appointed to hand out tickets and to handle seating arrangements, and admission was free. Space was limited in Beit Ha'am: out of 756 seats, about 470 were reserved for the press and others – mostly survivors – so there was not enough room for the general public.[16] The proceedings were broadcast on closed circuit television at the Ratisbonne Monastery, about 500 metres from the hall at Beit Ha'am, which enabled 570 additional viewers to see the proceedings live on screen.

The only ways to *see* the trial in Israel were at Beit Ha'am, at the Ratisbonne Monastery, or in the newsreels shown at the cinema; these used edited clips acquired from Milton Fruchtman, after the events had taken place. Research at the Herzliya Studios Archive revealed that there were only eleven Geva or Carmel newsreels that mentioned the Eichmann case (Carmel and Geva were the only two companies whose newsreels were screened at theatres, alternating weekly). The relevant newsreels included items not necessarily related to the proceedings taking place in Beit Ha'am. For example, a June 1960 newsreel reported about the "06 Unit" of the Israel Police Department set up to investigate Eichmann, which received documents from Yad Vashem; another reported on the investigation itself, showing memorial plaques at Bergen Belsen and a press conference given by the commander of the "06 Unit," Major General Avraham Zelinger. Other references to Eichmann included an update about the progress of the investigation; an August 1960 report about the conflict with the Argentinian government as a result of the kidnapping, and the return of the Argentinian and Israeli ambassadors to their home countries, a conflict settled by determining that Israel would pay damages to Argentina; the arrival in Israel of Dr. Robert Servatius, Eichmann's defence counsel; the reaction of the Israeli public to the trial, and more. Of course, the opening session of the trial, the reading of the verdict on 11 December 1961, the sentencing, and the appeal were also covered in the newsreels. Thus, cinema newsreels provided viewers throughout Israel with a narrow view of the "highlights" only. I was unable to find any newsreels presenting the main corpus of the trial – the 108 survivor testimonies given during the 114 sessions.[17]

The direct result of the two communications-related sagas described above is that *there is no complete audiovisual recording of the Eichmann trial available to us today.* It is only because of the public reactions to the trial in Israel – reactions that no one in power then could foresee –that live radio broadcasts were added, but these were also few in number. Perhaps the Israeli establishment was afraid of being accused of holding a show trial; or, maybe there was a failure to understand the importance of the role of visual media. Or, perhaps it was simply a lack of professional understanding and nothing more. Yet the arguments related to the professionalism of Capital Cities and its cameramen come into sharper focus today, sixty-one years later, when one watches the footage.

Much has been written about the reactions of the Israeli public to the trial, the effect of the trial on the survivors and its attitude toward them, the role of the survivor in the trial, and the many layers of meaning ascribed to personal testimonies. One comment by Haim Gouri is quoted over and over again in scholarly research, and it can be related to the character of the audiovisual documentation. The personal testimonies presented during the trial, according to Gouri, have the power of truth, and the uniqueness of each Shoah story brought before the listeners released "a tremendous energy of 'now I understand.'"[18] According to Gouri, the Shoah "was taking place now," during the course of the trial. I believe that the filmed documentation serves as an extension of that continuous present; despite its limitations, it perpetuates the significant moments and transforms them into the audiovisual iconography of the trial and of the Shoah.

So, what record did Capital Cities studios create, and what mark has this record left on us and on history? The state-of-the-art format of the time was the 2-inch quadruplex videotape reel, a reel of magnetic tape with a standard length of 4,800 feet or about 1,500 metres, which allowed for one hour of continuous filming. The sound was recorded on the magnetic tape itself, on separate soundtracks recorded by a microphone in the hall where the trial was held (most of it in Hebrew, and some of it in German and other languages). One of the soundtracks was used for simultaneous translation into English. The quality of the 2-inch tape is still considered standard analogue broadcast resolution.[19]

In an interview in *Ha'aretz* in April 2011, the eighty-five-year-old Milton Fruchtman talked about the preparations for the documentation of the trial. He recalled how he insisted on filming the trial on videotape and not on film, to make it easier to edit and transmit the materials. Four cameras were placed in the hall, and Israeli cameramen were hired to do the filming. The cameras were hidden in special booths so that no one would be able to detect them, and the cameramen filmed from behind a screen. A control room was set up on the other side of the street, and it was there that Fruchtman, the director Leo Hurwitz, and a team of technicians set to work and instructed the cameramen. Four monitors presented four camera angles from inside the hall,[20] and in real time Hurwitz and the technicians edited the documentation using camera-to-camera editing, recording the edited version onto one 2-inch tape. This method is similar to the work of the technical director, or vision mixer, in studio programs broadcast today on television.

Leo Hurwitz was an American well known for directing special programs, news, and documentaries, mostly for CBS. He had been blacklisted during the McCarthy era and unable to work in the United States. Hurwitz was called in to direct the filming of the trial, although he did not understand a word of Hebrew or German. Fruchtman, the producer, spoke both languages, and Hurwitz heard the simultaneous translation on his headphones. It is important to remember the delay in understanding what is being said when watching the unedited footage of the documentation of the trial. The editing choices made by Hurwitz, and perhaps also by Fruchtman (who claimed to be the co-director as well as the producer,[21] and as such, is responsible for some of the difficulties that the documentation presents), determined to a large extent the way the trial is remembered and also its credibility as a reliable reflection of what actually took place in the hall.

Many iconic moments are left out of the video documentation, including parts of Hausner's opening speech, and key testimonies like Rivka Yosselevka's account of the killing pits and the *Einsatzgruppen,* Joel Brand's account of the negotiations with Eichmann, Rachel Auerbach's account, and other stories of partisans and the heroes of the ghetto uprisings. Despite what has been written in many history books, the trial was not recorded in full on video- or audiotapes, and many sessions are partially or fully absent. For instance, Shandler describes audience reactions during Brand's testimony: ironic laughter that swept throughout the hall in response to Eichmann's forced confession that he was morally responsible for the murder of the Hungarian Jews but not legally responsible – a reaction not recorded by the camera but described by journalist Jim Bishop in his half-hour daily report broadcast on Friday, 7 July 1961, on WABC radio in New York.[22] An equally powerful moment is the iconic scene of "Ka-tzetnik" (author Yehiel Dinur) fainting on the witness stand. A sequence etched into collective memory in Israel and the United States is the series of shots documenting the exchange between "Ka-tzetnik," Hausner, and Judge Moshe Landau, who try to convince the restless "Ka-tzetnik" to sit down and tell his story. The moment at which "Ka-tzetnik" faints, images of Judge Landau were recorded. We hear the audience cry out in surprise, and the camera returns to "Ka-tzetnik" sprawled on the floor, while two policemen attempt to pick him up. The precise moment when "Ka-tzetnik" faints is not documented. The viewer fills in the gaps in his or her mind, but the heavy hand of the editor is felt here in its failure to capture the crucial moment.

In Israel, as noted above, the trial was broadcast on radio; in the United States, it was broadcast on television. Shandler describes the television "climate" in the United States at the time: "In the wake of scandals surrounding rigged quiz shows and corrupt FCC officials during the late 1950s, television networks made special efforts at the end of the decade to demonstrate their commitment to responsible broadcasting in the public interest."[23] The televised broadcast of the trial in the United States meant that the medium had progressed to covering international news, and that the role of the journalist as intermediary and commentator of events for the local audience was geared to the local agenda or consciousness. Shandler asserts that it was during the televised coverage of the trial that the American public first heard the word "Holocaust."[24] The coverage of the trial on American television (but also in Germany, and, in part, in Great Britain and France) took place primarily in daily newscasts shown at prime time on all of the major networks. In addition to the daily broadcast using footage of the trial from Capital Cities, some of the networks broadcast weekly news magazine summaries.[25] Shandler quotes a *TV Guide* item describing how edited copies of the 2-inch tapes were sent by car from Jerusalem to Lod Airport on a trip lasting an hour and a half, and in an agreement with many of the airlines the tapes were flown to Europe and the United States the same day. When there were particularly "hot" materials, a helicopter was rented to take the tapes from Jerusalem to the airport within minutes, considered "speed of light" transmittal in the days before satellite broadcast.

Before, during, and immediately after the trial, many related programs were shown on television. These include documentary films; specials about Israel, Eichmann, and even Hitler and Mengele; docudramas; and feature films about Eichmann and especially about Nazi crimes against humanity during the Holocaust. For example, the feature film *Operation Eichmann* was broadcast in the United States for four weeks prior to the beginning of the trial.[26] This docudrama, produced by Samuel Bischoff, was quickly completed and released in mid-March 1961 to take advantage of the trial's topicality. The story unfolds in several large segments. In the first part of the film, Eichmann (played by Werner Klemperer), as head of the Department for Jewish Affairs and Evacuation, personally supervises the extermination of Jews in Germany and the nations under its occupying forces. The second half deals with Eichmann's escape from an American POW camp; his four years under cover in Germany, aided by an association of Nazi SS members (ODESSA); his escape in 1950 to Argentina through Italy; and his capture on 11 May 1960. Another film, the CBS docudrama *Engineer of Death* was broadcast as part of the Armstrong Theater Circle in October 1960. There was even a special episode of *The Twilight Zone* in its third season, in which an SS captain returns to a death camp and meets the spirits of his tortured victims.

When the trial was over in Jerusalem, Capital Cities edited the half-hour-long documentary *Verdict for Tomorrow*, which was broadcast on American television, and presented by the eminent CBS reporter Lowell Thomas, who had covered the racial laws and their climax in *Kristallnacht*, the Final Solution, and now the Eichmann trial. In Europe, related programs and films, perhaps less well known in the United States, were shown during and after the trial.[27]

Unedited trial footage filmed by Capital Cities has appeared in many films on the topic throughout the years. The database of the Yad Vashem

Visual Centre includes information about more than 258[28] films related to Eichmann, most of them documentaries that use materials filmed and edited by Fruchtman and Hurwitz. For example, Haim Gouri and Jacko Ehrlich's trilogy, made in Israel in the 1970s, starting with *The Eighty-First Blow*, uses testimonies from the Eichmann trial as its soundtrack. Also notable are Danny Setton's *Eichmann, the Nazi Fugitive*, and Eyal Sivan's controversial *The Specialist*, among many others.

But the 2-inch tapes did not end as images and soundtracks of later documentary films. In 2011, they were all made available to the public for direct viewing on a YouTube channel as a joint project of the Israel State Archives and Yad Vashem. The 241 hours of tape deposited by Capital Cities in the State Archives after the trial were digitized by Yad Vashem and uploaded to YouTube. Eighty-four of the hours cover segments of testimonies and 154 hours comprise the trial sessions in chronological order. The "Eichmann trial" channel on YouTube invokes the original intention of those who carried out the documentation and serves as a collection of authentic testimonies, allowing us to see and hear the stories of survivors when they were still young, only fifteen years after the war was over. The channel was launched in April 2011, marking fifty years since the opening of the trial. Since then, there have been more than 190,000 online visitors on the Hebrew channel and some 631,000 on the English channel.[29] Most of the users come from Israel, the United States, Germany, France, and Canada.

Making the audiovisual documentation accessible on YouTube recalls the essence of the trial as Hausner had envisioned it then: the creation of a corpus of eyewitness testimonies describing murderous Nazi crimes and their impact. Sixty years later, these testimonies have taken on more historical significance, especially since most of those documented are no longer around, and there are not many survivors left who can be met face to face. In addition, social networks and other new media platforms inform, shape consciousness, and impact or even determine the audiences' points of view. The way an event is represented in the media, its distribution and consumption, the ways in which it is broadcast, streamed, uploaded, and shared via the web and social networks, has potentially a greater impact on the way people interpret the consequences of that event than its mere occurrence. Therefore, the importance of the accessibility of the Eichmann trial testimonies on YouTube in this age of media-savvy generations cannot be overestimated, as this is a unique corpus of a primary source of first-hand accounts of Holocaust survivors, recorded some fifteen to seventeen years after the crimes occurred. Or, as Haim Gouri put it so well in 1961, the survivors giving testimony at the trial were "one hundred and eleven proxies, each taking his or her turn on the witness stand and leading us across the desolate landscape ... in the length and breadth of the world that was and is no longer."[30]

NOTES

1 Avneri cited in Ora Herman, "Broadcasting from the Other Planet: The Eichmann Trial, the Establishment and the Electronic Media" (MA diss., Hebrew University of Jerusalem, 2004), 125.
2 Anita Shapira, Hannah Arendt, and Haim Gouri, *Two Perceptions of the Eichmann Trial* (Jerusalem, 2002), 9.
3 Herman, "Broadcasting from the Other Planet," 9.
4 Ibid., 9–10.
5 Israel State Archive, 804/13/3, Teddy Kollek to Yekutiel Keren, 10 February 1961; see also Herman, "Broadcasting from the Other Planet," 12.
6 Ora Herman estimates about that there were 12–16 live broadcasts, not all of which were preserved in the archives of Kol Yisrael. Herman states that "for the sake of caution, I stick to the estimate of 12 live broadcasts, although, as has been said, it is possible that the number was even less than that by half." Herman, "Broadcasting from the Other Planet," 38.
7 Many authors note the Israeli establishment's lack of understanding of the communications media at the time, especially television. Of course, David Ben-Gurion, who thought of television as a "destructive weapon," was responsible for this trend, and he opposed television's introduction into Israel. Ora Herman, Jeffrey Shandler, Anita Shapira, and many others have discussed this matter in depth.
8 Hanna Yablonka, *The State of Israel vs. Adolf Eichmann* (Detroit, 2004), 58.
9 In a letter from Teddy Kollek, the director general of the Prime Minister's Office, to former Mossad agent Isser Harel, discussing the forthcoming book, *How Eichmann Was Caught by Moshe Pearlman*, Kollek set out Ben-Gurion's involvement in the preparation of the book, and added: "The book should appear and be distributed before the trial, so that it will help to shape public opinion before the event." Israel State Archive, 804/13/3, Teddy Kollek to Isser Harel, 2 November 1960.
10 A short parenthetical remark regarding this matter: In 1961 as the trial was approaching its conclusion, the Foreign Office, through the Israel Film Service, commissioned David Perlov, a young filmmaker and a new immigrant from Brazil, to make a film for worldwide release that would add to the Israeli efforts to shape public opinion. Perlov made a short film (17 minutes) entitled "In Thy Blood Live," which was his response to Alain Resnais' *Night and Fog*. The film won the Critic's Award at the

Venice Film Festival in 1962. Though the film ends with a sequence about the trial, it actually deals with the magnitude of the Holocaust and its commemoration in Israel. Only in 1978 did the Israel Broadcasting Authority Channel One commission Perlov to make yet another film. The finished product, *Memories of the Eichmann Trial*, took a completely different point of view than that which the trial organizers had hoped for when they imagined "an official film about the trial and its importance." In the latter film, Perlov interviews Israeli Holocaust survivors Rivka Yosselevska and Stephania and Henryk Ross, who testified at the trial; Raffi Eitan, who took part in Eichmann's capture in Argentina; and many young Israelis, including members of the second generation, to learn how the trial changed their perspectives and formed their identity.

11 Jeffrey Shandler, *While America Watches: Televising the Holocaust* (New York, 1999), 90.

12 Israel State Archive 440, Hanoch Givton to the director of the European Broadcasting Service, Mr. Gillarion, 14 November 1960, cited in Herman, "Broadcasting from the Other Planet," 17.

13 Herman quotes an urgent telegram to the director of the Government Press Office, David Landor, from the vice presidents of the television networks (James Hagerty of ABC News, the vice president of CBS News, and Julian Goodman from NBC News). The telegram, undated, is preserved in a file at the Government Press Office. Herman later quotes Lander's response to the directors of the networks, in which he announces the final arrangements decided upon by a meeting of the trial organizers on 27 January 1961, and asks them to turn to Capital Cities regarding the prices of videotape recordings of the trial. See Herman, "Broadcasting from the Other Planet," 21, 23.

14 Israel State Archive 804/13/3, Geva Films to Teddy Kollek, 6 February 1961.

15 Shandler, *While America Watches*, 91.

16 Yablonka, *Israel vs. Eichmann*, 61–2.

17 What other news did cinema audiences see in these newsreels? The announcement of the capture of Adolf Eichmann, which was screened in movie theatres as the first item after advertisements for a new "electric hotplate" manufactured by the Israeli Bezek Company based on a Swedish patent, with the slogan "It's easy to cook with electricity," and an advertisement for a garbage disposal. After the report on Eichmann's capture, two items were broadcast about the filming in Israel of Otto Preminger's *Exodus* with Paul Newman. There was also an item about the "honeymoon week" of 100 couples married on Lag Ba'Omer; a report on the Red Magen David prize; news of archaeological findings near kibbutz Afikim; an item on the marriage of Princess Margaret; the story of a car that burst into flames; and an item about an antidote to snakebites discovered at Tel Aviv University.

18 Haim Gouri, *Facing the Glass Booth: The Jerusalem Trial of Adolf Eichmann* (Detroit, 2004), 270.

19 Today standard broadcast quality is digital video recording, with high-definition digital video files stored on hard disks. But in terms of analogue broadcasting, 2-inch tape was much better quality than most of the later formats, like U-matic, and even some of the early Betacam tapes.

20 Yablonka describes three cameras in the courtroom, whereas Fruchtman mentions four. I find Fruchtman's number more reliable than Yablonka's, because her sources are news items in local newspapers of the time (*Yediot Achronot* and *Haaretz*). I believe that Fruchtman describes the de facto situation, whereas the newspapers may reproduce the authorized official version that was published at the time.

21 Shani Litman, "Milton Fruchtman, the Man behind the Camera at the Eichmann Trial," *Ha'aretz*, 15 April 2011.

22 Shandler, *While America Watches*, 101–2.

23 Ibid., 97.

24 Ibid., 85.

25 For example, a weekly summary was broadcast on Sundays at four o'clock in the afternoon on ABC's New York station, which also broadcast a half hour of the trial daily and an hour on weekends.

26 Data regarding films and programs are taken from the Yad Vashem Visual Centre Online Film Catalogue (as of March 2021), available at https://library.yadvashem.org/index.html?language=en&mov=1

27 Regarding Israel, David Perlov made *In Thy Blood Live* in 1961, and though it won awards abroad I could not find any information on the Israeli audience and their reception of the film. From talks with Mira Perlov I conclude that the film may have garnered critics' praise and was known to cinephiles, but was not distributed locally. Other European films from the time include *Eichmann and the Third Reich* (Erwin Leiser, Switzerland, 1961), *The Story of Joel Brand* (drama by Franz Peter Wirth, Germany, 1964), *Personal Portraits in Question and Answer: Günter Gaus in Conversation with Hannah Arendt* (ZDF, Germany, 1964).

28 Number as of March 2021.

29 Number of visitors as of November 2013.

30 Gouri, *Facing the Glass Booth*, 140.

Contributors

Liat Benhabib is director of The Visual Center at Yad Vashem – the world's largest digital library and collection of films, survivor testimonies, and information on the Holocaust and cinema. She earned a BA (with honours) in the Faculty of film and television and in psychology, Tel Aviv University. She is a founding member of the Forum for the Preservation of the Audio-Visual Memory in Israel, and a member of Israel's Cinema Council since 2014. She has worked as a researcher, casting director, assistant director, and producer for Israeli feature films, documentaries, and television series by directors Eran Riklis, Ari Folman, David Ofek, and Yossi Madmoni, among others; as a film instructor for adults with special needs – script adviser, director, and producer at film workshops organized by Nitzan (a non-profit for people with special needs); and as a producer of the Video-Art installations by Michal Rovner and Uri Tzaig, and as co-producer, with Belfilms Productions, of 118 short films for the permanent exhibition of the Holocaust History Museum at Yad Vashem.

Michael Berkowitz is Professor of Modern Jewish History at University College London and editor of *Jewish Historical Studies: Transactions of the Jewish Historical Society of England*. His books include *Jews and Photography in Britain*; *The Crime of My Very Existence: Nazism and the Myth of Jewish Criminality*; *The Jewish Self-Image*; *Western Jewry and the Zionist Project, 1914-1933*; and *Zionist Culture and West European Jewry before the First World War*. His most recent co-edited books are, with Martin Deppner, *The Jewish Engagement with Photography*, and with Avinoam Patt, *"We Are Here": New Approaches of Jewish Displaced Persons in Postwar Germany*.

Ruth Bettina Birn served as chief historian of the Canadian War Crimes and Crimes against Humanity Section of the Canadian Department of Justice from 1991 to 2005, and was involved in the investigation and prosecution of Nazi crimes and modern political crimes. She is the author of numerous books and articles on the SS and Police, the German occupation of Eastern Europe, the prosecution of political crimes, transitional justice, the Eichmann trial. She is the author of *Die Höheren SS- und Polizeiführer: Himmlers Vertreter im Reich und in den besetzten Gebieten* and *Die Sicherheitspolizei in Estland 1941–1944: Eine Studie zur Kollaboration im Osten.*

Leora Bilsky is a Benno Gitter Professor of Law at Tel Aviv University and is the director of the Minerva Center for Human Rights. She is the author of *Tranformative Justice: Israeli Identity on Trial* (University of Michigan Press, 2004) and *The Holocaust, Corporations, and the Law: Unfinished Business* (University of Michigan Press, 2017). Professor Bilsky was the editor-in-chief of *Theory & Criticism* (*Teoria U'vikoret*), *Iyunei Mishpat,* and *Mishpatim.* Her current research is on genocide and cultural restitution.

Boaz Cohen, a historian, is head of the Holocaust Studies Program of the Western Galilee College in Akko and a lecturer at the Shaanan College in Haifa, Israel. His work focuses on the development of Holocaust memory and historiography in their social and cultural context and on Jewish and Israeli post-Holocaust society. His current research is on early Holocaust historiography, Holocaust testimonies, and early children's Holocaust testimonies and the adult interest in them. He is the author of *Israeli Holocaust Research: Birth and Evolution,* and co-editor of volumes on Holocaust and film and on survivor historians. Dr. Cohen is the convener and organizer of several Holocaust studies conferences at Western Galilee College, including the international conference series "The Future of Holocaust Testimonies."

Laura Jockusch is the Albert Abramson Associate Professor of Holocaust Studies at Brandeis University, where her research and teaching focus on the social, political, cultural, and legal histories of European Jews before, during, and after the Holocaust. Jockusch holds a doctorate from New York University and was a research fellow at the United States Holocaust Memorial Museum, Yad Vashem, The Hebrew University of Jerusalem, and the Radcliffe Institute of Advanced Study at

Harvard University. Her first book, *Collect and Record! Jewish Holocaust Documentation in Postwar Europe* (Oxford University Press, 2012), won the National Jewish Book Award and the Sybil Halpern Milton Book Prize. She coedited (with Gabriel Finder) *Jewish Honor Courts: Revenge, Retribution, and Reconciliation in Europe and Israel after the Holocaust* (Wayne State University Press, 2015) and (with Andreas Kraft, Kim Wünschmann) *Revenge, Retribution, Reconciliation: Justice and Emotions between Conflict and Mediation* (The Hebrew University Magnes Press, 2016). Her ongoing research project investigates how Jews conceptualized legal redress after the unprecedented crime of the Nazi genocide of European Jews. She is currently working on a book entitled *The Trials of Stella Goldschlag: Nazi Victim, Holocaust Survivor, and War Criminal?*

Thomas Pegelow Kaplan (PhD, 2004, University of North Carolina at Chapel Hill) is the Leon Levine Distinguished Professor and director of the Center for Judaic, Holocaust, and Peace Studies, as well as Professor of History at Appalachian State University in North Carolina. Pegelow Kaplan's work focuses on histories of violence, language, and culture of Nazi Germany and on the 1960s global youth revolts. His present research projects include an exploration of the genocide imageries and terminologies of leftist German and American protest movements from the 1950s until the early 1980s and a study of the transnational dimensions of German Jewish journalism in the 1930s and early 1940s. Pegelow Kaplan is the author of *The Language of Nazi Genocide: Linguistic Violence and the Struggle of Germans of Jewish Ancestry* (Cambridge University Press, 2011) and co-editor (with Juergen Matthaeus) of *Beyond "Ordinary Men": Christopher R. Browning and Holocaust Historiography* (Schoeningh Verlag, 2019) and (with Wolf Gruner) of *Resisting Persecution: Jews and Their Petitions during the Holocaust* (Berghahn Books, 2020).

Roni Stauber is an associate professor at the Department of Jewish History and the academic head of the Wiener Library for the Study of the Nazi Era and the Holocaust, both at Tel Aviv University. Stauber is also a member of the Yad Vashem Scientific Committee. He has published and edited books and numerous articles on the Holocaust and its memory, particularly on the politics of memory in Israel and its role in the diplomatic arena.He is the author and editor of numerous books including *Lesson for this Generation* (Jerusalem, 2000); *The Holocaust in Israeli Public Debate in the 1950s, Ideology, and Memory,* (2007); *Laying the*

Foundations for Holocaust Research – The Impact of Philip Friedman (2009); *The Roma: A Minority in Europe, Historical, Political and Social Perspectives* (2007), and *Collaboration with the Nazis: PublicDiscourse after the Holocaust* (2010). His newest book, is *Diplomacy in the Shadow of Memory – Past, and Present in Israeli–West German Relations, 1953–1965* (Yad Vashem and Zalman Shazar Center, Jerusalem, 2021). His current research examines the joint efforts of West German and Israeli law enforcement officials, in cooperation with Jewish organizations and institutes, to bring Nazi criminals living in West Germany to trial.

Fabien Théofilakis undertook his PhD studies in history jointly at the University of Paris Ouest Nanterre La Défense and the University of Augsburg. He is currently an assistant professor in contemporary history at the University of Paris 1 Panthéon Sorbonne. He defended his thesis on German prisoners of war in France and their repatriation to Germany (1944–9) in 2010. He has received several prizes for his work, including from the Université franco-allemande and the French-German Historian Committee. His book *Les prisonniers de guerre allemands, France (1944–1949): Une captivité de guerre en temps de paix* was published by Fayard in 2014. He has published several articles on the subject of POWS and co-directed a work on captivity, *Wartime Captivity in the 20th Century: Archives, Stories, Memories* (Berghahn Publishers, 2016, for English version) as well as a Franco-German volume about the concentration camp Dachau. In 2011, Théofilakis worked on the exhibition "The Eichmann Case, Jerusalem, 1961," organized by the Mémorial de la Shoah in Paris. Since then he has continued his research on Eichmann and the notes he took during his trial. His book on that topic should be published in 2022.

Dominique Trimbur is the senior program associate for the Fondation pour la Mémoire de la Shoah, Paris, and Associate Researcher at the Centre de Recherche Français à Jérusalem (CRFJ). He is a historian of German-Israeli relations, and of the European presence in Palestine/Israel. His numerous publications include *De la Shoah à la réconciliation?: La question des relations RFA-Israël (1949–1956)*; *De Bonaparte à Balfour: La France, l'Europe occidentale et la Palestine, 1799–1917*, edited with Ran Aaronsohn; *Une École française à Jérusalem: De l'École pratique d'Études bibliques des Dominicains à l'École Biblique et Archéologique Française de Jérusalem*; *Entre rayonnement et réciprocité: Contributions à l'histoire de la diplomatie culturelle*; *Europäer in der Levante: Zwischen Politik, Wissenschaft*

und Religion (19.-20. Jahrhundert) /Des Européens au Levant – Entre poli-
tique, science et religion (XIXe–XXe siècles); De Balfour à Ben Gourion: Les
puissances européennes et la Palestine, 1917–1948, edited with Ran Aaronsohn; *Europa und Palästina 1799–1948: Religion – Politik – Gesellschaft /*
Europe and Palestine 1799–1948: Religion – Politics – Society, edited with
Barbara Haider-Wilson.

James E. Waller is the Cohen Professor of Holocaust and Genocide
Studies, and chair of the Holocaust and Genocide Studies Program, at
Keene State College. In addition, he serves as Director of Academic Pro-
grams for the Auschwitz Institute for the Prevention of Genocide and
Mass Atrocities, an international NGO devoted to atrocity prevention.
He is the author of six books, most notably his award-winning *Becom-*
ing Evil: How Ordinary People Commit Genocide and Mass Killing (Oxford
University Press, 2nd ed., 2007), *Confronting Evil: Engaging Our Respon-*
sibility to Prevent Genocide (Oxford University Press, 2016), and *A Trou-*
bled Sleep: Risk and Resilience in Contemporary Northern Ireland (Oxford
University Press, 2021). Waller has held numerous visiting professor-
ships, most recently as an honorary visiting research professor at in
the George J. Mitchell Institute for Global Peace, Justice and Security at
Queen's University in Belfast, Northern Ireland (2017). In 2017, he was
the inaugural recipient of the Engaged Scholarship Prize from the International Association of Genocide Scholars in recognition of his exemplary contribution in advancing genocide awareness and prevention.

Esther Webman (d. 2020) was the head of the Zeev Vered Desk for the
Study of Tolerance and Intolerance in the Middle East, and a senior
research fellow at the Dayan Center for Middle Eastern and African
Studies and the Stephen Roth Institute for the Study of Antisemitism
and Racism at Tel Aviv University. Her research was focused on Arab
discourse analysis, mainly Arab perceptions of the Holocaust and Arab
antisemitism. She was the editor of *The Global Impact of a Myth: The Proto-*
cols of the Elders of Zion. Among her recent articles are "The War and the
Holocaust in the Egyptian Public Discourse, 1945–1947," *Arab Responses*
to Fascism and Nazism: Attraction and Repulsion, edited by Israel Gershoni; "Mixed and Confused: Egyptian Initial Responses to the Holocaust," in *Lessons and Legacies XI: Expanding Perspective on the Holocaust*
in a Changing World, edited by Hilary Earl and Karl Schleunes; "Tread-
ing in Troubled Waters: Seeking the Roots of Muslim Antisemitism," in
Bustan: The Middle East Book Review. The Hebrew version of her book
From Empathy to Denial: Arab Responses to the Holocaust, co-authored

with Meir Litvak, was the recipient of the Washington Institute for Near East Policy's Gold Book Prize for 2010.

Rebecca Wittmann (PhD, University of Toronto) is Associate Professor of History at the University of Toronto and chair of the Department of Historical Studies at University of Toronto Mississauga. Her research focuses on the Holocaust and postwar Germany, trials of Nazi perpetrators and terrorists, and German legal history; her most recent work looks at generational memory and shame. She has received fellowships from the Alexander von Humboldt Foundation, the Social Sciences and Humanities Research Council of Canada, the United States Holocaust Memorial Museum, and the DAAD (German Academic Exchange Service). She has published articles in *Central European History, German History,* and *Lessons and Legacies.* Her book *Beyond Justice: The Auschwitz Trial* (Harvard University Press, 2005) won the Fraenkel Prize in Contemporary History. She is currently working on a book project entitled *Guilt and Shame through the Generations: Confronting the Past in Postwar Germany.*

GERMAN AND EUROPEAN STUDIES

General Editor: Jennifer L. Jenkins

1 Emanuel Adler, Beverly Crawford, Federica Bicchi, and Rafaella Del Sarto, *The Convergence of Civilizations: Constructing a Mediterranean Region*
2 James Retallack, *The German Right, 1860–1920: Political Limits of the Authoritarian Imagination*
3 Silvija Jestrovic, *Theatre of Estrangement: Theory, Practice, Ideology*
4 Susan Gross Solomon, ed., *Doing Medicine Together: Germany and Russia between the Wars*
5 Laurence McFalls, ed., *Max Weber's 'Objectivity' Revisited*
6 Robin Ostow, ed., *(Re)Visualizing National History: Museums and National Identities in Europe in the New Millennium*
7 David Blackbourn and James Retallack, eds., *Localism, Landscape, and the Ambiguities of Place: German-Speaking Central Europe, 1860–1930*
8 John Zilcosky, ed., *Writing Travel: The Poetics and Politics of the Modern Journey*
9 Angelica Fenner, *Race under Reconstruction in German Cinema: Robert Stemmle's Toxi*
10 Martina Kessel and Patrick Merziger, eds., *The Politics of Humour: Laughter, Inclusion, and Exclusion in the Twentieth Century*
11 Jeffrey K. Wilson, *The German Forest: Nature, Identity, and the Contestation of a National Symbol, 1871–1914*
12 David G. John, *Bennewitz, Goethe,* Faust: *German and Intercultural Stagings*
13 Jennifer Ruth Hosek, *Sun, Sex, and Socialism: Cuba in the German Imaginary*
14 Steven M. Schroeder, *To Forget It All and Begin Again: Reconciliation in Occupied Germany, 1944–1954*
15 Kenneth S. Calhoon, *Affecting Grace: Theatre, Subject, and the Shakespearean Paradox in German Literature from Lessing to Kleist*
16 Martina Kolb, *Nietzsche, Freud, Benn, and the Azure Spell of Liguria*
17 Hoi-eun Kim, *Doctors of Empire: Medical and Cultural Encounters between Imperial Germany and Meiji Japan*
18 J. Laurence Hare, *Excavating Nations: Archeology, Museums, and the German-Danish Borderlands*
19 Jacques Kornberg, *The Pope's Dilemma: Pius XII Faces Atrocities and Genocide in the Second World War*
20 Patrick O'Neill, *Transforming Kafka: Translation Effects*
21 John K. Noyes, *Herder: Aesthetics against Imperialism*

22 James Retallack, *Germany's Second Reich: Portraits and Pathways*

23 Laurie Marhoefer, *Sex and the Weimar Republic: German Homosexual Emancipation and the Rise of the Nazis*

24 Bettina Brandt and Daniel L. Purdy, eds., *China in the German Enlightenment*

25 Michael Hau, *Performance Anxiety: Sport and Work in Germany from the Empire to Nazism*

26 Celia Applegate, *The Necessity of Music: Variations on a German Theme*

27 Richard J. Golsan and Sarah M. Misemer, eds., *The Trial That Never Ends: Hannah Arendt's* Eichmann in Jerusalem *in Retrospect*

28 Lynne Taylor, *In the Children's Best Interests: Unaccompanied Children in American-Occupied Germany, 1945–1952*

29 Jennifer A. Miller, *Turkish Guest Workers in Germany: Hidden Lives and Contested Borders, 1960s to 1980s*

30 Amy Carney, *Marriage and Fatherhood in the Nazi SS*

31 Michael E. O'Sullivan, *Disruptive Power: Catholic Women, Miracles, and Politics in Modern Germany, 1918–1965*

32 Gabriel N. Finder and Alexander V. Prusin, *Justice behind the Iron Curtain: Nazis on Trial in Communist Poland*

33 Parker Daly Everett, *Urban Transformations: From Liberalism to Corporatism in Greater Berlin, 1871–1933*

34 Melissa Kravetz, *Women Doctors in Weimar and Nazi Germany: Maternalism, Eugenics, and Professional Identity*

35 Javier Samper Vendrell, *The Seduction of Youth: Print Culture and Homosexual Rights in the Weimar Republic*

36 Sebastian Voigt, ed., *Since the Boom: Continuity and Change in the Western Industrialized World after 1970*

37 Olivia Landry, *Theatre of Anger: Radical Transnational Performance in Contemporary Berlin*

38 Jeremy Best, *Heavenly Fatherland: German Missionary Culture and Globalization in the Age of Empire*

39 Svenja Bethke, *Dance on the Razor's Edge: Crime and Punishment in the Nazi Ghettos*

40 Kenneth S. Calhoon, *The Long Century's Long Shadow: Weimar Cinema and the Romantic Modern*

41 Randall Hansen, Achim Saupe, Andreas Wirsching, and Daqing Yang, eds., *Authenticity and Victimhood after the Second World War: Narratives from Europe and East Asia*

42 Rebecca Wittmann, ed., *The Eichmann Trial Reconsidered*